Cross Theology

Cross Theology

The Classical *Theologia Crucis* and
Karl Barth's Modern Theology of the Cross

Rosalene Bradbury

Foreword by
Murray Rae

James Clarke & Co.

James Clarke & Co.
P.O. Box 60
Cambridge
CB1 2NT

www.jamesclarke.co
publishing@jamesclarke.co

ISBN: 978 0 227 68030 8

British Library Cataloguing in Publication Data
A record is available from the British Library

Copyright © Rosalene Bradbury 2011

First Published, 2011

This edition is published by arrangement with
Pickwick Publications

All rights reserved. No part of this edition may be reproduced, stored electronically or in any retrieval system, or transmitted in any form or by any means, electronic, mechanical, photocopying, recording, or otherwise, without prior written permission from the Publisher (permissions@jamesclarke.co).

This book is presented in memory of my mother, who encouraged it.
Leah Ruby Newman, 9 July 1918–12 January 2007

Contents

Foreword ix
Preface xi
Acknowledgements xiii

Introduction 1

PART ONE
Identifying the Classical *Theologia Crucis*, its Dogmatic Shape, Theological Content, and the Marks Characterizing its Theologians

1. Recent Conceptions of the Theology of the Cross: Reviewing the Secondary Literature 13

2. The Classical Epistemology of the Cross 33

3. The Classical Soteriology of the Cross 70

4. Identifying the Classical *Theologia Crucis*, its Dogmatic Shape, Theological Content, and the Marks Characterizing its Theologians 130

   Excursus: The Systematic Foundation to the Heidelberg Disputation 135

PART TWO
Karl Barth's Modern Theology of the Cross

5. From Luther to Barth 149

6. Recent Conceptions of the Theology of the Cross in Karl Barth: Reviewing the Secondary Literature 168

7. Karl Barth's Modern Epistemology of the Cross 196

8. Karl Barth's Modern Soteriology of the Cross 247

9. In Final Conclusion 293

Bibliography 303
Subject and Name Index 317

Foreword

Setting out the "task of dogmatics" in the opening pages of his *Church Dogmatics,* Karl Barth insisted that the criterion for all Christian utterance is to be found in Jesus Christ, in the one who is in person "God's gracious and revealing address to humanity."[1] The church must always ask in respect of its own utterances, "Does Christian utterance derive from Him? Does it lead to Him? Is it conformable to Him?"[2] Although some have contended that Barth did not always follow his own advice, no one has doubted Barth's intent to be thoroughly christocentric at every point of the theological endeavor. But should we also regard Barth's theology more specifically as crucicentric? Should we see Barth as upholding and developing the "thin tradition" of a *theologia crucis* that is represented before him in the likes of St. Athanasius, St. Bernard of Clairvaux, Johannes Tauler, Nicolas of Cusa and Martin Luther?

An answer to that question will depend, first, on our being able to say with an acceptable degree of clarity what distinguishes a *theologia crucis* from any other kind of theology, and second, upon our being able to show whether or not Barth's theology shares those distinguishing marks. The consequent and vitally important question, is whether any particular instance of a *theologia crucis* can faithfully answer "Yes" to Barth's own questions: Does such a theology derive from Christ? Does it lead to Him? Is it conformable to Him?

Consideration of these questions is the task admirably undertaken in this volume by Rosalene Bradbury. The particular task of clarifying what a *theologia crucis* consists in is addressed first. Such a theology is distinguished first, Bradbury contends, by an epistemological commitment to set aside the self-glorifying attempts by the creature to know

---

1. Barth, *Church Dogmatics,* I/1, 4.
2. Ibid.

and to encounter God on its own terms, and second by the associated soteriological conviction, that all anthropocentric methodologies for achieving salvation are negated by the vicarious, cruciform work of Christ. Bradbury's development of these insights in Part One of this work serves well in clarifying the distinctive features of a *theologia crucis* and gives cause to ponder whether these features ought to be distinguishing marks of every theology that claims to be Christian.

In the second part Bradbury engages specifically with Barth and considers whether the epistemological and soteriological convictions evident in the crucicentric tradition before him are decisive within his own theological project. Here Bradbury shows that Barth may be judged a theologian of the cross, not simply on account of his conformity to the received tradition but also on account of his profound and creative development of it. The case is made, and made well, that the generative power of a *theologia crucis* in Barth's theology deserves much more attention than it has commonly received.

What difference might this project finally make? It will serve undoubtedly to direct readers' attention to a neglected theme in Barth and will thus aid our comprehension of Barth's theological contribution as a whole. Comprehending more adequately a theologian of Barth's stature, however, requires also that we attend once again to the great themes of the Christian gospel, hear again the saving Word addressed to us in Christ, and ponder again what may be required of us in response. We have cause to be grateful to Rosalene for directing us again to that task.

Murray Rae
Associate Professor
Department of Theology
and Religious Studies
University of Otago

Preface

This book began as a doctoral thesis, which was accepted by the University of Auckland in 2009. The work is presented in two parts. Part One identifies the shape and content of a system of Christian thought predicated on the theology of the cross (*theologia crucis*) of Jesus Christ, and proposes the marks typifying its theologians. It does so with reference to the system's classical formation in the period bracketed by the early church and the Reformation. In the hermeneutical light shed by that classical crucicentric system Part Two finds the project of twentieth century Swiss theologian Karl Barth to exhibit many familiar crucicentric characteristics, and Barth himself to be fairly deemed a modern theologian of the cross. He crucially recovers, reshapes, and reasserts the classical system as a modern theological instrument, one answering enlightened theology's self-glorifying accommodation to modernity with the living Word of the cross.

The database for this investigation includes selected primary materials in the Apostle Paul, Athanasius, a group of medieval mystical theologians, the Reformer Martin Luther—particularly here his Heidelberg Disputation, and Karl Barth. It also pays attention to the recent secondary literature peripherally or more concertedly connecting itself to the theology of the cross, of whatever period.

In this literature numerous suggestions for the content of the theology of the cross arise, a major methodological task in Part One being to bring these together systematically. The secondary literature also contains conflicting assessments as to Barth's crucicentric status, and an important methodological task in Part Two is to analyze why this disagreement occurs. (The evidence will be that misunderstanding the theology of the cross *per se* correlates with misunderstanding the theology of the cross in Barth.)

It appears then that to date the inner structure of the system carrying the cruciform Word has not been made explicit, and Barth's crucicentric status not finally determined. To the extent that the present work now clarifies these matters it breaks fresh ground. In the process a new test by which to decide the crucicentric status of *any* theological project is developed, and a further and crucicentric way of reading Barth is proposed.

Acknowledgements

Dogmatics summons the listening Church to address itself anew to the task of teaching the Word of God in the revelation attested in Scripture. It can do this only as it accepts . . . and is therefore claimed by the Word of God.[1]

—Karl Barth

With profound gratitude for Barth who accepted that claim and continues to teach.

I wish to thank the editorial staff of Wipf and Stock for chancing a new author from a distant shore. Especially here I am grateful for the critical insight and guidance of my editor, Robin Parry. Profound thanks go also to Heather Carraher for her expert presentation skills. You have all been superb to work with.

With deep appreciation I also thank Dr. Martin Sutherland now of Laidlaw College, Auckland, and Associate Professor Murray Rae of the University of Otago. Dr. Sutherland graciously supervised the doctoral research on which the present work depends. Professor Rae was involved in the examination processes that ensued; his generous ongoing interest, and his kindness in preparing the Foreword here, are very greatly appreciated.

I owe a considerable debt of gratitude to the staff of the University of Auckland Central Library, the Ayson Clifford theological library, and the John Kinder theological library. All have been unfailingly helpful and efficient.

More personally I am most grateful to my family and friends near and far, whose continual interest in the face of imponderable questions has been both assiduous and very kind. Above all I thank my husband,

1. Ibid., I/2, 844.

Graham Bradbury, for his unstinting encouragement and practical support.

May the solely glorious God of the Bible, of the Reformation, and of Karl Barth, bless you all.

Rosalene Bradbury
One Tree Point

Introduction

Dogmatics is possible only as a *theologia crucis*, in the act of obedience which is certain in faith, but which for this very reason is humble.

—Karl Barth[1]

The term "the theology of the cross"[2] is intriguing; it comprises a definite feature within the contemporary theological landscape even as its meaning, via its classical tradition,[3] seems little understood. For every work implicitly or explicitly forwarding one theme or set of themes as its essential explanation, others will advance different themes with equal assurance, and without apparent awareness that alternate proposals exist. Some central elements of crucicentric[4] theology receive little scholarly attention, while others are diametrically reversed.[5] Likewise in the contemporary literature there appear to be no explicit criteria for designating someone a "theologian of the cross." By broad consent various theologians past and present enjoy this status, but apparently do so for differing reasons—some because they embrace issues of class suffering, others because they focus on the dogmatic significance of the crucified Christ. At the same time the crucicentric status of otherwise prominent theologians passes with little comment, and what there is is confused.

1. Ibid., I/1, 14.

2. Or simply "theology of the cross."

3. What may be called "the classical era" of the theology of the cross stretches from the early church to the Reformation.

4. Here "crucicentric" means "pertaining to the theology of the cross," (whereas "cruciform" recalls the cross itself.)

5. Wells points out that many liberation theologians co-opt crucicentric elements in support of anthropocentric theologies, diametrically reversing their classical application thereby. See Wells, *Cross and Liberation*, 161.

Such is the case with pre-eminent twentieth century Swiss Reformed theologian Karl Barth (1886–1968).

Lack of comment on Barth's crucicentric status is especially curious given the voluminous nature of the Barth secondary literature. It may simply be that the sheer magnitude of Barth's project means that the significance of the opening note in his mature theology, *viz.* "dogmatics is possible only as a *theologia crucis*,"[6] is overlooked. But it may also be that the current confusion regarding the nature of the theology of the cross means alertness to its presence in Barth, or indeed elsewhere, is simply not present.

Two central questions and associated proposals stem from the above. First, "In view of the first sixteen centuries of Christian tradition what is signified by the term theology of the cross?" In response, it is suggested:

> That the theology of the cross (*theologia crucis*) is an ancient system of Christian thought conveying the message of the cross of Jesus Christ, that in it alone all—necessarily self-glorifying—creaturely attempts to know and be as God are overcome, that the proper glorification of human knowledge and being may proceed.

Second, "On the basis of the theology of the cross as defined in Part One, can Karl Barth's project be called a theology of the cross and Barth himself a theologian of the cross?" Here it is considered:

> That the crucicentric system provides a pervasive, pivotal, and generative influence in the twentieth century orthodox theology of Karl Barth, who crucially recovers, reshapes and reasserts it as a peculiarly modern instrument—in so doing further advancing the system itself.

A subsidiary question and proposal follow, "Given that Barth is fairly adjudged a theologian of the cross, in the secondary literature why is there a nuanced appreciation of him as such?" ("Why is his crucicentric status not commensurate with his stature otherwise?") Here it is suggested:

> That where the crucicentric nature of Karl Barth's project has been missed or misassigned, and therefore he himself not considered crucicentric, there has likely been failure properly to comprehend

---

6. Barth, *Church Dogmatics*, I/1, 14.

the shape and content of the system structuring the crucicentric tradition, and to perceive the marks of its theologians.

The first proposal here suggests that a dual disciplinary foundation undergirds crucicentric thought. One of the leading mid-twentieth century German commentators on the *theologia crucis*, Walther von Loewenich, points to such a foundation when commenting on the meaning of the cross for the person Luther scholarship generally considers to be the first crucicentric theologian. He writes, "In the cross [the Apostle] Paul sees both the rule that governs God's Revelation as well as the rule that governs . . . the life of the Christian. The entire thought of Paul is controlled by the thought of the cross, his is a theology of the cross."[7] This observation is interesting in itself, but important now because here von Loewenich finds dual theologies of divine revelation and creaturely transformation, epistemology and soteriology therefore, to rule Paul's crucicentric perspective.

Soteriological and epistemological foundations also undergird the crucicentric perspective of the great patristic theologian Athanasius (c.296–373). In his early work *De Incarnatione* he speaks explicitly of two ways in which "our Saviour had compassion through the incarnation."[8] These are firstly that he "puts away death from humankind and renews [it] through the resurrection, and secondly [that] he makes visible what is invisible, that is, that he is 'Word of the Father, and the Ruler and King of the universe.'"[9] Athanasius' whole project subsequently becomes an elaboration of these two ways.

Clear evidence for a dual disciplinary foundation to crucicentric thought may too be found in Martin Luther (1483–1546). The Heidelberg Disputation (April 1518) particularly illustrates this, it being widely considered the culminating document of the classical crucicentric tradition. Within the disputation's deeper levels Luther delineates, systematizes, and for the first time codifies[10] the ancient crucicentric idea that the cross itself proclaims a self-disclosing and a saving Word, each emphasis

---

7. Von Loewenich, *Luther's Theology of the Cross*, 12.

8. Athanasius, *De Incarnatione* §16, in Thomson, *Contra Gentes and De Incarnatione*, 173.

9. Ibid., §17. See also, Weinandy, *Athanasius*, 36.

10. Barth serves to illustrate the point. He declares that "The man who thought out first, and with most originality and force, the basic anti-medieval and . . . anti-modern thought of the Reformation, that of the theology of the cross, [was] Luther." Barth, *Calvin*, 70. Quotation further cited here page 165–66.

being of equal importance.[11] Around the same time it is then Luther who retrospectively designates this idea, as also the dual disciplinary system predicated on it, *"theologia crucis."*[12]

Barth similarly sees both soteriological and epistemological importance in the theology disclosed from the cross. For instance he says that the effectiveness of the intervention "which took place on the cross of Golgotha . . . consists in the salvation of the sinner from judgement and the Revelation of faith in which he may grasp this salvation."[13]

As the literature review in Part One will show, many commentators effecting to write on the theology of the cross do not however recognize a dual disciplinary foundation systematically structuring it. Rather, and as already noted, explicitly or implicitly they align it to one or a few theological sub-disciplines; of which epistemology is the most common. To foreshadow the review's conclusions, these commentators' perspectives are in fact too narrow to enable them to see the whole.

Recognizing dual dimensions (epistemological and soteriological) structuring crucicentric theology now though, the discussion finds that each of these dimensions is again further divided. Each is expressed *negatively* in opposition and negation, and *positively* in defense and advance.

The negative epistemology of the cross: The self-glorifying human attempt to reach up to the knowledge of God and know as God knows, but the inability to do so, and therefore the crucicentric rejection of that attempt.

The positive epistemology of the cross: The summons of the cross to vicarious death in and with the crucified Christ, in whom the creaturely presumption to know as God is overcome. In exchange union with Christ's mind, consolidated through an ongoing sanctifying process of death to the natural attempt to know as God. This leads to the receipt of Christ's true and crucicentric knowledge of God, a process completed eschatologically with the resurrection of the creature's mind in and with the exalted mind of Christ. Thus the creature is made participant in

---

11. The Excursus to Part One makes the disciplinary handling of the crucicentric idea within the Heidelberg Disputation explicit.

12. Luther scholar James Kiecker says, "As far as I can tell, Luther uses the phrase 'theology of the cross' for the first time in his *Lectures on Hebrews* (1517–1518) . . . The complementary phrase, theology of glory, however, does not yet appear." Kiecker, "*Crucis et Gloriae*," 182.

13. Barth, *Church Dogmatics* II/1, 405.

Christ's glorious wisdom and governance, becoming thereby not God but fully humanly cognizant.

The negative soteriology of the cross: The self-glorifying human attempt to merit salvation by natural means, but the inability to do so, and therefore the crucicentric rejection of that attempt.

The positive soteriology of the cross: The summons of the cross to vicarious death in and with the crucified Christ, in whom the creaturely presumption to be as God is overcome. In exchange union with Christ, consolidated through an ongoing sanctifying process of death to the natural attempt to be as God. This leads to conformation to Christ's faith and obedience, a process completed eschatologically with the resurrection of the creature in and with the exalted Christ. Thus the creature is made participant in Christ's glorious person and kingship, becoming thereby not God but fully relational, fully human.

This negative and positive theology is grounded in three fundamental principles. The first and overarching principle holds that "God alone is glorious." Contingent on this an epistemological principle holds that "God alone truly knows God so as to reveal God truly," and a soteriological principle holds that "God alone can condition God and therefore the electing will of God." Defence of these principles results both in radical opposition to all anthropocentric epistemologies and soteriologies, and powerful reassertion of the centrality of the crucified Christ. Only in him is there true knowledge of God in Godself, and of the creature in relation to God. Only in him is salvation *already* worked out.

As a discrete system of theological thought each element—major theme or simple notion—of the theology of the cross corresponds with every other element, the same concepts constantly re-emerging and re-engaging from different angles. But the crucicentric system is always open to the inbreaking Word it proclaims. For in the deepest sense by *theology* the crucicentric theologians traditionally understand a divine *Theology* or *Word* or *Message* articulated from the cross. Ultimately for them this *Theology* has an ontological character, that is, Jesus Christ himself. Hence for example Luther's bold declaration, "*Crux Christi unica est eruditio verborum dei, theologia sincerissima.*"[14] [The cross of Christ is the only way of learning the words of God; it is the purest theology.]

---

14. Exegesis of Ps 6:11, "*Operationes in Psalmos,*" in Luther, *Luther's Works,* 14:342f. See also Oberman, *Luther,* 248. *Note*: The definitive German collection of Luther is: *Martin Luthers Werke.* [WA]. Its definitive English translation is: *Luther's Works* in 56 volumes, [LW].

As Wells says, "The theology of the cross, with its primary source in Paul and developed explicitly by Luther, is a minority tradition in Christian theology."[15] It forms a subsection within wider Christian theology. In the view of the present investigation a similar idea might be expressed by characterizing the theology of the cross as a system within a system, a distinctive word within the broader system of Christian belief, with the special service of distinguishing the boundaries between Christian thought and that of the world.

In line with its minority status the theology of the cross is sometimes referred to as the *narrow* or *thin* tradition, the contention being that it runs like a fine gold thread down the centuries of Christian thought and history. Hall explains, "[There] has been in Christian history a thin tradition which tried to proclaim the possibility of hope without shutting its eyes to the data of despair . . . This is, we must emphasize, a *thin* tradition. It has appeared only here and there, now and then, it never really belonged to Christendom."[16] Tomlin agrees, "Sometimes forgotten, sometimes remembered, this 'thin tradition' . . . has functioned like an antiphon beneath the high triumph song of Christendom."[17]

That antiphon sounds back and forward across the ages with greater or lesser force. Barth too notes its fluctuation. Anticipating later twentieth century commentary on the thin tradition, in 1922 he speaks of "a straight if for long stretches broken line [of ideas leading up] to Luther's view of . . . the theology of the cross."[18]

This long thin tradition is so described for another reason also—those marking it are not numerous. As already indicated, in its classical period it originates with the Apostle Paul and continues through a narrow line of theologians. Among these are Athanasius, and later a group of medieval mystics including: St Bernard of Clairvaux (1090–1153), the anonymous writer of the *Theologia Germanica* (c.1350), Johannes Tauler (c.1300–1361), and Nicholas of Cusa (1401–1464).[19] In turn the

15. Wells, "Holy Spirit", 479.
16. Hall, *Lighten Our Darkness*, 113–14. (Italics Hall's.)
17. Tomlin, "Subversive Theology," 59.
18. Barth, *Calvin*, 65.

19. The figures listed will receive particular mention here. There are however other medieval crucicentric mystics, at the far end of the age notably including the Spanish Teresa of Avila (1515–1582) and her compatriot John of the Cross (1542–1591). Born after Luther and outside the Reformation, obviously they do not influence him nor likely he them; nevertheless the Luther secondary literature notes similarities between his thought and theirs.

crucicentric mystics indirectly, but nonetheless significantly, influence Martin Luther's crucicentric understanding.

Support not only for the narrowness but also for the antiquity of the crucicentric tradition is offered obliquely by John McIntyre. In setting out various models of atonement he notes a certain "classic idea," the recovery of which he attributes to Gustaf Aulen in the latter's 1931 Latin work, *Christus Victor*. Beginning with the New Testament writers and Irenaeus (c.130–200), this classic idea is said by McIntyre to undergird the first thousand years of Christian soteriology, and to be still present up to Luther.[20] The idea itself concerns the exclusivity of the sovereignty of God, the centrality of the cross in all properly Christian theology, and the unique character of the salvific work of Jesus Christ.[21] While McIntyre does not directly identify Aulen's classic idea with the soteriology of the cross, in the present view that identification may reasonably be made. If so, Aulen's discovery adds additional weight to the notion that crucicentric theology is rooted in the earliest centuries of Christian thought.

Luther's systematizing of this ancient and thin tradition within the Heidelberg Disputation takes place explicitly over against another equally ancient but broader system, *viz.* the *theologia gloriae* supporting human self-glorification. In fact here Luther walks an old way. Shaped in mutual dialectical engagement the two systems have kept parallel course across the millennia of Christian thought.

The centuries following Luther see explicit awareness of the theology of the cross fade again. Though not the first significant theologian of the cross of the twentieth century—arguably that honor belongs to P. T.

---

20. McIntyre writes, "Aulen claims that the 'classic theory' is the dominant idea in the [New Testament], being at the foundation of ransom theories, and the ruling soteriology for the first thousand years of the Church's history [as] illustrated chiefly in Irenaeus and Luther." McIntyre, *Soteriology*, 43.

21. McIntyre writes, "[The classic idea] consists of several clear and simple affirmations: the salvation of mankind is a divine conflict and victory in which Jesus Christ on the cross triumphs over the evil power of this world and of this age [which have kept mankind] in perpetual bondage and suffering ever since the Fall . . . This work of atonement is presented as being from start to finish the continuous work of God and of God alone, not partly God's work and partly man's." (Ibid., 42–43.) McIntyre adds immediately that through its history the sponsoring text for this idea is Col 2:11–14, which refers to believers being incorporated in the *circumcision* (or *cruciform death*) of Christ, being buried with him in baptism, and by faith being raised with him from the dead, the record against them now nailed to the cross.

Forsyth—it is Karl Barth who signally recovers the classical crucicentric tradition for twentieth century modernity and beyond.[22]

An opening caveat applies here. As Lovin rightly says, "Karl Barth's project illustrates the power of a few central ideas to shape a systematic project of remarkable scope."[23] That these few central ideas are indeed *crucicentric* ideas does not mean that Barth's entire project can be read only in this way. This discussion is not suggesting that Barth is primarily or only a theologian of the cross. Any such quick estimation of a figure as seminal, multifaceted and fecund as he must clearly fail.[24] But that Barth is *also* a theologian of the cross, and crucially so for the modern rediscovery of the crucicentric tradition itself, is being contended here.

Stylistic Considerations

A note concerning certain stylistic decisions connected with this study may be of interest to readers. These relate to its: structure, terminological explanation, and Barth quotation.

In keeping with its twin concerns the work is presented in two parts. Each commences with an appropriate literature review. Reflecting the structure of the crucicentric system itself the two ensuing discussions are each divided again into epistemology and soteriology, and then into negative and positive aspects of these disciplines. (As an added guide and summary here chapter 4 includes a chart diagrammatically depicting the crucicentric system.)

22. A possible argument that Barth is unsympathetic to the classical *theologia crucis* on the grounds of its systematic character cannot be sustained. As is well known he describes himself as a *dogmatic* rather than a *systematic* theologian. He does so in order to protect the integrity of a faithful theology open to and conveying the Word of its Object and Subject, and to deny the reverse—a closed and anthropocentric system in which God becomes the prisoner of human religion. Nevertheless Barth is himself powerfully systematic in actual procedure. Jüngel supports this. "Barth's theology," he says, "was, from the beginning, an avowed enemy of systems. It remained so even in the very systematically written *Church Dogmatics*." Jüngel, *Karl Barth*, 27. See also Barth, *Church Dogmatics* IV/3, 477–78.

23. See Lovin's preface to Barth's *The Holy Spirit and the Christian Life*, ix.

24. In his prologue to his 1991 reading of the *Church Dogmatics* around six selected *loci*, George Hunsinger reviews several previously tendered "overriding conceptions" or single "interpretive motifs" of Barth up to that point, and concludes that while all are of value, none is definitive. None catches "the complexity-in-unity and unity-in-complexity of Karl Barth's *Church Dogmatics*." Hunsinger's own work "proceeds on the assumption . . . that such a conception is unlikely to be found." This conclusion is now generally accepted. See Hunsinger, *How to Read Karl Barth*, 20.

Most terminological explanations are provided as the discussion proceeds. The paradigmatic terms *modernity* (or *modernism*) and *postmodernity* (or *postmodernism*) are defined now however. To turn to *The Oxford Companion to Philosophy* explanation:

> On the longest view, [modernity] in philosophy starts out with Descartes's quest for a knowledge self-evident to reason and secured from all the demons of skeptical doubt. It is also invoked—with a firmer sense of historical perspective—to signify those currents of thought that emerged from Kant's critical "revolution" in the spheres of epistemology, ethics, and aesthetic judgement. Thus "modernity" and "Enlightenment" tend to be used interchangeably.[25]

Note that it is now considered historically more correct to speak of multiple Enlightenments, mutually differing in form across time and place.

The associated entry on *postmodernity* begins:

> In its broad usage postmodernity is a "family resemblance" term displayed in a variety of contexts (architecture, painting, music, poetry, fiction etc.) for things which seem to be related, if at all— by a laid-back pluralism of styles and a vague desire to have done with the pretensions of high modernist culture. In philosophical terms postmodernism shares something with the critique of Enlightenment values and truth-claims mounted by thinkers of a liberal-communitarian persuasion ... There is a current preoccupation ... with themes of "self-reflexivity" [and with] puzzles induced by allowing language to become the object of its own scrutiny in a kind of dizzying rhetorical regress.[26]

The final stylistic consideration here relates to quotation from Barth. As often observed Barth has an unparalleled gift for theological imagination. He relentlessly probes everything he finds, constantly circling in on his object from many angles and in exhaustive detail. Jüngel, for instance, says that Barth "resolves to make progress precisely by constantly correcting, or else completely changing direction, ... beginning once again at the beginning."[27] This characteristic approach is rightly acclaimed for its theological merit, but it also makes it difficult

---

25. Norris, "Modernism," 583. Pre-eminent German philosopher Immanuel Kant, 1724–1804, is popularly termed the *Father of the Enlightenment.*

26. Ibid., "Post-modernism," 708.

27. Jüngel, *Karl Barth*, 27. See also Barth, "Evangelical Theology in the Nineteenth Century," 165, and Torrance, *Karl Barth*, 14.

to quote Barth succinctly. Accordingly in the following study some excerpts from him are abridged or paraphrased for ease of meaning, the intention being always to reflect the original faithfully. Such treatment is clearly indicated.

Conclusion

Currently the term *theology of the cross* (*theologia crucis*) is vested with a range of meanings, none of which is generally regarded as definitive. On the basis of the classical crucicentric tradition, the system it conveys, and the Word from the cross conveyed by that system, the first part of this work hopes to contribute towards a broadly accepted definition. An associated aim seeks to uncover the defining marks of the theologian of the cross. If achieved these objectives should enable a new and crucicentric hermeneutic for Christian thought and history, in light of which *any* theological project might be evaluated for its crucicentric content.

In the second part of this work it is argued that lack of clarity concerning the dogmatic shape and theological content of the classical crucicentric system, as also of the concomitant marks of the theologian of the cross, has contributed to current uncertainty regarding the crucicentric status of Karl Barth's project and of Barth himself. In distinction to this uncertainty, in light of its earlier conclusions the discussion seeks to demonstrate that Barth's modern, orthodox[28] and evangelical[29] theology stands within the long thin crucicentric tradition, and that he himself exhibits the defining marks of its theologians. If this is so a crucicentric hermeneutic should provide an additional lens through which to read Barth freshly. It should also enable twentieth century crucicentric theology to account properly for Barth's contribution to it.

To commence Part One the relevant secondary literature is reviewed to determine how the theology of the cross, ancient or modern, has recently been understood.

---

28. After Vincent of Lerins (d c.450 CE) *orthodoxy* is traditionally defined as, "What has been believed in all places, at all times, by all people." See Denney, *Death of Christ*, 73.

29. Barth himself calls his theology *evangelical*, stressing that he does not mean this in a confessional or denominational sense. Rather, "The qualifying attribute 'evangelical' recalls both the New Testament and at the same time the Reformation of the sixteenth century." Barth, "Evangelical Theology: An Introduction," 11.

PART ONE

Identifying the Classical *Theologia Crucis*, its Dogmatic Shape, Theological Content, and the Marks Characterizing its Theologians

1

Recent Conceptions of the Theology of the Cross: Reviewing the Secondary Literature

[We] find ourselves in a situation where there is increasing talk about the theology of the cross but little specific knowledge of what exactly it is.

—Gerhard Forde[1]

The Literature *In Toto*

No less than the classical crucicentric tradition itself, the secondary literature pertaining to it is comparatively thin compared to the broader secondary literatures with which it intersects. An examination of the international ATLA theological database reveals that between the late 1960s[2] and the beginning years of the present century some 244 articles make some reference to the theology of the cross (of any period), although perhaps only fifty of these focus intensively on it. In descending emphasis this literature ties the theology of the cross to: epistemology, divine and human suffering, radical sociopolitical reform, Christology, soteriology, the means of Reformation, the combating of evil or heresy or human sin, eschatology, ethics, human glorification—both true and false, mysticism, pneumatology, various doctrines of atonement, and

---

1. Forde, *Being a Theologian of the Cross*, viii. In the first decade of the twenty-first century Forde's 1997 comment remains apt, his own excellent account of Luther's *theologia crucis* notwithstanding.

2. The late 1960s has been chosen as a point from which to begin the current investigation, the twentieth century renaissance in interest in the classical crucicentric tradition beginning around this time.

lastly anthropology. Six more concerted works on the theology of the cross exist. These include an historical-theological treatment by von Loewenich,[3] a short monograph by Prenter,[4] a major book each by McGrath and Forde seeking to explicate Luther's *theologia crucis*,[5] and a volume from Tomlin again with attention to Luther, but also Paul and Pascal.[6] The sixth work, by Hall, is less tethered to tradition and places the theology of the cross in a late-modern context.[7] A thin literature then, notwithstanding which it has grown significantly in recent decades, being increasingly associated with contemporary socio-political and liberative theologies.

The investigation in respect of Part One of this discussion depends generally on this collected literature, but as a way into it particular attention is accorded the just mentioned works by McGrath, Forde, and von Loewenich. McGrath in 1985 is chiefly concerned with questions of Luther's theological development and of Luther scholarship. Forde's 1997 popular but nonetheless scholarly paraphrase of the Heidelberg Disputation brings out the disputation's inner structure. Von Loewenich is widely recognized as providing the definitive mid-twentieth century treatment of Luther's *theologia crucis*, his seminal 1929 work being subsequently reworked by the author over almost forty years and appearing in several German and English editions

Having described the shape of the literary database to be used in Part One of this investigation, the discussion now turns to its content. Broadly speaking how has the theology of the cross been understood in recent decades?

The foregoing Introduction indicates that under the nomenclature "*theologia crucis*" Martin Luther gathers an otherwise diverse set of epistemological and soteriological ideas, connected by their common foundation in the noetic and ontological Word proclaimed from the cross of Jesus Christ. Particularly since 1983 and a new wave of scholarship occasioned by the five hundredth anniversary of Luther's birth, Luther's *theologia crucis* has been recovered and even popularized. Nevertheless

3. Von Loewenich, *Luther's Theology of the Cross.*

4. Prenter, *Luther's Theology of the Cross.*

5. McGrath, *Luther's theology of the Cross*, and Forde, *Being a Theologian of the Cross.*

6. Tomlin, *The Power of the Cross.*

7. Hall, *Lighten Our Darkness.*

database analysis shows that some themes once associated with classical crucicentric theology receive little scholarly attention, while others are appropriated in ways Luther would likely have found uncongenial. What is clear is that an inverse relation exists between the increasing volume of recent articles on the theology of the cross and the strength of their historical underpinnings. This is the first insight gained in overviewing the relevant literature as a whole.

The second is that there appears to exist something of a debate in the literature concerning what the theology of the cross *is*, and what it is *for*. Is it a divine or a human tool? Is it designed to defend or to advance the gospel? Does it constitute an instrument to announce a temporal and eschatological kingdom of social justice, or to call the church to evangelical reform? Is it all of these or something else altogether?

But if a debate *is* present, it is not one in the usual sense of committed exchange between advocates of opposing positions. Rather its presence is understated, existing overwhelmingly in the sub-structure of the collected texts. Its points often take the form of casual comment aside some principal concern; they are seldom backed by concerted scholarly support; behind them there seems little awareness that contrary opinions exist elsewhere.

These understated points gravitate finally to one of two debating sides, characterized now as the 'confined' versus 'extended' conceptions of crucicentric theology.

Position one: the confined position

The confined (or narrow) position associates the theology of the cross with either a single theme or narrow set of themes, that are usually said to encapsulate its meaning in entirety. These definitions may or may not explicitly appeal to classical crucicentric notions. With various shades of radical and dogmatic emphases: Dalferth (1982), Fiddes (1988), Neufeld (1996) and Richardson (2004) understand the theology of the cross to be first or solely an epistemological instrument for the revelation of divine truth. Moltmann (1972), Godsey (1982) and Hunsinger (1999) understand it as solely or overwhelmingly to do with a theology of divine suffering. Cornwall (1997), or at least his ATLA cataloguer, connects it with the ethical value of Christian suffering. Schweitzer (1995) and Wells (1992 and 2001) see the theology of the cross simply as an instrument of radical social critique. Mattes (1999) views it as divine methodology enabling proper human glory. Schweitzer (1998) now connects it to eschatological hope and justice. Hall (1989) and Kärkkäinen (2002) agree, but also find it a theology of sanctification. Barker (1965), Solberg (1997), Hagan (1997), and Hinlicky (1998), allow it a more multi-layered set of meanings, variously combining epistemology, radical political critique, and atonement / soteriology, but without intermeshing these systematically. It follows that those viewing the theology of the cross as just described do not find it a comprehensive theological system.

Position two: the extended position

As does the confined view the extended side of the debate looks back to the classical crucicentric tradition, but it understands that tradition quite differently. Now the theology of the cross is seen as a multivalent theological system centered in the broad river of Christian thought. No doctrinal statement in this system takes priority, rather each is rooted in the fundamental dialectic of the cross—in the tension between the exclusive divinity of God and the utter creatureliness of the human creature. This extended position also holds the theology of the cross to be methodology, a way of doing theology, an instrumental touchstone with which to anchor that thought which is properly Christian and to exclude that which is not. As such the theology of the cross is understood to engage a parallel system militantly.

Modern advocates of the extended conception reach back to von Loewenich (1929). More recently they include: Moltmann (1974), Kiecker (1995), Bayer (1995), Forde (1997), Hendel (1997), and Tomlin (1997 and 1999).

Even theological dictionaries bear out these confined and extended conceptions. The ecumenically orientated and theologically neutral *A New Dictionary of Christian Theology* locates the theology of the cross historically but restricts its meaning, in this case to epistemology. It declares shortly, "'Theology of the cross' is Luther's name for the doctrine that our knowledge of God must be drawn from the suffering of Christ in his humiliation."[8] In contrast the self-consciously evangelical source, the *New Dictionary of Theology*, forwards a more extended meaning. "[The theology of the cross] refers not simply to the doctrine of the cross, in

---

8. Richardson, "*Theologia Crucis*," 566.

which the cross is seen as the focal point of Christ's work of salvation (see Atonement), but to an understanding of the whole of theology as theology of the cross, in that the cross is seen as the focal point of God's revelation of himself and therefore as the foundation and centre of all truly Christian theology. In the theology of the cross the cross becomes a methodological key to the whole of theology."[9]

Finally now, if confusion exists as to the meaning and purpose of the theology of the cross, review of the database literature suggests that almost no attention has been paid to identifying the marks of crucicentric theology's theologians. That matter remains to be addressed.

The Literature Viewed Chronologically

Examination of the database also reveals how in recent decades conceptions of the theology of the cross have developed over against the contemporary theological and ideational ethos.

Lutheran Walther von Loewenich in his 1929 account of Luther's *theologia crucis* reasserts the crucicentric system as the methodological centre of Christian thought.[10] His words bear quoting in full. "The theology of the cross is not a chapter in theology but a specific kind of theology. The cross of Christ is significant here not only for the question concerning redemption and the certainty of salvation, but it is the centre that provides perspective for all theological statements. Hence it belongs to the doctrine of God in the same way as it belongs to the doctrine of the work of Christ. There is no dogmatic topic conceivable for which the cross is not the point of reference."[11]

But in the ensuing decades von Loewenich's embracing conception, viz. "a specific kind of theology," becomes gradually lost. By the early 1970s a disparate collection of foci each attempt to encapsulate the theology of the cross in its entirety.

Major German Reformed theologian Jürgen Moltmann in his 1972 article *The Crucified God* explores eschatological and trinitarian themes in relation to the death of Jesus Christ. In doing so Moltmann melts God's triune work on the cross and the theology of the cross, so that the

---

9. Bauckham, "Theology of the Cross," 181.

10. The next section of the discussion will examine this classical tradition more closely.

11. Von Loewenich, *Luther's Theology of the Cross*, 18.

latter is effectively a theology of triune sacrificial atonement. Moltmann says for instance, "At first glance there seems to be a vast difference between the doctrine of the Trinity and the theology of the cross. In reality, however . . . the most concise statement of the Trinity is God's work on the cross, in which the Father lets the Son be sacrificed through the Spirit."[12] Here Moltmann joins many commentators who do not really distinguish the theology of the cross from the work of the cross in and of itself.

In 1974 Moltmann broadens his earlier explanation. In reference to Luther the theology of the cross is now not only soteriological in importance, but a peculiarly Reformational gospel of liberation over against an opposing theology. He says, "The 'theology of the cross' is the explicit formulation that Luther used in 1518 in the Heidelberg Disputation, in order to find words for the Reformation insight of the liberating gospel of the crucified Christ, by contrast to the *theologia gloriae* of the medieval institutional church."[13] Here Moltmann effectively extends von Loewenich's 1929 understanding to include both an instrumental and peculiarly *social* use for the theology of the cross—*social* in a theological rather than a secular sociological sense. It is a liberative weapon to found new and eschatological society under the lordship of Jesus Christ. In Moltmann's words it comprises "a practical doctrine for battle, and can therefore become neither a theory of Christianity as it is now, nor the Christian theory of world history. It is a dialectic and historical theology, and not a theory of world history. It does not state what exists, but sets out to liberate men from the inhuman definitions and their idolized assertions, in which they have become set, and in which society has ensnared them."[14]

In 1982 major German Lutheran theologian Ingolf Dalferth[15] shows that Luther centrally distinguishes theology from all other disciplines, and with this theological method from philosophical method. For Luther the cross of Christ rather than human reason becomes the sole legitimate starting point for the knowledge of God. Christian truths can be verified only by faith in Christ and him crucified. They cannot be validated by "a unified theologico-metaphysical system which tries

---

12. Moltmann, "The Crucified God," 291.
13. Moltmann, *The Crucified God*, 70.
14. Ibid., 72.
15. Dalferth, "The Visible and the Invisible."

to verify theological truth-claims by incorporating faith in a general ontological scheme as one of its orders, nor a metaphysical dualism which adds faith as a separate realm of truth to the otherwise self-contained realm of natural truth."[16] It is, says Dalferth, this insistence on a strictly *theological* method for theology which characterizes and identifies Luther's *theologia crucis*. Extrapolating from Luther, he goes on to claim the critical importance of the cruciform starting point for late-modern theology.

In Dalferth's conception the theology of the cross is identified as an epistemological instrument with which to defend a strictly christological and crucicentric starting point for theology, particularly now *modern* theology, and conversely to oppose the metaphysical starting point with its intrinsic homage to human reason. Again then, (recalling Moltmann), the theology of the cross is an instrument of combat. As such it is *methodology* before it is strictly *theology*.

In 1987 American Bonhoeffer scholar and Barth student, John Godsey,[17] designates Dietrich Bonhoeffer a theologian of the cross on the grounds that Bonhoeffer emphasizes the humanity of the God who is *"pro nobis,"* who suffers in, with and for the world. He cites passages from Bonhoeffer's *Christ the Centre* in support, in so doing contrasting Bonhoeffer and Barth. Godsey writes, "Bonhoeffer's theology quite evidently is a *theologia crucis* in order to ensure the *costliness* of God's grace in Christ."[18] Leaving aside for now the accuracy of Godsey's comparative reduction of Barth as a crucicentric theologian, here Godsey identifies the theology of the cross exclusively with Christ's atoning suffering.

The increasing volume of works concerning the theology of the cross from the mid-1980s on announces a growing renaissance in interest in the crucicentric idea—if not always tethered to earlier tradition. Contributions now come not just from Luther scholars, but from feminist, liberation, and contextual theologians across the denominational divides, and including Roman Catholic and Eastern Orthodox scholars.

The year following Godsey's comments, 1988, sees leading British Baptist theologian Paul Fiddes suggesting that in Luther the theology of the cross and the theology of glory antonymously structure each other. Their antithetical relations expose both the inner nature and instru-

---

16. Ibid., 19.
17. Godsey, "Barth and Bonhoeffer."
18. Ibid., 26–27. (Italics Godsey's.)

mental purpose of each perspective, these being each finally reduced to epistemology. Fiddes writes, "Luther's distinction between a 'theology of glory' and a 'theology of the cross' [is respectively] the attempt to find God by the exercise of human reason, deducing all aspects of the invisible God from the visible things of the world, and by contrast a reflection on the way God himself has chosen to be found—in the suffering and humiliation of the cross of Jesus."[19]

In 1989 Canadian United Church contextual theologian Douglas John Hall understands the theology of the cross in terms of sanctification, or ongoing "spiritual crucifixion in the cross of Christ." Hall says that via a long line of crucicentric theologians, but particularly Luther, crucicentric theology proclaims the need for the creature to die with Christ if it is to rise in him and live for him. "[Luther's] is a theology of the cross, not first of all because the cross of Golgotha plays such an important part in it (though of course it does) but because the person who is doing this theology lives in a situation of spiritual crucifixion. He is torn between two accounts of reality one negating and the other affirming."[20] There is an important ethical note here. For Hall the theology of the cross is not a static set of propositions, so much as a dynamic process by which believers are brought into sacrificial relation with God and the community. In this Hall insists that the theology of the cross is more than a doctrine of atonement, although he does not go so far as identifying it with an embracing theological system.

Harold Wells is, like Hall, a radical Canadian United Church theologian. In 1992 he states, "The theology of the cross, with its primary source in Paul and developed explicitly by Luther, is a minority tradition in Christian theology that emphasizes the radical difference between the gospel of Jesus Christ and human wisdom."[21] In this Wells understands the theology of the cross as a form of logic. It declares itself the starting point for true knowledge of God and, consequently, for recognizing the foolishness of an anthropocentric beginning for that knowledge. As such the theology of the cross becomes a revolutionary soteriological, pneumatological and integrally social instrument, pointing to divine truth, pointing up falsehood, capable therefore of "profound systematic critique." This is so even although, "Luther himself did not appear to

19. Fiddes, *Creative Suffering*, 30.
20. Hall, "Luther's Theology of the Cross," 8.
21. Wells, "Holy Spirit."

realize the sociopolitical implications which some have found in [his *theologia crucis*] for church and mission."[22]

The temptation to debate Wells now will be foregone, other than to note that he appears to stretch both Paul and Luther in unusual ways, and his passing estimation of Luther as lacking any awareness of the sheerly political and social implications of his *theologia crucis* is arguable.[23] The point now though is that by the 1990s the theology of the cross is becoming less an instrument for defense of strictly dogmatic perspectives and procedures, and more an epistemological tool for radical social critique.

Don Schweitzer,[24] another Canadian and United Church theologian, in 1995 returns to Jürgen Moltmann's definition of the theology of the cross and the antecedents of that definition in von Loewenich and Luther. He explains, "The theology of the cross was traditionally one topic amongst others in Christian theology. With Luther this changed. As Walther von Loewenich has shown, the theology of the cross is more than a topic; it is the guiding principle of all Luther's theology. God, self, and world are all understood by Luther in terms of what the cross reveals about human sin and divine grace."[25] Similarly Schweitzer says, "*Theologia crucis* seeks to understand all theological topics in terms of this divine / human situation. In Luther's view the cross not only says something about God and humanity, it determines how everything else is to be understood as well."[26] Through Moltmann Schweitzer also draws on the social and liberative associations being attached to crucicentric theology contemporarily. Moltmann, he says approvingly, extends Luther's *theologia crucis*, adding a note of eschatological and corporate hope patterned on God's saving relations with Israel. The cross and resurrection together comprise the event in which the promised future breaks into the world, so that all suffering including death, social oppression and humiliation, is overcome.[27]

---

22. Ibid., 480.

23. Luther's excellent recent biographer Heiko Oberman concludes that from its start Luther perceived the Reformation to result in two consequences, the one eschatological and the other political. See Oberman, *Luther*, 72.

24. Schweitzer, "Jürgen Moltmann's Theology."

25. Ibid., 95.

26. Ibid., 96.

27. See ibid., 98.

It follows that for Schweitzer the theology of the cross forms a comprehensive system of ideas connected with social as well as spiritual liberation, corporate as well as individual redemption.

The same year, 1995, North American Lutheran scholar Gaylon Barker also writing of Luther's *theologia crucis*, states that the theology of the cross "is not limited to Christology, but rather, with Christology as its foundation, it shapes all of theology. Its intention was and is to make clear that God comes to us as a hidden God, hidden in lowliness and suffering in Jesus Christ, thereby meeting us in our weakness, in our guilt, in our suffering. It is for this reason the phrase, 'the cross alone is our theology,' becomes Luther's motto."[28] He then adds, "What we have in [Luther's *theologia crucis*] is a methodological statement with a strong christological orientation. It is a way of doing theology that has as its focus the revelation of God in Jesus Christ crucified. But even more so [it unfolds] what lies at the heart of the Christian tradition's insistence on how and where God is to be found, [that is] in the cross and suffering."[29]

For Barker the theology of the cross is first Christology centered on the suffering of Christ. But it is also methodology—a way of doing theology, and then epistemology. After Luther who opposed the Aristotelian starting point of scholastic metaphysics, the theology of the cross stands in radical antithesis to all anthropocentric starting points for the knowledge of God. True knowledge begins with suffering and the cross.

Again in 1995 American Lutheran James Kiecker investigates contentious questions in connection with the historical development of Luther's *theologia crucis*.[30] He provides a careful historical account of Luther's theological evolution, examining the medieval penitential system in detail and charting Luther's increasing disgust with its layers of theological and ecclesiastical corruption. In concert with commentators such as Moltmann, Dalferth, and Wells, Kiecker finds Luther's *theologia crucis* to be an instrument of radical social and ecclesiastical reform.[31]

---

28. Barker, "Bonhoeffer, Luther," 13.

29. Ibid.

30. This development will be addressed in the following section of the discussion, when introducing Luther himself.

31. This said, a radical social analysis of the theology of the cross in the 1990s possibly owes more to the late-modern emphasis on social equity than to structural radicality in the late-medieval world; Luther was hardly a social democrat.

Structurally it takes the form of a multi-thematic system, this for Kiecker being most true to Luther's crucicentric foundation.

Still in 1995, German Lutheran Oswald Bayer concisely sets out the Pauline foundation for crucicentric theology. Paul, he concludes, touches on many crucicentric elements that those following him gradually systematize. The purpose of Bayer's article is not however to explicate Paul's founding of a crucicentric system, but to define the essential *Word* or *Theology* of the cross. He declares with Kiecker and others that this cruciform Word or Theology is not self-evident, universally intelligible. Rather its very hiddenness is of crucial significance; it means that the Word of the cross can only be heard from within the locale of the cross.[32] Here (recalling Moltmann) it reveals itself to be a profoundly unified, christological and trinitarian Word, a Word which is both ontological and concrete, a confronting Word which is rooted both temporally and eschatologically. What Bayer shows therefore, is that on the basis of its most ancient foundation the theology of the cross is not only an extended systematic instrument, but something more. It carries an ontology of its own, it is a system fused with Revelation, a vehicle for Jesus Christ.

The following year, 1996, Canadian Franceen Neufeld[33] plots the theology of the cross as it passes from Paul, through the medieval mystical tradition, to Luther. In her introduction she appeals to noted British Anglican evangelical theologian Alister McGrath, finding with him that the central feature of the *theologia crucis* is "a rejection of all speculation in the face of God's concealed revelation in the cross of Christ."[34] For Neufeld the theology of the cross is finally mystical epistemology.

In 1997 a raft of articles on the theology of the cross appear, and six are reviewed now. In this year American Protestant Pastor Robert Cornwall[35] publishes an article addressing various understandings of atonement through Christian tradition, concluding that Christ's redemptive suffering provides a pattern for modern Christian living. This article is formally associated in the major ATLA database with the search-term *theology of the cross*, although the text does not actually present the nomenclature itself. This suggests that towards the end of the twentieth century *theology of the cross* is becoming increasingly severed from its

---

32. See Bayer, "Word of the Cross," 47.
33. Neufeld, "The Cross of the Living Lord."
34. Ibid., 135. See also McGrath, *Luther's Theology of the* Cross, 150.
35. Cornwall, "The Scandal of the Cross."

classical crucicentric foundation. It is sometimes now a generic term able to support whatever notion those employing it wish to accord it—in the ATLA theological-cataloguer's case, ethical prescription.

This chapter began by highlighting American Lutheran Gerhard Forde's 1997 remark that the theology of the cross is not well understood. He asserts this in the introduction to his major book, *On Being a Theologian of the Cross*. In an accompanying and hard-hitting article bearing the same title he argues that the theology of the cross is not some sentimentalized conception of "Jesus identifying with the suffering of the world." Rather it constitutes a rigorous and embracing hermeneutical lens[36] through which the world may be viewed realistically in all its sinful rebellion and self-deceit. What is also interesting is Forde's attention to and critique of *language*. For him the theology of the cross radically confronts the late-modern notion that meaning is purely subjective. This is one of the few places where the debate as to the nature and purpose of the theology of the cross surfaces. Forde explicitly reacts to the confined understanding of it, powerfully reasserting the extended soteriological, epistemological, and integrally realistic meaning which, he says, Luther actually intends.

Similarly to Forde, again in 1997 American Lutheran Kurt Hendel examines the Heidelberg Disputation.[37] As Forde, Hendel finds that while much modern crucicentric scholarship has fixed on divine suffering as the key element of the theology of the cross, Luther's conception is actually far more complex, being to do with the whole methodology and theology of the gospel of salvation.

Still in 1997, American historical theologian Kenneth Hagan returns to Luther's crucicentric conception. But unlike other commentators his implicit position is that Luther's doctrines of atonement, reconciliation, expiation of sins, the suffering of Christ, joyful exchange, the worm,[38] the

---

36. Forde writes, "[The theology of the cross is] "a particular perception of the world and our destiny, what Luther came to call looking at all things through suffering and the cross." Ibid., 949. See also the Heidelberg Disputation, Thesis 20.

37. Hendel, "Theology of the Cross." Forde focuses on a point by point examination of each of the Heidelberg Disputation theses, whereas Hendel delineates the Disputation's major themes.

38. Luther's theology of the worm and the devil, influenced by Ps 22:6, is a major sub-theme in his *theologia crucis*. Forsaken by God, Christ takes on worm-like human nature so as to defeat the devil. As Luther explains, "[Jesus Christ] degrades himself so profoundly and becomes a man, yes, even degrades himself below all men, as it is

devil, and similar, do not contribute to his *theologia crucis*. Rather Hagan thinks atonement in and of itself is Luther's central organizing concept,[39] and the *theologia crucis* alongside other doctrines comprises one strand of that. Its contribution to atonement is to oppose the dual attempts by the creature to avoid the work of the cross in its life, and to control God equating itself to God. Here there is no suggestion that rather than the theology of the cross being an aspect of atonement, atonement might be an aspect of the theology of the cross. It follows that Hagan joins those understanding the theology of the cross narrowly.

In 1997 American Lutheran feminist theologian Mary Solberg shows that Luther links power, the control of knowledge, and the methodologies for obtaining that control. In his *theologia crucis* he radically questions reigning epistemological power structures, proposing a cruciform counter epistemology. Similarly modern feminists are concerned with the ethical implications of possessing knowledge, and with developing counter epistemologies or *epistemologies of suspicion* for understanding reality.[40] Thus, Solberg says, strange as it may appear there is a place for fruitful dialogue between the epistemology of the cross and feminist epistemology, and she goes on to develop the lessons feminists might take from Luther. Behind these she conceives of Luther's theology of the cross narrowly; it constitutes above all a radical epistemological instrument for deconstructing the oppressive epistemologies of powerful elites.

Solberg has an ally in English Anglican academic Graham Tomlin. The same year, 1997, he writes, "The thin tradition . . . has impressive credentials as a kind of theology possessing an inbuilt resistance to the abuse of power."[41] Tomlin employs "the thin tradition" to dispute what is

---

written Psalm 22[:6] 'I am a worm and no man, scorned by men and despised by the people.' In such physical weakness and poverty, he attacks the enemy, lets himself be put on the cross and killed, and by his cross in death, he destroys the enemy and the avenger." (*Psalms of David* c.1537.) Lull, *Luther's Basic Theological Writings*, 110.

39. Hagan writes, "Atonement for Luther serves as an important interpretative tool for packaging many genuine Luther articles [of faith]". Hagan, "Luther on Atonement," 253.

40. Solberg offers an example here: both Luther and contemporary feminists agree that knowing "and not-knowing affect what we do and don't do, and how we justify what we do and do not do. Ethics is as integral to epistemology as science is." Solberg, "Epistemology of the Cross," 14.

41. Tomlin, "The Theology of the Cross: Subversive Theology for a Postmodern World?", 59.

an integrally postmodern assertion: since by definition the objectivity of truth cannot be known any proposal countering this is necessarily oppressive. Rather for Tomlin it is the postmodern assertion, falsely claiming truth and homage for itself, which is oppressive. He adduces Paul in Corinth, Martin Luther, and Blaise Pascal in support. For each the *Theology* or *Word* of the cross is ontologically Absolute Truth, moreover Absolute Truth which far from being coercive, humbly serves and emancipates. This being so Tomlin concludes, "[The thin tradition] has shown itself on several significant occasions to be capable of mounting a serious critique of theologies which are used to legitimize claims to power, and to offer instead an alternative vision of both God's use of power and that of those who claim to be his people."[42]

Clearly Tomlin like Solberg is returning to the historical and theological roots of the theology of the cross, although he views it as a comprehensive system, one grounded ontologically and christologically. In this profound sense it comprises a subversive political instrument capable of sustaining the objectivity of paramount counter-meaning.

The last years of the twentieth century bring a number of articles taking a broadly similar view of the theology of the cross to Solberg's and Tomlin's. That is, it constitutes a divine weapon with which to attack anthropocentric theologies, especially now late-modern anthropocentric theologies.

In 1998 American Lutheran Paul Hinlicky defines Luther's *theologia crucis* as a christological and soteriological instrument, which in the hands of twentieth century modern orthodox theologians has been reshaped and welded against contemporary descendants of nineteenth century anthropocentricism.[43]

Still in 1988, by means of reviving an old debate,[44] Canadian United Church pastor Don Schweitzer now investigates the shape of the mod-

---

42. Ibid.

43. See Hinlicky, "Luther's Theology of the Cross—Part Two," 46–61.

44. In 1971 John Douglas Hall argued controversially that Jürgen Moltmann's theology of hope was meant to confront the autonomy and sinful self-confidence of contemporary modern society. In North America, however, it was being misappropriated to support exactly this autonomy and self-confidence—doing so on the grounds that the kingdom offering freedom from individual and corporate oppression *already* existed there. In 1998 Schweitzer accepts Hall's analysis of North America's self-affirming use of Moltmann's position, but argues that far from this being a travesty of his intention, Moltmann can fairly be read in the North American way. Schweitzer says, "The escha-

ern theology of the cross, and questions the way it might be employed in contemporary North American culture. He warns first against a simplistic assessment of the modern liberal theological programme as fundamentally opposed to the primacy of the gospel, arguing that in significant ways, ethically and politically, the liberal programme takes its lead from the revolutionary nature of the gospel. Schweitzer then finds that the *theology* (*message*) from the cross announces a radical shift in human affairs, whereby sin and suffering are overcome and equity and eschatological hope commensurably increase. As such there are points at which the theology of the cross functions as a bridge between modern theologies on the left and on the right.

In this Schweitzer is rather far from the typical crucicentric distrust of all anthropocentric theology—which is not to dismiss completely his insight that a reshaped and peculiarly modern theology of the cross, securely grounded in the classical crucicentric tradition, might function as an instrument of reproachment. This also means that in the late nineties the *social* implications of crucicentric theology are increasingly to the fore for both the theological left and (in the North American case) right. The point for present purposes however, is that Schweitzer's conception of the theology of the cross lies at the "confined" end of the spectrum. He identifies it with a single theme, in this case inbreaking justice and commensurate eschatological hope.

In 1999 Graham Tomlin publishes his doctoral monograph *The Power of the Cross: Theology and the Death of Christ in Paul, Luther and Pascal*, (the author's earlier 1997 article foreshadowing this work). In *The Power of the Cross* Tomlin continues to take a holistic view of crucicentric theology, and to bring out its political implications, past and present, for the community of Christ. "The theology of the cross," he says, "has . . . been used both to offer comfort and to challenge complacency in the post-war West. This is a truly versatile theology, which can speak in different historical settings, both to those who exercise power and those who are on the receiving end of its operation."[45] And, "[The] *theologia crucis* [is] a polemical theology directed against theologies of power."[46]

---

tological outlook of Moltmann's theology enables a more nuanced assessment of North American culture [than Hall allows.]" Schweitzer, "Douglas Hall's Critique," 7.

45. Tomlin, *The Power of the Cross*, 4.

46. Ibid., 6.

As per his title Tomlin focuses on Paul, Luther, and Pascal—the latter providing a later counterbalance to Luther as each independently attacks the oppressive structures of his time. Tomlin also notes the contribution of medieval mysticism to the onward crucicentric tradition. Along with these investigations, throughout the volume Tomlin identifies certain dialectically contrasting elements in the *theologia crucis*, including the way suffering and "bringing low" precedes glorifying and "raising high," not only in the life of Christ but in the life of his followers. The author also brings out the significant philosophical elements of the tradition. Finally there is a parting discussion on the socio-political meaning of a crucicentric orientation in a postmodern world.

In all of these emphases Tomlin implicitly identifies the shape and content of the classical *theologia crucis*, (so-called here), although he does not stop to set out its shape and content formally. If any criticism is to be mounted of this penetrating work it is that in pursuing the theology of the cross first as political theology, rather than as systematic theology, Tomlin emphasizes its social and moral meanings, but misses its embracing eschatological power.

The same year, 1999, major American Presbyterian theologian, George Hunsinger, delineates those ways in which Luther influences Barth. One strand of that influence concerns the *theologia crucis*. He begins, "Another powerful theme that Barth absorbed from Luther involves the theology of the cross. In the last four or five decades, theologians have shown an increasing interest in the suffering of God."[47] For now what is interesting is simply that a theologian of Hunsinger's stature and background should view the theology of the cross exclusively in terms of the suffering of God, and thence narrowly.

Also in 1999, American Lutheran Mark Mattes reviews Gerhard Forde's 1997 book, *On Being a Theologian of the* Cross. In part he writes, "One important result of the renaissance of Luther scholarship for Lutheran theology in the twentieth century has been the retrieval of the eschatological character of Luther's theology of the cross (*theologia crucis*) and the attempt to evaluate and construct new presentations of Lutheran theology and other contemporary theologies in light of this discovery."[48] By "eschatological character of Luther's theology of the

---

47. Hunsinger, "What Barth Learned from Luther," 132. The excerpt is further cited, see here p. 189.

48. Mattes, "Gerhard Forde," 373.

cross" Mattes means Luther's reassertion that in and with Jesus Christ the "old man" must be crucified so that the "new man" may arise, new made, fully human and participant in Christ's risen glory. Mattes then advances human re-creation and proper glorification as the central meaning of Luther's *theologia crucis*. In doing so he faults Forde for missing the eschatology of Luther's *theologia crucis* almost entirely. Forde has been caught into "the new orthodoxy" of the theology of the cross as a theology of the suffering and dying of God. (Mattes says that the one value of conceiving the theology of the cross as a theology of divine suffering is that it points to the God who is not against, but emphatically and personally *for*, humankind.[49])

Three things can be said here. First, this is one of the very few examples in the literature being reviewed when an explicit debate as to the central meaning of Luther's *theologia crucis* actually occurs. Second, later discussion will suggest that a true *theologia gloriae* is indeed an important crucicentric notion in Luther. Third, as it happens Mattes is wrong in his estimation of Forde. Forde certainly does hold that the theology of the cross concerns divine suffering, but he does not allow this to be its only meaning so as to exclude eschatology, or in fact a whole range of theological elements. Indeed Forde's broad and systematic understanding of the theology of the cross is in marked contrast to Mattes' own perspective identifying it narrowly primarily with eschatology.

In 2001 Harold Wells continues his long interest in the radical social potential of the theology of the cross. Now he clarifies the methodological interconnection between Luther's *theologia crucis* and the late-modern liberation theologies. Not only have the liberation theologies borrowed from the crucicentric tradition, they have contributed to its recent radicalization as an instrument countering theological and social oppression. Wells writes, "Theology of the cross . . . is most authentically itself in our time when it appropriates the key insights of theology of liberation."[50] *Vis à vis* the current discussion, it would seem that at the beginning of a new century the transformation of the theology of the cross according to its contemporary context is continuing apace. Moreover the first critical question to it no longer concerns its shape and content, but its function.

---

49. Ibid., 387.
50. Wells, "Cross and Liberation," 147.

There are broad similarities between the 1999 review by Mattes proposing in part that eschatology governs and thus elucidates Luther's *theologia crucis*, and a 2003 article by Finnish-American theologian Veli-Matti Kärkkäinen. Writing out of the Mannermaa school of Finnish Luther research,[51] Kärkkäinen explains that a principal aim of this school is the provision of a new hermeneutic for Luther studies based on Luther's *leading idea*. The presumption is that as such, that idea must provide a key to the whole.[52] Mannermaa is said by Kärkkäinen to find such an idea in Luther's theology of true creaturely glory. The latter is said to dominate Luther's *theologia crucis* in the Heidelberg Disputation, and then to epitomize his lifelong crucicentric approach.[53] What is significant now, however, is that Kärkkäinen does not interrelate this particular crucicentric notion with other such notions, and thus (like Mattes) leans towards a narrow conception of the theology of the cross.

The penultimate discussion here notes a 2004 Barth introductory text by North American evangelical Kurt Anders Richardson. In passing reference to Luther's *theologia crucis* Richardson pronounces shortly, "[This] is the method of knowing and reflecting on the revelation of God through the cross-destined life of Jesus Christ."[54] From reading him further it seems that for Richardson reflection on the death of Christ leads to the action of *knowing about* God, reflection on the knowledge of God leads to the further action of *knowing* God. Reflection on knowing God leads to the supreme action of *trusting* God—who is axiomatically the God of the cross. In short the theology of the cross not only proclaims a

---

51. Prof. Tuomo Mannermaa held the chair of theology at the University of Helsinki 1980–2000.

52. See Kärkkäinen, "'Evil, Love,' 218.

53. While debate has taken place among Luther scholars as to the ongoing significance of his *theologia crucis* for his whole project, the consensus of recent opinion is that from his early theology on Luther never departs from his *theologia crucis*. Ebeling, for instance, says, "[Although in his later theology Luther] did not make constant use of [the terms *theologia crucis* and *theologia gloriae*] as slogans to represent his theological outlook, but only took them up again on rare occasions, they are a very accurate expression of his understanding of theology." Ebeling, *Luther: An Introduction*, 226. Similarly Forde, "[In] respect to the Reformation [the Heidelberg theses] remain determinative . . . It is not too much to say . . . that they are almost a kind of outline for Luther's subsequent theological program." Forde, *Being a Theologian of the Cross*, 20–21. Likewise von Loewenich, "There were a number of shifts of emphasis but Luther never gave up the theology of the cross." Von Loewenich, *Luther's Theology of the Cross*, 90.

54. Richardson, *Reading Karl Barth*, 126.

knowledge inculcating trust, but actually brings about that which it proclaims. On this reading the theology of the cross is defined principally as divine epistemological methodology. In this, therefore narrow, conception Richardson continues the late-modern stress on the function rather than the structure of the theology of the cross.

Since 2004 contributions to the literature on the theology of the cross have continued to appear.[55] Alongside familiar systematic, pastoral, and historical foci, the theology of the cross is now being related to such *topics du jour* as: climate change, the rehabilitation of torture as a legitimate instrument of power, the emergence of Africa, and the rise of post industrial society. These latest materials need not be reviewed in detail here. An overview of them shows that they stand in the same narrow course as the items considered above. That overview also suggests that as the second decade of the twenty-first century approaches, the theology of the cross continues to be understood variously—sometimes systemically but more often not. The case remains that no widely accepted explanation of its shape and content currently exists.

Concluding the Review

Almost all the conceptions of the theology of the cross of the past fifty years can quickly be placed towards one or other end of a continuum. One polarity narrowly identifies the theology of the cross with one or a few crucicentric elements. The other denotes an encompassing system of these elements. Advocates of the narrow conception quite simply do not appear to be aware that the broader and systematic conception of the theology of the cross exists. Conversely, from the perspective of that broader conception, to understand the theology of the cross in a narrow way necessarily misses its systemic breadth, shape, and involved theological content and purpose. Neither does a narrow view do justice to the historical depth of the crucicentric tradition. Indeed into the new century conceptions of the theology of the cross restricting it to radical methodology tend to sever it from its classical foundations altogether.

Taking all this into consideration it is the extended systemic understanding of the theology of the cross in the recent literature that, at this

---

55. According to the ATLA database between 2004 and 2009 the literature bearing in some way on the theology of the cross includes 18 journal articles, three essays, and five books plus their associated reviews.

juncture, appears truest to the classical tradition Luther culminates. The next two chapters aim to substantiate this conclusion further, beginning with consideration of the multiple epistemological strands of the classical *theologia crucis*.

2

The Classical Epistemology of the Cross

God can reveal himself only in concealment—
in the humility and shame of the cross.

—Martin Luther[1]

Epistemology has often been treated as an adjunct to the classical *theologia crucis*. In contrast the current study finds it to be one of two core dimensions systematically structuring it. This "epistemology of the cross" is itself divided in two.

In its negative aspect crucicentric epistemology stands in opposition to a parallel system holding it possible for the creature to obtain direct knowledge of God by anthropocentric means. This the classical crucicentric theologians consider foolish, impossible, and sinful. They argue critically that God alone possesses the knowledge of God in Godself, thus God alone can disclose God as God really is.[2] It follows that there can be no direct access to such knowledge. The creature's attempt on it is necessarily the attempt to know as God alone can know, and therefore to be glorious in its own right.

In its positive aspect classical crucicentric epistemology asserts and defends a revelatory solution to the ancient question as to how true knowledge of God in Godself might become available to the creature.

---

1. Luther, *Luther's Works,* 31:52–53. (Thesis 20, Heidelberg. Disputation.)

2. Influenced by Paul in 1 Cor 2:11, Athanasius for example says that no one "knows what pertains to God except the Spirit of God." Anatolios, *Athanasius,* 179. (*Letters to Serapion* 1:22.)

Drawn through the cross the creature's mind is absolutely identified with the mind of Jesus Christ, and thence with the mind of God. It participates in Christ's cognitive orientation, his self-knowledge, his wisdom, it sees with his eyes. This cognitive union is finally completed eschatologically. Then the creature's mind is totally transformed and renewed, becoming not divine but within Christ's noetic humanity fully human.

Dialectical tension within crucicentric epistemology and soteriology lends these dimensions internal coherence and strength, methodologically and theologically. In respect to crucicentric epistemology contrary pairs include: darkness and light, falsity and truth, the back and the front, the weak and the strong, revelation 'under the opposite'—or in the opposite place to that reasonably expected, revelation and hiddenness, wisdom and foolishness, humiliation and exaltation, time and eternity. The juxtaposition of these polarities unbalances natural expectations as to how things actually are, and therefore what is really true.

These pairs hinge on the cross. Von Loewenich explains:

> The cross puts everything to the test. The cross is the judgement upon all of man's self-chosen thoughts and deeds. In view of man's actual situation this means the radical reversal of all human assumptions. What is foolish is wise, what is weak is strong, what is disgrace is honor, what appears hateful to man is to be desired and loved in the highest degree. Does it not follow as a matter of course when we are told that lack of understanding is the true understanding of God? When we plunge into lack of understanding then we go the way of the cross.[3]

Similarly Wells, for whom the essential epistemology of the cross revolves around its radical revelation of knowledge regarding the man-God Jesus Christ—a God far different from the isolate, unknowable, deistic entity[4] of speculative metaphysics. Or in Wells' own words, "[The] theology of the cross, with its primary source in Paul and developed explicitly by Luther . . . emphasizes the radical difference between the gospel of Jesus Christ and human wisdom"[5]—"human wisdom" here

---

3. Von Loewenich, *Luther's Theology of the Cross*, 75.

4. According to *A New Dictionary of Christian Theology*, "'Deism' [refers] to belief in the existence of a supreme being who is regarded as the ultimate source of reality and the ground of value but as not intervening in natural and historical processes by way of particular providences, revelations and salvific acts." Pailin. "Deism," 148. The deistic god is the propositional god of metaphysics.

5. Wells, "Holy Spirit," 479. By "human wisdom" is meant speculative methods for deriving the knowledge of God.

connoting speculative methodologies for obtaining the knowledge of God. Wells continues, "The gospel proves to be not simply one more instance of general human religious wisdom, but a reversal of the wisdom . . . of the world. It is *evangelion*."[6] It is *the news of God proclaimed by God*, overturning the methodologies of the world for accessing that news.

Before turning to examine the negative and positive dimensions of this radical crucicentric *evangelion* however, two general background explanations are useful. The first concerns Luther's distinction between the theologian of glory and the theologian of the cross, the second relates to the classical crucicentric understanding of faith.

For Luther the *theologia crucis* is not simply a theoretical construct, even a divinely inspired one, but a living knowledge articulated through living beings. For him, as Gerhard Forde writes, "When the cross conquers, it becomes clear . . . that there is a quite different way of being a theologian."[7] It is then a commonplace of Luther scholarship that in Luther's recovery of the crucicentric tradition the distinguishing of theologians rather than of theological systems is of first importance.

Luther initially makes this distinction in his Heidelberg Disputation. "That person does not deserve to be called a theologian who claims to see into the invisible things of God (Thesis 19)," he says. "He deserves to be called a theologian, however, who comprehends what is visible of God through suffering and the cross (Thesis 20)." "The theologian of glory calls [the knowledge of God, deduced from the creature which is] evil, 'good', and [the knowledge of God revealed from the cross which is] good, 'evil'. The theologian of the cross calls the thing what it actually is (Thesis 21)."

But it is in his *Explanations of the Disputation Concerning the Value of Indulgences* the same year as the Heidelberg Disputation, 1518, that Luther is generally considered to set out his two theologians' characteristics, or marks, most succinctly. Here he bears quoting at length:

> A theologian of glory does not recognize, along with the Apostle, the crucified and hidden God alone. He sees and speaks of God's glorious manifestation among the heathen, how his invisible nature can be known from the things which are visible and how he is present and powerful in all things everywhere. [This theologian] learns from Aristotle that the object of the will is the good and

---

6. Ibid.
7. Forde, *Being a Theologian of the Cross*, 10.

the good is worthy to be loved, while the evil, on the other hand, is worthy of hate. He learns that God is the highest good and exceedingly lovable. Disagreeing with theologians of the cross, he defines the treasury of Christ as the removing and remitting of punishments, things which are most evil and worthy of hate.

In opposition to this the theologian of the cross . . . (that is, one who speaks of the crucified and hidden God) teaches that punishments, crosses, and death are the most precious treasury of all and the most sacred relics which the Lord of this theology himself created and blessed, not alone by the touch of his most holy flesh but also by the embrace of his exceedingly holy and divine will, and he has left these relics here to be kissed, sought after, and embraced. Indeed fortunate and blessed is he who is considered by God to be so worthy that these treasures of Christ should be given to him."[8]

In sum the major distinction between Luther's two theologians is that they each perceive reality differently. The philosopher-theologian of glory looks at God directly from around the back of the cross, thereby circumventing it; the theologian of the cross looks at God indirectly through the cross of Jesus Christ. The theologian of glory learns from natural methodologies that the knowledge of God can be reached speculatively; the theologian of the cross learns from the cross that God ultimately reveals the knowledge of himself in the crucified Christ. The theologian of glory looks towards the invisible things of God with the eyes of the intellect; the theologian of the cross looks towards the visible things of God with the eyes of faith.

The theologian of glory charges the theologian of the cross with foolishly beginning with that which is not tethered naturally, leading to the embrace of that which God in his perfection rejects: suffering and punishment. The theologian of the cross charges the theologian of glory with an equivalent foolishness for beginning with false and anthropocentric premises, leading to false vision, false discernment, and—disastrously—false proclamation.

Luther's point is that it is the theologian of the cross who is really wise, for in looking at God *through* the cross such a theologian correctly perceives reality. The metaphysical methodology of the theologian of glory produces not God, but only the image of its blinded creator.

8. Luther, *Luther's Works*, 31:225f. (Here "crosses" references that of Christ, and that of the creature.)

There is a second introductory matter. Generally the classical crucicentric theologians hold faith to be a capacity originating in God and graciously gifted to the creature. Faith is not a capacity to derive propositional truth or formulate dogma, (that being in the province of natural reason), but the capacity to trust the One who alone makes patent the knowledge of God in Godself, and who grants salvation through the darkness of death. From the crucicentric perspective faith is thus the antithesis of lack of trust, of hopelessness, of blindness to what actually is the case.

For Paul faith has a profound objective and christological character. It is always first *Christ's* faith, and that means finally that the gift of faith is one with the gift of Christ himself. So Paul writes, "For by grace you have been saved through faith, and this is not your own doing; it is the gift of God, not the result of works, so that no one may boast (Eph 2:8–9)." Paul's understanding of faith is also usefully interpreted by Barth when explaining Gal 2:20, (the square brackets below are his). "I have been crucified with Christ. I live; and yet no longer I, but Christ liveth in me. And the life which I now live in the flesh, I live in the faith of the Son of God [to be understood quite literally: I live—not in my faith in the Son of God, but in this—that the Son of God had faith!] who loved me and gave himself for me."[9]

For Athanasius too faith is not a human construction.[10] Rather it is a gift of the Father, mediated by the Scriptures, the saints, and supremely

---

9. Barth, "Gospel and Law," 7. The excerpt is further cited, see here pp. 198–99.

10. Athanasius (c.296–373), Patriarch of Alexandria from 328, is generally regarded as one of the four great patristic doctors of the Eastern Church. In retrospective overview, against the backdrop of a tumultuous age, one which saw him exiled from his patriarchate five times, Athanasius worked out his doctrines of the Son and Word of God, defending the full divinity of the Son and his consubstantiality with the Father. Athanasius also insisted on the full divinity of the Holy Spirit, and with this the triunity of the Godhead, a triunity which enhanced rather than compromised essential unity in God. In doing so he upheld the creed of the Council of Nicea (325), which council he had himself attended. In addition Athanasius contributed significantly to the orthodox doctrine of creation, holding that the Son and the Father are together creative in the power of the Spirit. He maintained, as had Irenaeus (c.130–200), that the world came into being *out of nothing* [*ex nihilo*]. In line with this he taught a fundamental distinction between the Creator-God and his creation. Creation included both the human body *and* soul; until this point the soul had being considered an aspect of the spiritual realm. Contra Gnosticism and the Manicheans Athanasius argued that creation was the work of a good God and so itself good; this was also important because at this time monasticism was questioning the spiritual value of Christian involvement in the affairs

the Son at the point of the cross. It follows that reason dictates a starting point with "the faith of the cross."[11] It is this God gifted cruciform faith which enables the human soul to know and confess Jesus as the incarnate Word and Son.[12] Thence Athanasius refers to Christ's death as "the capstone of our faith."[13] A comment in his *Vita Antonii* well expresses his position: "[Certain Greeks came to Antony] to dispute concerning the preaching of the divine Cross . . . [Antony asked them, 'Which] is better, faith which comes through the inworking (of God) or demonstration by [speculative] arguments?' And when they answered that faith which comes through the inworking was better and was accurate knowledge, Antony said, 'You have answered well . . . We Christians therefore hold the mystery [of the cross] not in the wisdom of Greek arguments, but in the power of faith richly supplied to us by God through Jesus Christ.'"[14]

Luther's understanding of faith closely follows that of Paul and Athanasius. In summary faith for him is the capacity to see that which is not visible to natural sight but rests in secret in Jesus Christ, above all in the cross. Or as von Loewenich explains, "[According] to Luther's Heidelberg theses . . . faith can be directed only to what is concealed, hidden, and invisible."[15] Such faith "stands in permanent conflict with perception. Its object is nothing perceptible, nothing visible, but their very opposite."[16] In turn this means that faith is not naturally founded. It

---

of the world. Athanasius set such notions out in a number of treatises, orations and pastoral letters. These include the early two-part work *Contra Gentes and De Incarnatione Verbi*, in which he described the epistemological and soteriological foundations to his thought. They also include anti-Arian writings declaring the full divinity of the Son, letters defending his doctrine of the Spirit (*Letters to Serapion* and *On the Holy Spirit*), and an inspirational biography of Antony the Great, *Vita Antonii*, of value to contemporary and later monasticism. There is too a corpus of exegetical studies. (Note that the so-called *Athanasian Creed* is actually a late fifth or early sixth century Latin work, likely related to Augustine's *De trinitate*.) See Pettersen, "Athanasius," 41–42, and Weinandy, *Athanasius*.

11. See Thomson, *De Incarnatione* 28.2 and 28.5.

12. Athanasius says of Jesus Christ, "[He] is himself wisdom, himself Word, himself the very power of the Father, himself light, himself truth, himself justice, himself virtue, the very type, brightness and . . . unchanging image of the Father." *Contra Gentes* (46.8). See Weinandy, *Athanasius*, 23.

13. Thomson, *De Incarnatione* 19. See also Anatolios, *Athanasius*, 57.

14. Schaff, *"The Life of Antony"*, IV:74–78.

15. Von Loewenich, *Luther's Theology of the Cross*, 36.

16. Ibid., 91–92.

The Classical Epistemology of the Cross 39

"does not have its origin in any of the given abilities of the soul. [Neither can it] be classified with the rest of the psychic functions."[17] Faith then is not a flight into nothingness but faith in another, in a higher reality which is the genuine reality.

Faith for Luther is vested in Jesus Christ. He is the subject and object of faith, its divine originator and ontological content. This being so, faith is "Christ given and Christ inhabited."[18] Von Loewenich says here, "[For Luther] Christ is not only the principal object of faith but also the ground for making it possible . . . Christ is related to faith as form to matter . . . This does not express identity between Christ and faith, but reduces their belonging together to its most acute form."[19] It follows for von Loewenich that on the basis of Luther, "Both 'through Christ' and 'through faith' must be said. Neither may be separated from the other."[20]

This unity means for Luther, as von Loewenich also says, that "faith is not a leap into a vacuum. It perhaps gropes in the darkness—and precisely there runs into Christ. It moves away from all experience and experiences Christ. And Christ is the firm possession of this faith."[21] A later Luther scholar comes to very much the same conclusion. Jenson says shortly, "[For] Luther faith has trust in Christ as its ground and centre. Only through faith can Christ be seen as the God who is hidden in the incarnation and cross."[22]

It is then for Luther not possible for the creature to *have* faith so as to trust in God, apart from receipt of Christ who *is* faith and trust. With this in mind faith and trust "directly" in God rather than by way of Christ, and him crucified, can only be false trust in a false god. Or as Luther himself says bluntly, "[Those] who approach God through faith and not at the same time through Christ actually depart from him."[23]

How then can authentic faith—faith that is originated, gifted and inhabited by Christ, be received? Luther's answer is via passage through the cross in which creaturely faithlessness and its corollary self-trust are

17. Ibid.
18. Ibid., 90.
19. Ibid., 104.
20. Ibid., 103.
21. Ibid., 106.
22. Jenson, "Karl Barth," 18.
23. Luther, *Luther's Works*, (Lectures on Romans), 25:287.

put to death, that Christ's faith may be received in their stead. Only by such deadly exchange can faith be had. Only via passage through the cross can faith disclose the meaning of the cross, first faith and then understanding; understanding is always predicated on faith and never the reverse. In McGrath's words, "[For Luther the] correlative to *Crux sola* is *sola fide*, as it is through faith, and *through faith alone*, that the true significance of the cross is perceived, and through faith alone that its power can be appropriated."[24]

This all has significant consequences for Luther's understanding of epistemology. As Dalferth explains, authentic epistemological knowledge is not for Luther a system of rationally verifiable axioms, but of objective truths asserted and verified on the basis of faith in Jesus Christ, and him crucified.[25] It follows too that Luther (as the classical crucicentric theologians generally) is deeply suspicious of all methodologies for the knowledge of God which bypass, or otherwise relativise, receipt of gifted faith as the precursor to all true knowledge of God, all true epistemology.

The Negative Epistemology of the Cross

The classical crucicentric theologians reject all anthropocentric starting points for the knowledge of God, including starting points in human experience, the law, a self-engendered mysticism, and the several strands of natural theology. In doing so they take up arms in—as Torrance notes in immediate reference to Athanasius—"a conflict between underlying frameworks of thought, an objective [thoroughly crucicentric] way of thinking from a centre in God and a subjective way of thinking from a centre in man."[26]

The first two of these starting points may be disposed of very briefly. Crucicentric epistemology regards *human experience* as the subjective product of either the senses or the reasoning mind. Starting with experience the creature cannot attain objective knowledge of God as God really is, for then it would be as God. The knowledge of God is attainable only by way of faith. Faith perceives that which experience subjectively cannot perceive; it validates that which experience subjectively cannot

---

24. McGrath, *Luther's Theology of the Cross*, 174. Italics McGrath's.
25. See Dalferth, "The Visible and the Invisible," 24.
26. Torrance, *Karl Barth*, 163.

The Classical Epistemology of the Cross 41

validate. McGrath (thinking of Luther) explains this further. "[The] theology of the cross draws our attention to the sheer unreliability of experience as a guide to the presence and activity of God. God is active and present in the world, quite independently of whether we experience him as being so. Experience declared that God was absent from Calvary, only to have its verdict humiliatingly overturned on the third day."[27]

Similarly, crucicentric epistemology denies the employment of the *legal* starting point for the knowledge of God, and therefore for truth.[28] For Paul and Luther the prime revelatory task of the law is not to declare the truth of God, but the truth of humanity in its fallen state before God. (The following chapter on soteriology will take this further.) It follows that those who would use the law to condition their access to God's knowledge of God merely disclose the knowledge of their own sinfulness.

To turn in greater detail to the third of the matters listed above, the classical crucicentric theologians also reject *the mystical starting point* for the knowledge of God, this being prominent in the medieval world.

A New Dictionary of Christian Theology defines *mysticism* as follows, "[The] main characteristics of mysticism seem to be: 1) [A] profound, compelling, unforgettable sense of union and unity; 2) the successive character of time is transcended in an awareness of simultaneity; 3) the experience is not felt to be a mere subjectivity; rather it is a disclosure ... 4) There is always a sense of enhancement of joy, exultation, ... 5) there is also an overwhelming sense of "presence," of the utter nearness of the transcendent."[29]

In the western branch of Christendom the broader ascetical and dogmatic traditions part at an early date, developing on parallel paths. In contrast in the eastern church mysticism develops in dialectical response to dogmatic theology. In both geographical spheres however, it is a particular strand of the ascetical tradition that keeps the crucicentric tradition alive during the Middle Ages, in due course coming to influence Luther's *theologia crucis* strongly.

---

27. McGrath, *The Enigma of the Cross*, 159.

28. As set down in Holy Scripture, divine law can be found chiefly in the decalogue (Exod 20:1–17, Deut 5:6–21), the interpretation of the decalogue in the Sermon on the Mount (Matt 5–7), and the instruction concerning these commands given by the Apostles. Luther gives first attention to the Mosaic law.

29. Tinsley, "Mysticism," 387.

To recap, stretching between the eleventh and fifteenth centuries major crucicentric mystical theologians include: St Bernard of Clairvaux (1090–1153), the anonymous writer of the *Theologia Germanica* (c.1350), Johannes Tauler (c.1300–1361), and Nicholas of Cusa (1401–1464). Together these figures hold certain commonalities of approach epistemologically and, to foreshadow future discussion, soteriologically. On the grounds that creation is fundamentally of God and so "good" they advocate a moderate discipline rather than an extreme asceticism, one which respects the physical body. They follow the Pauline tradition of the New Testament worshipping not the cross in and of itself, but its victim. Thence they reject much popular contemporary piety,[30] along with that practice meant to imitate Christ's passion in order to win justification.

In their epistemology the crucicentric mystics do not despise the use of reason, far from it, but they recognize that as a natural capacity reason is appropriate to the natural sphere only. Its limited sight cannot perceive God directly. Rather, and as Neufeld says, "Crucicentric mysticism recognizes no other way to discover the glory of God than to follow Christ through darkness."[31] The crucicentric mystics propose a *via negativa*, a negative path leading *through* the cross in and with Jesus Christ, as the sole way by which the creature might attain the knowledge of God in Godself, knowledge therefore of his glory. Moreover the knowledge received in this dark way is itself held to be glorious, (and not simply the content of that knowledge), just because it is the exclusive possession and gift of God. Cruciform passage is then the one route by which the creature's mind can be mystically united to Christ's mind, cognitive union made glorious because it is God and not the creature who has brought it about.

It follows that the medieval crucicentric theologians, as after them also Luther, rail against a very different and broader strand of medieval mysticism, one seeking direct knowledge of God by means of self-induced union with God. A key representative of this anthropocentric mysticism is Meister Eckhart (1260–1329), and a brief examination of his position might indicate what it is the crucicentric mystics so dislike.

---

30. Late-medieval piety centred on a eucharistic re-presenting of Christ's sacrifice and otherwise involved contemplation of the sufferings of Christ, in order to attain union with God.

31. Neufeld, "The Cross of the Living Lord," 136.

Theologically Eckhart holds to a pantheistic *union mystica*, the mysterious union of God and creation in which all things are in God and God is in all things. This conception gives rise to a contemplative practice in which human desire for the things of the outer and sentient world is channeled into desire for the things of the inner and spiritual world. So the soul becomes radically detached from creaturely being, losing its individually. Its inner *uncreated light* finally illuminates God "without a medium, uncovered, naked."[32] In Eckhart's conception the soul is then a *seed of God*, growing to become one with "the immovable cause that moves all things."[33] Indeed humankind *is* God, being neither beneath nor above where God is.[34] Given such identity between the human soul and deity, God can be known by looking within with the aid of the intellect. Thence Eckhart advocates reason as a direct pathway to God.[35]

From the perspective of the crucicentric mystics however, Eckhart's mystical path represents a straight nullification of the message from the cross concerning the revelatory work of Jesus Christ. It is a blatant attempt at self-glorification. As Neufeld puts this, the crucicentric theologians see that Eckhart's "eager abandonment to mystical thought without a corresponding halt before the cross of Christ, led him towards an unbridled acceptance of a theology of glory."[36]

---

32. Eckhart, *The Essential Sermons*, 198.
33. Ibid., 203.
34. See ibid., 187.

35. To stray into soteriology, Neufeld says, "Eckhart's definition of sin as the 'dissolution of order, and fall from the One,' corresponds with his depiction of salvation as a reintegration of the universe, the soul being brought 'back to conscious realization of its divine ground.' What is striking about this unbiblical doctrine of sin is its lack of 'appreciation for the demonic power of evil' without which it is impossible to perceive the profound significance of God's work of redemption." Neufeld, "The Cross of the Living Lord," 142. See also Eckhart, *The Essential Sermons*, 44–45.

36. Neufeld, "The Cross of the Living Lord," 133. Barth is also instructive here. Laying Eckhart's mystical abnegation of self at the door of Plato, he writes, "Note how Eckhart . . . does not cease to be a theologian of glory. [For him, as for Plato,] the basic aim of the philosopher is to die and be dead, his work being no other than that of detaching and separating the soul from the body. In my view [this mystical abnegation of self] for Eckhart was in the last resort simply Platonic purification." Barth, *Calvin*, 64–65.

To turn to him, Luther too has little time for Meister Eckhart,[37] but it is sometimes taught that Luther despises *all* mysticism and that it plays no part in his *theologia crucis*. As already indicated this is not the case. Von Loewenich suggests that Luther's "theology of the cross is inconceivable without mysticism, [for medieval monasticism of itself] does not provide an adequate explanation for the distinctiveness of Luther's theology of the cross."[38] Similarly Tomlin says, "[It] would not be true to say that [Luther] simply rediscovered [the *theologia crucis*] by sitting alone in his Wittenberg monastery with St Paul. Luther gained his interest in the cross as the heart of Christian life and thought not so much from mainstream academic theology, which had largely forgotten this type of theology, but from popular traditions of practical spirituality and piety."[39]

A note by Luther's recent biographer, Heiko Oberman, clarifies the nature of this mystical influence on Luther's *theologia crucis*. That influence is indirect but nonetheless significant. "Reading the Young Luther, one keeps expecting a clear profession of mysticism. And it comes, but in an unanticipated form and tenor, without the goal of ascending to God. Luther . . . read Tauler and the *Theologia Germanica* as striking examples of genuine, personal, living theology, . . . a signpost in Luther's search for life by faith in the world."[40] Davidson makes a like point, "There are obvious similarities in Luther's thought with the mysticism of men like Tauler, whom he read, but it is most improbable that the *theologia crucis* was directly influenced by the medieval mystical tradition; rather, Luther appropriates ideas from mysticism and reshapes them to suit his own theological arguments."[41]

Luther is then an academic theologian influenced by crucicentric mystical knowledge of God, rather than a crucicentric mystic interested in academic theology. As Neufeld explains, "Luther drew the dividing

---

37. A teaching note of Barth's is relevant here, "Luther heard what the school of Eckhart was saying. He understood it. It was alive in him. But because he heard and understood it, he tuned aside from the path of Eckhart as such. There can be no success along that path in terms of the theology of glory, but there is success a hundredfold in terms of the theology of the cross for those who have ears to hear what medieval mystics must surely grasp when they let themselves be taught." Barth, *Calvin*, 48.

38. See von Loewenich, *Luther's Theology of the Cross*, 166.

39. Tomlin, "Subversive Theology," 63.

40. Oberman, *Luther*, 180.

41. Davidson, "*Crux-probat-omnia*," 161 n.17.

line [between mystical and academic theology] with the cross of Christ, perceiving that the theology of the cross is pivotal to the soundness of mystical theology."[42]

Indeed, Luther's *theologia crucis* obliquely owes much to late-medieval crucicentric mystical theology, especially the writings of Tauler and the anonymous author of the *Theologia Germanica*. From his earliest period there are many similarities between these mystics and himself epistemologically and, as later discussion will suggest, also soteriologically. Both the crucicentric mystics and Luther see the human condition as depraved and in need of renewal through the cruciform work of Christ, if true knowledge of God is to be attained. Both they and he understand the cross as the continuing place of deep communion and fellowship within which that knowledge may be received. Both therefore reject any starting point for the knowledge of God apart from the cross—here alone God is *fully* revealed even as he is hidden in darkness. Both also reject the pious imitation of the suffering of the cross so as to condition both divine self-disclosure and creaturely salvation.[43] Both hold that faith alone receives the message of the cross; its cruciform light illumines the way of the soul through the darkness of death and hell to the greater light of the risen Christ. Allied to this, both the crucicentric mystics and Luther understand God to use the bitter experiences of life to lead the creature to the knowledge of himself; Luther's notion of God's alien work [*opus alienum*] owes much to the *via negativa* of crucicentric mysticism.

There is a further and major epistemological starting point, or strictly set of starting points, rejected by classical crucicentric theology. That *God alone possesses the knowledge of God in Godself, revealing Godself exclusively in Jesus Christ and above all at the point of the cross*, means that all *natural* paths to the knowledge of God necessarily fail. This is so whether the latter are vested speculatively in philosophy, or metaphysics, or in reason, or in natural creation. They are *impossible*

---

42. Neufeld, "The Cross of the Living Lord," 132.

43. Rather Luther reworks contemporary passion-contemplation piety such that the penitent identification with Christ's suffering becomes a *consequence* of, not *path to*, light and life. See his *Good Friday Sermon 1518* and his *Hebrews Commentary* of the same year. Tomlin says here, "[Luther insists] that meditation on the cross is not meant merely to evoke sentimental sorrow for Christ, but sorrow for one's own sins which put him there, and a sense of thankfulness for God's love and forgiveness." Tomlin, "Subversive Theology," 63.

because the creature is naturally without divine capacity and so cannot know what God alone can know. They are *foolish* (illogical) since leading around the back of the cross (as Luther says) they begin where truth is not found and ignore the place where truth actually resides. They are *sinful* because they dismiss grace, presuming to the creature God-likeness or even Godhood.

The thin tradition sees that to the extent the creature attempts to attain the knowledge of God via some innate capacity, the creature prefers and constitutes itself the natural starting point for that knowledge, bypassing the revelatory epistemology of the cross.[44] In such a case creaturely receipt of cruciform revelation is fatally compromised. Beside the Word from the cross there can be no *second* way to obtain the knowledge of God as God truly is, no *legitimate* way to a proper knowledge of God for those claiming Christ's lordship. It follows that crucicentric theology steadily defends the existence of an utter epistemological divide between the creature and God bridgeable solely by God, while it resolutely opposes and repudiates all natural words to the contrary.

But what exactly is natural theology? It can be understood in various ways,[45] all proposing a commonality between the created or natural realm and the Creator, so that relying on the created or natural order the human creature might speculatively attain to the knowledge of God as God really is. Here the presumption is that the knowledge of God is available partly or entirely by way of natural human initiative and by natural rational means. It follows that for its part, natural theology opposes the idea of a fundamental divide between creature and Creator. The various natural theologies, plural, may now be further explored.

To recall Luther's image two diametrically opposing sight lines exist, one directed to God *around* the cross, and one properly *through* it. Given this, given the crucicentric view that *God* must reveal God if true knowledge of God in Godself is to be made available to the creature, the classical crucicentric theologians reject all speculative instruments for attempting such knowledge. Philosophy and its admixture with theology in metaphysics ascribe to the human intellect a natural ability

---

44. See Busch, *Great Passion*, 89. See also Barth, *Church Dogmatics* II/2, 135.

45. Natural theology takes various forms including but not limited to: nature-religion, animistic and pantheistic modalities, intuitive awareness of the divine, *a posteriori* methodologies for the knowledge of the Creator by way of speculative reason and observation, and general revelation in nature and conscience and history. See also Thompson, *Christological* Perspectives, 187 n. 91.

to derive the knowledge of God. The issue reduces to the fundamental epistemological argument down the length of the classical crucicentric tradition. Any "God" made visible through speculation is logically the prisoner of human speculative capacity. (Or in modern variance, any deity reasonably established must reasonably be restricted to the scope of human reason.) Such a naturally constructed "God," the argument goes, cannot be the objective God of Jesus Christ.

Paul illustrates this reasoning. He condemns contemporary Greek deism with its speculative methodologies for direct knowledge of God as illogical and thence foolish. Analogy drawn on creation, and not least the created human intellect with its natural limitations, bypasses the real Word of the cross as it relativises the work of Christ.

Athanasius also rejects that logic which sees in the fallen creature the perfect image of its Creator. He considers this unreasonable not now because the creature is lesser than its Creator by definition, but for the properly theological reason that while prior to the fall the creature possessed a natural capacity to derive true knowledge of its Creator's nature from its own nature as created,[46] now, besmirched by sin, its own nature provides but an inadequate reflection of the nature of its Creator. Illustrating this, in *De Incarnatione* Athanasius explains that because "transgression [has] overtaken them, men [are] now prisoners to natural corruption and . . . deprived of the grace of being in the image [of God.]"[47] On this basis he argues that "by the weakness of their nature [humans] are not capable by themselves of knowing the Creator or of taking any thought of God."[48] It is no longer logical for them to start with themselves and expect to obtain true knowledge of God. On the contrary a quite different procedure is called for.

The medieval crucicentric mystics likewise exemplify the thin tradition's deep suspicion of the reasonable starting point for the knowledge of God. For example the fourteenth century writer of the *Theologica*

---

46. Athanasius says for example, "For God . . . inasmuch as he is good and exceedingly noble, made the human race after his own image through his own Word, our Saviour Jesus Christ. Through this likeness to himself, he constituted man able to see and to know essential realities, giving him also a conception and knowledge of his own eternity." See *Contra Gentes* 2.2, in Weinandy, *Athanasius*, 13.

47. A Religious of CSMV, *On the Incarnation*, 7. See Anatolios, *Athanasius*.

48. Ibid., 11.

Germanica[49] denounces that reason "which climbs so high in its own light and in itself that it fancies itself to be the eternal true light."[50] It fancies itself to be God! Around the same time Johannes Tauler[51] makes a similar criticism, sounding a cruciform call for the death of such conceit, as Neufeld explains. "Tauler [contrasts] the 'outward brilliance' of natural reason, which reflects human pride and worldly conceit, with the profundity of the divine light, which teaches the soul its creaturely need and dependence upon God. He [maintains] that speculation and natural reason 'bring confusion'; and 'a false peace,' whose only remedy is in dying to self through 'following the steps of Our Lord Jesus Christ.'"[52]

Nicholas of Cusa takes a similar stance. Brilliant himself,[53] Nicholas has a high regard for the intellect as an attribute of divine creation, and argues strongly that mystical ascent to the knowledge of God must not

---

49. *The Theologia Germanica*, also known as the *Theologia Deutsch* or *Der Frankfurter*, is a mystical treatise composed anonymously around 1350, probably by a priest of the Teutonic order in Sachsenhausen. It was discovered in 1516 by Martin Luther who again anonymously edited it, named it, and instigated its printing. As with other contemporary mystical theologies it teaches that the soul progresses towards God and the knowledge of God in stages: purification, illumination, and mystical union. But it pursues the minority crucicentric mystical tradition in warning that any self-motivated procession of the soul involves self-delusion and self-exaltation—dangers born of diabolically inspired self-reliance and a concomitant rejection of the demand of the cross. The essential human decision is therefore the renunciation of self-confidence, which can take place only as the soul wedded to Jesus Christ passes through death into his truth.

50. Winkworth, *Theologia Germanica*. See also Neufeld, "The Cross of the Living Lord," 136.

51. Tauler is considered one of the major figures of medieval German mysticism. Entering a Dominican Order at the age of 15, he became a teacher, preacher, and pastor, and travelled widely. Tradition has it that he underwent an inner conversion at the age of forty. While this has not been confirmed, it appears there was a fundamental spiritual maturing in mid-life. In his preaching and teaching Tauler was himself influenced by Paul's mystical understanding of the double indwelling of Christ—"Christ in us and we in Christ," as also Augustine's concept of the "hidden abyss"—that by divine design a place is made for God within each heart. Of this preacher-monk Luther said, "I have found more true theology in him than in all the doctors of all the universities." See Wakefield, *Christian Spirituality*, 370.

52. Neufeld, "The Cross of the Living Lord," 135–36. See also Shrady, *Johannes Tauler*, 90.

53. Nicholas of Cusa/Cues, Moselle Valley (1401–1464). Nicholas is noted for his genius, receiving his doctorate in canon law from Padua at the age of 22. He understands God as "the absolute maximum of creation," creation being the unfolding of all that God had previously enfolded.

be intellectually blind. Nevertheless he holds that the intellect may *not* derive the knowledge of God. To teach otherwise is tantamount to teaching that the mind can derive its own Creator, that the creature is exalted, that God is not God and infinitely superior intellectually, that the dull are prevented from the knowledge of the truth.[54] Accordingly Nicholas designates the attempt by the human intellect to derive the knowledge of God as intellectually foolish and idolatrous, "a worship of ourselves." Thence he calls for the destruction of the "most proud spirit of reason."[55] God alone may dispense the truth of God.

But it is with the scholastically trained Luther that the classical crucicentric condemnation of anthropocentric epistemology reaches its zenith. To understand this condemnation it is necessary to locate Luther within his intellectual context. The latter turns on late-medieval scholasticism. Of its various schools two dominate, the *via antiqua* and the *via moderna*.

The *via antiqua* looks back to St. Thomas Aquinas (1225–1274). He had sought to construct a coherent view of reality predicated on both Christian faith and classical Greek, particularly Aristotelian, philosophy.[56] Observing that in Christ grace and nature are combined, Aquinas argued that a commonality exists between God and the creature whereby grace perfects nature, and nature serves as a vehicle for grace. Thence an *analogia entis* exists,[57] the knowledge of God being derivable from

54. Nicholas argues that high intellectual capacity is not required to obtain true knowledge of God, for if so even the brightest mind would be too dull to derive a knowledge that is necessarily beyond it.

55. Neufeld, "The Cross of the Living Lord," 136., quoting Salter, *Vision of God*, 43.

56. Dalferth explains, "Thomas had constructed an impressively comprehensive and harmonious intellectual system, which integrated in a highly balanced form: biblical tradition, neoplatonist thought as represented by Pseudo Dionysius and Proclus, and Aristotelian philosophy. He thus managed to overcome the *prima facie* tension between philosophy and theology, reason and revelation, nature and grace[.]" Dalferth, "The Visible and the Invisible," 15–16.

57. "The medieval Roman doctrine of the *analogia entis* embraces both constitutive ontology and noetic procedure. As ontology it holds both the existence of the Creator God and of the human creature of God, and that an essential commonality necessarily connects them such that they correspond to each other. As epistemology it holds that given this correspondence, the creature is naturally capable of knowing the Creator, at least to some extent, by analogy drawn on itself to the nature of God." This definition draws on several sources including Hunsinger, *How to Read Karl Barth*, 283, and Richardson, *Reading Karl* Barth, 126. See also Barth, *Church Dogmatics* I/1, x. (For a definition of the dialectically corresponding *analogia fidei* see here p. 139, n. 12.)

nature and so amenable to necessary proof. But this also means for the later Thomists that reason is a necessary staring point for theology,[58] and that philosophy and theology are completely intertwined.

In contrast to the Thomists the *via moderna* of the Nominalists leaves open the question of the coherence of reality, of the commonality between the Creator and the creature. The *via moderna* holds faith to be a separate realm of truth from propositional (necessary or speculative) knowledge, and so not subject to the same methods and standards of proof. This also means that reason is not a necessary starting point for theology, and that a diastasis between theology and philosophy is maintained.

Where then does Luther position himself? Although trained under the *via moderna* at the university of Erfurt, by the time of the *Ninety Five Theses* (October 1517) he rejects both the *via moderna* and the older path as creaturely mechanisms usurping the glory of God. With the Nominalist *via moderna* Luther rejects the continuum between theological and philosophical truth as proposed by the *via antiqua*. Theological truth is not of the same order of truth as philosophical truth. With the Thomist *via antiqua* Luther rejects the metaphysical dualism holding theological and philosophical truths alongside each other as proposed by the *via moderna*. Theological truth is not simply one more order of truth.

Indeed both schools fail to grasp reality properly. They know nothing of the rift in creation at the fall, or of consequent human blindness to God, or of Jesus Christ. At bottom their common problem is that in their self-glorifying reliance on the speculative starting point they miss the concrete theology proclaimed from the cross. Von Loewenich explains this further. For Luther, "Metaphysics does not lead to a knowledge of the true God."[59] Rather for him, "all religious speculation is a theology of glory. He condemns this theology of glory because in it the basic significance of the cross of Christ for all theological thinking is not given its due."[60] "For the cross cannot be disposed of in an upper story of the

---

58. As Hagan notes, in practice the *via antiqua* begins with faith seeking understanding, regarding its formal starting point in reason as "convincing to those already convinced." See Hagan, "Luther on Atonement," 274.

59. Von Loewenich, *Luther's Theology of the Cross*, 27.

60. Ibid.

The Classical Epistemology of the Cross 51

structure of thought,"⁶¹ in the speculative realms of philosophic reason. "It makes plain that there is no direct knowledge of God for man."⁶² Its cruciform Word radically transcends all philosophy's subjective verities. It speaks *the* truth, not *a* truth continuous with or alongside propositional belief. Herein the cruciform core of Luther's epistemology.

The metaphysical methodology Luther particularly dislikes relates to the *analogia entis* (mentioned above.) He treats the notion that "what the fallen creature is like, God is like" with considerable distain. Dalferth says here, "[For Luther the] God who is the subject of this sort of theology is a result of speculative argument and not the living God of the Bible. It is an abstract entity, a theoretical postulate which may be needed to secure the coherence of a metaphysical system and is inferred by going from the *visabilia* of this world to the *invisibilia* beyond it. Yet inferential reasoning and postulation will never lead to knowledge of the invisible things of faith."⁶³

In Luther's view such inferential reasoning and postulation can infer only the creature's image of itself. In his *Sermon on the Mount* (1521) he puts this with characteristic vigor. "[You] should realize that when a monk in the monastery is sitting in deepest contemplation, excluding the world from his heart altogether, and thinking about the Lord God the way he himself paints and imagines him, he is actually sitting . . . in the dung, not up to his knees but to his ears."⁶⁴ Those who argue for and from an *analogia entis*, who predicate the knowledge of God on themselves, cannot be *Christian* theologians. They do not start with the true God manifest in Jesus Christ and him crucified. Their powers of reasoning are fatally contaminated, thus their methodology is fatally flawed.⁶⁵

Bound up with this condemnation, Luther rejects the starting point for the knowledge of God in human reason. He does so on reasonable grounds. Reason knows it cannot command that which alone has complete knowledge of itself; it knows too that in its finitude it cannot embrace the infinite mind of God. It follows that reason cannot be true to itself and presume to reach up to the knowledge of God. But in Luther's view the reasonable starting point presents even more serious problems

61. Ibid.
62. Ibid.
63. Dalferth, "The Visible and the Invisible," 24.
64. Luther, *Luther's Works*, 21: 33–34.
65. See Hagan, "Luther on Atonement," 266.

for theology. It undermines divine revelation, and it exalts the creature as God. For if reason could attain the knowledge of God proclaimed from the cross, the proclamation from the cross would not be required. If it could attain the knowledge of God proclaimed by the crucified Christ, the revelation of Christ would not be required. Moreover in these instances the reasoning creature would be uncovering what God alone can uncover. Reasonably therefore the reasonable starting point for the knowledge of God must be denied.

Luther is not however against reason *per se* in the service of theology. Created by God it occupies a vital place in understanding the things of God, accepting that this can never be a *prior* place. Von Loewenich again explains. "Reason [for Luther] is valid in its domain, but reason is a human work, and therefore judgement is pronounced upon it. For the cross is the judgement of all human glory. The way of the cross means the surrender of human glory and a plunge into foolishness. One who has caught something of the wisdom of the cross knows that reason is a 'dangerous thing.'"[66] Elsewhere von Loewenich observes, "Luther never changed in his critical attitude towards the role of reason in theology, although he could hail it as 'the most excellent of all things; in its own field, the affairs of this world.'"[67]

All this means for Luther—as indeed for the classical crucicentric tradition generally—that the reasonable science of philosophy is in no position to govern theology, and neither may it dictate theological method. Conversely however Luther thinks theology free to make *ad hoc* use of philosophical axioms where these are useful to it. Theology always takes prior place to philosophy. Thus Luther writes, "Philosophy treats of the things which can be known by human reason. Theology treats of things which are believed, i.e., which are apprehended by faith."[68] Faith for Luther is always superior to reason.

Dalferth's further explanation here bears quoting at length:

> Philosophy, [Luther] says, always talks about the visible and apparent things and about the conclusions which it can derive from those. The subject matter of philosophy . . . comprises everything that can be experienced by the senses and that can be inferred from experienced reality. It is the realm of knowledge accessible

---

66. Von Loewenich, *Luther's Theology of the Cross*, 75.
67. See ibid., 2.
68. Luther, *Martin Luthers* Werke, 26–28.

to the natural faculties of man, his senses (*sensualitas*) and reason (*ratio*), and it includes everything that belongs to the visible, apparent, present, and temporal things (*visibilia, apparentia, praesentia, temporalia*). On the other hand, it is utterly unable to treat of the invisible, non apparent, future, eternal, and spiritual things (*invisiblilia, non apparentia, futura, aeterna, spiritualia*) which are the subject-matter of theology and accessible to faith only.[69]

Finally in this overview of the negative crucicentric epistemological tradition, related to their broad opposition to natural theology the classical crucicentric theologians oppose the starting point for the knowledge of God in *natural creation*.

Here Paul has often been misunderstood. He neither advocates grounding the knowledge of God in natural creation, nor dismisses creation's revelationary capacity.[70] Its witness to the existence of a Creator, obvious even to the non-believer, cannot however lead to full spiritual truth. It cannot reveal the work of the cross or bring about surrender to Christ, rather it diverts attention from these things. The starting point in natural creation is therefore ultimately futile. Hiding God, it leads to the darkening of the mind.

As already suggested, Athanasius too follows this line of argument. In *Contra Gentes*—his early polemic against his Greek interlocutors—he declares, "as though in written characters [creation] declares in a loud voice, by its order and harmony, that God is one."[71] This one God is rational, his Word is Truth.[72] Athanasius then postulates that since the creature has been created in the image of the rational and truthful God, it ought to be able to derive true knowledge of such a God rationally, beginning from itself. This is particularly so since it has received an immortal soul, and an intellect under the direction of that soul equipping it to perceive and contemplate God. (Indeed, Athanasius says, it is ir-

---

69. Dalferth, "The Visible and the Invisible," 23.

70. See for example, Rom 1:20 "Ever since the creation of the world [God's] eternal power and divine nature, invisible though they are, have been understood and seen through the things he has made."

71. Thomson, "*Contra Gentes and De Incarnatione*," 34.4. In context Athanasius is arguing against polytheism. He goes on to say that "the order of the universe could not exist with more than one God governing it."

72. Placher, *Readings in the History of Christian* Theology, 49–50.

rational to deny the existence of such an intellect since the whole way the body is constructed witnesses to intelligence in its design.[73])

Yet for Athanasius there exists an inbuilt objection to the usefulness of such a procedure. Given the fall creaturely capacity to perceive and contemplate God, genuine as it may be, is clouded by stains of sin, marks from which the human creature cannot cleanse itself.[74] Thus practically the creature cannot derive an adequate knowledge of the Creator God from its own pattern. Neither from that pattern might it obtain the knowledge of God in Jesus Christ.

It is rather for Athanasius the doctrine of Jesus Christ, shining brighter than the sun, that reveals truth.[75] This brilliant doctrine lights the whole of creation with the knowledge of God made manifest in Jesus Christ—knowledge conveyed above all from the cross.[76] It is then a mark of foolish ignorance to deny that by the cross of Christ "the effects of the knowledge of God are made manifest to all."[77] The final incapacity of creation to reveal God adequately also means that creation is not to be worshipped. Indeed creation itself metaphorically "raises its voice against [such idolatry, pointing] to God as its Maker and Artificer, who reigns over creation and over all things, [who is] the Father of our Lord Jesus Christ."[78]

Luther likewise is suspicious of a starting point for God in natural creation. As Paul he does not reject it entirely, his opposition to the mooted commonality between the Creator and the creature notwithstanding. The natural world *can* point to the nature of God, to divine goodness, natural justice, godliness and so forth. Nevertheless as Paul, Luther thinks that to rely on natural creation for the full knowledge of God, rather than to rely on "the visible and manifest things of God seen through suffering and the cross,"[79] is not the way of wisdom.[80] Such

---

73. See also Schaff, *Contra Gentes,* 30–31.
74. Ibid., chapter 34.
75. Schaff, *Contra Gentes*. See vol. IV:1.1.
76. Schaff, *"The Life of Antony,"* 1.5.
77. Schaff, *Contra Gentes,* 1.3
78. Ibid., 27.3.

79. Thesis 20, Heidelberg Disputation. Luther adds polemically that the theologian who advocates such a direct and natural epistemology is blinded by pride and presumption, a barb not missed by his opponents.

80. Luther says, "virtue, godliness, wisdom, justice, goodness, and so forth[, the] recognition of all these things does not make one worthy or wise." Proof Thesis 19

a procedure exalts the capacity of the creation to reveal God over the capacity of the Creator to do so. In so doing it idolizes the creation. Commensurately it misses the place where the knowledge of God is supremely available, relativising the revelatory Word of the cross. Hinlicky captures these objections when he writes, "Luther does not deny that there is something to be known about God from his works, e.g., that he is the glorious, invisible Creator of creation. . . . But such knowledge does no one any good, and without the theology of the cross it is misused in the worst way."[81]

This is a natural place to conclude this account of the negative crucicentric epistemological tradition with its rejection of all anthropocentric starting points for the knowledge of God. As seen these include: human experience, the law, self engendered mysticism, and all natural theologies—philosophy and metaphysical speculation, reason, and natural creation. In the end though, this negative position comprises but the threshold to that which the classical crucicentric theologians affirm positively epistemologically.

The Positive Epistemology of the Cross

The classical crucicentric theologians present an embracing and positive epistemology. Humans are created to know their Creator intimately, such knowledge being life-giving. Given the post-lapsarian incapacity to know God naturally however, God pities them. Athanasius for example, explains that God "did not leave [believers] destitute of knowledge of himself [but] bestowed on them of his own image, our Lord Jesus Christ."[82] Instrumentally and ontologically it is then the cross of Jesus Christ which in the crucicentric view supremely discloses "the light of the knowledge of the glory of God" (2 Cor 4:6).

Once again multiple crucicentric elements interplay in this light. The first to be considered here relates to the dialectic between wisdom and foolishness. Others to be reviewed include: divine revelation in the suffering and humiliation of Christ, the dialectic between hiddenness and cruciform revelation, revelation "under the opposite," in consequence the fact that the knowledge of God is only available indirectly,

---

Heidelberg Disputation. Lull, *Luther's Basic Theological Writings*, 43.

81. Hinlicky, "Luther's Theology of the Cross—Part Two," 59.

82. A Religious of CSMV, *On the Incarnation*, 11.

the sheer epistemological priority of the living Word of the cross, and the crucicentric understanding of union with the mind of Christ.

The dialectic between wisdom and foolishness is employed across both dimensions of the crucicentric system as a methodological device for accenting the system's intrinsic logic and coherence. As such it constitutes a major crucicentric motif. Its use epistemologically[83] is introduced now principally in relation to the Apostle Paul.

To set the background to this development it is observed that universally two questions present themselves. "How can that which is ultimate be known about?" "How can it be known in itself?" In the first century Judaism answers with the law, the neighboring Greeks with reason. In brief, for the Jews the law conveys the knowledge of divine command, consolidating covenantal relation with God; for the Greeks reason enables knowledge [*gnosis*] of the hidden order of the cosmos to be deduced speculatively. It is in correspondence with these epistemological notions and their cultural contexts that Paul develops his dialectical understanding of wisdom and foolishness.[84]

To explain further, in first century Judaism wisdom is objectified and personified, made not divine but nevertheless godlike. As such it is closely aligned with the *Logos*—the concrete self-revealing Word of God, and with divine law—the command of God which is itself identified with the *Logos*. Unlike the Jewish notion however, Greek wisdom is neither objectified nor personified. Rather the Greeks identify wisdom first with the logic hidden behind the cosmic order—logic itself being considered an aspect of the *logos*, and then with the speculative methodologies applied to disclosing that logic.[85]

Paul understands wisdom rather differently; it rests finally neither in divine law nor in cosmic logic, but is embodied in Jesus Christ and him crucified. For ontologically Jesus Christ is the divine *Logos*—both the Word of the cross and the Wisdom of the cross, both the cruciform Announcer and the cruciform Announcement concerning where God is. He is the wise cruciform warning that given God's "most stringent

---

83. See here pp. 74–76 for a discussion on wisdom and foolishness relating to soteriology.

84. While Paul utterly rejects the eloquently expressed philosophies of his opponents—their "lofty words of wisdom," he is quite capable of employing a similar level of rhetoric when advocating his own position. See 1 Cor 1:17, 2:1.

85. See Brown, "Apocalyptic Transformation," 432.

The Classical Epistemology of the Cross 57

rejection of all deification of self-willing power"[86] as Jüngel puts it, the creaturely power to know as God is necessarily divinely proscribed and condemned. He is also the wise cruciform rule that since the revelation of God is focused in the cross, the cross is necessarily the prior starting place for this knowledge.

It follows for Paul that those who are truly wise recognize this cruciform Word and logic, receive it, and begin with it. They start where truth is ultimately to be found. To them this Word is infinitely superior to all metaphysical and religious methodologies for attaining the knowledge of God; indeed by its sheer truth it overcomes them all. Paul therefore flatly declares, "I decided to know nothing among you except Jesus Christ, and him crucified" (1 Cor 2:2). Ultimately there is nothing else to know.

It follows too that those seeking to access and prove the wisdom of God religiously (the Jews), or religiously and speculatively (the Greeks), engage in a categorical error. Foolishly (illogically) they use *anthropocentric* methodologies and starting points for the knowledge of God that, as such, are unfitted for their task. They cannot provide the answers to which they are set. The first problem for Paul is that the Jews and the Greeks start in the wrong place—themselves, and miss beginning in the right place—cruciform Wisdom. Behind this the difficulty is that the one Word and Logic of the cross is not amenable to necessary proof rooted naturally, thus the Jewish and Greek intellectual worlds can make no sense of it. As a mark of God it appears to them foolish. But for Paul it is the Jews and the Greeks who in their blindness and presumption are unwise. Thence he declares his own position, "For Jews demand signs and Greeks desire wisdom, but we proclaim Christ crucified, a stumbling block [*skandalon*] to Jews and foolishness to Gentiles" (1 Cor 1:22).

This also means that a juxtaposition of divine and human logic lies at the heart of Paul's crucicentric epistemology. This is demonstrated in his conclusion in regard to the Jews and the Greeks: that those who perceive themselves as wise in their rejection of the Word of the cross are actually foolish, while those who know themselves to be foolish before the cross are actually wise. It is also demonstrated in his finding in regard to God: that the "foolishness" of God's cruciform logic is necessarily wiser than that human wisdom that would circumvent that logic.[87] Or as von

---

86. See Jüngel Eberhard, *God as the Mystery of the World*, 206.

87. Paul writes, "For God's foolishness is wiser than human wisdom, and God's weakness is stronger than human strength (1 Cor 11:25)."

Loewenich puts this, "The Word of the cross is indeed 'foolishness.' But this is Paul's great new insight, that God can manifest his wisdom only in foolishness."[88] This wise "foolish Word from the cross" is then for Paul the unique arbitrating point between the wise and the foolish person. Its alien logic radically divides and upsets.

For Athanasius too Jesus Christ is the self-disclosing creative Wisdom of God.[89] He writes, "For God willed to make himself known no longer as in previous times through the image and shadow of wisdom, which is in creatures, but has made the true Wisdom herself take flesh and become a mortal human being and endure the death of the cross, so that henceforth . . . all the earth is filled with his knowledge."[90]

In this view the recognition of Christ's deity by believers contrasts markedly with the foolish "wisdom" of the pagan world—the foolish logic that would deduce the knowledge of the Creator from the creature thereby exalting the creature as God. The burden of Athanasius' epistemology then becomes the rejection of the many strands of pagan idolatry with their false methodologies and illogical presumptions. Polemically he decries that natural wisdom which, alongside the Wisdom of God, merely reveals its actual foolishness. He rejects those who holding to such foolishness miss the true starting point of the Incarnation. "So now your boasting has been shown to be completely vacuous, you enemies of Christ, and your parading around and babbling everywhere about 'He created me as the beginning of his ways' (Prov 8.22) is foolish . . . For the passage in Proverbs [makes] it evident that the Son is not a creature by nature and being . . . but the Father's own . . . offspring who is true Wisdom and Word, 'through whom everything came into being, and without him nothing came to be' (John 1:3)."[91]

Luther gets his own juxtaposition of wisdom and foolishness directly from Paul. He holds that supremely in the cross of Jesus Christ

---

88. Von Loewenich, *Luther's Theology of the Cross*, 11–12.

89. Athanasius writes extensively on Christ as the Wisdom of God. For quick instance, "For since human beings had turned away from the contemplation of [divine revelation, instead] contriving gods for themselves . . . the Saviour of all and Word of God . . . submitted himself to being revealed through a body, so that . . . he might [direct the senses of human beings to himself, persuading them] that he is not only a man but God, and Word and Wisdom of the true God." *De Incarnatione* 15–16. Cited by Anatolios, *Athanasius*, 53.

90. *Contra Arianos* 81. Cited by Anatolios, *Athanasius*, 174.

91. *Contra Arianos* 82. Cited by Anatolios, *Athanasius*, 175.

The Classical Epistemology of the Cross 59

God demonstrates an infinitely superior wisdom, one which both confronts and separates out those who are in receipt of the knowledge of God. This divine wisdom equates to a revelatory methodology, one which the world can neither naturally perceive nor speculatively appropriate. As Paul, Luther therefore radically reverses the "wisdom" of the world concerning the nature of reality, and therefore of God.

The wisdom and foolishness dialectic also indicates that *crucicentric* epistemology is itself profoundly reasonable, beginning from the cross it finds reason operating where naturally none can be thought present. Its perception of a true logic operating behind suffering and death is a case in point.

As the literature earlier reviewed shows, a theology of suffering has sometimes been confused with crucicentric theology in its entirety. While such a narrow conception is found here to be inadequate, a theology of suffering nevertheless is of major revelatory significance within the crucicentric tradition. The logic of the cross demands that the creaturely attempt "to know as God" be crucified with Christ. Only as that attempt is negated can the truth contained in the cross be received in exchange.

For this reason the crucicentric mystics prescribe an ascetical practice enabling the inner identification of the creature's suffering with the suffering and death of Jesus Christ. In the twelfth century Bernard of Clairvaux[92] emphasizes that in the suffering of God in incarnation culminating in crucifixion Christ reveals *himself*, and not simply information concerning himself. The creature by its own suffering is unified with his suffering and therefore with his self-knowledge. Similarly, central to the theology of Johannes Tauler (c.1300–1361) is the notion of a twofold path, the *vita activa* and the *vita meditativa*. These inform each other in a continuing praxis so that out of active identification with the suffering and death of Christ the soul enters into his darkness, indeed the darkness of the glorious light of God. Out of meditative reflection on this experience the knowledge of God is received. This is so, Tauler says, because, "While God's light is 'pure and radiant everywhere . . . nowhere does it

---

92. St Bernard was a Cistercian monk who established a monastery at Clairvaux in 1115, and is generally considered the dominant spiritual influence of his age. He explored the psychology of human love for God, placing adoration solely for the sake of God at the apex of his system.

shine brighter than in the deepest darkness."[93] Likewise the anonymous writer of the *Theologia Germanica* speaks of the death and hell through which the soul must pass if it is to know Christ profoundly.[94]

The young Luther is to take crucicentric mysticism's way to the knowledge of God through identification with Christ's suffering still further. For him the passion of Christ and the knowledge of God melt in the cross. This is so since God is not different from the suffering Christ, humble and lowly rather than majestic and powerful.[95] Christ's suffering therefore uniquely discloses the divine nature. For this reason in the Heidelberg Disputation Luther teaches that "God can reveal himself only . . . in the humility and shame of the cross."[96] Similarly he says, "True theology and the knowledge of God are in the crucified Christ."[97]

A related classical crucicentric notion constitutes the second major crucicentric motif. It teaches that in Jesus Christ, at the point of the cross, the diastasis between the hiddenness and revealedness of God reaches its greatest extent. This is so because exactly where God appears most absent to the eyes of the world, to the eyes of faith he is most revealed. The sheer degradation of the cross, its darkness, discloses the inner nature of One whose power—as Davidson neatly expresses it—"is defined in weakness, whose holiness is defined in involvement with squalor, and whose self-sufficiency is defined in the brokenness and helplessness of a cross outside a city wall."[98]

The dialectic itself stretches back to Paul who sees that in the cross the glory of God in Jesus Christ is most concealed to the world. "If our gospel is veiled," he writes to the Corinthians, "it is veiled to those who are perishing" (2 Cor 4:3), to those who are blinded to it. But it is most revealed to the eyes of faith. Von Loewenich calls this, "Paul's guiding principle of revelation,"[99] a conclusion which can be equally applied to the crucicentric theologians following Paul.

93. Neufeld, "The Cross of the Living Lord," 135–36. See also Shrady, *Johannes Tauler*, 90.

94. See Hoffman, *The Theologia* Germanica, 63, 74.

95. See Tomlin, "Subversive Theology," 63.

96. Luther, *Luther's Works*, 31:52–53.

97. *Heidelberg Disputation* Proof Thesis 20. Lull, *Luther's Basic Theological Writings*, 44.

98. Davidson, "Response to Bishop John Spong," 30.

99. The context of this quotation reads, "The fact that the Crucified One is the Messiah—something unheard of for Jewish ears—opened [Paul's] eyes to *the rule that*

Athanasius advances a similar notion when, in *De Incarnatione*, he says that "what seems [Christ's] utter poverty and weakness on the cross . . . quietly and hiddenly wins over the mockers and unbelievers to recognize Him as God."[100] Elsewhere Athanasius suggests that the primary reason for Christ's hiddenness is that he be "manifested afterwards"[101] in the resurrection.

The crucicentric mystics similarly teach that God hides himself in Jesus Christ in the degradation of the cross—hiddenness being a fundamental attribute of God, but also reveals himself in this degradation—revealedness likewise being a fundamental attribute of God. It follows that only one hidden in the cross with Christ can receive Christ's self-revelation, a notion rooted in the thought of St Bernard of Clairvaux (1090–1153). The latter holds that confronted by God, the creature naturally can expect only divine anger. Yet it escapes that anger for of his love for it God protects it from himself, hiding it in the crucified Christ. In this Bernard draws on Exod 33:18–23, the story of Moses sheltering in the hand of God from the annihilating glory of the divine visage. Via Bernard this becomes an image and a text which is to capture Luther's imagination.[102]

For Luther the contrast of divine hiddenness and revelation in the cross has historical roots. At the beginning of human history God revealed himself generally, but in time this procedure encouraged the creature to worship the creation and thence its own substance, usurping the glory of the Creator. Foregoing general revelation therefore, God next chose to mediate the knowledge of himself indirectly through his law. When this second revelation went unheeded God assumed the *clothes* or *masks* of the sacraments, of Holy Scripture,[103] and above all of

---

governs God's revelation. God reveals himself in concealment, God's wisdom appears to men as foolishness, God's power is perfected in weakness, God's glory parades in lowliness, God's life becomes effective in the death of his Son." Von Loewenich, *Luther's Theology of the Cross*, 11. Italics mine.

100. See A Religious of CSMV, *On the Incarnation*, 1.

101. Ibid., 38.

102. Tomlin notes here that, "Bernard's sermons on the Song of Songs, standard fare in the monastic circles in which Luther spent his early years, contain several themes which found their way into Luther's developing *theologia crucis,* for example . . . the idea suggested by Exodus 33 of God revealing his 'back' [to Moses], taken up by Luther in the *Heidelberg Disputation*." Tomlin, "Subversive Theology," 63.

103. The sacraments convey Christ's body and blood and the knowledge that the

the incarnation culminating in the crucifixion. Luther then stresses that in the degradation of the cross God *himself* is hidden and self-revealed, not some modalistic projection of God behind which the real God is eternally unknowable. The truth of God, he says, "can be found only in suffering and the cross."[104] Commenting here von Loewenich says that Luther "makes thoroughly clear that the hidden God cannot be a hypostasis in or behind God, but is the one living God who is manifest as he is concealed in the cross of Christ."[105]

In Luther's theology God elects to hide divine truth in the degradation of a cross for several reasons: i) Recalling the Moses story, to protect the finite creature from being fully exposed to a measureless knowledge it could not survive. ii) To prevent the inner truth of God being fathomable naturally, for then the creature would be as God knowing what God alone can know. iii) To require the true theologian to depend on God for the location of the truth of God. In conjunction with this, to direct this theologian to start epistemologically where that truth of God is actually revealed—the cross of Jesus Christ. iv) To enable the true theologian, the theologian of the cross, to distinguish true glory from its false portrayal by the world. v) Lastly, because hiddenness is integral to the God of the cross in the same manner that the finite is integral to the infinite.

But God also elects to reveal himself in the cross, to the eyes of faith not speculation. In his Genesis lectures (1535–1545) Luther concludes that precisely because God is *Deus absconditus* in the sufferings of the cross he can be *Deus revelatus* there, and precisely because he is *deus revelatus* in the cross he can also be *deus absconditus* there. Indeed—to again pick up the Moses analogy—the God who is hidden in the cross and the God who reveals himself there cannot be divided, any more than the "back parts" of God can be divided from the "front parts" passing before Moses.

The hiddenness and revelation of God in the cross bear on three closely related contentions undergirding the classical crucicentric epistemological tradition and gathered up finally by Luther. These are: that

---

believer is incorporated into divine death and resurrection. The Scriptures are the "swaddling clothes" which contain and reveal Christ. See Luther's 1537 Commentary on John. Luther, *Luther's Works*, 24:67.

104. Ibid., 53. Similarly Luther says, "True theology and the knowledge of God are in the crucified Christ." (Thesis 20, Heidelberg Disputation).

105. Von Loewenich, *Luther's Theology of the Cross*, 30.

The Classical Epistemology of the Cross 63

in the cross God "hides himself under the opposite," the indirect nature of divine revelation in Jesus Christ and him crucified, and the priority of the revelation from the cross.

First, as Forde states on the basis of Luther, "God's revelation can take place only under the form of the opposite, *sub contrario*"[106] in the cross of Jesus Christ. This strange methodology identifies its Subject as diametrically other than the God expected naturally by the world. For in its vaunted self-confidence and independence, its admiration of power and worldly majesty, the world imagines a God like itself. The cross is therefore meaningless to it. Von Loewenich summarises this rhetorically. "But what do we see when we see the cross? There is 'nothing else to be seen than disgrace, poverty, death, and everything that is shown us in the suffering Christ . . . There especially no one would of himself look for God's revelation.'"[107]

Second, by eternal decision God elects to reveal the knowledge of himself only *indirectly*, only through Jesus Christ, and only by way of the cross. Indeed as von Loewenich again says with Luther in view, "The cross makes plain that there is no direct knowledge of God for man."[108] Mattes, in commenting on Forde's treatment of Luther, reports similarly. "Our epistemological basis for discerning God's work in Christ . . . must be . . . grounded *a posteriori* in . . . what God in Christ has actually done, and not *a priori* in what God must do, given our prior metaphysical assumptions about God."[109]

It follows for Luther that the theologian who wants to circle round the back of the cross and see into the invisible[110] glory of God directly, drawing an analogy to God on the creature, presumes to itself godlike ability to disclose God. Moreover such a person reduces God to the level of the creature. Luther's condemnation is therefore cutting, "That person does not deserve to be called a theologian."[111] In distinction Luther's true

---

106. Proof thesis 4, Heidelberg Disputation. See Forde, *Being a Theologian of the Cross*, 31.

107. See von Loewenich's discussion of thesis twenty of the Heidelberg Disputation. Von Loewenich, *Luther's Theology of the Cross*, 28–29.

108. Ibid., 27.

109. Mattes, "Gerhard Forde," 383.

110. Note that Luther's understanding of the invisible is not the same as the idealist Aristotelian conception of a hidden unchanging world reachable speculatively. Luther denies the very existence of a second, invisible and independent realm of truth.

111. Thesis 19, Heidelberg Disputation. Lull, *Martin Luther's Basic Theological Writings*, 43–44.

theologian learns from the cross that God can be recognized only by looking *through* its cruciform lens. This is so since the cross instrumentally focuses both the truth of God, and the truth of God and the creature in their relation, through the crucified Christ. Indeed, for Luther, the cruciform starting point is *the* defining mark of the person who "deserves to be called a theologian."[112] So he summarises the matter, "Now it is not sufficient for anyone, and it does him no good to recognize God in his glory and majesty, unless he recognizes him in the humility and shame of the cross."[113]

This leads to the third contention undergirding classical crucicentric epistemology: that the knowledge of God is made available only by way of the cross means that the cross is—as McGrath says—the "final, decisive and normative locus of the revelation of God."[114] Classical crucicentric theologians agree that the message from the cross, (that is, concerning the identity of Jesus Christ and the meaning of his cruciform work), takes priority over similar theologies conveyed by other christological events—the resurrection or incarnation. Nevertheless views differ as to how this cruciform priority is itself established.

For Paul the *backward light of the resurrection* etches the paramount significance of the message from the cross (noting that the cross in its integral darkness immediately hides that significance). As McGrath puts this, "Paul treats the resurrection as a demonstration that Jesus is indeed the Son of God (Rom 1:3–4)—something which the cross initially seems to deny (Gal 3:13b)."[115]

By contrast in the fourth century Athanasius concludes that, notwithstanding the revelatory significance of the resurrection, *the forward light of the incarnation* points to the paramountcy of the cruciform message. Indeed for him the chief epistemological reason for the incarnation is that there be a platform from which the paramount priority of the message from the cross might be indicated and made sensible.[116]

This also means for Athanasius that Christ's divinity is revealed by the cross. Indeed that revelation constitutes its central epistemological

---

112. Thesis 20, ibid.
113. Proof Thesis 20, ibid.
114. McGrath, *The Enigma of the Cross*, 107.
115. Ibid., 31.
116. See Torrance, *Karl Barth*, 161.

message. He argues for example that in the crucifixion the "sun hid his face, and the earth quaked and the mountains were rent: all men were awed, [all things which prove] that Christ on the cross was God."[117] Weinandy and Torrance each direct attention to Athanasius at this point. Weinandy says that for Athanasius the cross "especially gives testimony that Jesus was God, for even the created order trembled in fear at the sight."[118] Torrance agrees. He finds that for Athanasius the cross reveals an exchange of love and obedience taking place in the work of Jesus Christ. It shows that the Father is the Father of the divine Son, and the Son is the Son of the divine Father, in their mutual self-giving through the Spirit. In so doing it also evidences the triune structure of its own revelatory Word.[119]

In the medieval mystical schools there is less emphasis on the incarnation and resurrection as events mediating the message from the cross. Rather the schools consider the cruciform message to be transmitted directly.[120] The cross stands alone as the one self-interpreting standard by which *all* theological knowledge, including that concerning christological events, is to be assessed.

Influenced by the mystics, in Luther too the theology from the cross need not be mediated by other christological events in order to be received. Rather, naturally hidden under the opposite, the cruciform Word is made directly patent to those who by the Holy Spirit look at the cross in faith.

If the cross stands at the centre of revelation then its cruciform *theology*—its explanation and demand, necessarily stands at the centre of all human theologies that seek to reflect revelation faithfully, that are indeed properly *Christian*. Explicitly and implicitly this insight forms an epistemological touchstone for the classical crucicentric theologians. Von Loewenich agrees. With Luther again in view he states, "Christian thinking must come to a halt before the fact of the cross. The cross makes demands on Christian thought, demands which must either be acted on or ignored. If Christian thought ignores the demands of the cross it becomes a theology of glory. If the cross becomes the founda-

---

117. A Religious of CSMV, *On the Incarnation*, 19.3.
118. Weinandy, *Athanasius*, 238.
119. See Torrance, *Karl Barth*, 161.
120. See Neufeld, "The Cross of the Living Lord," 136.

tion of Christian thought, a theology of the cross results."[121] Elsewhere von Loewenich declares that there is "no dogmatic topic conceivable for which the cross is not the point of reference,"[122] adding immediately that it is in this sense that Luther's theology "desires to be a theology of the cross."[123] Barker takes a similar position. In Luther the cross "is a way of doing theology that has as its focus the revelation of God in Jesus Christ crucified. [It unfolds] what lies at the heart of the Christian tradition's insistence on how and where God is to be found."[124]

If the cross is the prior place of revelation, its message at the centre of all properly Christian theology, the classical crucicentric theologians then hold that that message can only be received as the creature is drawn through the cross into the mind[125] of Christ. Cognitive union with him, and therefore with God, culminates the epistemology of the cross theologically, systematically.

Paul carefully does *not* command Christians to create within themselves a capacity to unite with the mind of God so as to know as God knows. Since the fallen human mind cannot naturally reach up to the mind of God, a *new* mind capable of God is required. But as such God alone can form it. Paul is therefore critical of those who by way of mystical or intellectual exercises would join themselves to the mind of God. Such self motivated practices trespass on the glory of God, revealing only the practitioner's enslavement to false spiritual power. Thus Paul concludes, "In their case the god of this world has blinded the minds of unbelievers, to keep them from seeing the light of the gospel of the glory of Christ, who is the image of God" (2 Cor 4:4). In their case such knowledge as they do have will be taken from them.

Rather Paul teaches that as the creature is drawn into the cross its self-glorifying desire to "instruct" (manipulate, determine, condition) God is put to death. In exchange it receives *the mind of Christ*. This is metaphorical language, but more than that. It is not that the mind of the creature is somehow deified, but that as the creature dies to its desire to control disclosure of the knowledge of God, its thought processes

---

121. Von Loewenich, *Luther's Theology of the Cross*, 27.

122. Ibid., 18.

123. Ibid.

124. Barker, "Bonhoeffer, Luther," 13.

125. After the Apostle Paul by *mind* here is meant not only the intellect, but also the psychic disposition towards or away from God.

are joined to and subordinated to *Christ's* glorious knowledge of and cognitive orientation to God. As Dunn explains Paul, this leads "to a wholly transformed perspective, a new awareness of God (1 Cor 14:25), a veil taken away (2 Cor 3:14–18), a complete reassessment of values and priorities (Phil 3:7–11). But also moral transformation . . . and transformation of social identity and community."[126] The creature is made to know what cannot be known naturally; it begins to see with new eyes; it comes into the knowledge of the gospel. Now it is the one instructed. Thence Paul marvels, "'For who has known the mind of the Lord so as to instruct him?' But we have[127] the mind of Christ" (1 Cor 2:16).

According to Brown's interpretation of Paul this cognitive union is an apocalyptic process. On the basis of Christ's cruciform work an inbreaking age has already formally overcome the age that was. The elemental powers binding the creature's false and speculative epistemology have already been defeated.[128] Formally the mind of the creature is therefore no longer captive to these "powers of the air"; rather in Christ it has been surrendered to the power of God. This state of affairs is worked out practically, Paul says, as in Christ the creature increasingly puts on the mind of Christ, discerning with *his* discernment "what is the will of God—what is good and acceptable and perfect" (Rom 12:2). This process of cognitive renewal will be completed finally, Paul adds, with the eschatological renewal of all creation.[129] Moreover that future completion is certain just because in the crucified Christ it has *already* taken place. With all this in view Paul now issues two complementary commands, "Do *not* be conformed to this world, but *be* transformed by the renewing of your minds" (Rom 12:2a).[130]

Subsequent to Paul the twofold notion of cognitive re-creation in this age, and full cognitive union with Christ eschatologically, does not appear to be pursued at the surface level of the crucicentric tradition.

---

126. Dunn, *The Theology of Paul*, 319.

127. The verb "have" here translates the Greek *eko* connoting *to hold or possess*. While this can be understood figuratively, a literal meaning is implied in this instance. Those who have passed through death with Christ concretely *hold* or *possess* his mind, they are actually cognitively united with him.

128. See Brown, "Apocalyptic Transformation," 435. Brown argues convincingly that Paul's is an apocalyptic outlook, and that for him the cross of Jesus Christ is the paramount sign of the future kingdom of God breaking into present reality.

129. See ibid.

130. Italics mine.

It remains present in that tradition's deeper levels however, where it is bound up with ideas concerning the creature's ontological renewal and heightening orientation to the divine will.

Athanasius serves to illustrate this deeper approach. He thinks that prelapsarian humankind was granted a *participatory share* in the mind of God.[131] If after the fall a vestige of that share remained enabling a certain natural knowledge of God, that share with its knowledge was necessarily flawed. In its consequent ignorance and separation from the Truth of God the creature was destined to die.[132] But the Son pitied its ignorance. Of his love for it he resolved to reveal himself to it, a decision and a revelation culminating in his obedience to the Father on the cross. By its cruciform means he, together with the Father, moved to renew the creature's prelapsarian state before God. Implicitly in Athanasius' thought such renewal extends to the state of the mind. So the creature comes to perceive the Son's self-revelation properly, and to know that to know him is to know God. (Later discussion will consider the eschatological implications of such cognitive renewal.)

Conclusion

Dichotomy and dialectic mark the classical epistemology of the cross. Here the knowledge of God is indirect, mediated through suffering, humiliation, hiddenness, and the unreasonable proposal that a crucified man comprises ultimate Truth. The theology explicating this epistemology covers a range of notions and themes. These may be divided into two groups, those associated with what the classical crucicentric theologians reject, and those associated with what they advocate.

As the foregoing discussion has shown, negative crucicentric epistemology embraces all anthropocentric methodologies and starting points for the knowledge of God related to: human experience, the law, a mysticism which confuses the knowledge of God with the self knowledge of the creature, and natural theologies based in philosophy,

---

131. Athanasius says here, "In creating them God caused human beings to share in the reasonable being of the very Word Himself, so that reflecting him, they themselves became reasonable, expressing the mind of God even as He does, though in limited degree." See A Religious of CSMV, *On the Incarnation*, 3.3. Slightly paraphrased.

132. "[Thence the Son] saw the reasonable race, the race of men that, like Himself, expressed the Father's mind, wasting out of existence, and death reigning over all in corruption." Ibid., 2.8.

metaphysics, reason, and natural creation. In the crucicentric view in common each of these finally produce not objective knowledge of God, but the self-glorifying creature's idolatrous reflection of itself.

Positive crucicentric epistemology includes themes related to: the wisdom of the cruciform starting point and the foolishness of God in asserting it, the revelation of God in the suffering and humiliation of Jesus Christ, the dialectic between divine hiddenness and divine revelation in the cross, revelation under the opposite—or where least expected, the indirect nature of revelation, the revelatory priority of the cross over other christological moments and therefore its centrality for Christian thought, and the cruciform provision for the creature of a new mind joined to the mind of Christ—a cognitive union to be actualized fully eschatologically.

These multiple negative and positive elements interweave around two key crucicentric principles, the overriding principle that God alone is glorious and the creature not so, and the specifically epistemological principle that God alone can truly know God so as to reveal God truly. It is then the classical crucicentric contention that it is uniquely in the man-God Jesus Christ, and supremely in the cross, that divine revelation takes place.

It is by being cognitively identified with Christ *in his death* that the creature receives this revelation; there is no other way for it to do so. The following discussion on classical crucicentric soteriology will take the ontological implications of deadly identification with Jesus Christ yet further.

3

The Classical Soteriology of the Cross

For the Word of the cross to those indeed perishing is foolishness, and to us (those being saved) it is the power of God.

—The Apostle Paul[1]

It is the theological ethos, the orientation, of classical crucicentric soteriology, as much as the specific theological proposals involved, which sets it apart from the soteriology of the wider orthodox tradition. At the heart of this ethos are two deaths and three sorts of glory. The deaths are those of Jesus Christ and of the creature in Christ, the glory is that of God and the true and false glory of the creature.

Two major principles and a particular set of themes and notions also contribute to this ancient and distinctive crucicentric ethos, each element standing over against parallel elements in the theology of glory. The prior crucicentric principle, (familiar here from the study of classical crucicentric epistemology), proclaims the absolute sovereignty of God and the utter creatureliness of the creature. The specifically soteriological principle insists that God alone can condition the salvific will of God.

At first glance the various crucicentric soteriological themes and notions can appear mutually disparate, but in common they each obey the above principles. Negatively they oppose the self-glorifying concept that the creature can determine the salvific will of God. Positively they

---

1. 1 Cor 1:18. (Young's Literal Translation.) In this older and literal translation the cross is presented as a mediatory instrument, its Word conveying Christ himself.

propose the centrality and certainty of the glory of God, the soteriological priority of Christ's cruciform work in satisfying the law on behalf of humankind, and the justifying, sanctifying and glorifying processes by which the creature benefits from this work.

This principled negative and positive soteriological message is proclaimed originally from the cross by Jesus Christ. He both issues it by his Spirit and comprises its cruciform content. This Christocentric cruciform proclamation is received by the creature as a divine Word impinging upon it from beyond itself and beyond time, drawing a line cleanly between the real and the non-real, death and life, the true and the false—especially the true and the false theologies of glory.

Three background considerations pave the way for substantive discussion of classical crucicentric soteriology. These are the nature of the western and crucicentric orders of salvation, the soteriological employment of wisdom and foolishness, and the priority of the cross soteriologically.

Mutually antagonistic orders of salvation continue down the centuries of the Christian tradition. The western *ordo salutis*[2] is *anthropocentric*. Predicated on the notion that the human will is free and unencumbered, it holds the creature capable of conditioning its justification. By dint of its own effort the creature satisfies God, earning and requiring its salvation. In the western order then, a self-engendered sanctification precedes justification. The electing decision rests with the creature, not the Creator.

In contrast what can be termed "the gracious *ordo salutis*," the crucicentric salvific order, is *theocentric*. It holds that prompted by the Spirit of God, faith, repentance, obedience to the law, do not precede the justifying action of God but respond to it. From the far side of justification the creature perceives that while it was yet sinful Christ died for it, thus—because of Christ and not itself—it is *already* justified.[3] It is this liberating realization which prompts the creature's acknowledgment of its justification, its glad response of obedience and penitence, and with this its increasing conformation to Christ—first to his death and then to his resurrection. In the gracious order then, a God-given sanctification

---

2. This is also known as the "western Protestant *ordo salutis*" since a strand of post-Reformation thought supports it.

3. See Rom 5:8.

succeeds justification. The electing decision rests with the Creator, not the creature.

This gracious salvific order lies at the heart of classical crucicentric soteriology. Rae captures its radicality when he says that the cross "is the unconditional affirmation that we belong to God, and as such, represents the contradiction of much Western theology and popular piety. God's forgiveness and reconciling love is not conditional upon our recognition of our sin nor upon our repentance . . . Repentance does not hope for forgiveness, but occurs because forgiveness has already been given."[4]

The crucicentric argument is that should this gracious order *not* be so, if in fact faith, repentance, obedience and so on were creaturely attributes preceding, warranting and conditioning justification, then salvific grace would not be free or certain. Neither would there be need for the cruciform work of Christ. Salvation would then become a matter of religious necessity, and the cross itself—as Paul warns—emptied of power.[5]

This crucicentric reversal of the western *ordo salutis* is not simply a theological nicety. To look back, in the sixteenth century the rebuke it posed to the theology of glory contributed powerfully to the cataclysmic upheaval in the European church now known as the Reformation. Here Hunsinger bears quoting at length:

> What Luther discovered . . . was not that grace is prevenient, for that would be nothing new. Nor was the novelty of Luther's discovery located in the idea that the sinner is justified by grace through an existential process of sanctification. That idea was as common in the middle ages as it was alien to the Reformation. Rather what Luther attacked was "the whole medieval tradition as it was later confirmed at the Council of Trent." All known scholastic doctrines of justification, whether nominalist, Scotist or Thomistic, finally saw justification as a goal to be obtained at the end of a purifying process *in nobis*. By contrast Luther saw justification as "the stable *basis* and not the *goal* of the life of sanctification." Justification by faith alone meant that our righteousness in God's sight is already our real spiritual possession. Although it has yet to become an inherent predicate *in nobis*, nonetheless we now possess it, whole and entire, *extra nos* in Christ by faith.[6]

4. Rae, "The Cross of Jesus Christ," Unpublished notes. Undated, 4.

5. See 1 Cor 1:17

6. Hunsinger, "What Barth Learned from Martin Luther," 131. Italics Hunsinger's. Here Hunsinger cites Oberman, *Luther*, 119f.

The Classical Soteriology of the Cross 73

With the Reformation in view Hunsinger subsequently continues:

> In a move whose significance can hardly be overestimated, Luther broke with every form of soteriological gradualism, that is, with every viewpoint which sees salvation primarily as a matter of gradual acquisition. Righteousness, he argued, was not essentially something that we acquire by degrees, but something that comes to us as a whole, just because Christ and his righteousness were perfect in the finished work he accomplished on our behalf.[7]

Put otherwise, the gracious *ordo salutis* was and is revolutionary.

Further, the western order of salvation is associated with the (aforementioned) *analogia entis*, and the gracious crucicentric order with an analogy of faith or *analogia fidei*.[8] From the perspective of the western order commonality between the Creator and the creature not only enables the creature to *know* God (again as earlier noted), but to *satisfy* God. Being godlike the creature can sanctify itself conditioning its justification. In contrast the gracious *ordo salutis* emphatically denies the *analogia entis* with its championing of an anthropocentric starting point for salvation. Rather the gracious order draws two analogies on the God-man Jesus Christ and him crucified. The first is from Jesus Christ to the sheer graciousness of the God who freely justifies the creature—for in the cross he corresponds exactly to this saving God. The second is from Jesus Christ to the *consequential* submission and obedience of the justified creature—for in the cross he corresponds exactly to the prototypical obedient human.

This also means that crucicentric theology employs not only dialectics[9] but analogy, the two methodologies complementing each other.

The gracious *ordo salutis* dictates the logic of relying salvifically solely on Jesus Christ and him crucified. By the same token salvific reliance by the creature on itself is considered by the crucicentric theologians to be illogical. The discussion now turns to the second preliminary matter, the crucicentric juxtaposition of wisdom and foolishness.[10]

---

7. Hunsinger, "What Barth Learned from Martin Luther," 140.

8. For a fuller definition of the *analogia fidei* see here p. 139, n. 12.

9. For the importance of dialectical tension in crucicentric theology see here page 34.

10. See here pp. 56–59 a discussion on wisdom and foolishness relating to epistemology.

For Paul's Jewish and Greek interlocutors foolishness characterizes not only the cruciform starting point for the knowledge of God, but the cruciform starting point for unity with God. They see nothing logical about a pathway to God via a cross. Brown explains, "[For] neither Jew nor Greek does the death by crucifixion of God's Son conform to [the] cosmic order. In neither system can what is antithetical to reason, to law, that is to *logos* itself, confer salvation. The 'logos of the cross' constitutes a contradiction in terms offensive both to the reasoned and to the religious mind."[11]

For the Jews to identify the powerful, holy and covenantal God with a man, let alone a crucified and therefore cursed man, constitutes transgression of the first commandment and so culpable blasphemy. Neither does the message of the cross—that through weakness power is manifest, and through death the covenantal kingdom restored—mesh with Jewish messianic expectations. Indeed the possibility that the crucifixion of Jesus is in any sense salvific appears nonsensical, and those advocating it likewise.

For the Greeks the proposal of the cross as a way to God, let alone the only way, seems equally foolish. Traditional Greek theism begins with the problem of human finitude and concludes that any god who brings release from it must reasonably be objective to the world—transcendent, unchanging, impassible, immortal, and so on. Faced with Paul's theology of the cross the Greeks therefore question how a man can be identified with the hidden wisdom of the cosmos, or aligned with the *Logos*. How should he "save" the world? How can *gnosis* originating in the world free the soul from bondage to the world? How can degradation and humiliation serve as a platform for glorification? All positive proposals here seem illogical to them. Moreover Greek cultural and philosophical objections exist to the idea of self-sacrifice for the undeserving and ungodly as a means of conditioning divine favor. If such unreasonable sacrifice is in fact the secret way to the ideal world, then the reasonable Greeks baulk at it.

Paul dismisses these objections as the product of poor logic and spiritual deception. His interlocutors, Jewish and Greek, engage in equal but opposite errors. Glorying in their righteousness before the law the Jews lift themselves to God. Glorying in their speculative methodologies

---

11. See Brown, "Apocalyptic Transformation in Paul's Discourse on the Cross," 432.

the Greeks reduce God to themselves. But for Paul these solutions cannot be. Rooted anthropocentrically, neither obedience to the law nor speculative reason can achieve the life-giving partnership with divinity they intend. In fact no commonality exists between God and the creature, and there is no possibility that the creature might create it. Enamored with their own "wisdom of the flesh," neither the Jews nor the Greeks can understand the wisdom of the cross, they lack the capacity to do so. In their hands law and reason—good in themselves—have become foundation pillars for an illogical self-glorifying theology of their own devising.

Paul attacks such worldly wisdom with the Word of the cross. It declares the meaning of the cross, that here there is neither conditionable deity nor the deistic god of some invisible realm, but divine Wisdom manifest in the crucified Christ. In his death he has powerfully and exclusively overcome the false wisdom of the world, the false notion that by the exercise of law or reason the creature can lift itself to God, so as to open the way of salvation to both Jews and Greeks. So Paul declares, "[But] to those who are called, both Jews and Greeks, Christ the power of God and the wisdom of God" (1 Cor 1:24).

Given that the cruciform defeat of worldly wisdom has already occurred, all creaturely attempts at bypassing the cross and attaining God on human terms, for self-glorifying human ends, must ultimately fail. Paul therefore also reiterates the certain warning of God, "For it is written, 'I will destroy the wisdom of the wise, and the discernment of the discerning I will thwart'" (1 Cor 1:19).[12]

What has happened formally must be made actual. The Word . . . of the cross demands that human wisdom really die if the Wisdom of God is to be received. The mark of the wise is that they perceive the inherent logic in this demand, of fools that they ignore it. Or as Paul—melting ontological Wisdom with the Word of the cross—states, "For the Word of the cross to those indeed perishing is foolishness, and to us (those being saved) it is the power of God" (1 Cor 1:18).[13] Of this statement Brown says decisively, "In this remarkable declaration is inscribed in

---

12. Von Loewenich summarises Luther at a similar point, "Reason and law . . . are toppled by the theology of the cross . . . For the cross is the judgement upon the pride of [human] wisdom. No self-glory can maintain itself in the presence of the cross." Von Loewenich, *Luther's Theology of the Cross*, 76.

13. Young's Literal Translation.

short-hand the whole of Paul's revolutionary gospel, so stated as to jar the careful observer into a startling new way of knowing. If we listen closely ... we begin already to hear in its strange turns and reversals, its unfamiliar constructions, the de-centering force of the cross against the falsely centered mind."[14]

As already noted, Athanasius has a great deal to say about the foolishness of his interlocutors, citing both their lack of logic and their personal absurdity. He commences his polemic against the Arians, for example, by declaring that, "Of all other heresies which have departed from the truth it is acknowledged that [the Arians] have ... devised a madness."[15] Since salvation is found solely in Jesus Christ, it is illogical for the Arians to attribute its source elsewhere, much less worship that source. It is unreasonable for them to seek salvation in gods they have themselves fashioned, gods which of themselves can be no more powerful than their human creators.[16] In any case the standard of true salvation is already given in the cross of Jesus Christ.[17] Wisdom dictates that it is here one must start soteriologically and methodologically.

In such arguments Athanasius relies heavily on Paul's soteriological insight. The true Wisdom of the cross reverses the "wisdom" both of the Jews and of the Greeks, uncovering its actual folly. Thence Athanasius says—and an older translation of him gives an extra cogency to his words, "[The mystery of the Word's becoming man] the Jews traduce, the Greeks deride, but we adore ... [By] what seems His utter poverty and weakness on the cross He overturns the pomp and parade of idols, and quietly and hiddenly wins over the mockers and unbelievers to recognize Him as God[, to renew creation, and to effect] the salvation of the world through the same Word Who made it in the beginning."[18]

This leads to the third matter setting the scene for an account of crucicentric soteriology, the salvific significance of the cross. As with the

14. Brown, "Apocalyptic Transformation," 432.

15. Newman and Robertson, *Against the Arians*, 1.1.

16. Athanasius says, for example in his *Contra Arianos*, "Now the so-called gods of the Greeks, unworthy the name, are faithful neither in their essence nor in their promises." An instrument of the creature, logically such gods are powerless salvifically. Ibid., 2.10.

17. As Meyer rightly says, "[The] most important motif for Athanasius [is] the propitiatory and expiatory sacrifice of Christ on the cross." Meyer, "Athanasius' Use of Paul," 150. See also A Religious of CSMV, *On the Incarnation*, 7, 9.

18. A Religious of CSMV, *On the Incarnation*, 1.

The Classical Soteriology of the Cross 77

centrality of the cross epistemologically, the centrality of the cross soteriologically is not everywhere recognized. Some within what is loosely called Christian orthodoxy preference the saving significance of Christ's incarnation for its atoning condescension. Some, Christ's resurrection for its demonstration of death overcome. For the classical crucicentric theologians however, the whole of the Christ event crowned by the cross is saving. The crucifixion is then the divine *raison d'être* for, and pivotal focus of, *all* other christological events—those coming before and those coming after it. It is then supremely in the cross that sin and death are finally and definitively overcome, and the creature freed and reconciled and transformed.

This being so the classical crucicentric theologians have no patience with the notion that the cross is, in McGrath's words, simply "one stage in the progress from Christ's earthly life to his exaltation at the right hand of God."[19] Such a notion reduces the significance of the cross, encouraging the frank denial of its claim in preference for a natural path to God and a resurgent theology of glory.

As they do epistemologically, soteriologically Paul and Luther comprehend the paramount significance of the cross from the perspective of the resurrection, while Athanasius understands it principally from the incarnation.

Paul gives full weighting to the salvific importance of the resurrection, while never losing sight of the prior significance of the cross. Denney says here that the resurrection does not qualify "in the slightest the prominence given in Paul to Jesus Christ crucified... There can be no salvation from sin unless there is a living Saviour: this explains the emphasis laid by the apostle on the resurrection. But the living One can be a Saviour only because he has died."[20]

In the fourth century the question of the soteriological significance of the cross becomes firstly the question of the personhood of the Son who bore the cross, and secondly the question of the Son's relation to the Father. (At this time *Sonship* itself is no longer at issue.) "Is the Son actually divine, one with God in being and nature?" "Is he actually human, one with humankind in time and space, such that his atoning work is truly mediatory, really vicarious?" Over against the complex metaphysi-

---

19. McGrath, *Enigma of the Cross*, 32. In the wider context of this comment McGrath supports the priority of the cross salvifically.

20. Denney, "Death of Christ," 73.

cal currents of his world Athanasius answers with the hypostatic union,[21] supported by the *homoousion*.[22] Only because Jesus Christ is fully human is he able to represent the creature, making its sin and death his own.[23] Only because he is fully divine, one in substance with the Father, is he able to overcome that creaturely corruption, freeing the creature vicariously.[24]

This also means for Athanasius that the incarnation is the necessary ground for the salvific work of the cross, while the work of the cross is the central reason for the incarnation. Supporting this, Anatolios warns that Athanasius' much noted emphasis on the incarnation should not be seen "as a de-emphasis on the death and resurrection of Christ, [these being for him] the very purpose of the Incarnation."[25] Athanasius himself simply says that Christ "came for this reason: that in the flesh

---

21. The doctrine of the *hypostatic union* holds that the two natures of Jesus Christ are joined *inconfuse, immutabiliter, indivise, inseparabiliter* [without confusion, without change, without division, without separation] such that he is fully human and fully divine.

22. Torrance usefully defines the homoousion as follows, "[The] *homoousion* gave precise theological expression to the truth that, while distinct from one another, the Father and the Son eternally belong to one another in the Godhead." Torrance, *Karl Barth*, 216–17. Italics Torrance's. Athanasius' argument for the substantial identity of Father and Son—the *homoousion*—is first soteriological. Put negatively, if Jesus Christ were not fully human and fully divine he would not represent God to the creature and the creature to God, mediating between them. He would not bear the creature's nature in all its sin, slavery, and condemnation, so as to vicariously represent it to God in obedience and repentance. He would not equally represent God to the creature in forgiveness and reconciliation.

23. Writing to Epicetus, Athanasius explains that the Son assumed the whole of human being that the whole of human being, body and soul, be saved. He argues that had the Son not been wholly human he could not have wholly represented the creature, and salvation could not have proceeded (Epic. 101.7.) In this Athanasius anticipates the famous dictum of Gregory of Nazianzus (330–390), "What is not assumed is not healed." Ep. 101, *Ad Cledonium*. See Weinandy, *Athanasius*, 95, and Norris, "Cappadocian Fathers,"114.

24. Athanasius writes, "For [the Son] suffered to prepare freedom from suffering for those who suffer in him. He descended that he might raise us up, he went down to corruption, that corruption might put on immortality, he became weak for us, that we might rise with power, he descended to death, the he might bestow on us immortality, and give life to the dead. Finally, he became man, that we who die as men might live again, and that death should no more reign over us." "Festal Letter 10.8," cited by Weinandy, *Athanasius*, 96.

25. Anatolios, *Athanasius*, 60.

he might suffer and the flesh be made impassible and immortal."[26] And similarly, "He who ascended the cross is the Word of God and Saviour of the World."[27]

Luther also awards central priority to the cross soteriologically, but for him it is again the resurrection of Christ which points to that significance. The backwards light of the resurrection identifies the cross as the place where sin and death are definitively overcome, enabling the resurrection of Christ and that of those in him to proceed. Or as McGrath explains, "[For Luther] it is the cross, interpreted in the light of the resurrection which must remain the key to our understanding of this world and our destiny within it. Christian existence in general, and Christian discipleship in particular, are governed by the cross . . . [To] give the resurrection priority over the crucifixion is to retreat from the realities of the world into the 'heavenly realms,' developing an idealistic view of the world and our place in it." [28]

Three background considerations to any discussion of classical crucicentric soteriology have been canvassed, *viz*. the nature of two dialectically opposing orders of salvation, the juxtaposition of wisdom and foolishness in the soteriology of the cross, and the salvific centrality of the cross itself. It can be seen already that the classical crucicentric theologians deny all soteriologies beginning anthropocentrically, a perspective to be further explored now.

The Negative Soteriology of the Cross

Denying the notion that the creature is fated, the classical crucicentric theologians also deny the possibility that human action can determine reconciled acceptance by God. There is but one determinate applying here, the vicarious cruciform work of Jesus Christ. His cross negates all anthropocentric methodologies for achieving salvation, including: the performance of meritorious good works (or "works-righteousness"), the conditioning of salvation by satisfying divine law, the use of speculative reason to condition the electing will of God, mystical exercises to reach up to divine union, the attempt by the individual to manufacture saving faith, or by the church to dispense salvific grace.

26. *Contra Arianos* 3.58. Cited from Anatolios, *Athanasius*, 60.
27. Schaff, *Contra Gentes*, 1.5.
28. McGrath, *The Enigma of the Cross*, 32.

In the view of the classical crucicentric theologians each anthropocentric path to salvation bears the mark of an old deception, one defining human maturity in terms of independence from God and self-governance.[29] This deception gives rise to two equal and opposite self-delusions, that salvation is not required for sin is not deadly,[30] and that salvation is required and can be attained naturally, by means of human capacity. Generally the crucicentric theologians see the latter delusion as the more dangerous; at its roots the desire to condition election is the desire to be like God.

For Paul human activity cannot help salvifically. This is especially so of *religious* activity for in it the greatest trap lies. What conventionally seems so admirable is actually the attempt to force divine favor, bypass the cross, and exalt the creature over God. Paul insists there is *no* requirement for the justifying work of Jesus Christ to be initiated by, or supplemented by, the creature. He warns that the attempt to do so is foolish—it cannot succeed. (Illustrating this, he cites the futile circumcising of Gentile believers to bring them into covernental relation with God.[31]) But it is also dangerous. As Paul knows from his own experience, the person religiously pursuing self-glorifying union with God must be thrown to the ground and broken.[32]

Athanasius similarly rejects any notion that the creature might satisfy God. Agreeing with Titus 3:4–5 he says directly, "But when the kindness and love of God our Saviour appeared, not because of righteous deeds that we had done but because of his mercy, he saved us."[33] Athanasius' objection to the possibility of conditioning salvation, even partially, is raised by him in order to protect the utter divide he per-

---

29. According to Mattes there are fewer differences between medieval and modern theological-anthropologies than might be supposed, for as the modern world will do, the medieval world lays claim to a form of self-actualization and its theology is influenced accordingly. See Mattes, "Gerhard Forde," 385.

30. In the Heidelberg Disputation Luther bitterly opposes the idea of a lesser, or *venial*, form of sin entailing lesser consequences than death. For him all sin separates the sinner from the one source of life, necessarily resulting in death. See theses 5 and 6.

31. "Listen! I Paul, am telling you that if you let yourselves be circumcised, Christ will be of no benefit to you" (Gal 5:2).

32. See Acts 9:1–9, Paul's conversion on the road to Damascus. See also Bayer, "Word of the Cross," 47.

33. Letters to Serapion 1:22. See Anatolios, *Athanasius*, 222.

ceives between the creature and the Creator, a divide that Christ alone can bridge. By its own efforts the creature cannot raise itself to God.

Supporting this, Athanasius insists on two natures in Jesus Christ, the divine nature rather than the human nature being salvifically efficacious. The contemporary notion of a purely human Son purchasing divinity in the cross Athanasius thinks modalistic. It compromises the personhood of Christ; it undermines the salvific efficacy of the cross; it opens the possibility that the creature might divinize itself. Even in Jesus Christ human nature cannot raise itself to be divine.[34]

The medieval crucicentric mystics likewise reject salvific human effort, and here especially introspective contemplation designed to unify the soul with God on human terms, for self-glorifying human ends. According to the anonymous writer of the *Theologia Germanica* for instance, such exercises can only strengthen diabolically implanted dreams of Godhood. The writer continues:

> [Mark how] the carnal man in each of us . . . first cometh to be deceived. It doth not desire nor choose Goodness as Goodness, and for the sake of Goodness, but desireth and chooseth itself and its own ends, . . . and this is an error, and is the first deception . . . Secondly, it dreameth itself to be that which it is not, for it dreameth itself to be God, and is truly nothing but nature. And because it imagineth itself to be God, it taketh to itself what belongeth to God; [that is, his glory. It says] "for the more like God one is, the better one is, and therefore I will be like God and will be God, and will sit and go and stand at His right hand," as Lucifer the Evil Spirit also said.[35]

Similarly Tauler, who holds that the soul is powerless to free itself from sin with the aid of mystical practices. The latter can only bring confusion and false peace. Indeed no work originating with the creature can condition salvation. God alone meets the condition for salvation since he alone has set it, and in the cross of Jesus Christ is himself the standard of it. It follows that relying salvifically on human works leads to death, but depending on the work of Christ results in life.[36]

---

34. See Ibid., 54.

35. Winkworth, *Theologia Germanica*, chapter 40.

36. See Neufeld, "The Cross of the Living Lord," 136, and Shrady, *Johannes Tauler*, 90.

The excursus to Part One sets out Luther's Heidelberg rejection of all human methodologies for conditioning salvation. That material need not be foreshadowed fully now, but one aspect is relevant here. Luther, like Paul, faults the use of *good* (or *religious*) works to gain salvific merit. Repentance, obedience, contemplative prayer, the display of faith and the like, are all especially deceptive just because they can seem so worthy of divine favor, so obviously efficacious therefore. In reality the fallen creature is unable to perform *any* work pleasing to God, requiring God to elect it. Works performed for this purpose are, Luther thinks, really aimed at controlling God. They constitute another form of the *theologia gloriae*. Moreover they negate the importance of the one really good work, that of Jesus Christ at Golgotha. "Work righteousness" is thus to be condemned; indeed the cross demonstrates that God has already done so. Luther is to maintain this judgement across his project.

If the classical crucicentric theologians deny the anthropocentric path to God, what do they affirm?

The Positive Soteriology of the Cross

The positive aspect of classical crucicentric soteriology relates to: justification, sanctification, resurrection, and true glorification eschatologically. Each of these doctrinal areas encompasses two or more significant crucicentric elements. A number of contingent crucicentric notions and themes attend each of these areas.

Justification

Viewed theologically, the classical crucicentric understanding of justification involves two real deaths, the death of Jesus Christ on behalf of the creature, and the death of the creature in Jesus Christ. Viewed methodologically, this understanding touches on five interconnected themes: the law, the vicarious suffering and death of Jesus Christ, the claim of the cross on the creature, the question of universal salvation, and the formal gift of new life in Christ. These themes are now outlined.

To set the scene for an account of Paul's forensic theology a methodological note is in order. From the latter part of the twentieth century forward New Testament scholars have keenly debated the validity of Luther's influence on Pauline studies. Rejecting the latter, a "new perspective on Paul"[37] has freshly located him within his religio-historical, particularly Jewish, context. Significant advocates of this position include figures such as Stendahl, Sanders, Dunn, and Wright—though they can also disagree amongst themselves. Opposing them scholars such as Westerholm, Schreiner, and Silva argue that a reading of Paul implicitly or explicitly indebted to Luther's prior reading of him, in fact has much to offer present scholarship.

It is not necessary to detail this now voluminous debate, but the "old perspective" will be sampled so as to indicate its flavor, and therefore that of the discussion as a whole.

In 1988 Westerholm concludes that if Luther had not understood the finer points of the cultural debates of Paul's own day, he had certainly not "perverted the apostle's larger meaning."[38] Westerholm still defends this position.

Schreiner contends that Paul is *not* primarily concerned with Jewish cultic practice. With the Abrahamic covenant in view it is the significance of the universal *moral* claim of the law that is uppermost in Paul's mind. "Paul's purpose . . . is to communicate the inability of the law to transform human beings. Unbelievers, since they are sold under sin, are unable to keep God's law . . . [They] are destined to die."[39] The so-called "new perspective on Paul" has its own flaws.

Silva however gives some credence to the new perspective. He sees in the opposition of the two perspectives a false dichotomy. They are in fact two sides of the same coin. Admitting that the Reformation emphasis requires greater consciousness of the Jewish-Gentile question, nonetheless Silva thinks—as Koperski reports him—that "full recognition of the redemptive-historical foundation of the message of Galatians does not require abandonment of the traditional Protestant understanding [that Paul opposes works righteousness.]"[40]

The present inquiry sympathizes with the above defensive positions, with the "old perspective" therefore. Paul and Luther are linked by

---

37. James Dunn originally delivered a lecture entitled "The New Perspective on Paul" in the University of Manchester on 4 November 1982. Thereafter he has continued to develop his "new perspective," setting it out again most recently in 2008, in a volume named after the original lecture.

38. Westerholm, *Israel's Law and the Church's Faith*, 222.

39. Schreiner, *Paul*, 267.

40. Koperski, *Paul and the Law*, 58.

their obedience to the same fundamental theological, indeed *crucicentric*, principles. If this is so, a reading of Paul obliquely through Luther must help clarify rather than hinder understanding of his fundamental thought, including his forensic theology.

To turn to that forensic theology directly, in the 2004 edition of his commentary on Romans, *Understanding Paul*, Westerholm begins by explaining the tremendous significance of the epistle for Luther, among others. Within this parameter he says, "[Adamic] humanity does not, and cannot, submit to God's law."[41] Yet "God (by giving the law) demands its obedience."[42] In Paul's theology the precepts of the law are non-negotiable. For the fallen human creature, however, they present an impossible standard. The creature cannot satisfy the law, but then neither does it wish to. It would rather promulgate its own law; *be* its own lawgiver. To this end the creature adopts one of two measures. Either it frankly disobeys the law, setting its own standard in place of the divine standard. Or, more subtly, it ostensibly submits to the law to force God to fulfill his covenantal promise to it. In both instances the creature is actually presuming to be as God. For Paul, however, pursuit of these dual procedures is doomed. The open attempt to be as God which denies the law reaps its own reward. The subtle attempt to be as God which conditions the law conditions only the penalty for the self-glorifying conceit involved. Thus Paul warns, "For 'no human being will be justified in [God's] sight' by deeds prescribed by the law" (Rom 3:20).

Paul is then utterly realistic in his assessment of the human condition and its outworking. "[All], both Jews and Greeks, are under the power of sin, as it is written, 'There is no one who is righteous, not even one'" (Rom 3:9b–10). "All who have sinned apart from the law will also perish apart from the law, and all who have sinned under the law will be judged by the law" (Rom 2:12). Paul proceeds to illustrate the point personally. If justification and thence salvation is achieved through obedience to the law, then he himself, a Pharisee schooled since birth in obedience to its divine precepts, might be expected to merit salvation. But he has exchanged such expectation for the truth that as all other humans, of himself he is incapable of meeting the righteous demand

---

41. Westerholm, *Understanding Paul*, 115.
42. Ibid.

of the law.[43] Indeed, the real effect of the law is simply to clarify what is required to break it, goading the creature's natural antinomianism and pointing up its natural sinfulness. Paul states this in several places including: "[Through] the law comes the knowledge of sin" (Rom 3:20). Similarly, "[If] it had not been for the law, I would not have known sin" (Rom 7:7b), and with a certain irony, "But the law came in, with the result that the trespass multiplied" (Rom 5:20a).

For the law rightly condemns the sinful creature. Here Paul reaches into the history of ancient Israel and the concept of the fall. At the dawn of history the Adamic attempt at independence from the claim and command of God leads inevitably to broken relationship, the imposition of suffering, atrophy, creaturely separation from God. Neither can the creature rescue itself. Condemned, it is nonetheless blinded and hardened to the one way out of its dilemma. Instead in gathering crisis it either rebels directly against God, or engages in the religious quest to placate God. Each of these strategies aims at domesticating God and avoiding the penalty of the law. Neither can succeed. The law can be contained neither by radical dismissal nor rigid pursuit of its letters. It is designed by a holy God not to feed the religious idea but to *crucify* it. The claim of the law is the claim of the cross, a legitimate claim on *the death* of the creature.[44] Thence Paul's own cry, "Wretched man that I am! Who will rescue me from this body of death?" (Rom 7:24)

But the law that kills is also the law that brings life. Paul holds that in both these capacities the law is wholly the work of a holy God. He

---

43. Paul denies the possibility of self-engendered righteousness. "If anyone else has reason to be confident in the flesh, I have more: circumcised on the eighth day, a member of the people of Israel, of the tribe of Benjamin, a Hebrew born of Hebrews; as to the law, a Pharisee; as to zeal, a persecutor of the church; as to righteousness under the law, blameless . . . But I do not have a righteousness of my own that comes from the law" (Phil 3:4b–9).

44. Death here does not imply simply the loss of temporal being, to which all are heir. Rather it means an eternal state characterized by continuing condemnation and separation from God. Indicating this Paul (envisioning Christ's apocalyptic return) writes, "[Those] who do not know God and . . . those who do not obey the gospel of our Lord Jesus . . . will suffer the punishment of eternal destruction, separated from the presence of the Lord and from the glory of his might" (2 Thes 1: 8–9). One commentary says to this verse, "Just as endless life belongs to Christians, endless destruction belongs to those opposed to Christ. The consequences of permanent separation from God come out forcibly in the phrase 'from the presence of the Lord' . . . Words cannot adequately express the misery of this condition." Gaebelein and Douglas, *Expositor's Bible Commentary*.

asks, "What then should we say? That the law is sin?" to answer directly, "By no means! . . . [The] law is holy, and the commandment is holy and just and good (Rom 7:7–12)." For it is the law of *God*, designed to bring the creature ultimately to him in surrender.

Demonstrating the life-giving purpose of the law in a further way, Paul appeals to a second ancient idea in Israel—that an executed criminal is divinely cursed.[45] It is not that having first transgressed the law the creature is rightly judged, condemned, excluded from the covenantal community, executed, and so cursed. Rather, cursed with fallen human nature, the creature inevitably fails the test of the law and so attracts its penalty. (Thus to the creature the law appears cursed.) For Paul the order here is significant, first curse and then condemnation. He argues that in his incarnation Jesus Christ first takes on the cursed inability of humankind to satisfy the law, and then in the crucifixion pays the penalty for the law's transgression. Thus Jesus Christ works out the curse so as to render it powerless; in him it is not avoided but exhausted. Christ does this on behalf of the creature, freeing it thereby from the weight of the law.

Paul refers to this complex of ideas around curse and law in several places. For example, "Christ redeemed us from the curse of the law by becoming a curse for us—for it is written, 'Cursed is everyone who hangs on a tree'" (Gal 3:13). Similarly, "For Christ is the end of the law so that there might be righteousness for everyone who believes" (Rom 10:4). And again, "For our sake [God] made him to be sin who knew no sin, so that in him we might become the righteousness of God" (2 Cor 5:21).

Under the law justification—embodied in and as Jesus Christ—is freely gifted to the creature. In Paul's words, "[This] free gift is not like the effect of the one man's sin. For the judgment following one trespass brought condemnation, but the free gift following many trespasses brings justification" (Rom 5:16). And with the free gift of justification comes the free gift of *faith* to acknowledge the receipt of justification—to acknowledge being saved. So Paul teaches the Ephesians, "For by grace you have been saved through faith, and this is not your own doing; it is the gift of God—not the result of works, so that no one may boast" (Eph

---

45. "When someone is convicted of a crime punishable by death and is executed, and you hang him on a tree, his corpse must not remain all night upon the tree; you shall bury him the same day, for anyone hung on a tree is under God's curse" (Deut 21:22–23).

The Classical Soteriology of the Cross 87

2:8–9). Similarly to the Philippians he explains that he himself does not have "a righteousness of my own that comes from the law, but one that comes through faith in Christ, the righteousness from God based on faith" (Phil 3:9). Finally then, bound up with faith and grace it is *because of Christ* and not the creature that the law is actually profoundly justifying and life-giving.

Athanasius too exercises a profound realism in regards to the declining human condition, the command of God, and the enforcement of that command by the law. Having succumbed to devilish[46] temptation at the fall, humankind has been excluded—individually and corporately—from life-sustaining connection with God. In consequence it descends back toward "non-being," the very state from which it had been called into being at its creation. That descent is marked by sin and decay, the one viciously compounding the other in a deepening circle of "de-creation."[47]

As an aside, by *sin* Athanasius does not mean pursuit of the sentient world—he considers the world as the creation of God to be axiomatically good. Nor for him is sin first to do with moral evil, reprehensible as that may be. Rather he understands sin as a direct consequence of the fall. In subsequent decline and de-creation the creature forsakes the true God for gods after its own design and calling; it claims for itself that worship rightfully belonging to God. Indeed the fallen creature would *be* God. Its preference is for itself, its own glory. Thus it "imagines and feigns what is not."[48] Or as Athanasius says, "[Forgetting] the knowledge and glory of God, their reasoning being dull, or rather following unreason, [men] made gods for themselves of things seen, glorifying the creature rather than the Creator (Rom 1:25), and deifying the works rather than the Master, God, their Cause and Artificer."[49] Sin, deeply conceived, is therefore for Athanasius *idolatry*.[50] Moreover sin is irrational, illogical

---

46. See A Religious of CSMV, *On the Incarnation*, 5.8.
47. See Anatolios, *Athanasius*, 48.
48. See Schaff, *Contra Gentes* 8.1. See also Weinandy, *Athanasius*, 16.
49. See Schaff, *Contra Gentes*, 8.3.
50. Weinandy states that Athanasius does not present a doctrine of original sin in the later Augustinian sense, "but does portray sin's cancerous nature." See Weinandy, *Athanasius*, 31.

in terms of itself.[51] It damages the creature ontologically, separating the latter from the Spring of Life. Thus, inevitably, it reaps its own reward.

To return to the principal discussion, Athanasius says that in its move towards de-creation, its sin and decay, the creature excites the penalty of the law. Moreover it is impossible for it "to flee the law since this had been established by God because of the transgression."[52] Thence Athanasius echoes Paul, in *this* circumstance the law becomes to it the law of death. He writes:

> God had made man, and willed that he should abide in incorruption, but men, having despised and rejected the contemplation of God, and devised and contrived evil for themselves . . . received the condemnation of death with which they had been threatened, and from thenceforth no longer remained as they were made, but were being corrupted . . . and death had master over them as king. For transgression of the commandment was turning them back to their natural state, so just as they had their being out of nothing, so also . . . they might look for corruption into nothing in the course of time.[53]

The remedy for such a dire situation, Athanasius thinks, requires more than just an outward repentance.[54] Ontological change is required. So God acts personally to save and transform humankind. God chooses to do so of his pity and mercy and love, because the doomed creature has no capacity to save itself, to prevent his own "handiwork in men" being brought to naught,[55] and because it is not worthy of God's goodness that

---

51. Referring to the Roman Senate's custom of creating gods, Athanasius declares that mortal humans who take to themselves the authority to *make* divine, clearly presume themselves to *be* divine. "[For] the maker must be better than what he makes, and the judge necessarily has jurisdiction over the judged, and the giver has to bestow what is in his possession." He adds sarcastically that "the remarkable thing is that by dying like men [Senators] prove their decree concerning those they deified to be false." In actuality, Athanasius says, the creature cannot manufacture that which is infinitely greater than itself. For it to suppose that it *can* marks its stupidity and its idolatry. See ibid.

52. See A Religious of CSMV, *On the Incarnation*, 9.

53. Ibid., 4.4. See Weinandy, *Athanasius*, 29.

54. Athanasius says, "If . . . there had been only sin and not its consequence of corruption, repentance would have been quite good. But, since transgression had overtaken them, men were now prisoners to natural corruption and they were deprived of the grace of being in the image [of God. Hence he who is] the Word of God [and] the Word of the Father was able to reconstitute all things and to suffer for all and to advocate on behalf of all before the Father." A Religious of CSMV, *On the Incarnation*, 7.

55. See ibid., 8.

the deceit practiced on humankind by the devil should be allowed to succeed.[56] God decides to do so before the world begins, predestining the creature for adoption by the Father through the One who is both Son and divine *Logos*.[57]

It follows for Athanasius that the "incorporeal and incorruptible and immaterial Word of God comes to our realm."[58] The Word comes in Jesus Christ, the perfect image of the Father. He comes in human form so as to suffer the penalty of death properly due other humans, that the penalty of the law might be duly lifted from them. He comes in love. Athanasius advances this explanation in many places, for example:

> [The Word], taking a body like our own, because all our bodies were liable to the corruption of death, . . . surrendered His body to death instead of all, and offered it to the Father. This He did out of sheer love for us, so that in His death all might die, and the law of death thereby be abolished because, having fulfilled in His body that for which it was appointed, it was thereafter voided of its power for men. This He did that He might turn again to incorruption men who had turned back to corruption, and make them alive [again.][59]

In Athanasius' estimation the law, now satisfied by the condescension and sacrifice of the Word of God on creaturely behalf, has become to the creature the law of life.

Turning to the far end of the classical crucicentric tradition, McGrath argues that the salvific operation of the law[60] remains Luther's "fundamental statement concerning the human situation and God's manner of dealing with it."[61] In the Heidelberg Disputation he sets out this fundamental statement with particular power, his forensic thought here forming an extensive footnote on Paul's own understanding.

In his proof to Thesis 24 of the Heidelberg Disputation Luther says that the law is not "to be evaded; but without the theology of the cross

---

56. See ibid., 2.6. See also Placher, *Readings in the History of Christian Theology*, 50.

57. See Newman and Robertson, *Against the Arians*, 2.76.

58. A Religious of CSMV, *On the Incarnation*, 2.8.

59. Ibid., 8.4.

60. Luther's theology of the law is set out in more detail in the excursus to Part One. See here pp. 143–45.

61. McGrath, *The Enigma of the Cross*, 176.

man misuses the best in the worst manner."[62] For in the face of human sin the law *continues to apply*. Those who would use the law to manipulate God for self-glorifying ends instead find themselves inescapably condemned under it. As Barth says, "[Luther leaves] no place for an 'also' or a 'but' or a 'nevertheless.'"[63] There is no escape from the law. Yet the law is not evil; in pointing to death it points equally to life. It indicates the gospel which absorbs and surpasses its own juridical imperative;[64] it declares the Good News that in the cross of Jesus Christ God graciously bears the full weight of the law on behalf of the condemned creature, satisfying its due penalty so as to justify the creature before it.

It is then solely in this way, via the cross, that true human life is gained. It is not that the creature is free *of* God, but freed by the law to live freely *to* God. The creature's liberation consists *negatively* in the fact that it need no longer attempt to manipulate the law to effect its salvation, in any case an impossible and sinful quest. It consists *positively* in the joy of reconciliation with the God who made the creature for himself.

No longer to gain justification but because of it, in glad response for Christ's cruciform work, subject to the cross, the creature at last relinquishes its attempt at self-glorification *and obeys the law*. It does so knowing it can neither boast that it has merited its justification, nor take credit for its new turn to obedience. Christian righteousness, Luther says, is "that righteousness by which Christ lives in us, not the righteousness that is in our person."[65] Justification, liberation, obedience, all are matters of forensic grace.

For all the classical crucicentric theologians the real satisfaction of the law involves the suffering of Jesus Christ. This is the second major element of the crucicentric understanding of justification being considered here. As already observed, the theology of the cross has at times

---

62. Lull, *Martin Luther's Basic Theological Writings*, 46.

63. Barth, *Calvin*, 43.

64. In many places Luther holds that the gospel of grace transcends the law. For example he interprets 2 Cor 3:9, "For if the ministration of condemnation hath glory, much rather doth the ministration of righteousness exceed in glory." Similarly in his Sermon on Galatians (1532) he teaches that "the difference between the Law and the gospel is the height of knowledge in Christendom . . . [After] the first Word, that of the Law, has done [its] work and distressful misery and poverty have been produced in the heart, God comes and offers his lovely, living Word." Thus for Luther the law in its graceless legalism is dead and the gospel alive.

65. Luther, *Luther's Works*, 26:166. See also 1 Cor 1:29.

The Classical Soteriology of the Cross   91

been treated as being synonymous either with a theology of suffering or with theodicy—the theology relating divine justice and mercy. While in the present view such identification is misplaced, nevertheless suffering, both that of Jesus Christ and that of the creature, forms an important crucicentric theme. Contra the zxworld which understands suffering as the product of blind fate or malicious deity, in a defined sense the crucicentric tradition perceives suffering as a mark of grace. The suffering of Christ is considered further now, that of the creature in due course.

To turn to Paul's world, as in the English the Koine Greek *pathema*, usually translated *suffering*, carries the dual connotations of pain and the endurance of pain. In the cross the God-man Jesus Christ is both afflicted with pain and endures pain, unlike the impassible deistic god. In his incarnation Jesus Christ empties himself of visible majesty (Phil 2:6–7), in the crucifixion he dies publicly exhibited (Gal 3:1), in humility (Phil 2:8), weakness and powerlessness (2 Cor 13:4), in bloody agony (Col 1:20), and in emotional despair. He dies in unimaginable spiritual distress, the divine Son given up to death by his own Father (Gal 1:4).

But as many scholars have observed Paul does not greatly dwell on the appalling physical details of the crucifixion of Jesus Christ. For him it is the passion's theological significance that is to the fore. Across the whole of his incarnation the Son suffers precisely because in identifying himself with the creature's condition, he identifies himself with the creature's presumption. This suffering reaches its crescendo in the cross. Here the Son experiences the ultimate consequence of human disobedience. Here his endurance becomes an inbreaking eschatological force disclosing divine power, defeating the gods of this world, overcoming human isolation, lifting the penalty of the law, bringing vicarious rescue. In short it is the suffering of Christ which inserts a great "No!" across the creaturely quest after its own way, and equally permits the promised "Yes!" to humankind itself to be concretely and eternally established (2 Cor 1:19–20).

Christ's suffering is then emphatically *not* the result of injustice. It is not an instrument used by a foolish God to beget justice, or by an angry Father punishing a guiltless Son in order to balance some celestial scale of justice,[66] these being arguments likely advanced by Paul's interlocutors. Rather Christ's suffering is one with the suffering of God,

---

66. For this reason Paul stresses Christ's *free* obedience toward the Father. See Gal 1:3–5.

"the way God's saving power is released,"[67] the primary demonstration of the power of God exacting the creature's redemption,[68] the evidence that true majesty and strength and humility are not different from each other. For Paul, as for later crucicentric theologians, it is then the message of the cross which vitally proclaims this revolutionary cruciform reality. Schreiner says of Paul here, the "theology of the cross reminds readers that salvation was accomplished through the suffering and death of Jesus of Nazareth."[69] It comprises a "message [which] teaches that God's power is revealed in and through weakness."[70]

To move to the fourth century, for Athanasius the suffering of Christ is profoundly redemptive. This is so in terms of both its forensic accomplishment and its sacrificial character. Torrance explains, "[Instead] of trying to explain away what the gospel tells of the weakness and mortality, the obedience and humiliation of Jesus in the form of a servant, Athanasius emphasized them and showed that it was human nature in this very condition that God had appropriated from us in its corruption and sin."[71]

It is then in the very powerlessness, weakness and humiliation of the cross that Athanasius, like Paul, perceives a great exchange to take place. The creature's sinfulness, suffering and death is replaced by its contrary, the power, strength and majesty of the Son's divine nature. Or as Athanasius himself says, "[The Son] became weak for us, that we might rise with power, he descended to death, that he might bestow on us immortality, and give life to the dead."[72]

Inspired by the biblical witnesses,[73] Athanasius places the sacrificial suffering of Christ at the common core of his Christology and soteriology. The sacrifice of the cross is the critical reason for the incarnation.[74] Without taking human form the Son could not have presented himself

67. Schreiner, *Paul*, 95.

68. Paul says of Christ, "In him we have redemption through his blood, the forgiveness of our trespasses" (Eph 1:7–8a).

69. Schreiner, *Paul*, 91.

70. Ibid., 97.

71. Torrance, *Karl Barth*, 160–61.

72. "Festal Letter 10.8" c.f. "Festal Letter 14.4," cited by Weinandy, *Athanasius*, 96.

73. Here Meyer cites the influence on Athanasius of both the story of Abraham and the ram sacrificed in place of Isaac (Gen 22:15), and of Paul's ransom motif (1 Cor 6:30; 7:23). See Meyer, "Athanasius' Use of Paul," 162.

74. See A Religious of CSMV, *On the Incarnation*, 9.

as a pure sacrifice on behalf of humankind; he could not have put an end "to the law that was against us."[75]

This does not mean that Athanasius considers the Son's sacrifice placatory, placatory sacrifice being normative for the cultures surrounding him. Rather he thinks that that sacrifice takes place to perfect the will and work of the Father.[76] As such the Son's death is a profoundly trinitarian act—the Father commands the Son and the Son obeys the Father, in the power of the Spirit of love. The sacrifice of the cross is then a radical weapon wielded by the triune God against devilish assault on humankind in order to preserve divine honor, just as a king might offer up his body to free his citizens, though themselves undeserving, in order to protect his own honor. This relevant contemporary image is expressed by Athanasius as follows: "A king who has founded a city, so far from neglecting it when through the carelessness of the inhabitants it is attacked by robbers, avenges it and saves it from destruction, having regard rather to his own honor than to the people's neglect. Much more, then, the Word of the all-good Father . . . by the offering of his own body . . . abolished [death and] restored the whole nature of man."[77]

Athanasius' theology of sacrifice is intertwined with his sacramentology. In his pastoral letters he teaches the church that the sacrificial rites of the Jewish law have been superseded by Christ. In the Eucharist believers partake of the true Lamb of God, who purifies them with his blood.[78]

The meaning of sacrifice raises the question of Athanasius' attitude to the suffering of the Son. Influenced by the Greek rejection of the possibility of divine suffering, he denies that the incarnate Son suffered. For instance he writes, "While the Son endured the insolence of men, he himself was in no way injured, being impassible and incorruptible and very Word and God . . . [For] men who were suffering, and for whose sakes he endured all this, he maintained and preserved in his own impassibility."[79] Rather Christ's human nature alone suffered *directly* in the cross. Athanasius says for example, "Suffering and weep-

75. Ibid., 10. See also Anatolios, *Athanasius*, 59.

76. See Newman and Robertson, *Against the Arians*, 1.59. See also Meyer, "Athanasius' Use of Paul," 170.

77. A Religious of CSMV, *On the Incarnation, Contra Gentes*, 10.

78. Meyer, "Athanasius' Use of Paul," 168.

79. See A Religious of CSMV, *On the Incarnation*, 54.3.

ing and toiling, these things which are proper to the flesh are ascribed to [Jesus Christ] together with the body."[80] And, "The Father commanded the Son to die *as a man* for us."[81] Athanasius' caveat here is that while the Son dies as a man, he does *not* die as other men. Rather his human nature is uniquely "complete in all respects,"[82] perfect and so acceptable sacrificially.[83]

Nevertheless Athanasius considers Christ's divine nature involved *indirectly* in the suffering of his human nature (a position Luther is also to share[84]). "Let it be known," he says, "that while the Word himself is impassible in his nature, [he is passible] because of the flesh which he put on."[85] "While the Word bore the weaknesses of the flesh as his own—for the flesh was his own—the flesh itself rendered service to the activities of the divinity—for the divinity was in the flesh and the body belonged to God."[86] Corresponding to this Athanasius considers that while Christ's human will naturally prefers to escape the suffering of the cross, his encompassing divine will is "well disposed" to obey God unto death, and directs his human will accordingly.[87]

To move briefly to wider patristic thought, Athanasius' debt to the great Alexandrian theologian before him, Origen (185–232), is well established. The question of the latter's approach to the suffering of God serves to illustrate this. Weinandy suggests that a seeming inconsistency in Origen's view of divine suffering arises because Origen wants to hold together, "maybe for the first time explicitly,"[88] the transcendent otherness of the impassible God and the immutable perfection of God's sacrificial love for humankind.[89] In fact however there is no contradiction here. What Origen sees is that suffering in God is an integral aspect of

---

80. Newman and Robertson, *Against the Arians*, 3.56.

81. See A Religious of CSMV, *On the Incarnation*, 7 and 22. Italics mine.

82. See "Festal Letter" 1.9, cited by Meyer, "Athanasius' Use of Paul," 152.

83. Athanasius' contemporaries, Cappadocian Fathers Basil of Caesarea (330–c.379), and Gregory of Nyssa (c.331–c.395), likewise proposed the impassibility of the Son's divine nature.

84. For Luther's doctrine of *communicatio idiomatum* which holds together the two natures of Christ in the suffering of the cross, see here p. 96.

85. Newman and Robertson, *Against the Arians*, 2.34.

86. Ibid., 3.3.

87. A Religious of CSMV, *On the Incarnation*, 21.

88. See Weinandy, "Origen and the Suffering of God," 459.

89. See ibid.

The Classical Soteriology of the Cross 95

divine perfection. In turn this insight influences not only Athanasius but the long tradition of crucicentric thought succeeding him.

Of those patristic figures who follow Origen and Athanasius chronologically, Bauckham notes that, constrained by Alexandrian Christology, some at least court the possibility of divine passibility. They lean toward a God who cannot suffer unwillingly or out of any lack in himself, but who is free to suffer voluntarily on behalf of his creation.[90] The distinction involved requires careful handling of passibility and impassibility in God, so as to advance the notion that the *Logos* is essentially unaffected by the suffering of Christ's human nature, but yet fully aware of and thus involved in it.[91] Here Bauckham notes that the theologians concerned deliberately use paradox to accent the delicate balance within their position. He cites Gregory of Nazianzus (330–390) and "the sufferings of him who could not suffer",[92] and Cyril of Alexandria (378–444) for whom "the *Logos* suffered impassibly."[93] It follows that this strand of patristic theology departs considerably from the remote, impassible God of prevailing Greek thought, a departure aligning it with developing crucicentric thought.

Luther continues this crucicentric direction in his own attitude to the suffering of God, striking a careful balance as he does so. That is, he departs from the contemporary scholastic schools which maintain an absolute divine impassibility, denying any real involvement by the Father or the divine Son in the atoning work of the cross, undercutting it thereby. Luther also rejects the notion of a wholly wrathful and vengeful Father punishing the Son. Human sinfulness merits divine punishment, dealt with by the aligned wills of the Father and the Son in the cross.[94]

---

90. See Bauckham, "Only the Suffering God Can Help," 8.

91. See ibid.

92. Wace, "Gregory of Nazianzus," Oration 27. The wider context here reads, "I adjure you by the name of Christ, by Christ's emptying Himself for us, by the sufferings of Him Who cannot suffer, by His cross, by the nails which have delivered me from sin, . . . in the name, I say, of this sacred mystery which lifts us up to heaven!"

Bauckham says at this point, and significantly for the present investigation, "Gregory anticipates Barth's view that God is 'not his own prisoner,' i.e., his impassible nature cannot be a constraint on his freedom. But Gregory still seems to think that the wholly voluntary 'suffering' of God in Christ is not experienced [to the full] . . . since he triumphs over his sufferings in the act of suffering them." Bauckham, "Only the Suffering God Can Help," 8, n.23.

93. *Apathos epathen*, cited by McGuckin, *St. Cyril of Alexandria*," 184 n.25.

94. Luther says for instance, "Christ . . . of his own free will *and by the will of the*

Nevertheless (the salient point here) this does not mean that the Father suffers in the cross; clearly Luther is not a Patripassian. It does mean though that the Father is involved in the work of the cross, if indirectly, while the divine nature of the Son is certainly affected by it. Making this last point, Hunsinger quotes Luther directly. "Confronted by the objection that the deity cannot suffer and die, Luther retorted: 'That is true, but since the divinity and humanity are one person in Christ, the Scriptures ascribe to the divinity, because of this personal union, all that happens to [the] humanity.'"95

Luther supports his position on logical grounds. Given the hypostatic union, it is not possible for Christ's divine nature to be divorced from what happens to his human nature. Vitally too, if divinity is not intimately involved in the suffering of the cross, its soteriological power is negated. Thence Luther declares at Heidelberg in 1518, "Now it is not sufficient for anyone, and it does him no good [salvifically] to recognize God in his glory and majesty unless he recognizes him in the humility and shame of his cross."96

Reinforcing this position, Luther advances his doctrine of *communicatio idiomatum*. The latter holds that the two natures of Christ in the one hypostasis interpenetrate each other and cannot be abstracted from each other, so that what happens to Jesus Christ affects both his natures. In this, as the crucicentric theologians before him, Luther stands in marked opposition to the classical Greek insistence on divine impassibility. But he also departs from other major Reformers, and notably John Calvin (1509–1564),97 who are sympathetic to the Greek view.

Contra some late-modern Lutheran scholars,98 Christ's suffering in incarnation, and above all in crucifixion, is not for Luther especially a mark of divine identification with the materially poor. Rather, in line with preceding crucicentric tradition, Luther holds Christ's suffering to be a mark of divine identification with the spiritually impoverished, in all

---

Father . . . wanted to be an associate of sinners[, being therefore] condemned and executed as a thief." *Galatians Commentary* (1535). Luther, *Luther's Works*, :278. Italics mine.

95. Hunsinger, "What Barth Learned from Martin Luther," 134., quoting Luther, *Luther's Works*, 37:210.

96. Proof Thesis 20, Heidelberg Disputation.

97. For the crucicentric influence of Luther as against Calvin, see here pp. 189–90 and associated notes.

98. For example, Wells (2001).

their devilish slavery, lowliness, and corruption. The very fact of Christ's endurance and pain overcomes the pain human sinfulness causes God. In doing so it reconciles the creature to God formally, *de jure*.

The question then becomes how reconciliation might be concretely realized in the creature. It is now that a third element in the crucicentric theology of justification comes into play. As already indicated the crucicentric theologians hold that only as the creature dies to its besetting religious objectives, *viz.* its desires to force its election and to usurp divine glory, that that which Christ has done for it *de iure* is made manifest for it *de facto*. It is the Word of the cross which summons the creature to this death; it declares that the path of salvation leads not around the cross but *through* it, not merely to its foot but to its very core.[99] *The claim of the cross on the life of the creature is then a fundamental crucicentric contention.*

Again Paul's personal experience bears this out. From the far side of death with Christ he can write, "[The] world has been crucified to me, and I to the world" (Gal 6:14). And similarly, "For through the law I died to the law . . . I have been crucified with Christ" (Gal 2:19). Or more inclusively, "We know that our old self was crucified with him so that the body of sin might be destroyed, and we might no longer be enslaved to sin. For whoever has died is freed from sin" (Rom 6:6–7). Neither is this language merely metaphorical. Drawn vicariously into Christ and into his death formally, Paul thinks that the creature must *really* die to its desire for itself if it is to know the freedom from sin and death which Christ has won for it, and if it is to be transformed. As von Loewenich explains Paul, "Only he who shares Christ's dying can attain fellowship with him."[100] This cruciform requirement is then the soteriological half of the cruciform rule Paul finds governing the life of the Christian.[101] Dunn agrees with von Loewenich, "Paul's teaching is *not* that Christ dies 'in the place of' others so that they *escape* death (as the logic of 'substitution' implies). It is rather that Christ's sharing *their* death makes it possible for them to share *his* death . . . [There is] a sense of a continuing

---

99. From the crucicentric perspective there is no biblical foundation for the notion that the creature somehow places its sinfulness at the foot of the cross, and passes on untroubled and untransformed behind it.

100. Von Loewenich, *Luther's Theology of the Cross*, 12.

101. For the cruciform rule governing the life of the Christian, see here p. 3.

identification with Christ in, through, and beyond his death which . . . is fundamental to Paul's soteriology."[102]

As for Paul so for Athanasius. He maintains, to quote Anatolios, "that the salvation worked by Jesus Christ does not take place *outside* us or extrinsically, by divine decree [as it were], but is a transformation from *within* the human being."[103] This ontological transformation commences in the incarnation, but is fully realized only in Christ's death.[104] *Co-bodied* with Christ's humanity, to use Anatolios' phraseology,[105] humankind is made participant in that death. Meyer makes a similar observation, "Based on an important theological insight of Paul, Athanasius affirmed that Jesus' sacrifice and the *co-crucifixion* of all Christians 'in Christ' (cf. Gal 2:19 & Rom 6:6–8) are connected."[106] Following Paul, Athanasius then holds that whereas those united with Adam die eternally, those united with Christ in the cross pass after him through death. Thence Athanasius instructs the church to "follow Him . . . who says to us, 'I am the Way'[, for he is] 'the First-born from the dead.'"[107] And in a festal letter he enjoins his flock to commit themselves entirely "to the Lord Who died for us, as . . . the blessed Paul did, when he said, 'I am crucified with Christ.'"[108]

This said, it is true that of itself "co-crucifixion" is not a major theme in Athanasius at the surface level of the text. His first concern is not to explain the need to take cruciform passage in and with Christ so as to know his life—apparently so obvious a need requires little elucidation—but to insist that that deadly passage could not exist if Christ were merely human.

The crucicentric mystics follow Paul and Athanasius here. Contra the broad stream of medieval mysticism they teach the need to die to self through union with the God who loves and suffers for the world. As the writer of the *Theologia Germanica* says, everything that was raised

---

102. Dunn, *The Theology of Paul*, 223.

103. Anatolios, *Athanasius*, 64.

104. See Newman and Robertson, *Against the Arians, by Saint Athanasius*, 2.69.

105. Commenting on John 17:2. Athanasius says that as the Son is ontologically one with the Father, so Christians are one body with the Son, and thence united with the Father. See Weinandy, *Athanasius*, 99. See also Anatolios, *Athanasius*, 61.

106. Meyer, "Athanasius' Use of Paul," 149. Italics mine.

107. Newman and Robertson, *Against the Arians*, 2.65.

108. Schaff, "Festal Letter 5."

and made alive in Adam must perish and die in Christ,[109] for in him human nature itself is put to death. And as already seen Luther presents a powerful theology of the necessity of creaturely death in and with Jesus Christ. Such death is consequent on divine justice and actively brought about by God. This putting to death Luther terms "God's alien work." Apart from cruciform death there is no other solution to the creature's predicament, no other passage to new life.

There is a final critical element in the classical crucicentric conception of justification. At the intersection of soteriology and anthropology the crucicentric theologians hold that the benefits of Christ's cruciform work apply to all people *formally*. But do they hold that Christ's benefits apply to all people *in practice*? This is equally the question as to whether the crucicentric theologians proclaim a doctrine Christian orthodoxy still regards as heretical: universal salvation.[110] What is at stake theologically is the meaning and power of the cross. If Christ's cruciform work does not actually save *all* people then the boundless nature of its power is thrown in doubt, leaving space for some other and anthropocentric path to salvation. What is at stake methodologically is the coherence of the classical crucicentric perspective, leaving space for a theology of glory. Given this significance the question of the extent of election in classical crucicentric theology will be considered here at some length.

Generally the classical crucicentric theologians adopt a position at least very close to universal election. (This is another place where Calvin falls outside the crucicentric tradition.) They can do so because the cross itself holds the scandalous exclusiveness and inclusiveness of Christ's cruciform work in tension.[111] Election is *exclusive* in that it is only available to those who by faith are drawn vicariously into the death

---

109. See Tripp, "Theologia Germanica," 376.

110. In Christian theology the term *universalism* is applied in two unrelated ways. It suggests either that the purposes of God are universal, or refers to the notion that election is universal. It is in the latter sense that it is used here. For a discussion of Barth's treatment of universalism see here pp. 264–69.

111. Paul announces "Christ crucified, a *skandalon* to the Jews and folly to Gentiles" (1 Cor 1:23). The "scandal" for Paul's interlocutors, Jewish and Greek, is not so much the claim that a particular man, time and place is the locus for the salvation of the world, but the illogical character of the argument being used to carry that claim. As previously noted, the Jews consider it illogical that a man put outside the community would be its means of salvation; the Greeks consider it illogical that a just deity would act to save the guilty, let alone do so self-sacrificially. For previous discussion on Greek and Jewfish attitudes to wisdom and foolishness see here pp. 56–59.

of Christ, but it is *inclusive* in that all human beings, indeed all things in heaven and on earth, are formally and potentially so drawn. Christ came to save the *whole* world! This exclusive-inclusive tension reflects the tension between the twin objectives of crucicentric soteriology: to protect the exclusive freedom of a sovereign God to elect whomsoever and however many God chooses, and to guard against any suggestion that the creature can circumvent the cross and elect itself.

Down the centuries to the Reformation the crucicentric tradition continues to balance this tension finely, powerfully protecting the sovereign freedom of God to elect all should God wish to do so, against a raft of alternative proposals. For example it stands against the hopeless notion that election for salvation or damnation is unalterably predetermined, just because that position infringes God's freedom to elect. For a similar reason it opposes the old idea that, suitably indulged, God *must* favor the petitioner. But by the same token the crucicentric tradition finally does not subscribe to a universalist position. That too declares what God *must* do, elect all, and so falls into the same self-glorifying trap as notions declaring election unalterably restricted to the few.

This careful approach to election may be illustrated by examining Paul, Athanasius, and Luther.

Scholarly debate exists concerning universalism in Paul's thought. Schreiner carefully examines all the passages in which Paul is said to be universalist,[112] finding some substance in the allegations. He gives the example of Rom 5:16,[113] in which "the many" benefit from the salvific grace of God in Jesus Christ, agreeing that here "the many" carries the force of "all." Nevertheless finally Schreiner concludes that the case for universalism in Paul cannot succeed. Paul recognizes that even as God's graciousness is limitless, the marks of the justified believer, repentance and faith, are not universally present.

---

112. See Schreiner, *Paul*, 182–88.

113. "For if the *many* died through the one man's trespass, much more surely have the grace of God and the free gift in the grace of the one man, Jesus Christ, abounded for the many" (Rom 5:16). Italics mine. Other Pauline texts said to demonstrate a universalist tendency in Paul include: "[Through Christ] God was pleased to reconcile to himself all things, whether on earth or in heaven, by making peace through the blood of his cross" (Col 1:20). "And he died for all, so that those who live might live no longer for themselves, but for him who died and was raised for them" (2 Cor 5:15). "In him we have redemption through his blood, . . . according to his [plan in Christ] to gather up all things in him, things in heaven and things on earth" (Eph 1:7).

Dunn takes a broadly similar view.[114] For him Paul maintains tension between the inclusivity and exclusivity of election in an analogous way to the manner ancient Israel maintains tension between the universality and particularity of her God. On the one hand Paul holds that Christ "died for all," (2 Cor 5:15). On the other he teaches that peace with God derives solely from the blood of the cross, (Col 1:20), implying that those outside its cruciform parameters have no such peace and are not justified. Dunn therefore concludes that Paul is not universalist, although he leans in that direction.

Wells however frankly preferences universalism in Paul. In his view Paul clearly holds that to deny the applicability of Christ's cruciform work to the whole of the *kosmos* is to make Christian truth provisional, negating the concrete reality of salvation itself. This is so since for Paul Christ occupies the first place in creation, he creates all things, he is Lord of all things, he sacrifices himself on behalf of all things. Accordingly Christ does not reject a portion of that which is already his. In support Wells quotes a number of texts including: "[The Son] is the image of the invisible God, the firstborn of all creation; for in him all things in heaven and on earth were created, things visible and invisible, whether thrones or dominions or rulers or powers—all things have been created through him and for him . . . [Through Christ] God was pleased to reconcile to himself all things, whether on earth or in heaven, by making peace through the blood of his cross" (Col 1:15–20).

In comparison to Wells, Schreiner's and Dunn's approaches seem the more balanced. While he recognizes an embracing graciousness in God, nevertheless Paul does not adopt any principle that might allow the creature to presume on that grace apart from the cross; he will not empty the cross of its power. Certainly too Paul does not find the marks of the justified believer to be universally present. Moreover, and in the present view, out of his regard for right logic Paul will not, even obliquely,[115] provide space for the self-glorifying attempt to necessitate divine action.

At first glance Athanasius, influenced by Origen,[116] also seems to favor a universalist approach to salvation, he speaks inclusively of elec-

---

114. See Dunn, *The Theology of Paul the Apostle*, 43–46.

115. If the free decision in God to elect all humankind in Christ does not actually compromise divine freedom, yet it lends itself to the tempting misconceptions that it does so, and that on its ground the creature may dare to direct God.

116. Balds concludes that Origen's position on election is influenced by his

tion in many places. For example he says, "[In] no other way except through the cross does the salvation *of all* have to take place."[117] In fact the oft-made charge that Athanasius is heretical at this point is likely anachronistic. It was not until the Origenist controversies of the fifth and sixth centuries culminating in the Fifth Ecumenical Council in Constantinople (553), that a doctrine intimately connected with universal salvation, *apokatastasis*, was explicitly repudiated—accepting that what the anathemas against Origen entailed is not completely clear.[118] But even if such a ruling had existed prior to Athanasius, a charge that he transgressed it could not have been successfully prosecuted. On closer examination Athanasius thinks salvation belongs to all *who respond to Christ*, not to all *regardless of response to Christ*. He considers a positive response to be marked by faith, belief, fear of God, possession of the Spirit, and above all death with Christ.[119] In this Athanasius' typically crucicentric concern is to protect the sheer freedom of God to elect, and then the freedom of the creature made aware of its election to accept or reject that gift. That being so, while Athanasius champions the liberality of grace, he does not provide for its *necessary* distribution, he will not presume on the electing will of God.

For comparative purposes brief reference may also be made to Athanasius' contemporary Gregory of Nyssa, who like him also looks back to Origen. Gregory shares Origen's notion of creaturely freedom to cooperate with the prior work of grace, the creature being unable

---

Platonism, but that it falls short of a full-blown *apokatastasis*. Origen, he says, holds that God will neither violate the creature's freedom to depart and return to him, nor compromise his own freedom to choose whom he will save. See Balds, "Apokatastasis," 78–79.

117. A Religious of CSMV, *On the Incarnation*, 26. Similar examples in Athanasius include the following: "[By] his death salvation was effected *for all* and *all* creation was saved. He it is who is the life *of all.*" Ibid., 37. "[Christ] brought *all* humanity to himself and through him to the Father." Ibid., 10. In respect to 2 Cor 5:14, "For the love of Christ impels us, when we consider that if one died for all then *all* have died." Ibid. In respect to Heb 2:9, "We see him . . . Jesus, crowned with honor and glory because of the passion of death, that by the grace of God he might taste death on behalf *of all.*" Ibid. Italics in all these instances mine.

118. See Balds, "Apokatastasis," 78–79.

119. For example Athanasius writes, "[Consider] the Apostle and High Priest of our profession Jesus, who . . . after offering Himself for us, . . . offers to the Father those who in faith approach Him, redeeming all, and for all propitiating God. Newman and Robertson, *Against the Arians*, 1.53. And "[It] pleased God by the foolishness of preaching to save them that believe" (1 Cor 1:21). Ibid. 2.16.

to save itself. "The power of human virtue is not sufficient in itself to cause the souls not sharing in grace to ascend to the beauty of [eternal] life,"[120] he says. Similarly too, Gregory of Nyssa hopes for the universal salvation of all rational creatures. For him this even includes the devil and all his angels, something Origen had entertained at one point and then rejected. Indeed Gregory of Nyssa's notion of universal salvation is effectively more rigorous than Origen's since unlike the latter he rejects the notion that once saved the creature might again fall.

To move again to the far end of the classical crucicentric era, Luther's position in respect to the number benefiting from the cruciform work of Jesus Christ is similar to those of Paul and Athanasius. He will not limit the sovereign freedom of God to elect or reject whomsoever and however many God wishes, hence he cannot be called a universalist. Luther's personal background to his doctrine of election is relevant to this decision, and may be briefly considered now.

Hinlicky and others indicate that the popular story concerning the young Luther's inability to receive certainty of salvation from the church is misleading.[121] In a sense, Hinlicky says, the opposite is true. Luther develops the view that sinful humankind can never please a holy and righteous God, and stands rightly condemned. He has no confidence therefore that he himself possesses salvation, thus God seems untrustworthy. Luther is then weary of the pastorally well-intentioned assurances of mercy provided by the *semi-Pelagian*[122] (though not called that) theology of the *via moderna* in which he is schooled. He views such assurances as scripturally ungrounded and based on a mechanical conception of grace. So his question stands, "Where do I find a gracious God?"[123]

---

120. Gregory of Nyssa, Saint. *On the Christian Mode of Life*, 131.

121. See Hinlicky, "Luther's Theology of the Cross—Part One," 46.

122. *Pelagianism*: Unaided by grace, of its freedom the creature is able to initiate faith, move towards God, and achieve salvation. At its root Pelagianism considers that human nature is not originally corrupt, so that the creature remains free to choose good or evil.

Semi-Pelagianism: Unaided by grace, of its freedom the creature is able to initiate faith, but God immediately infuses that faith with salvific grace, enabling the creature to move towards God and receive salvation. This movement is thus a cooperative process.

While the nomenclature itself stems from a celebrated dispute between Augustine of Hippo and the English monk Pelagius at the commencement of the fifth century, debate as to the existence of a natural human capacity to reach up to God goes back to the earliest period of the church.

123. See Tomlin, "Subversive Theology," 64.

The turning point for Luther comes under the influence of both the twelfth century Bernard of Clairvaux and his present spiritual director and superior Johannes von Staupitz. The former teaches Luther that it is only *in response* to justification that the heart begins to be purified by the Spirit and the soul to imitate Christ. The latter assures him that the sheer love of God evidenced in Christ's wounds means divine acceptance of every baptized individual *preceding* penitence.[124] Under this tutelage Luther eventually reworks late-medieval spirituality, taking it far beyond the schools and even the other Reformers. He concludes that no condition for justification exists other than that embodied in the proclamation from the cross. The crucified Christ alone is Reconciliation, Righteousness, Peace, Life, Salvation in all its fullness and priority.[125]

Luther can then understand election as free and secure for all sinners, provided only that they are baptized as a sign of the grace they have already received. Their salvation has not been merited but comprises unfettered grace, itself a typically crucicentric position.[126] Thus the mature Luther can counsel a dying man, "God has taken [Jesus Christ] the Victor unto Himself and has promised Him to us for our constant companionship, so that even the loneliest person is never alone in death but has Christ at his side. Long before we could extend our hand to Him, He reached forth, rescued us from the gulf which separated us from God, [that is] eternal death, and gained for us a home with God."[127]

Here Luther stands in marked contrast to the other Reformers, especially Calvin whose doctrine of double predestination he eschews. But he also completely reverses the doctrine of conditionable election presented by the schools. In Luther's view these mutually opposing positions equally bypass the sheer freedom of the salvation Christ conveys in the cross.

On the basis of the unconditionality of election Luther also counters Aquinas' doctrine that nature serves grace, concluding that there is no commonality between the creature and the Creator so that the creature might unify itself with God. The poverty of isolate human nature is the sole human attribute attracting (not necessitating) the gracious action of God. Thus in his commentary on Paul's epistle to the Romans (1522)

---

124. See Oberman, *Luther*, 182.
125. See Luther, *Luther's Works*, 26:151.
126. See Oberman, *Luther*, 323.
127. See Bornkamm, *Luther's World of Thought*, 130.

Luther writes, "God saves only sinners, teaches only the stupid, enriches only the poor, raises only the dead."[128]

Nevertheless, and to return to the question of universalism, the issue of free and secure justification "for all" as opposed to "for all the baptized" is not straight forward in Luther. What of those who have always been outside the gospel, or who have come deliberately to reject it? In Luther's world this means: Turks, papists, peasants, Jews,[129] and heretics. His answer here is that Christ's cruciform work is also efficacious for them *potentially*. The role of the church is thus to be an instrument, at times a very sharp instrument, in the conversion of nonbelievers. Finally though, God alone determines and knows their fate. For the creature to pronounce on that fate is for it to presume to know as God; the true theologian does not do so therefore. Once again Luther's concern is to avoid any suggestion that the creature might glorify itself. Overall, Luther's doctrine of election is similar to Paul's, if somewhat more restrictive in tone.

In final answer then to the question of the number of the elect in classical crucicentric understanding, it appears that the thin tradition carefully excludes universalism in order to protect the sovereign freedom and glory of God. At the same time, wanting to promote the sheer graciousness of God in the Person and work of Jesus Christ, the classical crucicentric tradition is not unfriendly to a very broad election indeed.

---

128. Luther, *Luther's Works*, 25:418. Lecturing on Luther at this point, Barth observes that when "the last and supreme possibility is that we are sinners [Luther's thinking becomes] an assault upon Scholasticism, upon its very heart." Barth, *Calvin*, 43.

129. Luther's theology in regard to the Jews attracts a considerable secondary literature, not least from German scholars remembering the Third Reich. Writing in the 1950s, Heinrich Bornkamm finds that Luther opposed Judaism on religious rather than racial grounds. Luther, he says, condemns Israel for rejecting her Messiah and so refusing to live in accordance with her divine election, law and promise. (See Bornkamm, *Luther's World of Thought*, 232–33.) By the end the twentieth century however the discussion is deeper and more shocking. Recalling the day of Christ's crucifixion historian Heiko Oberman tellingly titles his section on Luther and the Jews "Darkness at Noon." He argues that Luther's insight into election for all *potentially*, leads him to sanction any including brutal means of securing that election *actually*; the cross means God's ministers need have no fear. But, observes Oberman, where there is no fear of divine penalty for appalling deeds the darkness at noon may proceed; Luther's position leads inexorably toward the Holocaust. See Oberman, *Luther*, 392–97. As later discussion will indicate, in his concern at the removal of the constraint of the gospel on civil power Barth takes an analogous position to that of Oberman. See here p. 250.

There is one last matter for discussion here. The gift of new life to the creature is not strictly a facet of justification itself, as much as a consequence of it. A brief glance at Athanasius illustrates the classical crucicentric perspective here. As seen, for Athanasius human sinfulness leads towards "de-creation," a decline exacerbated by the application of the law.[130] Cutting across that downward procession the crucified Christ satisfies the law on the creature's behalf, liberating it. But Athanasius thinks still more is involved; the process of de-creation is not only halted by the satisfaction of the law but *reversed*. The freed creature now moves not towards de-creation but re-creation. Having been co-bodied with Jesus Christ in the cross it is now newly clothed in his humanity, made not divine but fully human. Illustrating this from John 15:5 Athanasius explains that as the Son "is the vine we are united to him as branches, not according to the essence of divinity (for that is impossible) but . . . according to the humanity . . . We are fitted into one body with him and bound together in him."[131]

In this way human existence begins to be utterly transformed. There is an ontological change, an inner reorientation to God, a completely new moral existence. As Anatolios expresses this, "[For Athanasius] the salvation worked by Jesus Christ does not take place *outside* us . . . but is a transformation from *within* the human being."[132] Weinandy similarly notes Athanasius' view that it is by being drawn *into* Christ that the "the lives of sinful men and women [are] transformed into lives of virtue."[133]

According to Athanasius the proof of this transformation is found in the changed and changing lives of Christ's followers: the adulterer who no longer commits adultery, the murderer who murders no more, the wrong-doer who gives up grasping, the profane person who starts praising God.[134] Quickened by the Spirit of God,[135] the Son's followers thus begin doing that which previously they could never have done, they begin to reflect his filial image.

---

130. For Athanasius' position regarding the law see here pp. 87–89.
131. Newman and Robertson, *Against the Arians*, 1.54.
132. Anatolios, *Athanasius*, 64.
133. Weinandy, *Athanasius*, 43.
134. See A Religious of CSMV, *On the Incarnation*, 30.5.
135. In this Athanasius is influenced by Paul's statement that "the last Adam became a life-giving spirit" (1 Cor 15:45). See Meyer, "Athanasius' Use of Paul," 161.

To conclude here, the law which cannot be conditioned except by Jesus Christ and him crucified, Christ's salvific suffering and death on behalf of a creature who cannot save itself, who has indeed no commonality with God, the claim of the cross on this self-exalting creature, the careful uniting of the sovereignty and the generosity of God to allow but not prescribe universal election, the formal gift of the life of Christ with its inherent promise, all these are themes interlinked within the classical crucicentric notion of justification. But justification is yet to be practically worked out.

Sanctification

The classical crucicentric theologians recognize that from an extra-temporal perspective, (if one can speak from such), the re-creation of the creature before God takes place in the one eschatological moment in which death is exchanged for life. Temporally considered however this moment is ongoing; Luther for example states that Christ has won forgiveness "once for all on the cross[, but] the distribution takes place continuously."[136] (McGrath rightly notes that the "sheer oddness" of a *continuing* moment of salvific exchange is often overlooked.[137]) In this unusual moment what has already been formally accomplished in the cross on behalf of the creature, that is its forgiveness encompassing its justification and reconciliation, becomes actual within it via a lifelong process of sanctification. Methodologically this sanctifying process comprises interconnected crucicentric elements: life in the cross and the suffering experienced by those living this life.

Paul summons the new believer to real life in the environment of the cross of Jesus Christ. He calls on this person to take up his or her own cross, to die to the old desire for self, to work out salvation before God practically thereby.[138] Death for Paul is then the one way by which the sanctifying life of Christ, already appropriated to it formally in the cross, can actually be received. McGrath again. "The full force of Paul's insight is missed if we interpret him as teaching that we can have life *despite* death and strength *despite* weakness: for Paul, the remarkable

136. Luther, *Luther's Works*, 40: 214.
137. McGrath, *The Enigma of the Cross*, 29.
138. Paul writes, "Therefore . . . work out your own salvation with fear and trembling" (Phil 2:12).

meaning of the enigma of the cross is that life comes *through* death and strength *through* weakness."[139]

In this Paul reiterates the summons of the cross itself. Bultmann usefully interprets Paul here. "[Will the creature] acknowledge that God had made a crucified one Lord; [will he] thereby acknowledge the demand to take up the cross by the surrender of his previous understanding of himself, making the cross the determinative power of his life, letting himself be crucified with Christ (1 Cor 1:18–31; Gal 6:14; cf. 5:24)?"[140]

It must be said immediately that for Paul the cruciform summons to life in the locale of the cross in no sense theologically undercuts the completed nature of Christ's cruciform work, or the completed nature of the benefits that work bestows. The justified creature need not retrospectively justify its justification, it does not sanctify itself. If the initial moment in which the creature is incorporated in Christ's death extends forwards throughout its temporal life, nevertheless because of Christ and him crucified its justification is always full, complete, and certain.

In the environment of the cross the followers of Jesus Christ are summoned, individually and corporately, to take on the radically different norms of life in the cross. They are called to become increasingly like Christ, increasingly filled with his Spirit. Since in the work of the cross Christ emptied himself and took on the form of a slave, so through the Spirit his followers are to do likewise. Since in his death and resurrection Christ intercedes for the church and for the world, so through the Spirit his followers are to pray ceaselessly for the church and for the fulfilled reconciliation of the world. Since Christ establishes his followers in just relationship with God, so through the Spirit they are to establish just relationships both in the church and in the world. Since Christ reconciled the world, so through the Spirit they are to work for reconciliation between all peoples, all classes, all creeds, knowing that in Jesus Christ there is no longer Jew or Greek, slave or free, male or female.

Paul himself exemplifies this incarnational way of being, as Tomlin explains, "Paul's own life has taken on a cruciform shape, sacrificing his own social power and status for the sake of others. [His is the life of sacrificial love, of] self-giving towards one's fellow-believers, and spe-

---

139. McGrath, *The Enigma of the Cross*, 30. Italics McGrath's.

140. Bultmann, *Theology of the New Testament*, 1:303. See also, Hinlicky, "Luther's Theology of the Cross—Part One," 48.

cially the poor. It is this pattern of life he recommends to . . . Christians, namely the way of servanthood, the way of the cross."[141]

Indeed numerous New Testament passages attest to Paul's pastoral concern in this regard, a concern reaching out to individuals and to their communities. He enjoins the Galatians, for example, to "Bear one another's burdens, and in this way you will fulfill the law of Christ" (Gal 6:2). Or again, "[Work] for the good of all, and especially for those of the family of faith" (Gal 6:10). But above all there is his great plea to the Roman believers, "I appeal to you therefore, brothers and sisters, by the mercies of God, to present your bodies as a living sacrifice, holy and acceptable to God, which is your spiritual worship" (Rom 12:1). This is cultic language. Paul implies not only that his listeners are to serve God and others sacrificially, but that they are to do so in full identification with Christ and with his sacrifice. In this way they participate with Christ in a divine function, the re-creation of a fallen world. In this way they worship God.

This said, and as McGrath observes, Paul "carefully excludes the theory that we share the fullness of resurrected life *here and now*."[142] Presently Christ alone has been raised; his followers remain caught between Easter Friday and Easter Sunday, between the now and the not yet. New life is being gained, but fulfillment of the promise of new and resurrected life lies ahead.[143] McGrath further explains, "In Paul's thought the resurrection remains a future event, a 'not yet' which illuminates and transforms the present without breaking into it with full force. The Christian is forced to concede that he must live and struggle with the reality of his earthly situation, while continually looking forward to the future resurrection and interpreting the present in its light."[144]

Athanasius does not speak of life in the environment of the cross as such. Nevertheless the notion of self-sacrifice as an ongoing dying to self in which the work of the cross is increasingly realized, is critical to his understanding of Christian development. Such sacrifice provides a means for the followers of Christ to identify experientially with him, and with the salvation he has won for them.[145] It enables those in Christ

---

141. Tomlin, "Subversive Theology," 62.
142. McGrath, *The Enigma of the Cross*, 33. Italics McGrath's.
143. See ibid., 32.
144. McGrath, *The Enigma of the Cross*, 31.
145. See Meyer, "Athanasius' Use of Paul," 162. Here Meyer appeals to *De Incarnatione* 54.

to reflect his image,[146] and it provides a proper basis for the practice of ethics, being the inculcation of Christ's "virtue, mortification and continence."[147] Sacrifice therefore offers an acceptable path to Christian maturity. Thence Athanasius teaches that as Christians, "[We should] cleave to our Saviour, [confess] our iniquities, and ... by the Spirit [mortify] the deeds of the body. [For] showing the dying of Jesus in our bodies ... we shall receive life and the kingdom from Him."[148]

There is though one important, and typically crucicentric, proviso here; Athanasius insists that to follow Christ's cruciform example is to become *not* divine but human as he is human. "[The] Saviour says; 'Be merciful, as your Father which is in heaven is merciful' ... and, 'Be perfect, as your heavenly Father is perfect.' And He said this ... not that we might become such as the Father; for to become as the Father is impossible for us creatures, [but that we might] by imitation become virtuous and sons ... taking an exemplar and looking at Him, [acting] towards each other in concord and oneness of spirit."[149]

Athanasius holds that at a practical level this self-sacrificial developmental process should center on both regular fasting and faithful attendance at the eucharist. As Weinandy explains him, fasting is "a foundational exercise by which one appropriates the salvific work of Christ into one's own life."[150] Or as Athanasius himself explains simply, it "allows one ... to die with Christ."[151] So too the communicant literally puts on the death of Christ, and thus his life.[152] To partake of the elements, Athanasius teaches, is to "draw near to the divine lamb, and touch heavenly food."[153] It is to be nourished by Christ himself.

For the crucicentric mystics life in the locale of the cross has a high ethical flavor. It means obedience to the teaching of the cross concerning the sacrificial imitation of Christ's love for God, for the church, and for the world. Bernard of Clairvaux, for example, emphasizes that love and

---

146. Ibid.
147. Ibid., 169.
148. Schaff, "Festal Letter 7."
149. Newman and Robertson, *Against the Arians*, 3:10.
150. Weinandy, *Athanasius*, 125.
151. Ibid.
152. See Schaff, "Festal Letter 4."
153. Ibid., "Festal Letter 5."

gratitude toward God must be worked out externally in selfless charity towards one's neighbor.

Influenced by the cruciform message transmitted to him through Paul and the mystics, Luther too summons justified believers to life in "the shadow of Calvary."[154] They are not to circle around the back of the cross to avoid its ethical demand, but rather to live sacrificially for God and for others. (Some late-modern commentators misinterpret Luther here.[155] Broadly speaking he does not take from the cross a primary injunction to believers to undercut oppressive *political* power, but the demand that their *own* power be cut away, freeing them more and more for direction by Christ.[156] The civil upheavals accompanying the Reformation are a by-product of Luther's position, not its first objective.)

For all of the classical crucicentric theologians though, life in the cross involves a particular attitude to the Person of Christ. They see that two equal and opposite errors are possible. Either believers focus on the divinity of the risen Christ and their triumph in him, missing the cruciform summons to live in the locale of the cross sacrificially. Or they focus on the humanity of the crucified Christ and their poverty in him, missing the summons of the cross to look towards their resurrection in joy and hope. Rather, the crucicentric theologians teach, a life lived fully to Christ in the cross attends to both his divinity and his humanity; it holds both cruciform claim and resurrection promise together. In consequence of Jesus Christ both sacrifice and joy mark the life of the true theologian.

Life in the cross inevitably involves human suffering. As seen the theology of suffering is not identical with the theology of the cross in its entirety. Nevertheless human suffering is an important crucicentric theme connected with sanctification, methodologically parallelling the suffering of Christ connected with justification. It will be considered now in some detail.

In overview the classical crucicentric theologians oppose any suggestion that of itself human suffering is atoning; such a notion empties the cross of its power while affirming the creature's ability to glorify itself. Nevertheless they still consider human suffering an integral element

---

154. "The shadow of Calvary" is a term used by McGrath on the basis of Luther. Barth is to speak of the "environs of Golgotha."

155. For example, Schweitzer (1995), and Wells (1992) and (2001).

156. See Forde, *Being a Theologian of the Cross*, 112.

in the soteriological process. It is part of the world order consequent on the fall; the dual residency of believers in the cross and in the world means that they are not excluded from the painful post-lapsarian legacy. In the case of believers however, the crucified Christ lends meaning to their suffering where otherwise there could be none.

Believers' suffering is first a share in *Christ's* redeeming and life-giving sacrifice. It is the message of the cross which teaches that this is so. Or as Hendel succinctly puts this, "The theology of the cross is a theology of suffering because it is a theology of life and salvation."[157] With Luther in view McGrath says similarly that, "The theology of the cross identifies the intimate relation between faith, obedience and suffering, and asserts that the greatest treasure bequeathed to his church by her Lord is the privilege of sharing in those sufferings."[158]

In line with this the crucicentric theologians also consider that the suffering of each individual believer is the suffering of the whole Christian community. This is so since each member of the church is in communion with every other member, and the whole church is in communion with its Head, who suffers with and for it.[159]

To set out the classical crucicentric theology of human suffering further the discussion commences once again with the first century Greek world. As earlier noted the Greeks hold human suffering to have no positive qualities. It may be the work of capricious deity; it certainly connotes evil; logically a loving deity would not allow it.[160] Over against this condemnatory perspective Paul, seeking to strengthen a young church under persecution from without and torn by dissension from within,[161] teaches that in a circumscribed sense human suffering can be profoundly redemptive. It is not atoning, the suffering work of Christ

---

157. Hendel, "Theology of the Cross," 230.

158. McGrath, *The Enigma of the Cross*, 179.

159. McGrath says, "Christ's obedience and sufferings are those of his body, the church, which must bear the marks of his nails in her flesh." Ibid.

160. Gerhard Forde writes, "[It] is almost universally the case that theologians and philosophers *include* suffering without further qualification among those things they call evil." Forde, *Being a Theologian of the Cross*, 84.

161. Unlike his opponents Paul does not consider human suffering objectively. Neither does he concern himself greatly with the suffering of those who remain outside of Christ, although he views their situation as dire, "These will suffer the punishment of eternal destruction, separated from the presence of the Lord and from the glory of his might" (2 Thes 1:9).

alone is that, but where it involves deliberate sacrifice on behalf of others it generates life and advances the gospel. Paul illustrates this by appealing to his own experience. "If we are being afflicted, it is for your consolation and salvation" (2 Cor 1:6), he tells the Corinthians. The greater the suffering, the greater the comfort received from God, the greater ability to share out that comfort, and therefore Christ himself. To quote Cornwall it is in this sense that Paul finds "our suffering is redemptive."[162]

Paul identifies two causes of human suffering, internal and external.

Internal pain inevitably follows the acknowledging of salvation, and with this the gaining of realistic self-knowledge. Past sin is seen for what it is, and the inescapable reality of present sinfulness perceived. Such insight is painful, as he can personally testify. At the commencement of his Christian discipleship he is physically blinded for three days and in great inner turmoil, he neither eats nor drinks.[163] As his discipleship matures so does an acute sensitivity to his own continuing sinfulness, and with this comes active struggle in the process of dying to self. Thus Paul cries in existential agony, "I see in my members another law at war with the law of my mind, making me captive to the law of sin that dwells in my members. Wretched man that I am! Who will rescue me from this body of death" (Rom 7:23–24)? As Bayer explains, "[Truth for Paul] can be imparted only in a rebirth through the death of the 'old man,' through baptism and a 'journey through the hell of self-knowledge.'"[164]

External suffering by believers can have several origins, including that of the spiritual realm. Again the latter is true to Paul's own experience, "Therefore, to keep me from being too elated, a thorn was given me in the flesh, a messenger of Satan to torment me, to keep me from being too elated" (2 Cor 12:7b).

But external causes of believers' suffering also include persecution. Indeed, in a fallen world Paul finds this inevitable. "[All] who want to live a godly life in Christ Jesus will be persecuted" (2 Tim 3:12), he says. Persecution is then one of the instruments God allows in order to conform believers to Christ; properly viewed it is sanctifying. Here again Paul teaches through personal illustration. "We are afflicted in every way, but not crushed; perplexed, but not driven to despair; persecuted, but not forsaken; struck down, but not destroyed; always carrying in the

---

162. See Cornwall, "Scandal of the Cross," 9–10.
163. See Acts 9:9f.
164. Bayer, "Word of the Cross," 48.

body the death of Jesus, so that the life of Jesus may also be made visible in our bodies" (2 Cor 4:8–10). And in similar vein Paul encourages the beleaguered Thessalonians, "[Your] persecutions and the afflictions that you are enduring [are] intended to make you worthy of the kingdom of God, for which you are also suffering" (2 Thes 1:4–5).

Endurance under persecution is then a strange confirmation of increasing maturity in Christ. Continuing to address the Thessalonians Paul summons them to respond to their salvation by standing firm in the face of their accusers (see 2 Thes 2:13). Similarly he enjoins the young Timothy, "Share in suffering like a good soldier of Christ Jesus" (2 Tim 2:3). This said, for Paul the enduring of suffering is not finally a human work, but a Spirit engendered participation in *Christ's* work of endurance and pain, a sharing in *his* suffering. The endurance of believers can therefore never be a source of pride.

Athanasius also presents a developed theology of human suffering, herein his third way to exist in Christ (after fasting and partaking of the eucharistic elements.) He recognizes a world divided in two comprising those who fight Christ—*the impious*, and those who fight for Christ—*the pious*. Athanasius thinks the pious normally subject to persecution, and in being persecuted normally identified with Christ's death and saving life—not only metaphorically but ontologically. Thence he teaches the Alexandrians that they must, in Weinandy's words, "realize that all suffering that comes upon them is to conform them to the image of Christ crucified,"[165] thereby strengthening their assurance of salvation. He adds, "Let us, then, rejoice in spirit, . . . knowing that our salvation is being stored up for us in the midst of the time of affliction. For our Saviour did not redeem us by resting but destroyed death by suffering for us. [Likewise] those who revere God will be persecuted."[166]

On further occasions too Athanasius similarly encourages his people. Since Christ "suffered to prepare freedom from suffering for those who suffer in him,"[167] far from being meaningless their own suffering enables them to know the freedom Christ has won for them. "At no time," Athanasius says, "should one freely praise God more than when [one] has passed through afflictions."[168]

165. Weinandy, *Athanasius*, 125.
166. "Festal Letter 13.6," cited by Anatolios, *Athanasius*, 38.
167. Schaff, "Festal Letter 10."
168. Schaff, "Festal Letter 7."

Turning to the understanding of human suffering held by the crucicentric mystics, Johannes Tauler finds the creature to be painfully trapped between time and eternity, between an instinctive longing for God as the one satisfaction of the human soul, and a natural inability to satisfy that yearning. In consequence frustration and suffering lie at the heart of the human condition. False solutions present themselves but are inevitably revealed as illusionary, their proffered answers incapable of working out peace with God. Of itself the creature, Tauler says, "can neither taste God nor know him, and since everything else is insufficient, he feels himself hemmed in between two walls with a sword behind him and a sharp spear in front."[169] The creature's true solution lies not in avoiding its dilemma, but in personally embracing it in the one place where its antitheses are resolved. In the cross of Calvary the desire for God and the attaining of God are uniquely synthesized in Jesus Christ. Entering into the crucified Christ, and into his suffering, provides the one path to inner peace. Thus Tauler sees beyond the tribulation and hopelessness suffering naturally engenders. Recalling the dialectic embracing hiddenness and revealedness in the crucified Christ, he writes, "[The] deeper we sink the higher we rise, for height and depth are here identical. [While God's light is] pure and radiant everywhere . . . nowhere does it shine brighter than in the deepest darkness."[170]

For the writer of the *Theologia Germanic* heaven and hell are interchanging states in human experience, alternatively afflicting and comforting the soul throughout its temporal existence. As Christ in his earthly ministry did not know "serene freedom from earthly woe," neither can the one believing in him expect to do so. Rather the believer is to follow Christ through suffering and the cross, passing with him through death and hell. In this way the believer is drawn into Christ's hidden, redemptive and ongoing suffering over the human condition, but also into his continuing peace amid "hardship, distress, much anguish and misfortune."[171] So the writer advises, "If you wish to follow Him you must take the cross upon you. The cross is the same as the Christ life, and that is a bitter cross for natural man . . . Christ's soul had to visit hell before it came to heaven. This is also the path for man's soul."[172]

169. Shrady, *Johannes Tauler*, 143.
170. Ibid., 144. This quotation previously referred to. See here pp. 59–60.
171. Hoffman, ed., *The Theologia Germanica of Martin Luther*, 74.
172. Wakefield, ed., *A Dictionary of Christian Spirituality*, 376.

Bernard of Clairvaux takes a similar position. His sermons on the Song of Solomon stress the need for contemplation and imitation of Christ's passion. By this means the soul already secured in Christ by Christ is made increasingly flexible and amenable to the direction of his divine love.

Influenced by Bernard's sermons Luther too emphasizes the importance of suffering in the development of Christian maturity.[173] He observes that the creature without Christ naturally tries to avoid suffering and therefore despises the cross, perceiving no virtue in either. Even the justified creature is likely to perceive the work of the cross in its own life as bitter failure. Nevertheless that ongoing "mortifying and vivifying" work humbles and strengthens the believer, conforming her or him to Christ. For this reason the believer is to value suffering exceedingly, understanding it as a necessary corollary to the life of faith.

Indeed for Luther those claiming to follow Jesus Christ can be divided sharply between those who reject and those who accept the suffering inherent in his discipleship. The theologian of glory "defines the treasury of Christ as the removing and remitting of punishments, [as] things which are most evil and worthy of hate."[174] But the true theologian, the theologian of the cross, "teaches that punishments, crosses, and death are the most precious treasury of all."[175] Von Loewenich explains Luther further here. Luther sees that in the cross the creature's "glory must present itself in lowliness, its nobility in disgrace, its joy in grief, its hope in despair, its life in death. The hiddenness of the Christian life does not remain something formal, but expresses itself in practice in a very perceptible way. In concrete terms, the hiddenness of the Christian life is a following of Christ's suffering."[176] Von Loewenich adds that for Luther, "life in the cross, that is, of death, and this only in its most shameful form"[177] marks the way toward Christian maturity. The believer may be made more certain in faith, and conformed more nearly to Christ, in no other way.

---

173. See Tomlin, "Subversive Theology," 63.

174. Luther, *Luther's Works*, 31:225f. *Explanations of the Disputation Concerning the Value of Indulgences*, 1518.

175. Ibid.

176. Von Loewenich, *Luther's Theology of the Cross*, 118.

177. Ibid., 79.

Neither is this a shallow prescription on Luther's part. With an historian's eye Oberman, making a similar point to von Loewenich's, movingly describes the existential struggle which Luther undergoes *after* his breakthrough realization that he cannot and need not save himself. In the middle of 1527 Luther is so tormented by doubts concerning his faithfulness and his worthiness before God that he comes close to death. To this Oberman says, "Certainly Luther was no longer questioning the Reformational discovery that God bestows justification by faith without anterior or posterior conditions. He had only just attested to the fact that 'I have taught correctly about faith, love, and cross.' But certainty of faith does not exist once and for all, it is not a virtue one can possess on which one can rely. Certainty of faith is a gift that 'exceeds my powers.'"[178]

This inner struggle finally leads Luther to appropriate more fully what his Reformational insight has already shown him—that the receipt of faith and of eternal salvation are entirely in the gift and power of a *gracious* God. As their corollary, deep assurance of salvation too is a gift. Indeed the very struggle for it is a sure sign of God's hand continuing to conform him to the cross.

In summary then, the formula that the life of God is born out of death—and not in any other way, and the observation that suffering is a necessary part of that deadly process, comprise major elements within the classical crucicentric understanding of sanctification. Any note of joy concerning the latter is yet muted however. Indeed the crucicentric understanding of sanctification would be a bleak prescription for inculcating Christlike maturity, if it were not for the glorious reality balancing it.

Resurrection and eschatological glorification

The final segment of crucicentric soteriology concerns resurrection and true glorification eschatologically. Crucicentric elements grouped here include resurrection life, the true *theologia gloriae*, and the eschatological service of the creature.

For the crucicentric theologians new life in Christ, while formally granted in justification and increasingly actualized in sanctification, is worked out fully only at the close of the creature's earthly existence.

---

178. Oberman, *Luther*, 323. Oberman refers to Luther's correspondence, Luther, *Martin Luther's Werke. Kritische Gesamtausgabe, Briefwechsel*, vol. 1–18 (Weimer: 1912–1921), 4.228.

Eschatological transformation is then a direct consequence of Christ's cruciform death. In considering it the discussion turns first to Paul, and to the principle of resurrection itself.

The idea that life arises out of death is rooted powerfully in the cult of ancient Israel. In the New Testament Jesus reflects it.[179] Paul asserts the principle throughout his letters—modifying it so as to set the way for the crucicentric theologians who follow. To the Corinthians he writes, "What you sow does not come to life unless it dies" (1 Cor 15:36). To the Romans he declares, "[If] you live according to the flesh, you will die; but if by the Spirit you put to death the deeds of the body, you will live" (Rom 8:13). But Paul does not define death and life generically. Not *any* death but "cruciform death in and with Christ" is meant, not *any* life but "the life of Christ" applies. So to the Galatians Paul states, "I died . . . and it is no longer I who live, but it is Christ who lives in me" (Gal 2:19b-20). And to the Romans, "Therefore we have been buried with him by baptism into death, so that, just as Christ was raised from the dead by the glory of the Father, so we too might walk in newness of life. For if we have been united with him in a death like his, we will certainly be united with him in a resurrection like his . . . But if we have died with Christ, we believe that we will also live with him" (Rom 6:4-8).[180]

Grounded in Scripture, the principle of resurrection is also integral to crucicentric mysticism. While other strands of mysticism seek a way *around* death to divine union, crucicentric mysticism holds passage *through* death in and with Jesus Christ to be the one path to resurrected life with God. The writer of the *Theologia Germanica*, for instance, says that the whole reason the creature is put to death is that it be "raised again and made alive in Christ."[181] Similarly Nicholas of Cusa speaks of "God's creative power and love" lifting the creature through the cross to a place "beyond the coincidence of contradictories," beyond the ideal realm. Here God "the undivided divine Trinity" encounters it, subdues

---

179. Jesus says, "Very truly, I tell you, unless a grain of wheat falls into the earth and dies, it remains just a single grain; but if it dies, it bears much fruit. Those who love their life lose it, and those who hate their life in this world will keep it for eternal life" (John 12:24-25).

180. See Gal 2:19 and Col 3:3.

181. See Wakefield, ed., *A Dictionary of Christian Spirituality*, 376. In this equation the influence of Rom 8:13 can be seen.

The Classical Soteriology of the Cross 119

it, and gives it new form. In this cruciform way the creature is liberated from "entrapment by reason's proud quest for God."[182]

Luther too has a strong theology of creaturely death as the sole and necessary condition for new and authentic human existence.[183] In this he is influenced by First Testament texts in which God kills in order to bring forth life,[184] by Paul's cruciform modification of the ancient Hebrew principle of resurrection, and, and once again by the twelfth century Bernard of Clairvaux. In regard to the latter Luther adopts Bernard's exploration of the dialectical relation between God's life-taking and life-giving works, between the *opus alienum* and *opus proprium*.[185] The alien work of God does not undermine but serves God's proper work of creaturely resurrection and renewal. Again the Heidelberg Disputation sets this out clearly. In his proof to Thesis 4 Luther writes, "God does his alien and wrathful work before he does his proper and loving work; he makes alive by killing, brings to heaven by going through hell, brings forth mercy out of wrath."

This raises the further point that generally in the crucicentric tradition the life produced out of death cannot simply be a remodeling or restoring of the old self-glorifying life. A mere restoration does not require death, while the fact of death makes restoration necessarily impossible. Rather the work of the cross reverses the ontological depths of the human condition. In its embrace the *lifeless* creature is completely re-created, totally re-made, radically transformed in the image of Christ, first formally and then actually.[186] This is creation *ex nihilo*, creation out of the nothingness of death. Paul, for example, writes, "God gives life to the dead and [out of death] calls into existence the things that do not exist" (Rom 4:17).

If this is so the utterly new creature has an utterly new identity. Paul says, "So if anyone is in Christ, there is a new creation: everything old has passed away; see, everything has become new" (2 Cor 5:17)! To this Bayer comments, "[The man brought into Christ] is created anew and has

---

182. See ibid., 279.

183. Luther writes for example, "To be born anew, one must consequently first die and then be raised up with the Son of Man." Proof Thesis 24, Heidelberg Disputation.

184. For example Deut 32:39, 1 Sam 2:6, and Heb 12:11.

185. For the *opus alienum* and/or *opus proprium* in Luther also see here pp. 45, 99, 144, and 255.

186. Bayer, "Word of the Cross," 47.

his identity permanently outside himself, in another, a stranger, in one who has replaced him in a wondrous change and exchange of human sin and divine justice."[187] From a creaturely perspective this metamorphosis, having commenced temporally, is completed eschatologically.

The crucicentric theologians hold that the creature's death takes place first formally in the crucified Christ, and then actually as the creature is made to identify with Christ's death—an identification marked by the sacrament of baptism and the ongoing process of sanctification. For those "crucified with Christ" the ultimate significance of physical death is a lesser matter; Luther indeed refers to it as "the little death" (*das Tödlein*).[188] But physical death does signify that that which in the environs of the cross had always lain ahead, resurrection to true and glorious union with the risen Christ has finally come to pass. Now the old self-glorifying ways of being have been completely and finally extinguished. Now death itself has died. Now what has been hidden—the life of the new person, the person in whom Christ ontologically is the new life, is made clear. But this also means that a true and eschatological *theologia gloriae* crowns the classical crucicentric understanding of soteriology.

By way of brief background *theosis* is the term normally applied to the notion that those in the man-God Jesus Christ therefore subsist in the triune God. Their glorification (deification) is increasing during temporal life, and will be completed in the life to come. It is for this purpose that those in Christ have been created. The notion itself relies on 2 Pet 1:3–4. The passage states that of his glory Christ has promised his followers "escape from the corruption of the world [that they may] become participants of the divine nature." Theosis is thus bound up with sanctification and eschatology. Though at times neglected, the concept has always existed below the surface of Christian orthodoxy, eastern and western, Roman Catholic and Protestant. At the point where theosis connotes the creature's participation in and reflection of *Christ's* glory, the notion has lent itself to classical crucicentric thought. Where that participatory stress has been missing theosis has lent support to the opposing notion that the creature is, or is becoming, divine in its own right—to which of course the classical crucicentric theologians are implacably opposed.

187. Ibid.
188. See Mattes, "Gerhard Forde," 382.

With notable exceptions—von Loewenich, McGrath, Mannermaa and Kärkkäinen interpreting him—true human glory as an element of the crucicentric tradition is generally overlooked by the secondary literature on the theology of the cross. In part this may be due to the narrowness of many conceptions of the theology of the cross. But even where a broad and systematic perspective does exist, the presence of a true *theologia gloriae* in classical crucicentric thinking often passes unremarked. Presumably it is hidden by the very power of crucicentric theology's opposition to human *self*-glorification. However that may be, generally for the classical crucicentric theologians salvation in all its moments is divinely directed to one overall purpose: Spirit empowered participation in the glory of the risen Christ, and thence of the triune Godhead.

In Rom 8:30 Paul holds that those whom God has predestined in Christ he has also justified in the cross of Christ, and those whom God has justified *he has also glorified*. Denney calls this, "the most daring verse in the Bible."[189] It is, he says, made all the more so by Paul's use of the Greek aorist tense to indicate that because of the *completed* nature of the work of the cross, in Jesus Christ human glorification has *already* taken place. It is a concrete reality, definite. It is this certainty which stands behind Paul's frequent injunctions to believers to live expectantly in the knowledge—to quote McGrath—"that the cross is the only gate to glory."[190] For example Paul writes, "Therefore, since we are justified by faith, . . . we boast in our hope of sharing the glory of God" (Rom 5:1–2). Similarly, "And all of us, with unveiled faces, seeing the glory of the Lord as though reflected in a mirror, are being transformed into the same image from one degree of glory to another" (2 Cor 3:18). Or again, "Therefore I endure everything for the sake of the elect, so that they may also obtain the salvation that is in Christ Jesus, with eternal glory" (2 Tim 2:10).

Athanasius too speaks of the glorification, or deification, of human nature. He begins with the progressive glorification of the human nature of Jesus Christ. (In the fourth century the christological and soteriological difficulties inherent in such a notion are yet to be fully understood.) Christ's humanity "advanced in wisdom, transcending by degrees human

---

189. See commentary on Rom 8:30 in Gaebelein and Douglas, eds., *Expositor's Bible Commentary Electronic Version*.

190. McGrath, *The Enigma of the Cross*, 165.

nature, being deified, [and] appearing to all as the . . . shining forth of the Godhead."[191] The high point of this glorious appearing was reached, Athanasius thinks, in the cross as the Son overcame sin. In consequence the Son could rise—in Weinandy's explanation of Athanasius—"fully deified as a glorious man."[192]

If the Son's human nature was progressively deified, Athanasius can then argue that the humanity of those co-bodied with the Son will be progressively glorified. Indeed he considers that the incarnation, and especially the crucifixion, took place fundamentally that human divinization might proceed. As Meyer explains him, "Jesus received death for us so we could become temples of God."[193]

Across his project Athanasius emphasizes the link between Jesus' death and the true glorification of believers. For quick example, "[The Son] was made man that we might be made God; and he manifested himself by a body that we might receive the idea of the unseen Father; and he endured the insolence of men that we might inherit immortality."[194] Again, "[A] union was achieved [in Christ] between the true nature of the divinity and human nature in order that salvation and divination might be assured."[195] Likewise, "He himself should be exalted, for he is the highest, . . . that he may become righteousness for us, and we may be exalted in him."[196] And finally now, "[The Son] became man that he might deify us in himself . . . and [so make us] partakers of the divine nature, as blessed Peter wrote."[197]

Using the parabolic image of the prodigal son Athanasius then insists that those in Christ are not glorious in and of themselves, but rather clothed in that glory that belongs always to the divine Son. "The father watched for his son's return, . . . providing shoes for his feet, and, what is most wonderful, placed a divine signet ring upon his hand; . . . by all these things [creating him anew] in the image of the glory of Christ."[198] As the father of the prodigal transforms the status of his contrite son,

191. Newman and Robertson, *Against the Arians*, 3.53.
192. Weinandy, *Athanasius*, 97.
193. Meyer, "Athanasius' Use of Paul," 168.
194. A Religious of CSMV, *On the Incarnation*, 54.3.
195. Newman and Robertson, *Against the Arians*, 2.70, cf. 3.5.
196. Ibid., 1.41.
197. *Ad Adelphium* 4. See Weinandy, *Athanasius*, 98.
198. Schaff, "Festal Letter 7.10."

Athanasius reasons, so too the Father of all transforms the status of those who turn to his Son in repentance and faith.[199] Believers are then "no longer earthly, but . . . *made Word* by reason of God's Word who for our sake became flesh."[200] They are ontologically "intertwined with the Word who is from heaven."[201]

But a vital if implicit proviso guides Athanasius' theology of human glorification. As Weinandy explains, he "argues that we can rightly be called 'gods' not in the sense that we are equal to the Son by nature, but because we have become beneficiaries of his grace."[202] Weinandy then adds, "[For Athanasius deification] is not . . . the changing of our human nature into something other than it is, that is, into another kind of being. Rather, deification . . . is the making of humankind into what it was meant to be from the very beginning, that is, the perfect image of the Word who is the perfect image of the Father. Moreover this deification is only effected by being taken into the very divine life of the Trinity."[203]

Lifting the creature into the divine life of the Trinity means in turn that for Athanasius creaturely glorification is always *participatory*. The creature shares in the glory of the triune God; *God's* glory, *his* deity, the glory pertaining to it is never first its own. Here Athanasius draws a fundamental distinction between the deification of Jesus' human nature and that of other humans; Jesus is the Word of God, the unchanging image of the Father "not by participation,"[204] Athanasius says, but in and of himself.

Creaturely deification takes place for Athanasius by the power of the Spirit of Christ. Because the Spirit is in the Word, and the Word is in the creature, the Spirit is in the creature. Because the Word is united with the Father by the Spirit, the creature united with the Word is also united with the Father by the Spirit, and therefore with the eternal Godhead.[205] So Athanasius says, "[Apart] from the Spirit [we] are strange and distant from God, yet by the participation of the Spirit we are knit into the Godhead. [For the Word] wills that we should receive the Spirit, that [on

199. Ibid.
200. Newman and Robertson, *Against the Arians*, 3.33. Italics mine.
201. See ibid.
202. Weinandy, *Athanasius*, 99.
203. Ibid.
204. See Schaff, *Contra Gentes*, 46.8.
205. See Newman and Robertson, *Against the Arians*, 2.59.

account of him] we too may be found to become one in the Word, and through him [one in the Father.]"[206] It is then the function of the Spirit to *sanctify* and *glorify* and *deify* and *exalt* the creature—in Athanasius these categories melt together—so that it might exactly reflect the perfect image of the Son and thence itself be made a son of God.

This conception of the gradual and participatory glorification of the creature consequent on the cruciform work of the Son, governed by the Father, empowered by the Spirit, is to continue to influence the crucicentric understanding of the theology of human glorification in the patristic era and beyond.[207]

The eschatological understanding of the crucicentric mystics likewise focuses on creaturely glory. Recalling the earlier reference here to their rejection of Meister Eckhart, the crucicentric mystics carefully distinguish their position on creaturely glory from the broader mystical stream he represents. As Eckhart they hold suffering to advance the soul towards divine union. But they do not agree that the soul, whether of itself or divinely aided, merges into God, losing its creatureliness and individuality.[208] Rather the soul is lifted by God through death and hell, to be increasingly embraced by the glory belonging to heaven. But *to heaven*! Here glory is never a property of the creature, and neither does the creature lose its creaturely aspect or its individuality.

For example the anonymous writer of the *Theologia Germanica* writes, "[Since Christ] became humanized and man becomes divinized . . . God must be humanized in me."[209] He then immediately explains this. It is not that the creature becomes as God, but rather "this means that God takes unto Himself everything that is in me, from within and without, so that there is nothing in me that resists God or obstructs his work."[210] The will of the creature is at last fully aligned with that of God, so that God is the directing power within it.

---

206. See ibid., 3.24.

207. The Cappadocian fathers exemplify this. Norris observes that Basil of Caesarea and Gregory of Nyssa "speak of humans becoming divine because the divine Son became human," while Gregory of Nazianzen redefines the term *theosis* in light of Athanasius' conception of true human glorification, frequently employing it. All three Cappadocian fathers insist that the term *theosis* best describes what is ultimately meant by *salvation*. See Norris, "Cappadocian Fathers," 114.

208. For an earlier reference to Meister Eckhart see here pp. 42–43.

209. *Theologia Germanica*, chapter 3.

210. Ibid. See also Tripp, "Theologia Germanica," 376.

Similarly Tauler, whose theology of light in deepest darkness has already been mentioned. He speaks of the soul's staged passage through suffering and death to be lost in God. Quoting Tauler, von Loewenich explains the latter's scheme:

> The lowest step is contemplation of the life and suffering of Jesus . . . [In] the second step . . . all that man's lower powers can comprehend drops away. . . . But he has not yet achieved peace. It is at this point that trials arise in full force . . . What rids the soul of them is [the third step,] the birth of God within the soul . . . All man's "individuality" is destroyed . . . [With the fourth and final step man] is submerged in God. "There the created nothing submerges into the uncreated nothing, . . . the created abyss into the uncreated abyss, . . . there the spirit has lost itself in God's Spirit."[211]

At first glance Tauler appears to present a theology of self-glorification, but on examination he begins with the work of the cross as God's prior way to the creature. The individuality the creature loses—doing so through painful trial after that of Christ—is its self-glorifying quest for independence. Reduced to "nothing" in this way it is finally embraced by the Spirit of God *as creature*. It has not initiated its own way to God, much less become God. In short, here human glorification is to do with the creature's cross-won and Spirit empowered participation in *God's* glory, not the manufacture of its own. The difference between Tauler and the Eckhart school is the difference between light and dark.

Paul especially, but also the *Theologia Germanica* and Tauler, are to influence Luther's own understanding of true human glory. If Paul, with pastoral concern, encourages a fledgling and persecuted community by pointing to the true glory awaiting its members individually and corporately, at the far end of the classical crucicentric era Luther, with equivalent concern, recalls an established and self-glorifying community back to the cross by stressing the cruciform command incumbent on its members to sacrifice, suffering and death. Exactly as Paul however, Luther understands the cross to be the one gate to glory, and suffering faith the one way that that gate might be entered in. In McGrath's words, "For Luther . . . Christ bestows upon us [i.e., those already saved] . . . the privilege of suffering with him in order that we may be raised with him; treading the same path as he once trod, leading first to the cross,

---

211. See von Loewenich, *Luther's Theology of the Cross*, 153–54.

and then to glory."[212] Von Loewenich agrees; he quotes Luther himself. "Faith unites the soul with the invisible, ineffable, unutterable, eternal, unthinkable Word of God, while at the same time it separates it from all visible things. This is the cross and the Passover of the Lord, in which He preaches this necessary comprehension [of faith]."[213]

To refresh an earlier reference here[214] Finish professor Tuomo Mannermaa similarly finds Luther's *theologia crucis* to culminate in the eschatological participation of the creature in the glory of the risen Christ. Such participation involves "real-ontic" union between the creature and Christ, and therefore God, this being for Luther the ultimate gift of divine love. *Future ontological union* is then said by Mannermaa to be Luther's leading idea. It culminates Luther's adaptation of the theology of the cross, and in doing so influences his whole direction. Mannermaa interpreter Kärkkäinen further explains, "For Mannermaa, the leading idea [in Luther is his insistence that] human glorification means the 'participation' of the believer in Christ which, because Christ is God, is also a participation in God himself. This deification is the result of God's love: human beings cannot participate in God on the basis of their own love; rather God's love effects their deification . . . though the substances themselves do not change into something else."[215]

But even in Mannermaa's extreme view of Luther's position, stretching him further than many are prepared to allow, the creature is never allowed to lose its creatureliness and rise to *be* God substantially, and neither does its "real-ontic" union with God reduce God to its own level. To be really deified in the sense Mannermaa (and by extension Kärkkäinen) finds Luther advocating, means that the creature participates in the risen Christ's glorious personhood *as creature*. Moreover Mannermaa stresses Luther's rejection of creaturely *self* glorification, including eschatologically; the operative deifying power is always the gracious love of God. Luther hardly engages in a false *theologia gloriae* himself.

Mannermaa's contribution though is not just to identify the formative significance of the true *theologia gloriae* in Luther's thought. In

---

212. McGrath, *The Enigma of the Cross*, 165.

213. "*Operationes in Psalmos*," in Luther, *Luther's Works*, 14:342f. See also von Loewenich, *Luther's Theology of the Cross*, 83.

214. For an earlier reference to Tuomo Mannermaa see here p. 30.

215. Kärkkäinen, "Evil, Love and the Left Hand of God," 218.

doing that he implicitly underscores the high place of the true *theologia gloriae* for crucicentric thought generally.

Eschatological participation in the glory of God does not exhaust the meaning and consequence of the true *theologia gloriae* for the creature—or for the classical crucicentric theologians. Culminating the Word of the cross is the promise that participation in Christ's glory means participation in his reign over a new heaven and a new earth, governing with his wisdom and at his direction. This is the great and eternal destiny to which the creature is called via justification, sanctification, resurrection and glorification.

Paul for example writes to Timothy, "The saying is sure, 'If we have died with him, we will also live with him; if we endure, we will also reign with him'" (2 Tim 2:11–12). After Paul Athanasius says similarly, "[On] rising from the dead . . . we shall no longer fear death, but in Christ shall reign forever in the heavens."[216] This reign is not simply to be that of individuals, but first that of the church itself, holy, perfect, and presented to the Father by the Son.[217]

For Luther too, the cross announces the certainty of the creature's eschatological reign as the culmination of its glorification in Christ. As early as 1516 when commenting on Rom 8:18–19,[218] he says that the justified creature is summoned to fulfill "the mandate of Easter" to usher in the kingdom of God presently, and to rule with Christ eternally. Then "we shall easily issue laws, and judge all things aright, and even make a new decalogue, as Paul does in all his epistles, and Peter, and above all Christ in the gospel."[219] According to von Loewenich the promise of this glorious eschatological rule comes to full form in the deeper levels of the Heidelberg Disputation, and from there extends forward into Luther's mature theology. Von Loewenich then concludes that this "part of the theology of the cross is too intimately entwined with Luther's central thought ever to be given up."[220]

---

216. Newman and Robertson, *Against the* Arians, 2.67.

217. See ibid.

218. Paul writes, "I consider that the sufferings of this present time are not worth comparing with the glory about to be revealed to us. For the creation waits with eager longing for the revealing of the children of God" (Rom 8:18–19).

219. Luther, *Martin Luthers Werke*, 39. 1.47.

220. Von Loewenich, *Luther's Theology of the Cross*, 90–91.

There is one final point to be made here, and of relevance to the whole classical crucicentric soteriological tradition. Profoundly within crucicentric soteriology there sounds a note of triumph over adversity, a note of joy. This triumphant joy is not grounded in the creature for the creature has no cause to boast—its justification, continuing sanctification and true glorification are not its own doing. Rather soteriological triumph and joy are rooted ontologically in the glorious Word breaking into the creaturely realm in the incarnation of Jesus Christ, and proclaimed above all from his cross. This note of triumphant joy, too often overlooked or erroneously called "uncrucicentric," is in fact a touchstone shaping the crucicentric theologian's demeanor towards God, the community, and the world.

Conclusion

The classical soteriology of the cross conveys a sharp negative word; the creature may not be as God. All attempts at self-glorification are divinely denied, doomed, and ultimately negated. This negative word is however embraced in a powerful and hopeful cruciform message, the saving Word from the cross of Jesus Christ. The cruciform message is first of justification. In his cross Jesus Christ satisfies the penalty of the law on behalf of the creature, formally freeing it, lifting it into himself. The cruciform message is then of sanctification. In exchange for taking up its own cross and dying to itself more and more, the creature is drawn increasingly into Christ's new and risen life, not just formally but actually. So the creature has passed *through* cruciform death and not around it. The cruciform message is finally of resurrection and eschatological glorification. At the close of earthly life the sanctified creature is lifted into the risen life of Jesus Christ, to be made eternally that which God has decreed and created it to be from the beginning, fully human, participant in Christ's eternal glory, enlisted forever in his eschatological service.

Methodologically this cruciform soteriology comprises a system of interlinking themes and doctrines. Negatively these oppose human works, particularly *good* works, as a way of conditioning the electing will of God. Positively they include the following. Under justification: the law of death and the law of life, the suffering and death of Jesus Christ on behalf of the creature, the claim of the cross on the creature, and the question of universalism. Under sanctification: continuing death in the realm of the cross, and the suffering and death of believers. Under resurrection and glorification: new and resurrected life, the true *theologia gloriae*, and the eschatological service of the creature. Other ideas span across all these elements, including the motif-like juxtaposition of wisdom and foolishness, the insistence that justification precedes sanctification, and an understanding of faith as divine gift. Separately and together the elements of this soteriological matrix respond to two principles, being the exclusivity of the glory (divinity) of God, and the attendant notion that in Jesus Christ and him crucified God alone graciously determines the eternal election of the creature.

The soteriology of the cross though is not first a theological sub-system. For all the classical crucicentric theologians it is supremely an ontological *Word* or *Theology* commanding the continuing death of the creature desiring itself. For only as the creature dies is it clothed in the true humanity of the risen Christ, new-made, to participate *as creature* in his eternal glory and service. As a theological sub-system the soteriology of the cross merely explicates this cruciform Word.

Having overviewed the principal lines by which crucicentric soteriology and before that epistemology proceed, the shape and content of the crucicentric system and the marks of its theologians may now be formally described.

4

Identifying the Classical *Theologia Crucis*, its Dogmatic Shape, Theological Content, and the Marks Characterizing its Theologians

A theologian of glory calls evil good and good evil. A theologian of the cross calls the thing what it actually is.

—Martin Luther[1]

The idea undergirding crucicentric theology is a simple one. It is that the cross of Jesus Christ proclaims a unique self-disclosing and saving Word. A major objective in Part One of this discussion has been to uncover the various theological strands depending on this cruciform Word, along with their mutual relations. The epistemological and soteriological system which results is informed by complementary analogical and dialectical methodologies: the analogy of faith in which God is known from the crucified Christ, and the dialectic of the cross with its asymmetric synthesis in which grace resolves sin. This system is located in the deeper textual levels of the work of the Apostle Paul and a thin line of theologians succeeding him down the centuries, the classical formation of this tradition concluding with the Reformer Martin Luther.

It is then Luther who is first to codify the crucicentric system deliberately, doing so in his 1518 Heidelberg Disputation. Around the same time he retrospectively designates that system, and by extension the long

---

1. Thesis 21 Heidelberg Disputation. Lull, *Martin Luther's Basic Theological Writings*, 44.

tradition carrying it, "*theologia crucis.*" Forde (1997) and Kärkkäinen (2003)[2] each suggest that the great importance of the *theologia crucis* for Luther means that it fairly constitutes a hermeneutical lens through which to view his entire project. The notion that the classical crucicentric system constitutes a hermeneutic through which *other*, including modern, theological projects might be evaluated for crucicentric content, is not however pursued in the relevant secondary literature. Such a generic application is though proposed here.

On the basis of the present discussion this classical, crucicentric, and hermeneutical system can now be presented diagrammatically, and the marks of its theologians formally delineated. The chart on the following page broadly illustrates the dialectical relationships within the crucicentric system, and the equivalent ways in which the epistemological and soteriological dimensions within this system relate to its central principles.

The Marks of the Theologian of the Cross

While the following marks are neither exhaustive nor prioritised, on the basis of the foregoing investigation they fairly indicate the demeanor of the theologian of the cross. Together they constitute a hermeneutical standard against which the crucicentric status (as traditionally understood) of any theologian can be determined. The marks are:

1. *Primary attention to the Word from the cross.* The theologian of the cross learns from the cross:

    i) that the knowledge of God and the salvation of God are each hidden in and disclosed by Jesus Christ, supremely at the point of the cross;

    ii) that it is only as the Holy Spirit brings the creature to die to itself that it receives this revelatory knowledge, and with it Christ himself and therefore salvation.

---

2. For Forde and Kärkkäinen respectively, see here pp. 24 and 30. As will be shown, Klappert (1971), Thompson (1978), and Barker (1995), also view the *theologia crucis* as a hermeneutic, Klappert and Thompson in relation to Barth, and Barker in relation to Bonhoeffer. See respectfully pp. 175, 179, and 185.

CROSS THEOLOGY

POSITIVE EPISTEMOLOGY

God alone can truly know God so as to reveal God truly.

3. God in the crucified Christ reveals God formally. Creature freed and reconciled cognitively to God *de jure*.

4. Passage through the cross entails the real death of the presumption to know as God, and so the receipt of Christ's mind *de facto*. Here faithful analogy is drawn on Jesus Christ to God, (the *analogia fidei*.)

5. Noetic transformation completed in eschatological participation in the glorious mind of Christ, (the true *theologia gloriae*.)

NEGATIVE EPISTEMOLOGY

The creature as creature cannot uncover the knowledge of God.

1. Rejection of all forms of natural theology, including speculative analogy drawn on the creature to the Creator, (the *analogia entis*.)

2. Behind this, opposition to the self-glorifying presumption to know God in Godself as God alone knows, (the false *theologia gloriae*.)

The creature of itself is not glorious.

God alone is glorious.

POSITIVE SOTERIOLOGY

God alone can condition the salvific will of God.

3. God in the crucified Christ determines election formally. Creature freed and reconciled to God *de jure*.

4. Passage through the cross entails the real death of the presumption to be as God, and so the receipt of Christ's life *de facto*. Here justification precedes sanctification, (the gracious *ordo salutis*.)

5. Ontological transformation completed in eschatological participation in the glorious being of Christ, (the true *theologia gloriae*.)

NEGATIVE SOTERIOLOGY

The creature as creature cannot condition the salvific will of God.

1. Rejection of the notion that sanctification precedes justification, (the western *ordo salutis*.)

2. Behind this, opposition to the self-glorifying presumption to determine election, sanctification, and glorification as God alone determines, (the false *theologia gloriae*.)

THE SHAPE AND CONTENT OF THE CLASSICAL CRUCICENTRIC SYSTEM

2. *A particular way of seeing.* Allied to the above, the theologian of the cross is marked by a particular way of seeing. He or she looks indirectly at God, *through the cross*, receiving the revelation of God in the crucified Christ. Such a theologian does not look directly at God *from behind the cross*, beginning speculatively from the creature.

3. *Adherence to three central principles.* The theologian of the cross proceeds on the basis of three central methodological and strictly theological principles, the first giving rise to the other two.

    i) God alone is glorious.

    ii) God alone can truly know God in Godself so as to reveal God truly.

    iii) God alone can condition the salvific will of God.

4. *A wise regard for reason.* The theologian of the cross wisely elects to begin where the knowledge of God is disclosed in the cross, and not foolishly (illogically) where such knowledge is not available.

5. *A profound realism.* The theologian of the cross is marked by profound realism:

    i) Methodologically the crucicentric theologian grounds theology concretely rather than abstractly or speculatively.

    ii) Theologically the crucicentric theologian is utterly realistic about the human condition in all its frailty and sinfulness.

6. *Two stances toward human glory.*

    i) Citing a false *theologia gloriae* the theologian of the cross adopts a negative stance towards creaturely attempts on the glory of God.

    ii) Citing a true *theologia gloriae* the theologian of the cross adopts a positive stance towards Spirit empowered creaturely participation in Christ's glory.

7. *A particular watchfulness at the threshold of the church and the world.* Since the theology of glory impinges on the church in the world, the theologian of the cross stands guard at the threshold of the church and the world. In this sense the theologian of the cross is not so much an apologist for Christian truth in the world, as a defender of it in the church.

8. *Insistence that the gospel take priority over the age.* Allied to the above point, the theologian of the cross defends the gospel against a compromising accommodation to the age, insisting rather that the age be accommodated to the gospel for the gospel rightly judges the age.

9. *Existence in the realm of the cross.* The theologian of the cross exists in the environs of the cross, in the place of continuing death to self-idolization and continuing surrender to the lordship of Jesus Christ.

Enough has now been done to validate this discussion's first substantive proposal:

> That the theology of the cross (*theologia crucis*) is an ancient system of Christian thought conveying the message of the cross of Jesus Christ, that in it alone all—necessarily self-glorifying—creaturely attempts to know and be as God are overcome, that the proper glorification of human knowledge and being may proceed.

Excursus:
The Systematic Foundation to the Heidelberg Disputation

Crux probat omnia.

—Martin Luther[1]

Crux sola est nostra theologia.

—Martin Luther[2]

As seen, central to Martin Luther's lifelong project is an argument with the metaphysical and anthropocentric starting point of the prevailing scholasticism. On the basis of preceding tradition he uncovers an epistemological and soteriological method, and attendant dogmatic, for theology. These derive not from human logic but from the logic of the God who, from the cross of Jesus Christ, speaks a self-revealing and a saving word. Accordingly Luther calls this word and its message *theologia crucis*.

While it is in his *Lectures on Hebrews* (1517–1518) that Luther first starts to bring his *theologia crucis* together, it is with his disputation[3] at Heidelberg around the same time, April 1518, that his crucicentric understanding flowers. Within the disputation's surface and deeper textual levels he delineates and systematically relates the epistemological and

1. "The cross is the criterion of all things." Luther, *Martin Luthers* Werke, 5.176.

2. "The cross alone is our theology." Ibid., 5.179.

3. In the medieval university the disputation was a form of debate; indeed a student was not considered to have completed academic training without standing victoriously in one. The person wishing to defend a set of disputation points (or theses) simply posted them on a bulletin board in the university precincts, inviting all comers to dispute them at a particular time and place.

soteriological dimensions of the Word from the cross more succinctly than anyone before him. As such the Heidelberg Disputation is now generally considered a key document in the onward transmission of the crucicentric tradition and the system that tradition carries.

In the view of a number of commentators this transmission starts with the critical influence of the Heidelberg Disputation's encapsulation of crucicentric thought on the Reformation. Forde, for instance, agrees that the disputation "is theologically much more important and influential . . . than the Ninety-five Theses, even though the Ninety-five Theses caused more of an ecclesiastical and political stir. [The Heidelberg theological theses] remain determinative . . . It is not too much to say . . . that they are almost a kind of outline for Luther's subsequent theological program."[4] There is therefore surprise that the disputation is among the least known of Luther's works.

Given the Heidelberg Disputation's crucicentric and historical importance, an overview of it is offered now as an adjunct to Part One. This overview adds support to the conclusions already drawn here concerning the shape and content of the classical crucicentric system—the disputation itself comprising the original digest of that shape and content.

Space forbids expanding on the wider historical backdrop to the Heidelberg Disputation,[5] but the immediate circumstances surrounding it are as follows. Subsequent to the declaration of the Ninety-five Theses, 31 October 1517, which popular history now marks as the commencement of the Reformation, Pope Leo X hoped to silence Luther conventionally by having him degraded academically and anathematized ecclesiastically. Luther was duly summoned to defend his position in open debate before the General Assembly of his German order, the Augustinian Hermits, meeting at Heidelberg on the 26 April 1518. In preparation for this his monastic superior and spiritual director Johannes von Staupitz instructed him to prepare theses, avoiding contentious issues and sticking to such dull and academic matters as sin, free-will and grace. In fact these issues were central to Luther's developing attack on scholasticism,[6] including the penitential practices it supported. He

---

4. Forde, *Being a Theologian of the Cross*, 19–21.

5. For a fuller historical account see Oberman, *Luther*, 223, 258.

6. In his *theologia crucis* Luther challenges several contemporary scholastic platforms. These include the notion that those elected for salvation cannot sin, the idea that some sins are in a lesser category and therefore *venial* (forgivable), scholastic support for the western *ordo salutis*, and the belief that the human will is neutral or free.

duly prepared twenty eight theological and twelve philosophical theses,[7] posed in a series of terse antitheses reflecting the dialectical tension within his position. In the event Luther did not defend these theses himself but appointed fellow Augustinian Leonhard Beier to do so. Luther himself presided over the debate. No decision was reached, the younger brothers approved Luther's position while the older brothers did not.

Building on a traditional picture,[8] methodologically the Heidelberg Disputation itself can be regarded as a gracious bridge with supporting pillars at each corner. The pair of pillars on the "epistemological side" represent the hiddenness of God, arching to divine self-revelation. The pair of pillars on the "soteriological side" represent the law of death, arching to the law of life. It follows that Luther's theological theses are mainly focused epistemologically or soteriologically, although other disciplinary areas impinge upon these perspectives.

To make patent the disputation's underlying systematic structure, its content is now presented under appropriate disciplinary headings.

Christology

Generally in the Heidelberg Disputation Luther does not explore the internal relation of Christ's hypostatic natures in the atoning work of the cross, (as twentieth century ontological theories are wont to do), or otherwise pay particular attention to the personhood of Christ. A "Christology of the cross" is not finely worked out, nor is there a separate section of the disputation that might be called Christology. At the same time the disputation is all Christology. Luther's crucified Christ is the inbreaking Word of God. As such he is a *prophetic* Word, warning that new life is possible only by passing through the cross. He is a *commanding* Word, compelling exactly this passage. He is then a *mortifying* and *vivifying* Word, a Word that kills and makes alive again, a Word of re-creation, the new and eternal Adam remaking the old and dying Adam. He is a profoundly *eschatological* Word. Coming from the future Jesus Christ stands proleptically in the present, drawing those he summons by faith through the cross back into his future. Finally for Luther the crucified Christ is a *majestic* Word, the Lord of the creature, standing over

---

7. It is the theological theses that are now generally considered to be of more significance for Luther's Reformation decisions.

8. See Forde, *Being a Theologian of the Cross*, 20 n.20.

against the foolish and sinful human effort to circumvent his revelatory Person and cross so as to usurp his glory.

Epistemology

In theses 19 to 21 of the disputation the question as to the human knowledge of God elicits the fundamental assertion guiding crucicentric epistemology down the centuries, an assertion developed in dialectical correspondence with the *theologia gloriae*. In its Reformational form—via Luther—it declares that any deity made visible by speculative analogy drawn on the creature is logically the prisoner of human capacity. Speculation cannot objectively establish its deistic god. All it can do is reinforce the foolish human presumption to know as God, while circumventing the place where God's self-revelation is supremely available, the cross of Jesus Christ.

Luther then holds that the true theologian, *viz.* the theologian of the cross, learns from the cross what can only be foolishness to the theologian of glory, that God ultimately reveals the knowledge of God *sub contrario*, under the form of the opposite. Against all human expectation and reason God makes himself known at the point where to natural vision he is most hidden—in the suffering, shame and humiliation of the cross of Golgotha. God chooses this alien methodology for two reasons. Negatively, to confound the self-glorifying pretension of the theologian claiming to possess a natural capacity to know God as God knows. Positively, to enable the theologian who has submitted such pretension to the cross, who sees by faith, to identify the contrary place wherein the knowledge of God is actually made available.

Indeed the cross demolishes the legitimacy of all methods outside itself for knowing God as God really is. In support of this, in his proof to Thesis 20 Luther co-opts the story in Exod 33:18–23 in which Moses is forbidden to view the glory of God directly.[9] Similarly the creature may not view the invisible things of God directly by speculation, but

9. "Moses said, 'Show me your glory, I pray.' And [the Lord] said, 'I will make all my goodness pass before you, and will proclaim before you the name, *The Lord*. . . . [But] you cannot see my face; for no one shall see me and live.' And the Lord continued, 'See, there is a place by me where you shall stand on the rock; and while my glory passes by I will put you in a cleft of the rock, and I will cover you with my hand until I have passed by; then I will take away my hand, and you shall see my back; but my face shall not be seen' (Exod 33:18–23)." *Punctuation changed.*

Excursus: The Systematic Foundation to the Heidelberg Disputation

solely by faith with the aid of a cruciform lens.[10] True knowledge of God cannot rely on an *analogia entis*[11] with its natural way to the knowledge of God; if it could Christ's work on the cross would be negated and the glory of God usurped. Rather the knowledge of God relies on the aforementioned *analogia fidei*, in which faith sees Jesus Christ as analogous to God because one with God.[12]

In Thesis 21 Luther presses home his epistemological attack. The two theologians are distinguished not just by the starting point they choose and the knowledge acquired in consequence, but by the way they convey that knowledge. The theologian of glory calls evil good and good evil; the cross is "evil" and the human circumvention of the cross "good." Here false perception leads invariably to false proclamation. Grace received is unaccompanied by inner transformation, obedience, or sacrifice. (Taking his lead from Luther, a later theologian is to speak at this point of "cheap grace."[13]) In contrast the theologian of the cross "calls a thing what it actually is." The cross is "good," and its circumvention "evil." True discernment of good and evil leads to true proclamation. The theologian of the cross properly proclaims the gracious Word of the cross, that through suffering and sacrifice the one being conformed to it is being reconciled to God.

---

10. See Luther's *On the Bondage of the Will*.

11. For a definition of the *analogia entis* see here p. 49, n. 57.

12. "As with the dialectically corresponding *analogia entis*, the *analogia fidei* embraces both constitutive ontology and epistemology. Similarly also it holds the existence of the Creator God and of the human as the creature of that God. But it rejects that logic whereby the human creature being created in the image of God necessarily corresponds to its Creator, an essential commonality existing between them. Neither does the *analogia fidei* support the corresponding epistemological idea that, given their commonality, the creature is necessarily capable of knowing its Creator by analogy drawn on itself. An authentic correspondence, commonality, and knowing does exist however. Reversing the direction of the *analogia entis*, the *analogia fidei* draws an analogy to God not on the creature but on the man-God Jesus Christ, and him crucified. By grace faith perceives him to be the one Person corresponding exactly to the Creator God, utterly identical with and analogous to him. In this model therefore creaturely action: faithful perception, knowing, and speech, corresponds to *prior* divine action: gracious revelation in Jesus Christ." This definition draws on several sources including Hunsinger, *How to Read Karl* Barth, 283, and Richardson, *Reading Karl Barth*, 26.

13. The opening section of Bonhoeffer's *The Cost of Discipleship* begins "Cheap grace is the deadly enemy of the Church. We are fighting today for costly grace." Bonhoeffer, *The Cost of Discipleship*, 43.

Soteriology

As a late medieval man Luther accepts certain aspects of the dominant Anselmian theory of atonement, including the latter's stress on the gracious righteousness of the Father in appointing the Son a substitutionary sacrifice, satisfying the penalty properly due human sinfulness, atoning for humankind thereby.[14] But, as Hagan points out, Luther does not fully subscribe to any one of the atonement theories tradition offers him.[15] He distrusts attempts to explain a mystery that, as such, he thinks necessarily incapable of theological explanation. It is not the *how* but the *givenness* of atonement which Luther finds vital.

In the Heidelberg Disputation it is Luther's understanding of this *how* that lies behind his rejection of the need to perform salvifically efficacious works. For him the most enticing and therefore most serious form of sin attaches to those works performed by the *righteous*, those who know of their justification, those who should know better! These are works genuinely inspired by God but offered in the quest to control the favor of God, and thence God himself. (Theses 5 and 6.) Luther warns such theologians that their works will not gain them the control they seek; rather their works will lead to their condemnation. In trusting in them the righteous engage in the error of failing to fear God. They fail to acknowledge their inability to merit the justification they have received, they fail to depend continually on the grace of the cross (Thesis 7).

Though the righteous bear the greater responsibility before the law, works meant to secure divine favor performed by a further group,

---

14. In rejecting a singularly wrathful deity in favor of a righteous and gracious one, Luther bears marked similarity to Anselm of Canterbury (1033–1109). Until relatively recently Anselm was said to lay the basis for the later penal substitution theory: the Reformation notion that the crucified Son bears the Father's punishment for human sin, thereby satisfying the righteous anger of a just and holy God toward humankind, thereby enabling divine forgiveness to flow to humankind without compromise to divine justice and holiness. Now though, it is generally agreed that Anselm teaches the need for punishment 'or' satisfaction [*aut poena 'aut' satisfactio*] as the remedy for human disobedience. It is not by bearing divine anger and associated punishment, but by satisfying divine honor in free obedience unto death, that Jesus Christ is vicariously salvifically efficacious. Indeed Anselm rejects the notion that an honorable deity would punish an innocent man. It is likely then, that Anselm would not have approved the harshest form of the later penal substitution theory with its cold and holy justice. In due course neither would Luther.

15. See Hagan, "Luther on Atonement," 253.

the *unrighteous* or nonbelievers, likewise result in the condemnation of those proffering them (Thesis 8). *Ignorance* of the law is no excuse!

Indeed all works aimed at conditioning divine favor bypass the cross, mark human sinfulness, and further separate the creature from God. Luther adds that it is not possible to "have it both ways," to trust partially in the salvific power of works and partially in the cross (Theses 9 and 10). All works originating with the creature—whether that person is among the *righteous* or *unrighteous*—encourage arrogant self-worship and are therefore deadly (Thesis 11). No creaturely work of itself is ever 'good' so as to be salvifically efficacious (Thesis 25). Works are "good" only in so far as on the far side of salvation they are inspired by and infused with grace, so that all credit for them goes to God. Luther is careful here. Such genuinely good works cannot recommend the creature to God, but because of the cross of Jesus Christ they need not do so.[16] The true purpose of good works is to honor God's law, and therefore indicate and honor him. In all this Luther flatly rejects the western *ordo salutis* presenting salvation as a necessary consequence of such human works as faith and repentance.

Luther's faithful understanding of the *how* of atonement also lies behind his position on the salvific use of the will. To explain this it is necessary to describe the prevailing scholastic understanding of the will. The Nominalist position—which Luther encountered as a student at the University of Erfurt—holds that God is bound by his own nature to love his creation. God therefore obliges himself to infuse salvific grace into each creature who wills to do its best to imitate the divine (Aristotelian) attributes, or in scholastic terms who wills "to do what is in one," [*facere quod in se.*] The creature is able to will to obey because its will is inhabited by a 'spark of divinity' enabling that obedience.

Nominalist evidence for the existence of this resident spark is found in the fact that at the fall God held the creature responsible for sin. Logically, so the argument goes, a just God would not have done so unless prior to the fall the will had possessed a God-given capacity to choose or reject the command of God. After the fall God allowed a spark of that prelapsarian capacity to remain, precisely that the creature might retain its earlier ability freely to will to obey the commandments.

---

16. In this Luther opposes Aristotle who in his ethics holds that righteousness is a human capacity acquired in the performance of righteous deeds. See Forde, *Being a Theologian of the Cross*, 104–5.

While in their theology of the will the Nominalists do not mean to countermand the supreme right of God to elect for salvation, and although the pastoral reasons for what is their semi-Pelagian position might seem morally valid, in his Heidelberg Disputation Luther sharply denies their position. There is no residual spark of divinity inhabiting the will and enabling the creature to will obedience. Before the fall and enslaved to God the will actively chose to do good, being inactive (in Luther's terms "passive") towards the willing of evil. The fact that temptation was avoided before the fall was therefore due entirely to God. After the fall and enslaved to sin the will actively chooses to do evil, being inactive towards the willing of good. Moreover the will is powerless to reverse its sinful orientation. Thus for Luther the will never has been free or neutral. In the post-lapsarian period the devil determines all but the minutiae of life. (Theses 13 and 15.) Luther therefore closes every loophole, even prelapsarian loopholes, which might otherwise allow the creature freedom to will to and actually keep the commandments, and therefore to merit salvation.

What then of the theologian recommending the salvific capacity of the will? Luther holds that such a theologian "adds sin to sin so as to be doubly guilty" (Thesis 16). He warns that the person who in accordance with prevailing scholastic advice "does his or her best" to obtain salvation, adds the sin of attempting to condition God to the sin of believing it actually possible to do so. That the church must prescribe, judge, and be satisfied concerning the achievement of "the best" before that achievement becomes salvifically efficacious, only compounds the problem. It makes the church an accomplice in the self-glorifying, Christ denying, endeavors of its members. Luther thus attacks the heart of the scholastic penitential system,[17] and with it the spiritual and temporal power of the Roman church.

---

17. For those who fall short and whose consciences are troubled, the scholastics provide a complicated system of restoration. This involves absolution on the performance of "works of satisfaction," or on payment to the church in lieu of such works. The problem with this for Luther is that it shifts salvific power from God to his creation in the form of a worldly church. Kiecker further explains. "Early on the idea arose that, if the [work of] satisfaction proved too severe, it could be lessened or removed. The church might be indulgent to the penitent . . . To gain the church's indulgence the penitent might perhaps visit a shrine to view the relics, or endow a monastery, or go on a crusade. Or he might borrow from the 'treasury of merits,' a sort of heavenly bank account containing the over-and-above good works of the saints. Upon payment of a service charge, an indulgence would be issued, and the work of satisfaction would be cancelled." Kiecker, *Crucis et Gloriae*, 180.

Nevertheless Luther teaches that the will of the fallen creature can be acted on from beyond itself. The grace of God deriving from the cross of Jesus Christ might steadily bring it under captivity to Christ, returning it to an earlier prelapsarian orientation toward God. This is so since in the cross the creature does not choose God through the exercise of its will, but God chooses it through the exercise of his gracious willingness. So Luther appeals to John's account of the words of Jesus, "You did not choose me but I chose you" (John 15:16.) (Theses 17 and 18). For Luther the hope of the cross yet overshadows the question of the will.

Luther's understanding of the *how* of atonement also lies behind his position on the salvific use of law. Naturally the very existence of the law might suggest a human capacity to obey, pacifying divine wrath and gaining divine favor. But for Luther that natural perspective is predicated on false logic. The "wisdom of the law" merely affirms the religious[18] effort to find, contain and retain God in human service. *Theologia crucis* is then the antithesis of this legal "wisdom." It negates the misuse of the law and asserts in its place a true and ontological logic, that is, that salvation is possible only via the one Person with the power to effect it. There is no natural pathway to salvation, contra the position implied by the western *ordo salutis* sanctification does not precede justification. The creature cannot sanctify itself so as to condition its acceptance by God. All it can do is stand in fear of God,[19] accusing itself, pleading for mercy (Thesis 12).

What then of those who refuse to accuse themselves before God? What of those who trust in their own salvific merit, circumventing the cross and therefore grace? In Luther's view they are guilty of mortal (deadly) sin, and stand under condemnation. He refuses to classify the fault involved as merely "venial," a category of sinfulness attracting a lesser degree of punishment. Indeed Luther denies the existence of some less heinous category of sin (Theses 5 and 6). The law has been broken, and that break exposes transgressors to its full penalty. In this Luther again follows Paul, holding the prime purpose of the law to be the exposure of sin (Theses 1 and 2). For the law points to the inability of the

18. In the crucicentric tradition generally *religion* is a generic (and somewhat pejorative) term for idolatrous systems of belief fundamentally aimed at the glorification of the creature.

19. "The fear of God" is a critical notion in Luther. It denotes awe and terror before God, stemming from awareness that one is sinful, in deadly peril, and powerless to alter this condition.

creature to keep its commands perfectly, and therefore at all (Thesis 23). It tempts and goads its own transgression, so as to magnify and thence fully expose the depths of human sinfulness. Finally, inexorably, the law curses, accuses, grants no mercy, judges, *kills*, everything that does not glorify Christ.

Luther says that when the creature discovers its inability to effect its salvation through the law, and the peril in which it consequently stands, it is liable to react in one of two ways. It becomes either antinomian, or narrowly obedient. But the law can be contained by neither of these strategies; its penalty remains. Thence the creature is in crisis. Resist as it may it cannot free itself. What then can be done?

In setting out his solution Luther begins with a familiar question. "If the law cannot save us, is it evil?" Here he appeals to Paul in Rom 7:12, "The law is holy, and the commandment is just and good" (Thesis 24). In pointing to human sinfulness and salvific incapacity, the holy law points to the divine Solution to human disobedience and incapacity, it points to Jesus Christ. It indicates that by his cruciform death he has already formally lifted the penalty of the law from the creature, so as to free it formally.

Yet in spite of the freedom from the law therefore formally offered it, the creature unaccountably continues its resistance. In an assiduous quest after its own way, blinded and hardened to the cruciform solution before it, it still hungers after those desires which diametrically oppose the way of the cross: self-confidence, self-control, independence from and power over God, the appropriation to itself of divine wisdom and majesty and power. Thus Luther's blunt proclamation, "The remedy for curing desire does not lie in satisfying it but in extinguishing it" (Thesis 22). The cross does not feed the religious idea but proclaims its end.

Now Luther comes to the heart of the message proclaimed from the cross. "The Lord kills—performing his alien work which is of immediate value, in order to make alive—performing his proper work which is of eternal value" (Thesis 4). Through being actually identified with Christ's death the creature is freed from enslavement to false powers, to sin and to death. These no longer have any legal hold upon it (Thesis 26). Now before the creature there is nothing but resurrection and eternal life. Through the law both the ontological depths of the human condition and the creature's eternal destiny have been diametrically reversed (Thesis 24). Now the law of death has become to it the law of life.

From the far side of its justification the creature sees that it could never have satisfied the law to save itself. It could never have saved itself from the righteous application of the law. But the forensic work of God in the cross of Jesus Christ has done so for it, on its behalf. Christ's work has been to it entirely a work of grace.

In the power of the indwelling Spirit the creature now enters into a process of sanctification stretching over its remaining earthly life. It takes up its own cross, dying increasingly to itself, actually receiving the faithful life of Christ in exchange. More and more it is clothed in his humanity, conformed to him, to be participant in him, sharing in his glory. Thence it is made not God but fully human. "For through faith Christ is in us, indeed, one with us" (Thesis 26), Luther says.

In summary, for Luther the *how* of atonement is effected solely by Jesus Christ who was crucified. Salvation is a consequence of *his* good work on the cross, *his* willing obedience unto death, *his* justifying of the penalty of the law. This means that good works, the will, and the law, cannot and need not be used by the creature to condition its salvation. It is the cross itself that proclaims this logic.

Ethics

As is often acknowledged, Luther is the consummate pastor. As such he has practical as well as dogmatic ends in view. This is crucially so in the Heidelberg Disputation, which is orientated throughout towards the concrete provision of hope. At its conclusion Luther insists that on the far side of justification the creature is equipped to take up its cross, live sacrificially for others, and perform genuinely good works, *viz.* God's works, not its own. Here Luther's allusion is to the thirteenth century doctrine of *ex opere operato*. The latter teaches that the efficacy of a sacrament derives from the grace of Christ infused in its elements; such efficacy does not derive from innate qualities within the minister or recipient. Likewise in the performance of good works the justified creature has no positive ethical capacity of its own, but consequent on its justification by the grace of God *Christ's* ethical capacity, *his* obedience to the divine commandments, may now be expressed in and through itself (Theses 26 and 27).

Conclusion

By the end of the Heidelberg Disputation there is a note of exaltation in Luther. God has not sought out an attractive but an *unattractive* (sinful) people for his possession. This unattractive people has been formally and actually identified with Christ's death and resurrection and exaltation, to be made *attractive* solely because of him. Thence Luther exalts, "[Sinners] are attractive because they are loved; they are not loved because they are attractive" (proof Thesis 28.) It is the cross itself which proclaims this truth. Luther's case rests.

PART TWO

Karl Barth's Modern Theology of the Cross

5

From Luther to Barth

Perhaps one way to appreciate the powerful impact on Barth of the primacy Luther assigned to God's Word would be to say that it led Barth, almost alone among modern theologians, to grant uncompromising precedence to the Reformation over modernity itself.

—George Hunsinger[1]

It would seem that there is no legitimate way to remain within the crucicentric tradition and yet retrieve the anthropocentric theology Luther's *theologia crucis* so comprehensively confounded. But in the decades and centuries following Luther an attempt is made by some of his successors to do exactly this. The free and gracious benefits of Christ are proclaimed, but the costly requirement of the cross is ever more neglected in favor of a legalism on one hand, and a shallow triumphalism on the other. The Word of the cross itself loses its eschatological, prophetic and intrinsically ontological character.

Twentieth century Danish theologian Regin Prenter further explains, "[Post-Reformation] Lutheran theology quickly accustomed itself to separating Luther's theology of the cross from his theology of the word and began to preach the word about the cross in such a way that it no longer had anything to do with . . . the actual crucifying of the old Adam . . . The word about the cross became 'an objective doctrine,' it lost its character as a word which not only teaches something about the

---

1. Hunsinger, "What Barth Learned from Martin Luther," 137.

cross, but which actually works as the cross in connection with the cross in our own lives."[2]

It is not that there are no significant crucicentric theologians in the decades and centuries following Luther; clearly there are, even if they sometimes look back to the general ethos of the crucicentric tradition rather than to Luther himself. Closer to Luther's own age are figures such as the English Puritan John Owen (1616–1683) and the French Roman Catholic Blaise Pascal (1623–1662). Later on significant crucicentric theologians include the Scots divine John McLeod Campbell (1800–1882), or another Scot, Congregationalist Peter Taylor Forsyth (1848–1921). In the circumstances of time and place each conveys the negative and positive Word from the cross, opposing human self-glorification and proclaiming passage through the cross as the sole way in which true knowledge of God and true human glorification might be obtained.[3] Only the very briefest details of the crucicentric approaches of these major figures can be given here.

John Owen (1616–1683). Negatively Owen emphasizes that humans do not take the initiative in equipping themselves with the means of salvation. *Positively* he emphasizes (contra the Armenians) that in the cross of Jesus Christ a loving God not only provides the possibility of salvation, but actually brings salvation about. In a subtle defense but also amelioration of the Calvinistic doctrine of limited atonement, Owen

---

2. Prenter, *Luther's Theology of the Cross*, 6.

3. The question as to the crucicentric status of *other* Reformation figures receives little attention in the Luther literature. In the present view Calvin, for example, shares important commonalities with the thin tradition, including a high view of the distinction between God and the creature, and the supremacy of the christological starting point epistemologically and soteriologically. But his doctrines of: predestination, divine impassibility, penal substitution and its corollary in the Father's punishment of the Son, limited atonement, the perseverance of the saints, and his failure to balance an emphasis on the transcendent sovereignty of God with an equal emphasis on divine humanity, would seem to put him outside the ethos of crucicentric thought. The question of his personal affect (or emotional tone) also suggests the sharply ascetic Calvin's location beyond the thin tradition. By temperament the theologian of the cross is marked by an essential cheerfulness, the cross being synonymous with robust hope, whereas, as Barth says, over Calvin's vitality there rests a deep shadow. Barth adds darkly, "We cannot really learn to know the details of the Genevan system [of morality accompanying Calvin's theory, and] that is so much admired, without words like 'tyranny' and 'Pharisaism' coming almost naturally to our lips. No one who has proper information would really have liked to live in this holy city." (Barth, *Calvin*, 22.) Affectively then Calvin does not present as a theologian of the cross.

holds that all for whom Christ died receive the benefits of his atoning work, being equipped by the Holy Spirit with the means to do so: faith, holiness, and grace. Owen thereby stresses salvation as a work of divine prerogative and initiative. In so doing in a quintessentially crucicentric way he leaves open the possibility of something very close to universal election.[4]

Blaise Pascal (1623–1662). At the dawn of modernity Pascal stands *negatively* against all anthropocentric religion, with its epistemological roots in a natural knowledge of God. In its finitude human agency, no matter how reasonable, logically cannot capture the infinite knowledge of God. Pascal holds *positively* that if reason is insufficient an instrument for such knowledge, Christ is all-sufficient, epistemologically and soteriologically, for those inspired to accept him. Spirit empowered conformation of the believer to the suffering Christ comprises the one path to authentic knowledge of God in Godself, and to exalted Christian existence.

John McLeod Campbell (1800–1872). *Negatively* McLeod Campbell repudiates the human attempt to usurp the glory of God. Shortly into his important work, *The Nature of the Atonement*, (1856), he supports Luther's rejection of the creaturely attempt to "climb into heaven," Luther himself having got this from the *Theologia Germanica*. The creature cannot save itself, it cannot make itself as God. Thus McLeod Campbell writes, "[Christ] came down, was born, was conversant among men, suffered, was crucified, and died, that by all means he might set forth Himself plainly before our eyes, and fasten the eyes of our hearts upon Himself; that thereby He might keep us from climbing up into heaven, and from the curious searching of the divine majesty."[5] *Positively* McLeod Campbell presents a gospel of divine love and graciousness in Christ, worked out soteriologically in Christ's incarnation, but above all in his expiatory atonement on behalf of all humans.

Peter Taylor Forsyth (1848–1921). Scots Congregationalist Peter Taylor Forsyth is arguably the first major crucicentric theologian of the twentieth century. He is often compared to Barth, sometimes being known as "a Barthian before Barth." Although he did not come to international prominence until the re-publication of his works in the 1950s, Forsyth is immensely important for modern English evangelical

---

4. See Spence, "John Owen," 412–13.
5. McLeod Campbell, *Atonement*, 37.

theology. He stands *negatively* against contemporary anthropocentric theologies, whether Liberal Protestant or Roman Catholic, eschewing individual or churchly attempts either to derive the knowledge of God speculatively, or to condition salvation. Cruciform grace may not be cheapened and manipulated. Even if meant to prove and commend Christianity to the modern age, human reason and the historical-critical methodologies allied to it reveal not the truth of God in Jesus Christ, but rather the power of their own presumption. *Positively* Forsyth emphasizes the high priesthood of Jesus Christ in the cross. As Sykes explains him, he holds that in the cross of Jesus Christ "God has *done* something for humanity, not merely demonstrated, shown, or said something . . . What has been effected is a change of God's practical relation to humanity, carried out by God himself."[6]

Not discounting the contribution made by the above figures, nevertheless after Luther the thin tradition, having flowered briefly with his recovery of the idea that the cross proclaims a self-disclosing and a saving Word, proceeds on a downward cline towards near invisibility.

Into emergent modernity the ancient human desire to live independently of divine claim becomes increasingly justified by the western European relocation of humankind to the centre of existence. This occurs as figures such as Descartes (1596–1650), Hume (1711–1776), and Kant (1724–1804), seek to establish the upper limits of reality on the basis of reason and experience rather than divine revelation. English poet Alexander Pope (1688–1744) expresses the enlightened mood in his *An Essay on Man* (1733), "Know then thyself, presume not God to scan, the proper study of mankind is man." By the close of the eighteenth century general knowledge is being grounded anthropocentricly. Notions of the individual and of individual freedom of conscience are to the fore. In tandem with these developments dualistic distinctions arise between the public and the private, and the objective and the subjective, privileging the former and relegating the latter. In consequence there is an increasing marginalization of Christian faith discovered, after all, to belong to the individual, the private, and the subjective.

Yet a further theological consequence of the European Enlightenment(s) concerns biblical and ecclesiastical authority. As Christian faith becomes marginalized the actuality of an authoritative and cruciform Word speaking through the written and spoken proc-

---

6. Sykes, "Theology through History," 233. Italics original.

lamations of the Bible and the church becomes ever more doubtful. How then is Christian authority to be secured? It falls finally to German Friedrich Schleiermacher (1768–1834), and to the nineteenth century Liberal Protestant theologians following him, to defend "the Christian religion" against its perceived imminent collapse. They proceed by accommodating the faith to exactly the enlightened outlook which threatens it. Godsey explains, "In reaction to [secularizing] developments, German liberal theology, from Schleiermacher to the Ritschlian school, accepted the anthropocentric starting point and developed a theology that located God within the realm of human religion. This accommodation of Christian belief to modernity ended in what has become known as culture-Protestantism [*Kulturprotestantismus*] . . . Liberal theology made religion—or, better, the religious person—the centre of its attention, for it assumed that here was located God's presence in humans as an original datum."[7]

The major tenets of Liberal Protestantism can be summarized as follows. Having a perfect consciousness of God, imaging both the fatherhood of God and brotherhood of man, Jesus of Nazareth is the most spiritually and morally advanced human ever to have lived. He is not just a religious genius, but hero, leader, poet, and thinker. Thus he constitutes the quintessential prototype of modern self-absolutized human being, as he promises universal moral and spiritual perfection. On the pattern of Jesus human progress is inevitable, not just materially but morally. Assured of their divine calling to become glorious as God, assured too of the approving fatherhood of God, the children of God are evolving naturally to become more loving, just, and peaceful. In conjunction with the natural processes of human evolution each person can decide to actualize his or her higher religious nature, thereby achieving a more perfect consciousness of God. The kingdom of God will be built on earth by such perfected beings. In these notions Liberal Protestantism finds a manifesto for a new and modern religion in a new and modern age.

From the crucicentric perspective the gains accruing to this religious adaptation are illustrated by the nineteenth century development of important historico-critical methodologies for exegeting the biblical text, and their employment alongside a range of developing social and

---

7. Godsey, "Barth and Bonhoeffer," 18–20. Note that culture-Protestantism and Liberal Protestantism are terms for the same movement. The English speaking world tends to use the latter.

natural scientific disciplines in the search for the historical Jesus.[8] These also contribute to what for Liberal Protestantism's address to modernity is a crucial, and of itself valuable, message. As a properly scientific faith Christianity merits intellectual respectability.

But there are also losses. The modern realignment of Christian faith leads to two major outcomes. First, the gospel is submitted to the reigning intellectual paradigm thereby reversing Luther's method in which the reigning intellectual paradigm is submitted to the gospel. Second, the resulting syncretistic religion in its key particulars resembles an older, anthropocentric and self-deifying system predicated on godlike human perfection, spiritually, morally, materially. What the nineteenth century Liberal Protestants lose in this is the notion of a divine starting point for the knowledge of God, and the crucicentric reality that humankind is not the arbiter of its own destiny.

The inevitable reaction to Christianity's modern metamorphosis and the confidence that inspires it begins in a familiar way. War! In the European cataclysm of 1914–1918 the Christian nations of the world tear out each other's hearts. By the conflict's end the enlightened culture of the preceding two centuries, along with its confident religion, lies in fearful question. There is no "brotherhood of man," rather the new and modern race has revealed itself enslaved to old and primitive instinct. Far from evolving naturally to become more loving, just, peaceful, humankind has clearly regressed to embody diametrically different qualities. Scientific progress has brought not human advancement but terrible weapons. In their wake the economies of Europe stagger, none more so than Liberal Protestantism's German homeland laden down with reparations. In such an environment it becomes evident that humankind lacks the ability to actualize its mooted "higher religious consciousness." In any case God-consciousness appears to advance no one spiritually. The divine kingdom cannot presently be built on earth. Its cruciform standard is the mark of fresh dug graves. The Europeans lose their assurance of salvation, for there appears no salvation. If they are

---

8. By "the historical Jesus" Liberal Protestantism means the actual human figure of Jesus of Nazareth shorn of an improbable post-Easter, and positioned heroically before modern culture. Johannes Weiss (1863–1914) and Albert Schweitzer (1875–1965) argue convincingly that the "search" for this mythical figure merely reinvents Jesus of Nazareth in the image of the historians and theologians who seek him. See Mattes, "Gerhard Forde," 376–77.

children of God, God is at best capricious and perverse. The sense of God's approving fatherhood dissipates. A new truth prevails.

Karl Barth: A Modern Theologian

Into this disillusioned mindset explodes a new and positive way of seeing, a new and positive theologian. Separated from Luther by just over four centuries and the child of a very different age, nevertheless like Luther, Karl Barth is again to shatter the reigning theological paradigm. In 1922 the second edition of his *Der Römerbrief* falls "like a bomb in the playground of the theologians," as Roman Catholic theologian Karl Adam famously observes.[9] Indeed from the perspective of another century again, the re-formation of Christian faith Karl Barth engenders has yet to settle.

But to go back before *Romans* a little, in 1914 Barth despairs at the inability of the cultured European nations to avoid war. As Busch in his definitive biographical account of him reports, Barth's despair is exacerbated by the embrace of the Kaiser's war policies by virtually all his old teachers. In turn this leads him to question profoundly the Liberal Protestantism he has absorbed from them.[10] Over the next several years Barth turns instead to "the strange new world within the Bible."[11] Here he receives a radically new vision of God and the creature, *viz.*, human beings cannot bypass or overcome the man-God Jesus Christ, but Jesus Christ confronts, condemns and overcomes them. This occurs most immediately and most shockingly in the cross, being God's final "No!" to modern pride, arrogance, and the self-empowered pursuit of glory.

From this biblical, christocentric and crucicentric perspective Barth commences what is to be a lifelong engagement with the whole stretch of western intellectual tradition, and the various Christian theological intersections with that. But he remains above all in conversation with the modern intellectual programme, and the modern theological accommodation to it—especially the modest, reasonable theology of

---

9. Original comment in the June 1926 issue of the Roman Catholic monthly *Hochland*. See McKim, *How Barth Changed My Mind*, ix n.1, and Green, *Barth*, 16.

10. See Busch, *Karl Barth, His Life from Letters and Autobiographical Texts*, 81.

11. This is the title of an early Barth essay collected in *The Word of God and the Word of Man*, 28–50.

his old teachers.¹² This implies three questions. Accepting that over the course of his project there are various twists and turns of emphasis, what is Barth's attitude to modernity itself? What, in more detail, is his attitude to the nineteenth century theological reaction to modernity? Can Barth himself be judged a modern theologian, and if so in what sense?

What is Barth's attitude to modernity?

In commencing an answer two significant observations by Webster are noted. He says, "[It] is too easy to reduce the complexities by making [Barth] appear either merely dismissive and reactionary or a kind of mirror-image of modernity who never shook himself free of its grip."¹³ And, "Barth was referring to much more than his age when he wrote at the end of his life, 'I am a child of the nineteenth century.'"¹⁴

It is certainly true that Barth's relationship with modernity is complicated. The "child of the nineteenth century" attacks the Renaissance discovery that "man is the measure of all things including Christian things,"¹⁵ citing Descartes as the father of the theological crisis this provokes. Descartes' reasonable God is "dependent upon the self-conscious human I that conceives of him, thus making God a part of that I,"¹⁶ and the human I gloriously part of God. Such a deity lies hopelessly within.¹⁷ In fact it is impossible, Barth thinks, to deduce the real God starting with the "I" who knows. The real God cannot be proved or otherwise thought out; God is not a subjective human construct!

But Barth's protest is not only against the modern anthropocentric starting point for the knowledge of God as God really is. It is equally against its corollary, a subjectivism and an individualism isolating human beings from God and from each other. Under this scheme each

---

12. Later in his life Barth is to comment ironically that the Liberal Protestants encourage the very end they wish to avoid. Where the gospel assimilates to the age rather than confronts it, it has nothing new to say and becomes irrelevant. See Barth, "Evangelical Theology in the Nineteenth Century," 27.

13. Webster, *Barth*, 15. Note that along with T. F. Torrance, British Anglican John Webster, Professor of Systematic Theology at the University of Aberdeen since 2003, is instrumental in bringing Barth before the English speaking world.

14. Ibid. Webster's reference is to Barth, *Late Friendship*, 3.

15. Barth, "Evangelical Theology in the Nineteenth Century," 26.

16. See Busch, *Great Passion*, 26.

17. See Barth, *Church Dogmatics* III/1, 360.

person is lord of his or her own way, granting new form to the old theology of glory. Barth returns to this theme in many places, for example in his assessment of the eighteenth century. "[Eighteenth century] man recognizes himself as an *in-dividuum*, as undivided and indivisible, that means that he recognizes himself as a being who is at least similar, at least related to the ultimate reality of God. He finds himself, or he finds in himself . . . something eternal, almighty, wise, good, glorious . . . Individualization means the enthronement . . . of the man experiencing himself here and now as the secret, yet for himself supremely real king."[18]

Overall Barth sees that in the eighteenth century the external becomes internal, the once objective God merely a subjective property or quality of the creature, especially the modern individual creature. Commensurably "man projects what is within himself externally,"[19] that is, the creature equates itself with God. In both directions therefore the eighteenth century presumes equality between the creature and its God, this being but a short step from presuming the creature to *be* God. Either way for Barth God's glory is usurped and God controlled. Thus he writes, "Individualization means appropriation of the object [God] to be the purpose of his domination."[20]

What is Barth's attitude to nineteenth century theology?

As already described, the modern "domination of God" only gains further momentum in the nineteenth century, attracting the contemporary attention of Schleiermacher and the Liberal Protestants. In turn Barth reserves his sternest criticism not for the modern intellectual programme, but for the nineteenth century modern theological reaction to it. His attitude, in answer to the second question being asked here, is one of deep suspicion.

Barth's re-examination of Liberal Protestantism proves it to be "in sharp conflict both with the biblical message and with the real world," to quote Torrance's summation.[21] Consequent on their anthropocentric sympathies Liberal theologians disastrously miss the opportunity

18. Barth, *Protestant Theology in the Nineteenth Century*, 99.
19. See ibid.
20. Ibid.
21. Torrance, *Karl Barth*, 182.

to declare a proper starting point from below, a faithful theology beginning with the human grasped by God. Instead, Barth says, Liberal Protestantism's "starting point from below [becomes] a theology of self understanding [, it cannot] break through the general trend of the century."[22]

Moreover Liberal Protestantism's attempt to convert Jesus Christ to a figure of purely *human* moral authority, to make of him an imitable example of absolutized humankind, leads inevitably to the practical loss of God. It impoverishes the human heart while opening it to an inordinate self-confidence. In 1922 Barth finds this loss and its consequences to be signally responsible for the modern deification of nationhood. It has led to the terrible war just gone, and the terrible judgement still prevailing. In essence the ethical problem for the modern creature is its idolatrous intent on itself, its own way, its own lordship. Barth calls this "a sickness unto *death*."[23] This is not a position from which he is to depart. In 1959, after a second cataclysmic war, his earlier opinion of the disastrous legacy of nineteenth century theology is only reconfirmed. The preceding century's optimism has proved no foil at all to the adventures of his own day. Thus he concludes, "[The] sphere of our time and history is not then the theatre of a decrease of darkness as we might suppose, . . . but rather of its intensification and increase."[24]

From the start to the end of his project therefore, exercising a rare literary gift for theological expression, Barth sheets home his attack on Liberal Protestantism's concession to modernity, in its stead offering an older orthodoxy and a crucified God. His ground breaking Romans commentary sets the tone.

> Jesus stands among sinners as sinner; He sets himself wholly under the judgement under which the world is set; he takes his place where God can be present only in questioning about him; he takes the form of a slave; he moves to the cross and to death; his greatest achievement is a negative achievement. He is not [contra Liberal Protestantism] a genius, endowed with manifest or even with occult powers; he is not a hero or leader of men; he is neither poet nor thinker:—*My God, my God, why hast thou forsaken me?* Nevertheless, precisely in this negation . . . he is

---

22. Barth, "Evangelical Theology in the Nineteenth Century," 25.
23. Barth, "Ethics Today," 170. Italics original.
24. Barth, *Church Dogmatics* IV/3, 392.

recognized as the Christ; for this reason God hath exalted him; and consequently he is the light of the Last Things by which all men and all things are illuminated. In him we behold the faithfulness of God in the depths of hell. The Messiah is the end of mankind, and here also God is found faithful. On the day when mankind is dissolved the new era of the righteousness of God will be inaugurated.[25]

Thus Barth's real God, smashing into the far country of creation history, revealing himself concretely in Jesus Christ, fully human, fully divine, condemned on human behalf, crucified and really risen. Here the world's Messiah, righteous and rightly judging, glorious in his negative achievement, most visible where most hidden in humiliation and a cross. *This* God cannot be of human making, and neither may the creature use him as a guise for worshipping itself.

In the same year as *Romans*, 1922, Barth mounts a similar argument:

> Jesus Christ is not the crowning keystone in the arch of *our* thinking. Jesus Christ is *not* a supernatural miracle that we may or may not consider true. Jesus Christ is *not* the goal which we hope to reach after conversion, at the end of the history of our heart and conscience. Jesus Christ is not a figure of our history to which we may 'relate' ourselves. And Jesus Christ is *least of all* an object of religious and mystical experience. So far as he is this to us he is not Jesus Christ.[26]

Jesus Christ is not less than the objective God for Barth. He is rather the Christ of God—fully divine, fully human, his mediatory ontology tested and proved. Neither is he a "moral exemplar," but rather a sinner among sinners. (The mood after the 1914–18 war was correct at least in rejecting the possibility of human perfection.) His death is not heroic, but death for the sinfulness of all human beings—vicarious, formally substitutionary, expiatory, and mediatory. Far from being the noble hero of Romantic imagination, Jesus is the degraded slave of human opprobrium, deserted even by God. As *this* man he calls modern individuals not to be gods unto themselves but to cruciform death, not to die metaphorically in imitation of his moral example, but to really die so as to receive his life. He is the actual end and the new beginning of

---

25. Barth, *Romans*, 97. Italics original.
26. Barth, "Ethics Today." Italics original.

humankind, the one Word of God in death and in life, the Subject and Object of theology, he—and he alone.[27]

A truly modern theology must start with *this* Jesus. In not doing so nineteenth century theology not only fails to address the questions put to it in its own time, but fails the generations following it who depend on its answers. Moreover in not starting in the one place where truth is to be found it has not adopted a reasonable methodology; it does not therefore comprise the true theology of modernity.

In all this Barth does not reject the modern paradigm out of hand. As Hunsinger says, he simply transcends its religious skepticism "even as modernity's untold contributions [are] also welcomed and preserved."[28] In making a similar point Webster additionally notes that the nineteenth century ethos "sometimes [sets] the terms of the debate"[29] for Barth. Its drastic misrepresentation of Christian faith demands his attention just as it had that of the Liberal Protestants (with their very different answers) before him. And in his own review of it, in 1957, Barth himself recognizes that the challenges the previous century's tendency towards secularization set its theologians, "remain for us too."[30]

Can Barth himself be judged a modern theologian, and if so in what sense?

In short, no less than the theologians in the period just before him, the child of the nineteenth century is tasked with defending and explicating Christian faith in the modern ideological context. He does so in a

---

27. The images of Jesus presented by medieval theology and by modern theology have a certain similarity for Barth. In both ages Jesus is discovered to be a heroic figure demanding imitation, in both ages his cruciform message falls victim to the presumption of human glory, and in both ages the correction needed is the reassertion of the theology of the cross. Thus Barth says, "In contrast to the medieval picture of Jesus, the Christ of Luther is not the pious man but the man who is set in the ranks of sinners under judgment, in the shadow of hell and death, the crucified Christ. Not the crucified Christ of edification, who kindles our admiration as a martyr and hero, whom we are to imitate in his submission to the will of God, whom we can depict and tolerate in his tragic beauty, but the nonedifying crucified Christ of Grünewald [proclaiming] the strange work of God . . . [In him] a hole is made in the Gothic vault, and God's heaven is seen high above. He who sees me sees the Father [John 14:9]." Barth, *Calvin*, 61.

28. Hunsinger, "What Barth Learned from Martin Luther," 137–38.

29. See Webster, *Barth*, 15.

30. Barth, "Evangelical Theology in the Nineteenth Century," 12.

characteristically modern way, without apology[31] emphasizing reason, humanity, and the importance of the individual. That is, Barth is attracted by the integral logic of divine epistemology, and he reflects this by insisting on a rational methodology for theology.[32] Soteriologically he explores the humanity of God—something he is freer to pursue in his mature theology but which informs all his thinking. Beside these emphases Barth is deeply concerned with the humanity of the creature and therefore with human history, with true human existence as personhood in relation, with what it is to be an individual before God, and with the nature of true human freedom. These are all familiar modern themes, albeit handled rather differently from the way chosen by the nineteenth century theologians. Over against their distinctive response to the age lifting up the creature, Barth might fairly be said to present a peculiarly modern and modest theology of his own.

Nonetheless objections to designating Barth a modern theologian have arisen during his lifetime and beyond on the liberal *right*, the centre, and the evangelical[33] *left* of the theological spectrum.

The charge from the (actually conservative) descendants of the nineteenth century Liberals that Barth is not modern but reactionary is well known, and in the present view already well dismissed. Jenson says tellingly here, "Nothing could be more precisely mistaken than many English and American writers' assumption that Barth was a theological reactionary, who tried to save the faith from the acids of modernity by retreating to premodern habits of thought."[34]

The question from the middle ground admits Barth's modern location, but challenges its integrity. Godsey and others accuse him of shying

---

31. Barth regards apologetics as the Christian attempt to prove the veracity of Christian belief by beginning with a neutral starting point rather than with the crucified Christ. Thompson adds here, "Barth believes in the possibility and necessity of dialogue between the Church and the world [on the basis of Christ's cruciform reconciliation with the world, but neither] natural theology nor apologetics can help or lead men to faith; it is truth alone that wins converts." Thompson, *Christ in Perspective*, 190–91, n.126.

32. Barth admits the reasonable instruments of other disciplines—including philosophy—might be of assistance to theology, provided they are denied determinative authority.

33. For the term "evangelical" see here p. 10, n. 29.

34. Jenson, "Karl Barth," 22.

away from the life-questions posed Christian faith by the modern world, or of otherwise relativising these as "theologically uninteresting."[35]

In fact, and to extend what has been said above, as a modern theologian Barth meets the modern world head-on, albeit from a different and higher angle than some of his contemporaries—for instance Bonhoeffer to whom Godsey negatively compares him in this regard.[36] Barth's political, moral and ethical writings realistically engage with the concrete circumstances of the contemporary world. Witness for example his profound reflections on industrialization, the devastation of war, class relations, the Nazi state and with it the plight of the Jews, the relations of church and state, or his later observations on the cold war, to say nothing of his personal involvements here.[37] In these writings he locates the roots of the anxieties of the modern world in its defining malaise, its preoccupation with self: self-actualization, self-realized autonomy, self-lordship and its corollary—self-enfranchised independence from God. The modern world has sought to determine itself as if Jesus Christ had never been, and therefore unreasonably departs from the one real solution before it.

From the opposite direction to the reactionary charge has come the more insightful question as to whether, modernity's influence on him notwithstanding, Barth is better judged a *post* modern theologian. In 1976 Hall, writing of the early reaction to Barth's dismissal of Liberal Protestantism, makes exactly this observation. "There was a suspicion on the part of many in the Anglo-Saxon world that Barth's whole theo-

---

35. Godsey writes, "Barth—in his theology but not his personal life—shied away from the experientially orientated questions of the modern world that had engaged liberal theology, . . . this-worldly questions of human formation and community and participation in the sufferings of God in ordinary secular life." Godsey, "Barth and Bonhoeffer," 24–25.

36. In laudatory distinction to Barth, Godsey finds in Bonhoeffer a crucicentric approach starting from below. Bonhoeffer begins with an aged world, a persecuted church, a rejected neighbor, and a crucified Jewish Messiah identifying with and confronting the roots of all worldly suffering. See ibid., 25.

37. Contra Godsey and others, in recent decades significant Barth commentators including Webster, Clough, and Green, have pointed to the presence of a concerted social and moral concern in Barth. For instance in his own introduction to Barth, Green says, "Barth was as much concerned to develop a *social* and *public* theology as a *theocentric* (christocentric and trinitarian!) theology. From first to last his was a communal theology and politics was always intimate in his thinking." Green, *Barth*:18. Italics original.

From Luther to Barth 163

logical program was reactionary: a return to Biblicism, to the Reformers, to pre-modern orthodoxy (neo-orthodoxy). On the other hand, a few more astute commentators thought him post-modern."[38]

In 1989 Jenson starts to agree with the latter group, "Barth's thought is drastically 'modern' . . . Indeed, if there is such a thing as 'post-modernism,' Barth may be its only major representative so far, for his work is a vast attempt to transcend not merely the Enlightenment but also 'modern' Protestantism's defining way of making that attempt."[39] By the time of his 1997 revision of the above text Jenson has consolidated his position. "Barth's theology is determined in its structure and warrants by the Western church's continuing effort to come to terms with the eighteenth-century Enlightenment, that is, with modernity's founding event. Indeed, if there is such a thing as 'post-modernism,' Barth is its only major theological representative so far, for his work is an attempt not only to transcend the Enlightenment but to transcend nineteenth-century Protestantism's way of doing the same."[40]

So is Barth better understood as *postmodern*? While he certainly transcends Liberal Protestantism's response to the Enlightenment, the question as to whether he transcends the Enlightenment itself is more difficult to answer. Barth hardly reflects the mood of religious pluralism, denial of absolutes and spiritualized "self-reflexivity"[41] which has come to be associated with postmodernism. To use its idiom, the meaning of the self-disclosing text is concretely determined for him by the authorial Voice of the text; meaning is not forever fluid according to the whims of the reader. Neither does Barth transcend the modern regard for rationality. The logic of the cross, infinitely wiser than any human wisdom, founds and prioritises his procedure, as indeed all facets of his project.

It appears then that Barth does not depart from the modern age, but surmounts it while remaining intellectually rooted in it. Agreeing with Jenson's 1989 assessment therefore, in the present view it would seem that Barth might best be described as "drastically modern." Webster concurs. He constantly reiterates the message that the "work of Barth is central to modern western theology, both historical and constructive."[42]

38. Hall, *Lighten Our Darkness*, 135–36.
39. Jenson, "Karl Barth," 25.
40. Ibid., 22.
41. For a definition of *postmodernism (postmodernity)* see here p. 9.
42. Webster, *Cambridge Companion to Karl Barth*, xi.

If Barth transcends modernity's religious conceits, nevertheless he does not leave modernity itself behind. Rather his relationship with it is always conducted, as elsewhere Webster also notes, "from the inside."[43] In his own summary of Barth's contribution T. F. Torrance reaches a similar conclusion, "Not only does [Barth] recapitulate in himself in the most extraordinary way the developments of all modern theology since the Reformation, but he towers above it all."[44]

As a drastically modern theologian then, what Barth does not do is repeat the theological mistakes, as he sees them, of the theology of the preceding century. He does not fit Christian faith and thought to the prevailing epistemological paradigm; he does not mistake the self-absolutised individual for God. Rather, where the modern intellectual programme and its dependent theology are contrary to the gospel, he confronts them head-on *from within modernity* with the prior dialectic of the cross. That cruciform dialectic, the diastasis between God and the creature, is central to the final matter for discussion now.

In his opening lectures on Luther at Göttingen in the Summer of 1922, the young Barth lays out a crosswise epistemological and soteriological model with which to explore the theology of the Reformation. The model's vertical axis represents the eternity of God, while the horizontal axis represents the temporal realm—human finitude, sin, and death. As these lines intersect, as eternity connects with time, momentous consequences ensue. Negatively, the human attempt to know and be as God is denied. Positively, ignorance of God and death itself are vanquished, true knowledge of God along with life in God are received, and obedience to the command of God in response to the grace of God commences. In Barth's view this crosswise model does not merely depict reality, it is itself profoundly real. "The intersecting of the human horizontal line with the divine vertical line is a fact,"[45] he says, it is not a human construct but given.

The model itself is inspired by Luther's juxtaposition of the theologies of the cross and self-glorification in the theses of his Heidelberg Disputation. Barth's attendant explanation of that disputation, and including implicit acknowledgement of his crucicentric debt to Luther, bears quoting at length:

43. Webster, *Barth*, 15.
44. Torrance, *Karl Barth*, 1.
45. Barth, *Calvin*, 61. Italics original.

> What we have in these theses of Luther is truly and literally a theology of the cross. Luther, too, sees a horizontal line before him, our human striving, knowing, willing, and doing. The theology of glory thinks that somewhere on an extension of this line it will reach the goal of infinity, the invisible things of God. Its slogan [after Aquinas] is that grace does not destroy nature but perfects it. Luther does not deny that there is this wisdom, this beatific vision, much, much further along that line.[46] His objection is that one thing is overlooked, namely, that at the centre, where each of us stands, ... there is a break that throws everything into question. To say human is to say sin[!] ... What is radically set in question by this break in the middle of the line is not simply our banal everyday willing and doing, but just as much what we regard as our love of God, [our vaulted capacity to lift ourselves to see God directly, face to face. For rather what we see are] folly, death and hell. These fearful visible things of God, his strange work, the crucified Christ—these are the theme of true theology ... [For the] gap in the horizontal line, this disaster of our own striving, is the point where God's vertical line intersects our lives, where God wills to be gracious. Here where our finitude is recognized is true contact with infinity.[47]

Here at the intersection of the two lines the *Deus absconditus* is revealed in Christ, and not via speculation. Here sanctification is a consequence of forgiveness of sins, and not its cause. Here the church is the community of those graciously elected by God, and not itself the fount of electing grace. Here too the vertical way from God to the creature cuts incisively into "the horizontal path, of reason and good works,"[48] of human knowing and doing in the quest for glory, opening the way of faith.

The pedagogical point is obvious. "We see now why [Luther's *theologia crucis*] was so basically polemical and militant,"[49] Barth lectures. Luther's is a revolutionary theology. He demands that at all times "we halt at the sharply severed edges of the broken horizontal line,"[50] and in fear, humility, and naked trust, renounce the way of reason and good works. It is then Luther "who thought out first ... the basic anti-medieval

---

46. Barth has in mind the eschatological future of those in Christ.
47. Ibid., 45–46.
48. Ibid., 89.
49. Ibid., 47.
50. Ibid., 46.

and . . . basic anti-modern thought of the Reformation, that of the theology of the cross."[51] His crucicentric theology provides a "characteristic opening up of the way, the first turn of the Reformation."[52] But Barth is doing more here than simply expounding Luther's *theologia crucis* to his students; he is also revealing his sympathy with Luther's crucicentric approach, and projecting the dominant influence of that approach down the decades of his own thought.

There is a second Reformational turn. If Luther lives on the vertical line to the detriment of an alertness to the horizontal,[53] a little later Calvin lives on the horizontal line to the detriment of an alertness to the vertical.[54] If in his *theologia crucis* Luther brings the vertical and the horizontal lines of reality together negatively, Calvin is to do so positively. If Luther is orientated to the crucified Christ and "the forgotten cross at the beginning of our human way"[55]—the forgotten need for the creature to die to its presumption to glory; Calvin is orientated to the glorious God and the creature's regeneration in him.

For Barth these distinctions mean that neither Reformer properly balances the intersection of the horizontal and the vertical, the negative and the positive words of the cross. In time that joint failure will permit a resurgent theology of glory to skew the legacy of the Reformation for its own ends. In consequence and despite its distance from scholasticism, *modern* theology leaps at the same anthropocentric starting point for God. The promise of the Reformation—the lasting exposure of the false *theologia gloriae* and the definitive declaration of the true, is still to be fulfilled.

Given all of this, Barth perceives the need for yet a further turn in the history of theological reform. In the glorious religion of the meta-

---

51. See ibid., 70.

52. Ibid., 89.

53. Luther, Barth says, still maintained "a vestige of the otherworldliness of monasticism" so that he makes the step from faith to a concrete prescription for life before God hesitantly. See ibid.

54. Notwithstanding his awareness of the utter sovereignty of God, or perhaps because of it, Calvin stands firmly on the ground. He is deeply concerned with the nature of creaturely existence before God. Barth finds that in him "the absoluteness of faith was translated into the relativity of . . . new obedience." This time "the intersection of the two lines was made [from below, and] the theology of the cross had taken on its second sense." See ibid. 88.

55. Ibid. 47.

physicians there lurks "something primal, wild, undomesticated, and demonic," he says.[56] If given the modern rise of that alien word "the Creator Spirit brings on the stage *another* theology of the cross,"[57] negatively that further word will again have to rouse the anger of the alien word, rouse it and silence it sharply. But it will also want to identify the positive intersection of the vertical and horizontal lines of reality: to witness to the solely glorious God who summons the creature, and to indicate the creature who as such is summoned by this God. Barth's meaning is clear. The task he senses before him is nothing less than to complete the waiting Reformation promise in his own time. He must proclaim a re-formed theology of the cross, one that is radically placed to the age, that ultimately is fundamentally positive, and that therefore is rightly set between its axes.

Does he do so? The shape and content of Barth's drastically modern project will now be considered in the light of the crucicentric hermeneutic proposed in the first part of this study. Once again the discussion will begin with a question, followed by a review of the relevant secondary literature.

---

56. Ibid., 48.
57. Ibid. Italics mine.

6

Recent Conceptions of the Theology of the Cross in Karl Barth: Reviewing the Secondary Literature

Barth's is, therefore, very definitely and distinctively a *theologia crucis*.

—John Thompson[1]

In the end, Barth's theology tends towards a *theologia gloriae*.

—John Godsey[2]

The Database and its Positions

To answer the question as to how the secondary literature views Barth's interaction with crucicentric theology, a database has been prepared comprising relevant materials from the middle of the twentieth century up into the first decade of the twenty-first century. The mid-1950s do not constitute the earliest period of controversy bearing on Barth's crucicentric development,[3] but they do mark a period when the shape and

---

1. Thompson, *Christ in Perspective*, 157 n.6.

2. Godsey, "Barth and Bonhoeffer," 26.

3. Early assessments of Barth's development include that of Dietrich Bonhoeffer, who from his prison cell accuses Barth of engaging in a "positivism of revelation." Behind this Bonhoeffer perceives a tendency in Barth to triumphalism and an associated avoidance of negative human realities—suffering, death, evil, sin and so on. Later theologians, such as Hall (1976), read back into Bonhoeffer at this point the added criticism that, having begun with a theology of the cross, Barth then departs from it. See Bonhoeffer, *Letters and Papers from Prison*, 280, 286. See also Hall, *Lighten Our Darkness*,139, 240 n.65.

content of his project is being generally assessed,⁴ including by Barth himself.⁵ Therefore they provide a convenient place from which to start.

Materials selected for examination include some thirty one journal articles focusing on the theology of the cross but also somewhere mentioning Barth, six articles primarily concerned with Barth but also somewhere touching on the theology of the cross, and nine introductory texts to Barth. The texts either refer to the theology of the cross directly, or more often present Barth's treatment of traditional crucicentric themes without acknowledging these as such. All these materials appear in English originally or in English translation. In addition two related German language works referring to the influence of Luther's *theologia crucis* on Barth have been consulted.

The above database was unable to include books or articles dedicated solely to exploring Barth's project as a theology of the cross in line with earlier crucicentric tradition. These do not appear to exist. This absence seems strange given the late twentieth century renaissance of interest in crucicentric theology, classical and modern, and the otherwise voluminous nature of the Barth secondary literature. The discussion's subsidiary proposal suggests a possible reason here. That is, that there has likely been a failure properly to comprehend the true shape and content of crucicentric theology, so that it is missed in Barth.

As a way into this literature particular attention will be paid to three general Barth introductions, one each by John Thompson (1978),⁶ T. F. Torrance (1990),⁷ and Eberhard Busch (2004).⁸ Obviously other candidates exist but these introductions have been selected because together they cover Barth's context, sources, content, and the structure of his theology, and are indicative of his legacy. Combined they also embrace

---

4. In 1951 Hans Urs von Balthasar proposed that Barth's project can be divided into two methodological phases, the first *dialectical*—up until Barth's 1931 book on Anselm *Fides quaerens intellectum*, the second *analogical*—accounting for Barth's mature theology following the Anselm book. This "Anselm thesis" focused interest on the question of Barth's development, a matter subsequently debated through the 1950s and beyond. See von Balthasar, *Karl Barth*.

5. Refer Barth's retrospective 1956 lecture in which he summarises the shape of his own development. Barth, "The Humanity of God."

6. Thompson, *Christ in Perspective*.

7. Torrance, *Karl Barth—Biblical and Evangelical Theologian*.

8. Busch, *The Great Passion*.

nearly the whole period of scholarship since Barth's death in 1968 until the present, as also English and German speaking perspectives on him. Thompson's deep yet straight forward approach to Barth's mature theology, *viz* "The writer finds himself more in agreement with Barth than his critics and has himself only rarely and briefly entered a critical caveat,"[9] (an approach viewed sympathetically here), loses nothing for the three decades since it first appeared. The late Scots Presbyterian theologian T. F. Torrance needs no concerted introduction. As the leading British student of Barth he demonstrates a profound sense of Barth's place, and of the underlying structure of his thought. The personal insight of Barth's last research assistant, Eberhard Busch, into the man as well as his theology is highly acclaimed, as is his most recent Barth introduction.

In the opening pages of his seminal *Church Dogmatics* Karl Barth writes, "Dogmatics is possible only as a *theologia crucis.*"[10] The implication is that the *theologia crucis* is critical to Barth's project. But is it? In the light of the classical crucicentric tradition does his project actually constitute a theology of the cross? Does Barth himself demonstrate the traditional marks of a crucicentric theologian? What does the selected literature have to say?

Like many of the decisions concerning the nature of the theology of the cross itself, Barth's status as a theologian of the cross is not universally acknowledged. Judgments in the recent literature concerning the presence of a crucicentric perspective in his project are frequently assured yet poorly supported. Generally they appear to have been made without awareness that contrary opinions exist. Moreover they are usually expressed incidentally.

This said, examination of the selected database suggests that since the 1950s three broad positions have emerged on the question: i) Barth's project is a theology of the cross. ii) His project partially qualifies as a theology of the cross. iii) Barth's project is not a theology of the cross at all. With respect to these divisions the position of individual database commentators is as follows:

---

9. Thompson, *Christ in Perspective*, vii.
10. Barth, *Church Dogmatics* I/1, 14.

Position One—Barth's Project is a Theology of the Cross

According to Klappert (1971) Barth's project is fundamentally a *theologia crucis*, at the heart of which stands the forensic work of Jesus Christ. In this proposal Klappert directly influences Thompson (1978). The latter takes a systematic and historical view of the long crucicentric tradition, finding its influence in both Barth's early and mature theology.

Ten years later the debate turns on Barth's conception of divine suffering. Extending rather than contradicting Luther's position[11] Barth stresses that the *deity* of Christ does suffer in the cross, and for Bauckham (1988) and Fiddes (1988) this development reinforces Barth's crucicentric status. Bauckham calls him a crucicentric theologian who has lifted Luther's *theologia crucis* into the modern age. Fiddes likewise credits him with this, and with enabling the late-modern development of crucicentric theology to proceed.

Wells (1992) agrees that Barth is a crucicentric theologian, attributing to him a radical crucicentric epistemology inspired by the Creator Spirit of God, and rooted naturally.[12] Since however Wells' own conception of the theology of the cross is narrowly (as opposed to systematically) conceived, his designation of Barth as a crucicentric theologian is similarly circumscribed.

Two years later Klappert (1994) develops his earlier insight into the central importance of the *theologia crucis* for Barth, this time focusing on the implications of that stance for social equity in a disrupted world.

Schweitzer (1995) agrees with those like Barker (1995), who find Barth not particularly influenced by Luther's *theologia crucis*. But unlike them Schweitzer does not believe that distance from the classical tradition discredits Barth as a crucicentric theologian in his own right. Rather he calls Barth's whole project, both its early and mature theology, a distinctive theology of the cross, indeed one that significantly influences Jürgen Moltmann.

In contrast Hinlicky (1998), as Bauckham and Fiddes exactly ten years before, heralds Barth's rediscovery of Luther's *theologia crucis* as

---

11. As earlier discussed, in his doctrine of *communicatio idiomatum* Luther holds that since the two natures of Christ in the one hypostasis cannot be abstracted from each other, accepting that Christ's deity cannot suffer it must yet be bound up in the suffering of his humanity.

12. Contra Wells such a natural base is quite foreign to Barth. To be further discussed.

not only theologically important, but of huge political and social significance for twentieth century theology forward. Nevertheless, Hinlicky says, Barth leaves it to others to take his seminal rediscovery further.

Hunsinger (1999) joins a strand of this particular discussion. Like Hinlicky he finds Barth's project to be profoundly affected by Luther's *theologia crucis*, and therefore itself a theology of the cross. Since however Hunsinger understands Luther's crucicentric theology as being almost synonymous with a theology of suffering, his estimation of Barth as a theologian of the cross in Luther's train is—as for Wells (1992)—actually narrowly prescribed.

Tomlin (1999) finds Luther's crucicentric theology influences Barth profoundly. Here Tomlin qualifies neither the breadth of Luther's position, nor Barth's use of it.

Wells (2001) again picks up the question of the influence of Luther's *theologia crucis* on Barth's theology. In Wells' analysis Luther develops the *theologia crucis* as an instrument of Reformation and Barth recovers Luther's radical approach, wielding the theology of the cross against the theology of glory of his own time—Liberal Protestantism. Nevertheless unlike Luther, Barth never sufficiently recognizes the political potential of the *theologia crucis*, although in itself this does not deflect his essential crucicentric orientation.

For Richardson (2004) Barth's status as a crucicentric theologian needs no qualification. He holds Barth to be profoundly influenced by the classical crucicentric tradition mediated through Luther. The earlier crucicentric tradition comprises an epistemological instrument declaring the primacy of Jesus Christ, and Barth's recovery of this instrument is critical to his entire theological programme. Nevertheless Richardson's own conception of the crucicentric tradition is somewhat narrow, so that (as with Wells 1992 and Hunsinger 1999) the significance of his estimation of Barth is circumscribed to this extent.

This last observation may also be applied to Vorster (2007). He regards Barth as a theologian of the cross, while he understands the theology of the cross itself as a theology explaining suffering. Vorster's vision of crucicentric theology is not embracing, accordingly the crucicentric status he ascribes to Barth cannot be so.

Position Two—Barth's Project Partially Qualifies as a Theology of the Cross

Bound up with existing questions of Barth's development Berkouwer (1956) finds that the early Barth is influenced by Luther's *theologia crucis*, but in his mature theology moves somewhat away from that. There is in Barth an 'uncrucicentric' element of human glory.

Twenty years later Hall (1976) substantially agrees, but now the mature Barth completely breaks with the earlier crucicentric tradition.

Position Three—Barth's Project is Not a Theology of the Cross

Earlier reference was made to Bauckham (1988) and Fiddes (1988). For them Barth's development of Luther's crucicentric position—in this case concerning the suffering deity of Christ—demonstrates his credentials as a theologian of the cross in Luther's stead. For Godsey (1987) however the fact that Barth develops Luther's crucicentric position—in this case as regards human glory—means that he diverges from it; he cannot be considered a theologian of the cross.

Bayer (1995) effectively doubts Barth's integrity as a crucicentric theologian. Barth's theology may not bypass the cross, but it barely stops at it in its hurry to arrive at the resurrection. The cross is effectively a necessary construct in his thought. Bayer then echoes earlier criticisms by Berkouwer (1956), Hall (1976), and Godsey (1987), that Barth is finally concerned with human participation in the glory of the risen Christ. In their view that is something which can be no part of crucicentric thought.

In 1995 Barker finds that Luther's *theologia crucis* does not influence Barth, thus Barth is not a crucicentric theologian.

The implicit debate just summarized will now be laid out chronologically so that the intertwining of its strands over time can be brought out, so that the positions already described can be further explained, and so that some preliminary response can be made. In the process a number of issues will be touched on that later discussion on Barth's epistemology and soteriology will take further.

The Literature Itself

As part of a general Barth introduction, in 1956 Dutch Reformed theologian G. C. Berkouwer contributes a note on Barth's development as a theologian of the cross. Berkouwer finds that influenced by Luther, no less than other contemporary dialecticians Barth understands the *theologia crucis* chiefly as methodology, a way of thinking and working theologically, and after that as a theology of divine suffering. Berkouwer says, "By putting in the place of the theology of glory the theology of the cross, the dialectical theologians [including Barth] intended not so much to make the cross of Christ the center and content of their theology as to develop a certain method of theological thinking by means of which to approach God's revelation."[13]

Berkouwer then supports contemporary criticism that Barth's methodological approach is inconsistent and cannot be sustained. His particular thesis is that Barth builds his project on two equal but opposite foundations, a theology of the cross—understood by Berkouwer strictly as a theology of divine suffering, and a theology of human glory—albeit participatory glory in Jesus Christ testifying to divine grace. There is for Berkouwer an inbuilt conflict between these foundations.[14] In this Berkouwer explains himself carefully. Barth never completely breaks with his crucicentric foundation, "Such a break with an important aspect of past theological discussion is nowhere discernible in the development of Barth's [mature] thinking."[15] Rather in his later theology Barth tries to marry his earlier crucicentric and glorious foundations, so that the cross no longer signifies divine suffering but triumphant grace. It is Barth's "purpose to show that the triumph of grace is most intimately related to the cross and therefore to the *theologia crucis*."[16] Ultimately, however, this marriage is said by Berkouwer to be unsuccessful, Barth is unable to sustain both foundations. His continuing crucicentric concern becomes subsidiary to his continuing glorious one, divine suffering becomes a step on the way to human glory. Berkouwer therefore concludes that overall, "Barth's theology must *from its inception* be characterized as

---

13. Berkouwer, *Triumph of Grace*, 201–2.

14. Clearly Berkouwer does not see human participation in Christ's glory as any part of the theology of the cross.

15. Berkouwer, *Triumph of Grace*, 19.

16. Ibid.

triumphant theology which aims to testify to the overcoming power of grace."[17] On the basis of Berkouwer then, Barth can be called a theologian of the cross partially only.

One response to Berkouwer is that he is partially right. As later discussion will show Barth *is* influenced by Luther's theology of the cross, although contra Berkouwer neither Luther nor Barth understand it to be identical with a theology of divine suffering. Certainly too there is a note of triumph in Barth's project, but again discussion will show that this strengthens rather than lessens the consistency of his crucicentric perspective. It appears then that Berkouwer fails to estimate the integrity of Barth's crucicentric approach fully because he fails to estimate the nature of crucicentric theology broadly. Such misunderstanding is to arise repeatedly.

In 1971 German systematic and exegetical theologian Bertold Klappert publishes *Auferweckung des Gekreuzigten*.[18] In this work Klappert counters the idea that at the heart of his theology Barth presents "a modern revival of traditional incarnation theology."[19] Rather Barth's "basic thesis"[20] is said to be: *the pivotal importance of the meaning and message from the cross, its theology therefore, for unlocking the meaning of Christ's earthly history*. As such this "basic thesis" comprises an explanatory key with which to unlock all aspects of Barth's project. Herein Klappert's own basic thesis concerning Barth. (In this regard Klappert's proposal is similar to Mannermaa's suggestion that Luther's leading idea sheds a hermeneutical light on his Reformation theology.[21])

Klappert supports his own thesis concertedly, touching on many themes in Barth which, in highlighting the central importance of the theology of the cross for explicating Jesus Christ, recall the classical cru-

---

17. Ibid., 37. Italics original.

18. The full title of this work is *Auferweckung des Gekreuzigten: Der Ansatz der Christologie Karl Barths im Zusammenhang der Christologie der Gegenwart*, [*The Awakening of the Crucified: Karl Barth's Christological Approach in the Context of Contemporary Christology*].

19. Phraseology borrowed from a comment on Klappert in Ware, "The Resurrection of Jesus," 25. Italics mine.

20. See Klappert, *Auferweckung des Gekreuzigten*, 154, referred to by Thompson, *Christ in Perspective*, 52. Klappert's estimation of Barth's basic thesis is further discussed here, pp. 221–22.

21. For an earlier discussion on the Mannermaa school of Luther studies see here p. 30.

cicentric tradition and especially Luther. Such themes include Barth's accent on the antithetical relations existing within the event of the cross: the humiliation of the Son and exaltation of the creature, the presence of the judge and of the judged in the crucified Christ, and the hiddenness of Christ's identity *sub contrario* and his revealedness in the resurrection—particularly its first moment of awakening in the tomb.[22] Other such themes are: the absolute unity of Christ's Person and reconciling work, the recognition of twin natures in Christ from the work of the cross (and not vice versa), consequent advocacy for a theological starting point with what God has actually done in the cross, and allied to this insistence that God is not other than he is in the crucified Christ—Klappert notes that in Barth the *scandalon* of the cross is drawn into the very idea of God.[23]

To instance Klappert, towards the end of his work he concludes that "methodologically Barth . . . places the question of the Subject of the cross at the beginning of his reconciliation theology."[24] It is then the message of the cross which answers that question for Barth, a tenable answer because for him the theology of the cross and the Subject (also Object) of the cross come together in Jesus Christ. Klappert explains:

> [For Barth] Jesus Christ as he exists in history is the Subject who becomes the Object. In the reconciling event of the cross he is the Subject, the Qualitative Other, the Judge—who as such also judges. He is too the Object, the one "just" human being who identifies absolutely with the creature in all its sinful humanity—who as such is also judged. For in the cross Jesus Christ is made sinful and degraded that the creature be made just and raised up. He is then himself the dynamic Message of the cross concerning this exchange, the actual Subject of the *theologia crucis*.[25]

All this means for Klappert that the key provided by Barth's basic thesis is particularly helpful in unlocking his Christology and soteriology in their relation. But it also means that in his view Barth consistently evidences a profound understanding of the theology of the cross, one accounting for crucicentric theology methodologically and ontologi-

22. "The divine action in the passion—hidden *sub contrario*—reveals itself in the pure divine act of the awakening." Klappert, *Auferweckung des Gekreuzigten*, 298, cited by Thompson, *Christ in Perspective*, 90.

23. See Klappert, Auferweckung des Gekreuzigten, 180, referred to by Thompson, *Christ in Perspective*, 58.

24. Klappert, *Auferweckung des* Gekreuzigten, 386. My translation.

25. See ibid., 225. My translation.

cally. This last and positive assessment is to continue to influence Barth scholarship, including Klappert's own.

Two decades after first coming to prominence the question of Barth's theological development continues to be connected to that of his crucicentric fidelity. In 1976 Canadian contextual theologian Douglas John Hall agrees with Berkouwer—and falls into a similar trap. Hall holds that because Barth heralds the glorious triumph of the cross he is unable to sustain a crucicentric perspective. In doing so Hall explains that Barth's *theologia gloriae* is however quite different from the theology of human self-glorification which Luther attacks. "According to the well-known thesis of Berkouwer, Karl Barth was finally unable to sustain his *theologia crucis* . . . [This points] to an evident truth: Barth moved more and more away from the theology of the cross and toward something that must be called a theology of glory, even if it is not identical with the *theologia gloriae* that Luther attacked."[26]

Essentially Hall's argument is that in his celebrated turn towards the humanity of God, and in his announcement of resurrection hope for the creature, Barth necessarily leaves behind a pessimistic emphasis on the "No!" of the cross, and therefore the theology of the cross in its entirety. Hall says in part, "There can be no doubt that it is possible to distinguish between Barth's earlier writings, where the *theologia crucis* is the dominant theme, and his later works, in which the divine Yes is stressed and Barth fears the association of the theology of the cross with pessimism and 'Nordic morbidity.'"[27] Once again the real problem is that Hall is defining the theology of the cross narrowly, in this case restricting it to the atoning work of the crucified Christ.

To offer a preliminary response, later discussion will show that it is simply not the case that Barth identifies the *theologia crucis* exclusively with the atoning work of the cross. Rather, and in line with the classical crucicentric understanding, the *theologia crucis* forms a broad foundation in his thought, one which includes a true *theologia gloriae*. While Hall is correct in identifying the presence of a note of glory in Barth's project, that presence does not distance Barth from the theology of the cross as Hall thinks, but rather consolidates his crucicentric status.

Nor does Barth prioritise the significance of the resurrection over that of the cross. When he writes, "[We] have to do with the Crucified

---

26. Hall, *Lighten Our Darkness*, 139.
27. Ibid.

only as the Resurrected . . . There is no going back behind Easter morning!"²⁸—which Hall adduces in support of his thesis that Barth leaves the cross and thence also *theologia crucis* behind—in the same passage Barth declares that Christ's death and resurrection are an inseparable unity, "[In] all the forms of his life this living One is none other than the One who once was crucified at Golgotha . . . We also do not speak rightly of His resurrection and His being as the Resurrected if we conceal and efface the fact that this living One was crucified and died for us."²⁹ In fact Barth never departs from the centrality of the cross in the life of Jesus Christ, the high significance of the resurrection being that it points back to this cruciform priority.

In both Berkouwer and Hall, however, there is at least an insistence that Barth *starts out* as a theologian of the cross before, in their view, departing from it.

In 1978 Irish Presbyterian theologian John Thompson publishes his doctoral dissertation on the Christology of the *Church Dogmatics*. In this he draws frequently on Klappert's 1971 work *Die Auferweckung des Gekreuzigten*. As Klappert he does not focus on Barth's debt to the classical crucicentric tradition. He does however offer balance to many of the major criticisms of Barth's crucicentric status, including the suggestion that Barth departs from the theology of the cross in his mature theology.

Thompson is one of the few commentators reviewed to understand the theology of the cross as a discrete system of multivalent ideas running down the length of Christian tradition, and to find it present in Barth as such. In his exhaustive analysis of Barth's mature Christology he touches on Barth's adoption—under the influence of Luther particularly—of many of the key themes and notions found in the long history of cruciccentric thought. Thompson cites as evidence Barth's emphasis on the *a posteriori* character of revelation via the crucified Christ, and his understanding that in the cross judgement is embraced by grace.

A further key finding is that Barth transmits this crucicentric epistemology and soteriology to those following him, including German Reformed theologian Jürgen Moltmann.³⁰ Barth is therefore a generative influence on the late-modern development of the theology of the cross.

---

28. Barth, *Church Dogmatics* IV/1, 343–42. See also Hall, *Lighten Our Darkness*, 139.

29. Barth, *Church Dogmatics* IV/1, 343.

30. Thompson, *Christ in Perspective*, 162 n.81.

Thompson concludes with the important observation that, "Barth's is very definitely and distinctively a *theologia crucis*. This does not mean that other terms applied to his theology, e.g., that of the Word of God or Revelation are now inapplicable. Rather the cross and resurrection are God's word and revelation as the climax and content of his reconciling action."[31] Barth is not only a theologian of the cross, but he certainly is one.

Thompson's associated point, and significant for the current study, is that Barth's *theologia crucis* doesn't negate, but embraces and sets in relief all other acknowledged ways of approaching his theology. Effectively then, for Thompson the theology of the cross constitutes a hermeneutic through which to approach Barth.

In 1987 American Barth student John Godsey picks up the question of a *theologia crucis* in Barth's development. He judges that from the time of Barth's Romans commentary in 1922, the deepest constant in Barth's theology is the sheer *Godness* of God. This equates to a tendency in Barth away from the broken humanity and sheer suffering of the crucifixion, and thence from Luther's *theologia crucis*—which Godsey understands in these terms. Rather Barth is triumphalistic. Here Godsey agrees with Berkouwer, Hall, and others, that this note of triumph is quite different than that evidenced in the anthropocentric theologies and concomitant epistemologies which Barth opposes. Nevertheless it still means that Barth leans towards the *theologia gloriae* and so away from the *theologia crucis*. Adducing Barth himself in support, Godsey explains:

> In the end, Barth's theology tends towards a *theologia gloriae* in order to ensure the *graciousness* of God's action in Christ. As he says at one place in the *Church Dogmatics*: "We not only have a *theologia crucis*, but a *theologia resurrectionis* and therefore a *theologia gloriae*, i.e., a theology of the glory of the new man actualized and introduced in the crucified Jesus Christ who triumphs as the Crucified."[32]

Is Godsey correct? This is familiar territory. As in Berkouwer (1956) the *theologia gloriae* he perceives in Barth hinges on human participation in the glory of the risen Christ; as later discussion will show in this he is quite correct. But he then finds that *theologia gloriae* to be

---

31. Ibid., 157 n.6.

32. Godsey, "Barth and Bonhoeffer," 26. See also Barth, *Church Dogmatics* IV/2, 355. This excerpt is also cited in later discussion here on Barth's *theologia gloriae*, see here p. 283.

necessarily the antithesis of the *theologia crucis*, and in this Godsey is quite incorrect. What Godsey does not do is read the text he quotes. (See above.) In it Barth holds the *theologia crucis*, the *theologia resurrectionis*, and *a proper theologia gloriae* tightly together. For Barth a true theology of glory is intrinsic to the theology of human resurrection, which in turn is intrinsic to the theology of the cross. Barth therefore takes a much more embracing view of the *theologia crucis* than Godsey does.

More positively for the view that Barth can justifiably be understood as a crucicentric theologian, in a 1988 dictionary entry headed "theology of the cross" British New Testament Protestant scholar Richard Bauckham lists Barth, among others, as pressing crucicentric theology further than Luther; Barth contends that the cross points to the humiliation of *God* in Christ and thence to Christ's suffering *deity*.[33] As earlier noted, for Bauckham this advance on Luther does not invalidate Barth's status as a crucicentric theologian but rather emphasizes it. Bauckham writes, "The central and critical role of the cross in Christian theology has rarely been perceived as clearly as it was by Luther, but in modern times theologians [such as] K. Barth . . . have attempted to do justice to it, and in some respects have pressed it further than Luther. In particular, they . . . have sought to revise . . . preconceptions of God in the light of the cross."[34] In addition Bauckham says that Barth, "insists that it is in the humiliation of the cross that Christ's divinity is most fully revealed,"[35] thereby identifying the presence of a further powerful crucicentric theme in Barth.

British Baptist Paul Fiddes (1988) also affirms Barth as a significant modern theologian of the cross. In his *The Creative Suffering of God* Fiddes begins with an account of the resurgent German *Kreuzestheologie*—which he defines as "theology *from* the cross"—of the previous two decades.[36] *Kreuzestheologie* focuses on the cruciform disclosure of the suffering of God in Jesus Christ, and therefore on the

---

33. To recall a previous discussion, in his doctrine of *communicatio idiomatum* Luther proposes that because of the hypostatic nature of the union between the Son's two natures, the suffering he experiences humanly may equally be ascribed to his divinity. Luther accepts however that the Son's divine nature does not suffer in and of itself. See here p. 96.

34. Bauckham, "Theology of the Cross," 182.

35. Ibid.

36. See Fiddes, *Creative Suffering of God*, 12. The rise of the German *Kreuzestheologie* is part of the twentieth century renaissance of interest in Luther, already referred to.

cross itself as a divine epistemological instrument. Fiddes finds the precursors to the modern *Kreuzestheologie* first in Luther's *theologia crucis*, and then in Barth's development of Luther's position. Barth thinks that the *deity* of Jesus Christ (and not just the *humanity* as in Luther) submits directly to the cross, indicating the absolute freedom of God to be the loving and suffering covenantal partner of the creature.[37] For Fiddes, as for Bauckham, this development of Luther's *theologia crucis* consolidates Barth's own position as a theologian of the cross. Fiddes writes, "Those who offer a theology 'from the cross' affirm that the cross is not just an indication of an eternal truth about God, but that it actually expresses what is most *divine* about God . . . From this Lutheran background Barth formulated the dialectical statement that the divinity of God is displayed more clearly in the lowliness of the cross, while the glory of man is displayed in the resurrection."[38] Fiddes adds that Barth does not only recover and develop the earlier crucicentric tradition, he significantly influences those crucicentric theologians who come after him.

Major Scots Presbyterian theologian T. F. Torrance, in beginning his 1990 introduction to Barth, points up the latter's powerful opposition to all creaturely attempts at self-glorification, *viz.*, "When man is confronted by God, there is inevitably collision, crucifixion. The cross is seen [by Barth] to be the supreme and unique event of the meeting between a holy God and sinful man, and at the cross all the subtle attempts of man at self-deification and self-aggrandizement are exposed."[39] Nevertheless Torrance does not designate Barth a theologian of the cross on this basis. Neither does he do so later in his introduction, when he addresses what, in the present view, are powerful crucicentric themes in Barth's theology. It would appear then that the question of Barth's crucicentric status is not before Torrance.

In his 1992 paper on the Holy Spirit and the theology of the cross Canadian Harold Wells writes, "Karl Barth, notable for his uncompromising stance towards 'religion as unbelief' and his insistence on the 'one Word of God' which is Jesus Christ, also attempts a *theologia crucis* . . . [Barth affirms] that there are 'true words spoken in the secular world.' He does so on the basis of the resurrection of the crucified Christ, since

---

37. See ibid., 15, 67.
38. Ibid., 30. See also Barth, *Church Dogmatics* IV/1, 204, 555–58.
39. Torrance, *Karl Barth*, 7.

'all the powers and forces of the whole cosmos are subjected to him.'"[40] Barth is said to centre this *theologia crucis* epistemologically and theologically in the Son's relation with the Holy Spirit, a relation giving rise not only to the Son's particular work of the cross, but also to the Spirit's general operation in the world. Here Wells refers to Barth in support. "[Barth says that it] is as we look back and forwards from God's special presence that his general presence in the world is recognized and attested and the authenticity and efficacy of his general divine omnipresence consists always and exclusively in the identity of the God who is present generally with the God who is present in particular."[41]

The question is whether Barth really does modify or otherwise widen his starting point with the Son, to include the Spirit. Is his *theologia crucis* pneumatological and christological, or even at bottom solely pneumatological? As later discussion will evidence, Barth's *theologia crucis* does in fact move in a pneumatological direction; Wells' instinct about this is quite right. But Barth does not split the Trinity![42] Wells' added implication that Barth somehow permits a natural starting point via the Holy Spirit, bypassing the particular work of God in the cross, indicates a procedure that is in fact completely foreign to Barth.

In reaching his conclusion Wells utilizes traditional crucicentric language loosely. He can do so because by the 1990s such language has lost its strict tie to the classical crucicentric tradition.

Berthold Klappert, 1994, continues his interest in the central importance of the *theologia crucis* for Barth. In his *Versöhnung und Befreiung*[43] he collects fourteen discussions, half of which have previously appeared individually. In these Klappert continues to place the cruciform reconciling and liberating work of Jesus Christ, as seen from the resurrection, at the core of Barth's crucicentric approach. In doing so he further stresses the influence of Luther's *theologia crucis* on Barth.

---

40. Wells, "Holy Spirit," 490. See also Barth, *Church Dogmatics* IV/3, 113f.

41. See Wells, "Holy Spirit, 487. See also Barth, *Church Dogmatics* II/1, 478.

42. Barth is concerned to protect the Son as the one revelatory Word of God, the Revealer of the Father *and the Spirit*. This is one of the reasons that, at the risk of subordinationism in God, he supports the 1054 western addition of the filioque clause in the Nicene-Constantinopolitan creed, in which the Spirit proceeds from the Father *and the Son*. See ibid., I/1, 477f.

43. The full title of this work is *Versöhnung und Befreiung: Versuche, Karl Barth kontextuell zu verstehen*, [*Reconciliation and Liberation: Attempts to Understand Karl Barth's Context.*]

Now though Klappert's principal focus is on the contemporary significance of Barth's crucicentric position in light of the great ruptures of the twentieth century, noting especially the holocaust. From this perspective Klappert lays out the importance of Barth's position for what is effectively a modern crucicentric ethic. Negatively this ethic rejects war and mass destruction; positively it points to the need for Christian social responsibility and associated action to encourage economic equity and social justice.

Theologically the pursuit of such an ethic means that the forgiveness, reconciliation and freedom won in the cross are being worked out practically in a new generation, that the coming kingdom of God draw near. Methodologically it means that Barth's crucicentric position is being reshaped and reapplied. To instance Klappert here, an excerpt from his discussion on "God in Christ, the Reconciler of the World" runs as follows:

> Here we stand in the centre of Karl Barth's *theologia crucis*. Here indeed is the middle of his whole argument . . . That is, that God alone can satisfy the radical judgement of the divine court in which the creature stands condemned; the guilty creature cannot take the penalty of that divine court upon itself. But in that strange court the judge carries out his judgment in such a way that its execution falls upon himself. He does for the guilty creature what it could never do for itself—he provides and is himself the way of its acquittal. For God himself is the judge who has personally entered into our guilty situation on our behalf; this is the glad news of Good Friday.[44]

Here therefore Barth's "whole argument" is deemed to be a theology of the cross, at the heart of which stands the forensic work of Jesus Christ. For Klappert the need to attest to this forensic theology of the cross, to its unexpected grace and freedom, characterizes a prescription in Barth to heal the problems of the modern world. But it also means, and of interest presently, that in Klappert's assessment Barth continues unequivocally to be a theologian of the cross.

If there is any problem with this assessment it is that here, as indeed in his much earlier 1971 finding, Klappert relies chiefly on Barth's forensic position. In the present view forensic theology *is* a vital dimension in Barth's (or any) soteriology of the cross, but whether it comprises the

44. See ibid., 153. My translation.

central focus of Karl Barth's theology of the cross *in its entirety* is doubtful. As will be shown, that focus is actually carefully balanced between false and true theologies of glory with their dependent methodologies for *the knowledge of God* as well as for salvation; it looks to *epistemology* as well as to soteriology.

More positively in the present view, guided by Barth's crucicentric soteriology Klappert's exploration of Christian social responsibility is important in and of itself. It is also in tune with late century interest in the social and ethical implications of Barth's crucicentric position, albeit that position variously perceived.

1995 brings a significant paper by major German Lutheran Oswald Bayer, laying out the theology of the cross from its beginnings in Paul down time, and commensurably down the axis between theology and philosophy. Bayer voices concern that a bias in both doctrinal theology and Christian metaphysics towards a *necessary* conception of the work of the cross, (because required by the concrete reality of Easter Sunday), reduces the "brute historical fact"[45] of the crucifixion. In passing he also notes that Barth risks falling into this trap. In Barth the relations between the Son and the Father, time and eternity, the divine "No!" of the cross and the divine "Yes!" of the resurrection, equate to logical constructs enabling the righteous judgment of God to be lifted from humankind. Indeed the Word of the cross itself is the ultimate construct in Barth. Deeply conceived cruciform proclamation is required by his theologizing, which theologizing is therefore metaphysical, therefore mythological, therefore naturally derived, albeit "contrary to Barth's intention."[46] Bayer says here, "Barth's attempt in the *Church Dogmatics* to understand the Word of the cross as a self-corresponding of God (*Selbstentsprechung*) . . . takes the sting from the offence that the cross of Jesus continually gives, even to those who perceive it as both judgement and grace."[47]

But is Bayer right? What appears to be happening is that he misunderstands the way theologians rooted in the classical crucicentric tradition approach the cross. If the Word of the cross comprises a real and cruciform conduit by which humankind is actually changed from one form to another, this Word is by definition rooted in reality and cannot

---

45. See Bayer, "Word of the Cross," 49.
46. Ibid., 50.
47. Ibid.

be merely a naturally originated "construct." Neither can the theology explicating this Word be regarded as really untethered. To turn to Barth himself, he is totally *realistic* (which means also totally *crucicentric*) in his approach to the meaning of the cross. Nowhere does he lose sight of the sheer reality of the Word spoken from the cross, nowhere does he depart from the historical rootedness of his own proclamation concerning that Word. More specifically, in his theology of self-corresponding in God the corresponding 'elements' of the divine interrelation are *concrete*, and held together in *real* love and humility. All this hardly equates to the existence of the Word of the cross in form or activity as an object of human logic.

Also in 1995, like Thompson (1978) American Lutheran Gaylon Barker makes the important methodological observation for this discussion that the *theologia crucis*—in this case specifically Luther's, may serve as a hermeneutic through which to evaluate a theological project—in this case specifically Bonhoeffer's. Barker says, "By using the *theologia crucis* as a hermeneutic we will investigate the intensifying concentration on Christology which gives Bonhoeffer's theology its worldly orientation, sense of reality, and an urgent demand for faith's responsibilities in the world."[48]

The main focus of Barker's discussion is not however to present a new and crucicentric hermeneutical tool for theology, but the discoveries made possible in using it. He is mainly concerned with Bonhoeffer, but in passing also mentions Barth. Barker finds that while Luther's *theologia crucis* (which he understands purely as a theology of suffering) influences Bonhoeffer's theology, its influence cannot be found in Barth's project "with its inaccessible God" and lack of "due emphasis on man's concrete earthly plight."[49] Barth's theology is therefore *not* a theology of the cross. In support Barker adduces Bonhoeffer's suspicion that Barth actually departs from Luther's *theologia crucis*, adding, "Bonhoeffer resisted becoming a Barthian and his defense was Luther . . . [While Bonhoeffer] became a dedicated student of the new dialectical theology, he never abandoned his criticism of it."[50]

In the opinion of the current discussion though, the reason Barker (as also Bonhoeffer) does not find a theology of the cross in Barth is once

48. Barker, "Bonhoeffer, Luther," 10.
49. Ibid., 12.
50. Ibid.

again to do with the way the theology of the cross is being understood. Barker misses its integrally systematic form as also its note of triumph. He therefore also misses Barth's systematic treatment of the crucicentric idea, negative and positive. Furthermore, Barker's argument that Barth presents an inaccessible God and that he does not emphasize the plight of humankind, so that he cannot be considered a theologian of the cross, might be refuted at length. Sufficient now however to assert that for Barth the whole reason for creation, reconciliation and redemption is the rescue of humankind from its earthly plight by a self-sacrificial God. This reason exactly accords with that given by the classical crucicentric theologians.

In 1995 Canadian United Church theologian Don Schweitzer[51] asks chiefly about the influence of Luther's *theologia crucis* on Jürgen Moltmann, but in passing also considers Barth's crucicentric influence on Moltmann. Schweitzer first questions whether Barth himself is a theologian of the cross. He answers unequivocally in the affirmative. Barth's early theology of crisis is ultimately concerned with the climactic human confrontation with death, while his mature theology is concerned with the triune God who lifts human beings into resurrection life only by way of death. It follows that in both his early and mature theology Barth is vitally concerned with the relations between death and resurrection, this in turn being a hallmark of the theologian of the cross.

Schweitzer also considers that Barth's *theologia crucis* is quite different to Luther's,[52] so that separately Luther's and Barth's crucicentric positions are distinctively foundational for Moltmann. But Schweitzer does not draw out the differences between Luther's and Barth's crucicentric theologies. In fact it will be the contention of the current investigation that Barth's crucicentric position is not radically different from Luther's, rather Barth extends and modernizes Luther's *theologia crucis* in various ways. It may be that compared to Luther, Barth contributes to Moltmann not so much differing as additional crucicentric emphases, for example new eschatological and pneumatological accents.

To digress somewhat, in 1996 and almost three decades after his death Barth's legacy is generally being re-evaluated. In connection with this the question of developmental phases in his project is again visited

---

51. Schweitzer, "Jürgen Moltmann's Theology as a Theology of the Cross."
52. See ibid., 95.

in what has since become known as "the McCormack-Gunton debate."[53] Since it sets the backdrop for the continuing if quieter debate regarding Barth's crucicentric status of interest here, it is briefly outlined now.

By the 1990s von Balthasar's 1951 thesis concerning the two-stage development of Barth's project, the first stage terminating with Barth's 1931 book on Anselm, has become received wisdom.[54] In 1996 American Princeton professor Bruce McCormack, and his reviewer British Reformed theologian Colin Gunton, relitigate it. In *Karl Barth's Critically Realistic Dialectical Theology: Its Genesis and Development 1909–1936*,[55] McCormack argues against von Balthasar that Barth's early theology is not first constrained by his methodology and especially his idealist dialectics, and later constrained by the material content of his theology and especially his *analogia fidei*.[56] Rather, McCormack finds early methodologies continuing into Barth's mature work. The mature theology still employs dialectical method worked out over against the idealism of Kant, not least the veiling and unveiling of God in his self-revelation—a dialectical engagement reaching its zenith in the cross. In making this point, contra von Balthasar McCormack finds not two but four phases in Barth's development.

In his subsequent review of McCormack, Gunton accepts McCormack's analysis of Barth's developmental phases. He also agrees that Barth continues his use of dialectics into his mature theology; Barth's later emphasis on the humanity of God never loses sight of God's otherness and transcendent glory. But Gunton also suggests that continuities in Barth's method and material content go both ways. Not only do significant earlier emphases continue—as per McCormack, but significant later emphases begin earlier. Barth's employment of analogy reaches back well before *Fides Quaerens Intellectum*. His opening concentration on dialectical theology contains within it an awareness of the humanity of God, a concern that afterwards is to become a major focus of his mature theology. Gunton's position is to become the new received wisdom.

---

53. See Gunton, "McCormack," and McCormack, "Gunton."
54. For von Balthasar's thesis see here p. 169, n. 4.
55. McCormack, *Barth's Critically Realistic Dialectical Theology*.
56. For the *analogia fidei* see here p. 139, n. 12.

As we have seen, classical crucicentric theology is characterized by the mutually complementary use of both dialectics and analogy.[57] In terms of the deeper question at hand, Barth's crucicentric status, the notion that both dialectics and analogy extend throughout his project supports the presence of a consistent crucicentric methodological approach in his thought. Across Barth's whole project Jesus Christ, crucified, is always the culminating Synthesis. Via the cross the fundamental contraries pertaining to the human condition are resolved so that the "No!" of God to the human attempt to know and be as God, (which is finally what sin is), is embraced in the reconciling "Yes!" of God to humankind. But always too, analogous to the gracious movement of God toward the creature there is an answering movement of the creature toward God, in faith, gratitude, repentance and free obedience. That movement is patterned on the man-God Jesus Christ, and him crucified. The crucified Christ is then the culminating Analogy.

To return to the principal discussion, in 1998, against the backdrop of the McCormack-Gunton debate, American Lutheran Paul Hinlicky makes two claims. First, that it is Barth who crucially rediscovers Luther's *theologia crucis*. Exploiting the crisis in modern confidence created by the 1914–1918 war, in *der Römerbrief* he employs crucicentric theology's paradoxical and dialectal methodologies to counter modern Liberal Protestantism, a practice he is then to continue throughout his project.[58] Second, that via Barth the rediscovered tradition influences contemporary theologians towards the theology of the cross, especially Rudolf Bultmann (1884–1976), Paul Tillich (1886–1965), and Dietrich Bonhoeffer (1906–1945). They, rather than Barth himself, in various ways further develop the paradoxical and dialectical methodologies of the earlier crucicentric tradition, in turn passing these developments to their own successors.

It is not until 1999 and American Presbyterian theologian George Hunsinger, that the question of Luther's crucicentric influence on Barth

---

57. For discussion on dialectical tension in crucicentric theology see here p. 34.

58. Hinlicky writes, "At the end of the [first world] war, Karl Barth led the way in the rediscovery of the theology of the cross. [In his commentary on St Paul's epistle to the *Romans* he says that the cross is not an obstacle we can overcome.] Rather the cross of Jesus is God's *No*—no to human pride, arrogance and self-worship, but above all to any attempt to use God's Name to justify that pride, arrogance and self-worship . . . These ideas of Barth captured the post-war theological generation, and have been effective until the present day." Hinlicky, "Luther's Theology of the Cross—Part One," 47.

Recent Conceptions of the Theology of the Cross in Karl Barth 189

is addressed in any concerted fashion. Hunsinger devotes one and a half pages to this, being one of the longer explorations of Barth's crucicentric status in the secondary literature reviewed. The suggestion from Hunsinger is that while as a matter of course Barth would have encountered the theology of the cross in figures such as Hegel and various patristic theologians, it is immediately mediated to him via the Reformation, and here Luther rather than Calvin. In Hunsinger's words:

> Another powerful theme that Barth absorbed from Luther involves the theology of the cross. In the last four or five decades theologians have shown an increasing interest in the suffering of God. Despite a long and venerable tradition concerning divine impassibility and the heretical danger of patripassianism, a God who cannot suffer has rightly come to be seen as a God who cannot love. The God of the New Testament has been belatedly rediscovered as a God of suffering love. This striking rediscovery has arisen, it would seem, largely from the impulse of Karl Barth, and the most important source for Barth in the history of theology was undoubtedly Martin Luther.[59]

Hunsinger then stresses the point: Finding God in cruciform humiliation and powerlessness,[60] Barth follows Luther rather than Calvin.

> Remembering the abiding distinction of Christ's deity from his humanity, Calvin insisted on the impassibility of divine nature. Remembering the real unity of Christ's person, Luther affirmed the suffering of God. Although Barth respected Calvin's distinction, he moved far closer to Luther. For Barth the theology of the cross disclosed the suffering love of God.[61]

---

59. Hunsinger, "What Barth Learned from Martin Luther," 132.

60. See ibid., 134. Hunsinger points to the following extracts on the suffering deity of Jesus Christ to illustrate Barth's cruficentric debt to Luther as opposed to Calvin: "This [crucified] One, the One who loves in this way, is the true God. But this means that He is the One . . . whose omnipotence is so great that He can be weak and indeed impotent, as a man is weak and impotent" (Barth, *Church Dogmatics* IV/1, 129). "He is God in the fact that He can give Himself up and does give Himself up, [not away], not merely to the creaturely limitation but to the suffering of the human creature, becoming one of these men, Himself bearing the judgment under which they stand, willing to die and, in fact, dying the death which they have deserved. This is the nature and essence of the true God as He has intervened actively and manifestly in Jesus Christ." (Ibid., IV/1, 130.)

61. Ibid., 133.

There are in addition other distinctions between the two Reformers. Calvin emphasizes the divinity of Jesus Christ, whereas Luther emphasizes this but also Christ's humanity in all its vulnerability. Calvin in practice if not formally limits divine mercy and grace, whereas for Luther these are new every morning and limitless.[62]

While Barth's general debt to Calvin is of course immense, on the basis of all these comparisons Hunsinger thinks Barth's *peculiarly crucicentric* debt extends to Luther rather than to Calvin.[63] In this Hunsinger reflects the general tenor of recent scholarship on the Reformation mediation of the *theologia crucis*. Hunsinger additionally finds that Barth corrects and radicalizes Luther's *theologia crucis*, fitting it to the modern age. In turn this modern *theologia crucis* is said to pervade Barth's project.

This all appears strong support for the presence of a theology of the cross in Barth. Yet a familiar problem ensues, undercutting the scope and so validity of Hunsinger's conclusions. Hunsinger does not perceive the systematic breadth of Luther's *theologia crucis*, and thus cannot really appraise its significance in Barth. There is too the question of Luther's fine treatment of Christ's deity and humanity in relation to the suffering of the cross,[64] which Hunsinger does not bring out. That said Hunsinger well supports the influence of Luther's crucicentric theme of suffering in Barth, and his idea that Barth corrects and modernizes Luther's *theologia crucis* is important, being extendable to a more robust conception of the *theologia crucis* itself than Hunsinger's own.

Tomlin (1999) says that Luther's crucicentric theology influences Barth profoundly.[65] The comment arises in the course of ruling Barth out as a theologian influenced by Paul independently of Luther. Barth, it

---

62. See Hunsinger, "What Karl Learned from Martin Luther," 132. See also, Barth, *Church Dogmatics* IV/1, 129–30, in which Barth speaks of the God who becomes a creature, and IV/3, 478, in which he quotes the writer of Lamentations regarding the boundless mercy of God.

63. In his 1922 Göttingen lectures Barth declares *glory to God alone* to be "the essential message of Luther *and* Zwingli *and* Calvin" (Barth, *Calvin*, 189). The emphases here are Barth's; the observation itself accords with the central principle of crucicentric theology. It follows that the crucicentric influence on Barth of each of the major Reformation figures deserves investigation. That said, certainly Barth's crucicentric debt to the Reformation rests *primarily* with Luther.

64. Luther treats the relation between Christ's humanity and divinity in his doctrine of *communicatio idiomatum*, see here p. 96.

65. See Tomlin, *The Power of the Cross*, 6.

would seem, wields the theology of the cross comprehensively, polemically, and strictly in line with the Reformation. In a considerable volume on the *theologia crucis* in its classical era, but also touching on its modern social meaning, Barth receives little further attention.

As noted, in 1992 Wells had seen in Barth an embrace of a pneumatology of the cross, this opening the way for Barth's acceptance of a certain natural knowledge of God. In 2001 Wells returns to the theology of the cross, being now concerned with the influence of Luther's radical crucicentric methodology on three modern and progressive theologians of the cross, naming Barth as one. (The others are Latin American liberation theologians Elsa Tamez and Jon Sobrino.) Wells discusses Barth's *theologia crucis* "on the left" at some length. He begins, "The great originator of theology of the cross in the twentieth century . . . was Karl Barth (1886–1968) who pre-dated the liberationists, but whose theology can be seen as an antecedent and precursor to liberation theology."[66] In this Wells follows Hinlicky (1998) in finding Barth to recover the counter-cultural and Reformational emphases of classical crucicentric theology for twentieth century theology. It is then Barth who develops the narrow tradition into a tool with which to confront nineteenth century Liberal Protestantism, in the process laying a radical crucicentric theological and methodological foundation congenial to late-modern liberation theologies.[67] That is, while contemporary liberation theologians do not draw directly from Barth, his crucicentric foundation creates a certain environment, *viz.*, "God's preferential option for the poor," in which theological criticism of capitalist structural inequality can advance. Wells' criticism of Barth is that having provided this radical crucicentric environment, he himself proceeds elsewhere. "Despite the enormous preponderance of biblical material about injustice and oppression, there is relatively little to be found about these things in Barth's theological work."[68]

In response three points can be made. First, on the basis of the classical crucicentric tradition a bias toward the poor is not the single determining criterion of a theologian of the cross. Wells misreads Luther's

---

66. Wells, "Cross and Liberation", 155.

67. "[A] close reading of [Barth] . . . demonstrates an inherent congeniality between his theology of the cross and theologies of liberation, and a potential for fruitful affiliation." Ibid., 158.

68. Ibid.

theologia crucis and thence Barth at this point. As with Hunsinger two years earlier, Wells' estimation of Barth as a theologian of the cross, indeed a radical one, is not broadly based. Second, related to this Barth's political theology is not somehow lacking because it does not dominate a voluminous project spanning almost fifty years. In fact Barth's moral, ethical, and political thought is very significant, as evidenced by recent studies by John Webster and others.[69] This said, third, in picking up Barth's recovery of the classical crucicentric tradition, in noting his further development of it over against the nineteenth century, and in suggesting the founding importance of that development for the late-modern liberation theologies, Wells nevertheless supports the lasting influence of Barth's crucicentric stand very powerfully.

Not dissimilarly to Torrance (1990), when introducing Barth Swiss Reformed theologian Eberhard Busch (2004) does not consider the question of Barth's crucicentric status as such. Nevertheless he indicates the existence in Barth's project of what are in fact typical crucicentric themes and emphases, soteriologically and epistemologically. For example, concerning the overall soteriological path Barth takes, Busch comments, "[For Barth, God] does not develop the potential already present in our 'life,' but is rather the *death* of humanity as it knows itself, and the resurrection of the new humanity that is always totally alien to us. What we find here is a rediscovering of Luther [on which basis] Barth pressed far beyond the anthropocentric thinking that had become almost fateful for modern theology."[70]

As with the literature review in Part One of this study, the penultimate discussion in this review references American Lutheran Kurt Richardson's 2004 text introducing Barth to contemporary North America. Richardson concludes one section of his text by noting Barth's continuing recourse to three fundamental conceptual tools. He explains these as follows:

> The first of these three is *analogia fidei* (analogy of faith), whereby our speaking, through faith that receives and proclaims the Word

---

69. For example Webster writes, "Barth's interest in ethics, long left largely unnoticed [is] now coming to light as one of the clues to understanding his project as a whole . . . If one wishes to discover the sheer humanity of Barth's thinking one need look no further than his writings on ethics." Webster, *Cambridge Companion to Karl Barth*, 13–14. See also Webster, *Barth's Ethics of Reconciliation*, and Webster, *Barth's Moral Theology*.

70. See Busch, *Great Passion*, 22. Italics original.

of God corresponds as a human word of testimony to the Word of God that has been received. The second is the disjunction between *theologia crucis* and *theologia gloriae*, both terms derived from Martin Luther's writings in connection with the Heidelberg Disputation. The former is the method of knowing and reflecting on the revelation of God through the cross-destined life of Jesus Christ, the latter is the method of abstract contemplation toward the attainment of immediate and transcendent knowledge of God. Finally, there is the dialectical polarity between *Deus absconditus* (hidden) and *Deus revelatus* (revealed), whereby the way of the knowledge of faith as *theologia crucis* is ever an experience of the God who is at once revealed and concealed in the conditions of Jesus' life and death.[71]

Again three points can be made. First, Richardson is mistaken in considering the *analogia fidei* a conceptual tool distinct from the theology of the cross, rather the *analogia fidei* falls under the crucicentric umbrella, both classically and in Barth. As will be shown, Barth's rejection of the *analogia entis*, and his corresponding emphasis positively on an *analogia fidei*, are significant elements *within* his crucicentric perspective. Second, Richardson is quite correct in picking up the negative or oppositional tone in Barth's theology of the cross, though he largely misses Barth's attention also to its positive aspect. Third, as the literature review in Part One noted, Richardson defines the theology of the cross narrowly, in this case as epistemology.[72] In the present view this is the likely reason he misses the embracing nature of Barth's *theologia crucis*.

To draw this review to a close, between 2004 and 2009 direct attention to Barth's theology of the cross continues to be slight. A search of the ATLA database returns only one article associating Barth and the theology of the cross. In 2007 South African dogmatics Professor Nico Vorster is chiefly concerned with finding a crucicentric solution for the problem of theodicy. In the course of his discussion however he refers to Barth. He finds that over against the Enlightenment Barth presents a starting point with the cross, resurrection and parousia of Jesus Christ. This enables Barth to maintain the righteousness of God in the face of suffering and evil in the world.[73] It also means for Vorster that Barth is

---

71. Richardson, *Reading Karl Barth*, 126–27. For a further definition of the *analogia fidei* see here p. 139, n. 12.

72. For reference to Richardson in Part One here see pp. 30–31.

73. See Vorster, "Theodicy and the Theology of the Cross."

a theologian of the cross, a positive assessment—although once again circumscribed by the narrow conception of crucicentric theology (now as a theology of human suffering) held by the person making it.

Concluding the Review

Before summarizing the recent treatment of Barth in relation to the theology of the cross, attention is drawn to a separate but related matter. As Forde (1997) and Kärkkäinen (2003) in the earlier literature review,[74] now Klappert (1971), Thompson (1978), and Barker (1995), each offer the theology of the cross as a hermeneutical tool for estimating the crucicentric orientation of a given theological project. The latter three commentators do not stress this hermeneutical use, and different conceptions of the theology of the cross are involved. Nonetheless the implication that a theological system might serve as a lens through which to evaluate theological projects is an important one for them, as also for the present investigation.

To turn to the substantive matter, it appears that in the literature of the last five decades interest in the question of Barth's theology of the cross has been thin but ongoing. This slight treatment seems surprising given the voluminous nature of the Barth secondary literature overall, as also the contemporary renaissance of interest in the classical theology of the cross. On the basis of the literature that does treat the matter however, it is concluded that no broadly acknowledged decision concerning the crucicentric status of Barth's project, or of Barth himself, currently exists.

There are numerous indicators in the Barth secondary literature to what are, from the perspective of the classical crucicentric tradition, characteristic crucicentric emphases in Barth's thought. For example the introductions to Barth by Torrance (1990) and Busch (2004) include many such references. Nevertheless these crucicentric emphases are not explicitly identified as such.

Of those who do directly consider Barth in relation to the theology of the cross, some flatly deny his crucicentric status, see Godsey (1987), Bayer (1995) and Barker (1995). Others find a theology of the cross partially present in Barth's project, see Berkouwer (1956) and Hall (1976).

---

74. For Forde and Kärkkäinen respectively, see here pp. 24 and 30.

There are also those in support. What is noticeable about this latter group is that among its members quite different aspects of the classical crucicentric system prevail. In itself this relativises the significance of some of the individual decisions reached, even as taken together they place Barth squarely within the crucicentric tradition. Very broadly: Klappert (1971) views the theology of the cross as soteriology. As such it comprises a methodological key to Barth's project. Bauckham (1988) likewise associates Barth's crucicentric position with soteriology. Wells (1992 and 2001), Schweitzer (1995) and Hinlicky (1998) perceive a radical crucicentric approach in Barth politically, socially and theologically, one which influences both late twentieth century crucicentric and modern-liberative theologies. Similarly, and returning to him, Klappert (1994) now freshly joins radical-political and systematic perspectives, creating a platform from which to see the implications of Barth's *theologia crucis* for a late-modern theology of social justice. Tomlin (1999) connects Barth to Luther's comprehensive and polemical *theologia crucis*. Fiddes (1988) and Richardson (2004) associate a theology of the cross in Barth strictly with epistemology. Hunsinger (1999) and Vorster (2007) align Barth's theology of the cross with a theology of suffering.

A minority of recent commentators explicitly understand Barth as critical to the recovery of the classical crucicentric tradition in the twentieth century, modernizing that tradition in various ways over against the modern resurgence of the theology of glory. These commentators include: Thompson (1978), Fiddes (1988), Schweitzer (1995), Hinlicky (1998), Hunsinger (1999), and Wells (2001). Once again however, often these claims are not individually well supported.

The next two sections of the discussion, on Barth's modern crucicentric epistemology and soteriology, hope to ground support for a theology of the cross in Barth's project more concretely. As indicated previously, those inquiries will take place in the hermeneutical light shed by the classical crucicentric tradition.

7

Karl Barth's Modern Epistemology of the Cross

Who but God could or would reveal God? Hence the content of the pronouncement of this slain man is both the work and also the person and essence of God.

—Karl Barth[1]

T. F. Torrance considers Barth develops "a very powerful epistemological structure at the heart of his theology."[2] The explanatory power of this epistemology Torrance seats in its *oneness* as against scholasticism's two-tier epistemology. This last involves both general and special revelation, both natural theology operating outside the premises of revelation, and revealed theology operating within the premises of faith.[3] Unlike this scholastic model however, Barth's unitary epistemology holds together both creation and redemption, both the creature and the Creator in their relation—which relation is reflected in the man-God Jesus Christ. Thence Jesus Christ discloses both the knowledge of God and the meaning of the divine human relation. He does so above all from the cross.

In this Barth adopts the same central epistemological principle as that to which the classical crucicentric theologians ascribed: God is known through God and through God alone.[4] Barth does so for many of the same reasons, including the need to oppose a still resurgent counter-

---

1. Barth, *Church Dogmatics* IV/3, 412.
2. Torrance, *Karl Barth*, 144.
3. See ibid., 149.
4. See Barth, *Church Dogmatics* II/1, 44.

epistemology. In his 1922 Göttingen lectures he explains the character of that counter-epistemology *vis à vis* the Reformation. "[The] impression . . . I have gained of medieval theology," he tells his students, "may be summed up in a phrase coined . . . by Luther at the 1518 Heidelberg Disputation: it is a theology of glory. It attempts and achieves a knowledge of God in his glory, purity, and majesty."[5] It does so by following a path of its own devising, a speculative path straight to the heart of divine mystery. Barth then sarcastically "praises" the self-confidence of those medieval theologians, and especially Aquinas, who would ascend from the base idea of revelation to master the mystery of God, exchanging their place for his.[6] How astonishing, he says, that no "medieval teacher confessed the truth that the church's authority rests on that of the biblical revelation."[7]

In distinction to that earlier glorious position Barth declares that there is *no* independently obtained knowledge of God for the creature. Given this, Barth's own starting point "is not in any sense epistemological";[8] it is not a construction of human science. Rather disclosure of the knowledge of God takes place exclusively in Jesus Christ and supremely from the point of the cross; he is the ontological Content of its cruciform theology, its Pronouncement, its living Word. This is the clear message of the cross, of the Reformation, and so, Barth says, of his own proclamation.

The creature receives this cruciform Word by *faith*. As with the discussion on epistemology in Part One, before proceeding to the substantive discussion it is again useful to review the meaning of faith, this time as Barth understands it.

Towards the end of his project Barth states dryly, "Nineteenth-century theologians spoke of "faith," and we do well to trust that they meant Christian faith. But their assumptions compelled them to understand faith as the realization of one form of man's spiritual life and self-awareness."[9] Indeed Barth always rejects the subjective interpretation

---

5. Barth, *Calvin*, 27.
6. See ibid., 27–28.
7. See ibid., 32.
8. Barth, *Church Dogmatics* II/1, 44.
9. Barth, "Evangelical Theology in the Nineteenth Century," 26. English translation (1957) originally entitled "Panorama of a Century."

of faith. Instead from the New Testament he retrieves the same understanding of faith as did the classical crucicentric theologians.

An early comment illustrates this. In his Göttingen lectures Barth positively discusses Luther's attitude to faith in the Heidelberg Disputation. "The centre of [Luther's *theologia crucis*] is the demand for faith as naked trust that casts itself into the arms of God's mercy, faith that is the last word that can be humanly said about the possibility of justification before God; a faith that is sure of its object—God[. This faith is not] itself a human work but . . . an integral part of God's strange work, sharing in the whole paradox of it."[10] In this Barth sets the course of his own understanding. Faith for Barth is totally objective. It has its own concrete ontology, Jesus Christ *is* Faith. But faith is also divine *act* for the creature, which act inculcates trust in that which has already been done for it. As Barth put this, "[The] great work of faith has already been done by the One whom I follow in my faith, even before I believe, even if I no longer believe, in such a way that He is always, as Heb 12:2 puts it, the originator and completer . . . of our faith."[11]

To digress slightly, Barth often utilizes circular images.[12] In his epistemology he holds that, sent by the Son, the Holy Spirit[13] graciously conveys the Word of the cross to the creature from beyond it, and simultaneously receives this Word for the creature from within it. In this circular Spirit directed way objective knowledge of God becomes subjective. The hidden message conveyed from the cross is appropriated to the creature so as to be known by it.

Returning to the matter in hand, what is equally contributed in this Spirit-empowered circular process, is Christ's faith to receive and trust God.[14] *Christ's* faith. In this connection Barth interprets Paul in Gal 2:20, "I live in the faith of the Son of God [to be understood quite literally: I

---

10. Barth, *Calvin*, 46–47.

11. Barth, *Church Dogmatics* I/2, 559.

12. For example Barth pictures the Christian community as an inner circle within a broader outer circle representing civil community. In turn both these circles exist inside a third circle representing the Kingdom of God. Christ is the common Center of all three. This image made a vital contribution to Barth's political theory.

13. Barth finds "no incongruence between Christ and the Spirit." Ibid., I/1, 453.

14. Barth says here, "Our knowledge of faith itself is knowledge of God in his hiddenness." Ibid., II/1, 57.

live—not in my faith in the Son of God, but in this—that the Son of God had faith!]"[15] The bracketed comment here is Barth's.

To live faithfully is therefore to act faithfully in correspondence with Christ's prior act of faith. Barth explains what this involves, "By the act of faith we mean the basic Chistian act, . . . an acknowledgment, a recognition, and a confession, an active-knowing."[16] Elsewhere he says similarly, "[The] law and all its commandments are kept and fulfilled by us when they find in us [faith, this being] the work and gift of the Holy Spirit, which we cannot take to ourselves, [for faith cannot be contrived], but for which we can only pray."[17]

Thus in summary Barth melts Christ's faith and contingent act culminating in the cross, and the faith and faithful act of the creature in response. But the triune God not the creature initiates faith, while the cross is the prime instrument of faith's transmission. This compilation of what are integrally *crucicentric* notions around faith is found throughout Barth's project.

The Negative Epistemology of the Cross

Barth develops his epistemology in dialogue with the whole stretch of the western intellectual and theological tradition, including the two-tier epistemology of scholasticism, the modern intellectual paradigm, and the nineteenth century theological reaction to the latter. In so doing in his negative theology he rejects prior reliance by the church on all anthropocentric methodologies, at all times,[18] for the knowledge of God. These circumvent the one Word of God that the church has to hear, and the one place that revelation may be found, the cross of Jesus Christ. In the next section of the discussion this negative epistemology will be further considered in relation to: natural theology, philosophy, metaphysics

---

15. Barth, "Gospel and Law," 7. Previously cited here p. 37.

16. Barth, *Church Dogmatics* IV/1, 758. Barth's use the German verb *kennen*, to know, connotes the senses he lists.

17. Barth, "Gospel and Law," 13–14.

18. In his early Göttingen lectures Barth suggests that the medieval period, the Renaissance, and Liberal Protestantism, so different from each other in their particulars, are each located wholly on the horizontal line of human life in the world. Here each engage in a self-glorying pursuit of human willing and knowing. As such they have more in common with each other than they do with the Reformation. See Barth, *Calvin*, 65–66.

including the *analogia entis*, human reason, and with particular regard to Schleiermacher and the nineteenth century, felt human experience.

In overview, as the crucicentric theologians before him the presenting problem Barth finds in natural theology is that it proposes two sources for the knowledge for God, first natural and then revelatory, first general and then special revelation; the second source here augments and culminates the first.

In Barth's view this two-step procedure is impossible. If Jesus Christ is God in person and as such the primary form of revelation, if revelation is structured in this way, then other putative revelations must conform to him. Logically they can have no revelatory capacity of themselves. But more seriously for Barth, the proposal is also idolatrous. It cuts across the scriptural principle that God alone truly discloses God. Indeed even if nature "is never advanced except as a prolegomenon, it is obviously no longer the revelation of God, but a new expression (borrowed or even stolen) for the revelation which encounters man in his own reflection."[19] Here God is subdued "to some form of our own subjectivity."[20] Or as Busch says interpreting him, Barth considers that divine revelation "is not an object that is open to our capricious human grasping. If it were then revelation would in fact be an idol in our human hands."[21] On both counts therefore, the dismissal of the true Source of revelation, and the idolatrous attempt by the creature on the divine capacity to know God as God alone can know, natural theology is not to be countenanced.

To consider Barth's attitude to natural theology in more detail, it can be said first that his negative stance towards natural theology has often been misinterpreted. In fact Barth does not deny the God-givenness of the natural realm, holding as Torrance says, "a created correspondence to exist between God and the contingent rational order of the universe."[22] This created order, including everything within it, depends on and gives material form to the overflowing love and generosity of the God who created it. Thus it *is* possible for there to be a natural revelation vested in creation. But Barth insists powerfully that such a revelation cannot be the *starting point* for the knowledge of God as God is in Godself, or of

---

19. Barth, *Church Dogmatics* II/1, 139. See also See Busch, *Great Passion*, 71.
20. Torrance, *Karl Barth*, 139.
21. See Busch, *Great Passion*, 225.
22. See Torrance, *Karl Barth*, 132.

God as God is toward the world in Jesus Christ. God alone can provide that knowledge.

For the human creature cannot of itself reach up to the knowledge of God. God is not an object as other objects, susceptible to examination by the creature on its own terms and by natural means. Barth often quotes, "*Deus non est in genere.*"[23] [God does not belong to a general human category.] Rather there is no innate human ability to know God. Indeed, and as Busch says, for Barth the very Word of God contests the "idea that humanity, as such, naturally possesses the possibility of knowing God."[24] Busch then explains that for Barth no "human speculative or other parallel methodology . . . can arrive at true knowledge of God, no human epistemological starting point will suffice. Such starting points 'are intrinsically ambiguous,' since logically there cannot be two quite separate revelations of God—divine and human."[25]

This human *incapacity* to know God naturally is made clear at many points in Barth's project. He says for instance, "There is nothing in the created world or in man which could discover the God manifest in revelation."[26] Truth does not have "its source in man, so that to know and declare the truth, to establish the truth as such, to live by the truth and in the truth, does not lie in man's capacity and existence."[27] To claim to possess such an innate capacity is therefore the blatant refusal of grace. Or in Barth's words, "God's Word is no longer grace, and grace itself is no longer grace, if we ascribe to man a predisposition towards this Word, a possibility of knowledge regarding it that is intrinsically and independently native to him."[28] Indeed, Barth defines natural theology itself in these terms, "[Natural theology] is no more and no less than the unavoidable theological expression of the fact that in the reality and possibility of man as such an openness for the grace of God and therefore a readiness for the knowability of God in his revelation is not at all evident."[29]

---

23. See for example Barth, *Church Dogmatics* II/1, 310.
24. See Busch, *Great Passion*, 43.
25. Ibid., 148.
26. Barth, *Church Dogmatics* I/1, 368. See also for example ibid., iv/2, 133.
27. Ibid., II/1, 207.
28. Ibid., I/1, 194.
29. Ibid., II/1, 135.

Allied to his denial of a natural capacity to reach up to the knowledge of God, Barth denies the possibility of a natural methodology by which the creature might exercise such a capacity. Recalling an earlier discussion here,[30] both Augustine (354–430) and Aquinas (1225–1274) accept a commonality between natural creation and God, enabling the knowledge of God to be deduced from the creature, profoundly shaping Roman Catholic and then major strands of Protestant epistemology. Barth though detects in this established position "the fiery living heart"[31] of the human quest for glory. The possibility that God and the world exist on some graded way enabling direct creaturely knowledge of God bypasses the true way to that knowledge in Jesus Christ. Its attendant methodologies are therefore to be denied. Grace and nature are emphatically *not* on a continuum; the knowledge of God may *not* be derived from the creature. "God's revelation is not in our power, and therefore not at our command,"[32] Barth says. Elsewhere he adds, "[If] grace is alongside nature, however high above it [grace] may be put, it is obviously no longer the grace of God, but the grace which man ascribes to himself . . . [It] is obviously no longer the revelation of God, but a new expression (borrowed or even stolen) for the revelation which encounters man in his own reflection."[33] In such a case the creature idolizes itself.

Torrance explains this further. "[For Barth there] is no way of going behind revelation to know God, any more than we can know God behind his back."[34] To try to make that journey, to attempt nevertheless to go "behind the back of Jesus Christ in order to know God [directly, is] equivalent to trying to think beyond and above God himself, and to making ourselves as God."[35] In such a self-glorifying endeavor grace is being denied. Or as Barth himself says succinctly, "If man tries to gasp at truth of himself, he tries to grasp at it *a priori*. But in that case . . . he does not believe."[36] When theology makes that attempt it becomes anthropology, it deserts its post.

30. For a previous discussion on natural theology see here p. 45f.
31. Barth, *Calvin*, 29.
32. Ibid., II/1, 69.
33. Ibid., II/1, 137.
34. Torrance, *Karl Barth*, 94.
35. Ibid., 71.
36. Barth, *Church Dogmatics* I/2, 302.

For all these reasons Barth regards the subtle way natural theology tries to insinuate itself into the church with narrowed eyes. "[In] the sphere of the Christian Church . . . natural theology . . . at least for a start and in appearance makes a very unassuming and modest entrance . . . [It] not only acknowledges revelation and grace as well, but even gives them . . . precedence . . . The astonishing fact . . . is that natural theology can make an entrance and surrender in this way; that it can use this disguise."[37]

This also means for Barth that natural theology is neither necessary nor permissible for the community who bears Christ's name; bowing to its temptation is a massive step backward to an age predating Jesus Christ. Thence Barth bluntly declares, "If you really reject natural theology you do not stare at the serpent, with the result that it stares back at you, hypnotises you, and is ultimately certain to bite you, but you hit it and kill it as soon as you see it!"[38]

The irony for Barth is that since God alone can overcome the creature's illusion as to its natural possession of godlike capacity, any attempt by the creature to do so requires the assumption that it can be as God. Thus he warns, "The illusion that we can rid ourselves of our illusion ourselves is the greatest of all illusions. And a theology which thinks it can persuade man against natural theology . . . is still itself definitely a natural theology."[39]

There is one seeming caveat to Barth's position, although on closer examination it is not really a caveat at all. He writes, "There is no reason why the attempt of Christian anthropocentrism should not be made, indeed ought not to be made. There is certainly a place for legitimate Christian thinking starting from below and moving up, from man who is taken hold of by God [toward the] God who takes hold of man."[40]

---

37. Ibid., II/1, 137.

38. See Barth and Brunner, *Natural Theology*, 75–76. This comment comprises part of Barth's sharp 1934 retort to Brunner's desire for a measured natural theology. Among other concerns Barth fears that Brunner, albeit inadvertently, risks comforting the German-Christians by his advocacy of the Lutheran doctrine of the state as a divinely ordained natural ordinance.

39. Barth, *Church Dogmatics* II/1, 169. Barth adds immediately here, "[The only thing] that can help him is that the grace of Jesus Christ Himself in its revelation comes triumphantly to him, freeing him from the illusion and therefore from natural theology."

40. Barth, "Evangelical Theology in the Nineteenth Century," 24.

This anthropocentric starting point however has its genesis in divine not human initiative.

In interim conclusion, for Barth two major errors attach to natural theology. On the one hand it bypasses the self-revelation of God. On the other it claims for the creature an innate capacity, and a self-predicated methodology, for knowing what God alone can originally know. In his rejection of these errors Barth's reasoning is typically crucicentric. In obtaining true knowledge of God it is the action of *God* and not the creature which takes epistemological priority. As Thompson says, this means for Barth that apart from Jesus Christ all "other supposed sources of the knowledge of God are automatically impossible, unnecessary and so excluded."[41] Torrance interprets Barth similarly. "The fact that God himself has to become man in order to break a way though our estrangement and darkness . . . not only precludes us from entertaining other possibilities of a way from man to God, but actually invalidates them all."[42]

In opposing the natural starting point for the knowledge of God Barth rejects prior reliance on any of the capacities and disciplines of the human mind. The emphasis here is on *prior* reliance. He is of course not proscribing the use of the intellect in the service of Christian thought.[43] What he objects to is the notion that theology lacks a given and eminently rational starting point of its own, forcing it to build on purely human procedure—ideal construct or speculative analogy.[44] This raises for Barth the special case of theology's relation to philosophy.

The first inbuilt problem which philosophy presents Christian theology rests in the *realist* philosophical view that for knowledge to move beyond the subjective sphere, to exist really, there must be a subject actively or passively disclosing itself, and a knowing object able to receive

---

41. Thompson, *Christ in Perspective*, 111.

42. Torrance, *Karl Barth*, 144.

43. Barth's insistence on rigorous intellectual engagement in the service of theology is of course impossible to overstate. Met on one occasion by its self-congratulatory absence, he asks acutely, "Is [this] due, fundamentally, to mere laziness? Have we here the type of intellect that . . . excuses itself from going farther, with the inspired words, 'not doctrine, life!' . . . The first notes suffice for the whole melody of anti-intellectualism. Or is it simply a kind of godlessness[?]" Barth, "Ethics Today," 175.

44. See Torrance, *Karl Barth*, 225. Elsewhere Torrance says, "Barth will have nothing to do . . . with some kind of faith-knowledge . . . which needs rationalizing through borrowed forms of ethics and philosophy." Ibid., 45.

what that subject discloses. These twin variables constitute realism's ontic and noetic necessities.[45] Barth holds the premise itself to be sound, but finds that philosophic-realism tends to equate subject and object. In the case where the subject is God and the object is the creature, the creature is lifted to equality with God. Guarding against such creaturely glorification once again therefore, Barth finds philosophical-realism to be quite different from theological-realism; its premises needing careful handling by theology.

The second inbuilt problem presented by philosophy to theology comes from the opposite direction. Philosophical-*idealism* holds that reality is based not in an external world but in the hidden realm lying behind it.[46] In this ideal conceptual realm "God" exists as the ultimate presupposition or synthesis about which nothing can be known absolutely.[47] For Barth the divine Object is thereby reduced to a subjective construct, and so to the level of the creature. Once again creaturely glory is on offer.

From the "theologically-realist" perspective of his mature theology Barth thinks that the problems exhibited by philosophical-realism, (the loss of the *distinction* between God and the creature, elevating the creature to the level of God), and philosophical-idealism, (the loss of the *objectivity* of God, reducing God to a creaturely construct), resolvable only in the cross of Jesus Christ. Contra philosophical-realism the cross slashes all conceptions of equality between God and the creature, for in it Jesus Christ is supremely over against the creature. Here the cross preserves an utter disparity between them. Contra philosophical-idealism the cross slashes all conceptions of a synthetic God existing merely constructively, for here Jesus Christ is the *actual* Synthesis and presupposition of the external world. Thence the cross preserves divine objectivity.

---

45. Barth considers God imposes these necessities upon himself; it is not that they are imposed on God by the creature! See ibid., 70f.

46. Idealism asks after the possibility of moving beyond the external world to its ultimate validation or presupposition. It therefore questions the realist assumption that there is a direct correspondence between the knowing mind and its object.

47. Busch notes here, "Barth . . . opposes the understanding of the world as an appearance, as something that is merely thought, [giving rise to] the modern concept that it is an element in our human ego-consciousness which we can control, attracting it to us, or rejecting it, or tolerating it as we please." See Busch, *Great Passion*, 185.

Accepting that the problems philosophy poses theology are resolvable in this cruciform way, Barth does allow theology to employ philosophy on an *ad hoc* basis. Philosophy, he says, yet offers theology important critical questions and critical ways of thinking. But Barth still advises care. As Schwöbel explains him, theology must never forget its "nearness to philosophy—a nearness as necessary as it is perilous."[48]

Barth's typically crucicentric proviso follows. Philosophy must not dictate to theology, it must not confuse its own word with the divine Word. Torrance explains that instruction, "[Philosophical theology] will not employ any criteria in the testing and establishing of its knowledge in abstraction from its actual content, and will not elaborate any epistemology in abstraction from the full substance of theological knowledge—rather will a correct epistemology emerge, and a proper theological method develop, in the actual process of seeking full understanding of the object of faith and constructing a dogmatics in utter obedience to its object."[49] Here "content" and "full substance" and "object of faith" reduce definitively to Jesus Christ. A properly philosophical theology will begin not with a construct of its own devising, but with, and with obedience to, the concrete Object of faith who is Jesus Christ.

Barth makes the concomitant point that while philosophy cannot dictate to theology, the latter may, with all modesty, assist philosophy. From the perspective of the cross of Jesus Christ theology offers philosophy a unique, objective, and properly crucicentric Solution to philosophy's prevailing methodological difficulties, real and ideal.

In line with his careful analysis of the relations between philosophy and theology, Barth rejects the traditional admixture between the older theology and philosophy in metaphysics. His particular nemesis here is the ancient *analogia entis*. (To recap, this is a conceptual system for the knowledge of God proposing a necessary commonality between the creature and the Creator, allowing the creature to determine the nature of God via analogy drawn on itself.[50]) As Hunsinger says, "As the premise behind natural theology, the *analogia entis* seems to underwrite almost everything Barth takes to be theologically impossible."[51] Barth

48. Schwöbel, "Theology," in *The Cambridge Companion to Karl Barth*, 26. Here Schwöbel quotes Barth, "Fate and Idea," 32.

49. Torrance, *Karl Barth*, 72.

50. For a further definition of the *analogia entis* see here p. 139, n. 12.

51. Hunsinger, *How to Read Karl Barth*, 283.

himself calls it, "the source of the corruption at work in German theology for nearly two centuries,"[52] and damningly, "the invention of the Antichrist."[53]

There are two strands of the old theology of glory at work here. The first derives from the fact that the *analogia entis* bypasses the divine self-disclosure in Jesus Christ in favor of the creature thinking its own way to God. Torrance explains, "It was his analysis of nineteenth century theology in Protestantism and of neo-Thomist and neo-Augustinian theology in Roman Catholicism that prompted Barth to put his finger on the concept of *analogia entis* as the danger-point, for it led theologies on both sides of the [Protestant/Roman] divide to interpret the gospel in terms of an independent conceptual system reached before and apart from the actual knowledge of God given to us through his incarnate self-revelation in Jesus Christ."[54]

The "danger-point" is not only the rejection of revealing grace, bad enough in Barth's view, but that in bypassing the divine self-disclosure of God in Jesus Christ, the creature presumes to itself godlike power to do what God alone can do, truly know God. Barth thus re-emphasizes the sheer impossibility of the creature reaching to the inner truth of God on the basis of itself. As Busch explains him, "We cannot derive the truth of God from our own thinking anymore than we can derive his existence from our own existence."[55] Rather Barth insists that the real God, the God of Jesus Christ, is "no universal deity capable of being reached conceptually."[56]

A second strand of the theology of glory also connects to the *analogia entis*. On the premise that a creature must reflect its creator, the *analogia entis* claims a direct and necessary correspondence between the creature and God. This is just a step from claiming equality between the creature and God; as with the problem posed theology by philosophical-realism it certainly reduces the distinction between them. So Barth clearly emphasizes that the "being of God cannot be compared with that of man."[57] God is entirely objective to the creature, utterly Other. Any

52. Torrance, *Karl Barth*, 158.
53. See Barth, *Church Dogmatics* I/1, xiii. and ibid., II/1, 82–83.
54. Torrance, *Karl Barth*, 169. See also Busch, *Great Passion*, 80.
55. Ibid., 28.
56. Barth, "The Humanity of God," 48.
57. Barth, *Church Dogmatics* III/2, 220. See also Thompson, *Christ in Perspective*, 78.

correspondence between Subject and object which may have once existed has been destroyed by sin.

In denying the *analogia entis* with its reasoned identification of the attributes of God on the ground of the creature, Barth does not deny human reason itself as an instrument for understanding the things of God. In fact, bearing in mind Anselm's dictum *fides quaerens intellectum*, he mounts something of a side-defense of the place of reason in theology. At creation God pronounced the whole person, and therefore all human capacities *including reason*, "very good." Certainly post-lapsarian humankind stands under the judgement of God, a judgement falling also on and limiting human reason. Nevertheless this does not detract from reason's essential theological function, that is, to point to the availability of the knowledge of God where *God* discloses it.

That said, as earlier Reformers, Protestant and Roman Catholic,[58] Barth sees that at best human reason can only establish that which is within its province. It cannot derive the knowledge of God in Jesus Christ, which knowledge is by definition beyond natural reach. Since God is the presupposition grounding the knowledge of God,[59] and since God discloses this knowledge to faith,[60] it is by faith and not by reason that such knowledge is received. Thence, and right from the beginning of his project, Barth denies the reasonable starting point for the knowledge of God as a flight from properly grounded human reason.[61] Setting itself on high, reason produces not the real knowledge of God in Jesus Christ, but all manner of anthropocentric notions of God which—as Torrance explains Barth—"man thinks up out of the depth of his own being and

---

58. To instance someone fairly termed a Roman Catholic Reformer, Frenchman Blaise Pascal (1623–1662) essentially argues that reason is an insufficient instrument with which to acquire the knowledge of God. Only the God-given intuition of the human heart is capable of doing so.

59. Torrance writes that for Barth, "It is through God alone that we may know God in accordance with his nature." Torrance, *Karl Barth*, 213. See also Busch, *Great Passion*, 27.

60. It is here that Barth's study of Anselm in *Fides Quaerens Intellectum* is important. By it Barth sees that the Word of God establishes the conditions under which the knowledge of God can be received. See Alan Torrance, "Christian Experience and Divine Revelation."

61. Barth appeals here to Luther, who "admonished and warned us all to leave off speculating and not to float too high but to stay here below by the cradle and diaper in which Christ lies, in whom dwells all the fulness of the deity bodily." Barth, *Calvin*, 47.

from all the fanciful projections out of his own self-understanding."[62] The most reason can do with respect to the knowledge of God is to point to its incapacity to attain that knowledge.

But the fallen creature willfully persists in its attempt to determine the knowledge of God reasonably, and therefore to equate itself with God. Thence it attracts radical confrontation by the Word of God, a confrontation it resists in equal and opposite directions. Either the creature effects a cold rationalism, lacking humility and passion and engaging in an overbold assertion of its prowess to determine the truth both of God and of itself in relation to God. Or it declares the truth of God present amid emotion and "hype," saving itself the hard work of thinking out the faith—which Barth calls *laziness*.[63] Both these strategies Barth thinks exist in the modern Christian community. Against the Word of God neither can prevail.

If a starting point in human reason cannot attain the knowledge of God, neither can a starting point for God in felt (affective) human experience. In this regard Barth's particular nemesis is once again the theology of the nineteenth century. Schleiermacher and the Liberal Protestants hold that the creature can know God only by beginning with its own perception, its own ability to encounter reality. Barth mounts two objections to this. First, by definition the experiential starting point is tethered subjectively and so incapable of deducing any but relative truth. But even more seriously, second, the experiential starting point puts "into the hand of man the instrument with which . . . man becomes wholly master even of the self-revealing God."[64] Such a starting point is therefore ill-conceived, sinful.

Three areas bearing on these comments may now be canvassed: Barth's own understanding of human experience of God, Schleiermacher's theology of experience, and Barth's response to the latter. Since the matter well exemplifies Barth's clash with the modern epistemology of glory, it will be explored here at some length.

True experience of God Barth defines as that knowledge gained from "human acquaintance with an object whereby its truth becomes a

---

62. Torrance, *Karl Barth*, 17.

63. Generally Barth equates laziness and sin. For further comment by Barth on laziness, see here p. 204, n. 43.

64. Barth, *Epistle to the Philippians*, 228–29. See also Busch, *Great Passion*, 59.

determination of the existence of the man who has the knowledge."[65] As Torrance explains Barth,[66] this object is the one word intelligible solely in terms of itself, the ultimate impinging object, the Word of God therefore. As it is encountered by the ultimate object or Word the creature's subjective knowledge of the encountering other is determined, as also its knowledge of itself in relation to this other.[67]

In this experience the creature is forced to acknowledge that there really is another determining and confronting it, and that—contra the modern mindset—it itself cannot really be the centre of reality. Certain such creatures then respond in acknowledgment and humble submission. Or as Barth himself says, "In the act of acknowledgement, the life of man, without ceasing to be the self-determining life of this man, has now its centre, its whence [or reason to be], the meaning of its attitude, and the criterion whether this attitude really has the corresponding meaning—it has all this outside itself, in the Word of God acknowledged in and through Christian experience."[68] This for Barth is what constitutes authentic Christian experience of God, experience ultimately tethered objectively and not subjectively. To use Alan Torrance's phraseology, it follows for Barth that "When the Word of God is present to us . . . we are turned away from ourselves and towards the Word of God, . . . orientated to it."[69]

There is for Barth a commensurate point. The very experience of being encountered by the objective other, or Word, determines the creature's knowledge that it itself did not initiate that encounter. "If man lets himself be told by the Word of God that he has a Lord, . . . [the] specific content of the Word experienced by him will flatly prohibit him from ascribing the possibility of this experience to himself either wholly or

---

65. Barth, *Church Dogmatics* I/1, 198.

66. See Torrance, Alan, "Christian Experience and Divine Revelation," 9–10.

67. A common criticism of Barth's theology of experience is that he speaks of Christian experience in terms of an acknowledgement of encounter by the Word of God, but says little concerning the *experiences* (plural) of the creature caught up in this encounter. He makes little mention, it is said, of guilt, suffering, rejection, forsakenness, despair, disillusionment, and so forth. But in the present view this criticism is ill-founded. As later discussion will indicate it is simply not the case that Barth neglects the felt-experience of the creature pressed by God.

68. Barth, *Church Dogmatics* I/1, 208.

69. Torrance, Alan, "Christian Experience and Divine Revelation," 14.

in part or from dialectically equating the divine possibility actualized in this experience with a possibility of his own."[70]

Additionally, Barth says that while God initiates and thus determines the creature's subjective experience of being encountered, nevertheless the creature is not a strictly *passive* recipient of this experience. Rather, to experience God is to experience oneself being determined by, and consequently responding to God. So Barth says, "If God is seriously involved in experience of the Word of God then man is just as seriously involved too . . . [The] very man who stands in real knowledge of the Word of God also knows himself as existing in the act of his life, as existing in his self-determination."[71]

This distinctive theology of experience is formed over against that of Schleiermacher and the nineteenth century. From the latter part of the eighteenth century on the perceived aridity of the Enlightenment begins to engender a Romantic reaction privileging feeling, nature, a spirituality based on old gods and old religious paths.[72] But to the young Schleiermacher Romanticism merely compounds the relegation of Christian faith already under way in the wake of the Enlightenment itself. He therefore sets out to commend the Christian religion both intellectually and affectively to his own age.

Alan Torrance explains further. "[What] Kant had done for science in grounding and defending scientific principles before what he saw to be the philosophical skepticism of this age, Schleiermacher sought to do for religion in an age which seemed to be undermining more and more the importance and relevance of religious conviction, by setting out to establish unshakably the essential principle underlying all piety and religion."[73]

Schleiermacher agrees with Kant that all experience has a cause, but disagrees that religion is a form of experiential knowledge which, since it lacks empirical validity, is best categorized under moral and practi-

70. Barth, *Church Dogmatics* I/1, 200. In part Barth's position is a reaction to Schleiermacher's notion of dependence. See here pp. 212-13.

71. Ibid., IV/1, 200.

72. Romanticism is an artistic, literary, and intellectual movement c.1770–1850 in Western Europe. It reacts against the aristocratic, social, and political norms of the Enlightenment, including the scientific rationalization of nature in art and literature. Counter to these it emphasizes *emotion* as a source of aesthetic experience, arguing for an epistemology based on what exists naturally.

73. Alan Torrance, "Christian Experience and Divine Revelation," 3.

cal reason. Rather for him the human religious experience of God, the culminating form of which is specifically *Christian* piety, is not one type of human experience but *the* basic human experience. Similarly it is not one form of knowledge but *the* fundamental datum of human existence, the "*a priori* of personhood," to use Kantian language.

For Schleiermacher essential proof of this is presented by the evident existence of a special form of experience, *viz.* the feeling of absolute dependence on God, seated not in the senses but in the deepest levels of human self-consciousness. He argues that for there to be freedom there must be a corresponding other in relation to whom the creature is free. Since the creature feels free, this other must exist. Since however the creature also feels its freedom to be circumscribed this other must claim and determine it. Since the other claims and determines it the creature feels itself to be in a dependent relationship with one whom Schleiermacher then designates "God."

This experiential "feeling of absolute dependence" or "God-consciousness"[74] becomes Schleiermacher's epistemological proof not only of the existence of God, but of God situated beyond the creature determining and enabling it to experience God. Brilliantly therefore, Schleiermacher at once achieves an empirical basis for the Christian religion in deference to the scientific ethos of the Enlightenment, and distinguishes God from the creature correcting Romanticism where it confuses the two. Moreover in doing so he pays homage to the Romantic embrace of felt experience.

In this Schleiermacher never intends a way for the creature to determine God. For him God is not an object requiring definition against other objects in order to be experienced, indeed not an *object* at all to be thus determined. It follows, he says, that the "transference of the idea of God to any perceptible object . . . is always a corruption."[75] He adds that any "possibility of God being *given* is entirely excluded because anything that is outwardly given must be given as an object exposed to our

---

74. Schleiermacher goes on to show that it is "God-consciousness" that draws all human beings into a synthetic unity with each other, in which the distinctiveness between individuals vanishes. For him this is the essence of the Christian experience of communion.

75. Schleiermacher, *The Christian Faith*, 4:4. See also Torrance, Alan, "Christian Experience and Divine Revelation," 6.

counter-influence, however slight that may be."⁷⁶ This is something with which Barth would agree.

To digress slightly, there are indeed several similarities between Schleiermacher's and Barth's overall positions, as Barth himself acknowledges. Both are concerned with experience, and view it as theologically vital. Both hold that God is not an object in the control of the creature. Both reject the Kantian notion that religious knowledge is subordinate because non-verifiable; rather religious knowledge *is* verifiable and thence foundational to all other knowledge. Both want to recommend Christian faith to the modern age, and in the attempt to do so both seek an intrinsically modern, reasonable and empirical, method for theology.

But, to return to the matter at hand, in his theology of experience Schleiermacher's underlying concern is however quite different to that of Barth, or of the crucicentric theologians generally. Unlike Barth, Schleiermacher's prior intention is not to undercut a theology of glory, but to defend the Christian religion in a scientific age.

Barth in his response to Schleiermacher and the nineteenth century first insists on honoring the theologians of the past, even and perhaps especially those whom he considers misguided. All are in the church by virtue of the same forgiveness, all have made their contribution. For Barth himself to criticize them *as Christians* would mean that he has not heard the Church in them as he should.⁷⁷ Or as Barth himself explains, "One must speak with equal reverence of the human and scientific attitude of many if not all the representatives of [nineteenth century theology. What] scholarly figures they were . . . I say this in order to emphasize that . . . we are faced with a type of person that merits our highest respect. This in itself is reason enough for our listening to them even today."⁷⁸

Of Schleiermacher specifically Barth stresses that only those who can love him have any right to criticize him. Barth can empathize with Schleiermacher's concerns and otherwise admire the genius he brings to his task. But in founding God experientially, subjectively, Schleiermacher relegates God to the level of the creature, further relativising the very

---

76. Ibid. Italics original.
77. See Barth, *Protestant Theology in the Nineteenth Century*, 14.
78. Barth, "Evangelical Theology in the Nineteenth Century," 16–17.

religion he had wanted to defend and build up. Thence Barth regards Schleiermacher's general approach with profound suspicion.

Early in his own project, in 1922, Barth asks acerbically whether for Schleiermacher and the nineteenth century "to speak of God means something other than to speak of man with a loud voice."[79] Around the same time he lectures:

> I have no reason to conceal the fact that I view with mistrust both Schleiermacher and all that Protestant theology became under his influence, that in Christian matters I do *not* regard the decision that was made in that intellectually and culturally significant age [i.e., to make God a postulate of the creature] as a happy one and that the result of my study of Schleiermacher . . . may be summed up in that saying of Goethe: "Lo, his spirit calls to thee from a cave: be a man and *not* follow me."[80]

Towards the far end of his project Barth's suspicion of Schleiermacher has not diminished. In his 1956 retrospective essay *The Humanity of God* he declares, "For [Schleiermacher's] theology to think about God meant to think in a scarcely veiled fashion about man . . . his revelations and wonders, his faith and his works. There is no question about it: here man was made great at the cost of God—the divine God who is someone other than man . . . This God was in danger of being reduced to a pious notion—to a mystical expression and symbol of a current alternating between a man and [man's] own heights or depths."[81]

Schleiermacher's experiential theology is, in Barth's view, really anthropology. Formally and materially, the starting point in a feeling of absolute dependence leads not to the knowledge of God but to the creature's self-reflection. Thence Barth says, "The great formal principle of Schleiermacher's theology is at the same time its material principle. Christian pious self-awareness contemplates and describes *itself*: that is in principle the be-all and end-all of this theology."[82] Barth further finds that Schleiermacher's theology is "a theology of self-understanding [which therefore does] not break through the general trend of the century,"[83] that trend which gives first place to the creature, relativising

---

79. See Barth, *The Word of God and the Word of Man*, 196.
80. Barth, "The Theology of Schleiermacher," xiv-xv. Italics original.
81. Barth, "The Humanity of God," 39-40.
82. Barth, *Protestant Theology in the Nineteenth Century*, 443. Italics original.
83. Barth, "Evangelical Theology in the Nineteenth Century," 24.

God. Moreover for Schleiermacher "faith in Christ" is merely a mode of human cognition, a way of thinking about Christ, rather than the gracious gift of the divine Son. That understanding of faith means the creature appropriating divine capacity to itself. Further still, Schleiermacher's desire to interpret Christianity so that it does not conflict with modernity subjects the gospel to modern culture, something Barth regards as a disastrous mistake.[84]

All this leads inevitably to an interpretation of the divinity of Christ whereby Christ merely culminates the divinity nascent in humankind. Here Barth says, "According to the premises of his concept of religion [Schleiermacher] was bound to renounce the idea of the Deity of Christ, to put it differently, to understand the Deity of Christ as the incomparable climax and decisive stimulator within the composite life of humanity."[85] Herein the self-glorifying end of all Schleiermacher's prodigious endeavors.

Given these multiple compromises the church is no longer able to stand over against the world. Impoverished spiritually and theologically, it becomes orientated towards a psychological interpretation of faith. These reversals also mean that contrary to his own claim, Schleiermacher is not true to the Reformers. The latter express the ground motifs "God" and "man" as "the Word of God" and "faith," but Schleiermacher has exchanged the Reformation expressions for "human religion," "human religious consciousness," and "human piety." He mediates a modern theology of glory, one that subjugates the gospel to the age, reduces Jesus Christ to the level of the creature, and raises the creature to the level of God. Thus Barth concludes flatly, "The basic concern of evangelical theology could not find a genuine expression in these terms."[86]

But it is not just what Schleiermacher *does* that disturbs Barth. The problem is equally what he does *not* do. In his recourse to anthropocentrism Schleiermacher misses the opportunity to present a real answer to the modern age. He says nothing of the God who actually *is* the objective Other, who confronts the self-glorifying pretensions of modern men and women. He does not stop at Jesus Christ. He does not halt before the cross. So Barth says with regret, "If only the need for an approach

---

84. See Busch, *Great Passion*, 58, and Torrance, *Karl Barth*, 30.
85. Barth, *Protestant Thought*, 349.
86. Barth, "Evangelical Theology in the Nineteenth Century," 24.

from below had been genuine, and had grown out of a new examination of the authentic concerns of theology!"[87]

From the outset therefore, Barth not only criticizes Schleiermacher's bent toward false human glory, but consciously sets out to end what is finally a catastrophic influence spilling into the twentieth century. As early as 1916 he announces this intention. ["Under the influence of Schleiermacher and the nineteenth century, with] a thousand arts we have made ourselves a god in our own image . . . It is clear that such a god is not God . . . [It] is high time for us to declare ourselves thoroughgoing doubters, skeptics, scoffers and atheists in regard to him. It is high time for us to confess freely and gladly: this god, to whom we have built the tower of Babel, is not God. He is an idol. He is dead." And to this sentiment he later adds, "None of the laughter or head-shaking of our contemporaries and none of our faint-heartedness ought to keep us from at least recognizing the task."[88]

At the far end of his life in 1968 Barth provides an epilogue to his 1923–1924 lectures on Schleiermacher's theology of experience. His editor Dietrich Ritschl notes Barth's now more balanced, even "critically resigned" attitude to Schleiermacher. Ritschl then adds, "But the content of the argument remains the same. Man has been made the subject of theology and Christ his predicate. And what Barth's earlier interpretation of Schleiermacher clearly leads us to is now [in the 1960s] fully confirmed, namely that [Schleiermacher's influence] is now extended [such] that modern twentieth century German theology is "a new and vigorous Schleiermacher renaissance."[89]

Dismissing Schleiermacher's attempt to recommend Christianity to the age therefore, it is Barth's lasting position that way must continuously be made for a proper and faithful kind of modern theology. That is, for a theology beginning reasonably with the Subject and Object at the centre of reality, who alone knows its divine self, and who therefore exclusively determines the creature's experiential knowledge of itself as Other.

Discussion on the theology of experience draws this sketch of Barth's negative epistemology towards its close. Busch says that in Barth's theology, "God's Word, which is outside any human grasp, chal-

---

87. Ibid.
88. Barth, Karl, *Göttingen Dogmatics*, 3–5. See also Busch, *Great Passion*, 61.
89. Barth, "The Theology of Schleiermacher," x. See opening epilogue.

lenges all human attempts to posit oneself as absolute."[90] Included here is the attempt to control the knowledge of God as God. That attempt is unreasonable; it ignores the given starting point in divine revelation in Jesus Christ culminating in the cross. It is also culpably sinful; any knowledge of "God" so obtained cannot be knowledge of the true God, the God of the Bible, but of an idol of the creature's own making after its own likeness and understanding.

At the same time, a point not always recognized, the negation of false epistemologies is for Barth scarcely the first task of theology. Rather they are to be dismissed *a limine*, at the threshold of serious theological reflection. Epistemologically the first task for a properly modern epistemology is *positive*, the reassertion of a christocentric and crucicentric way to the knowledge of God grounded logically in the place that knowledge is really proclaimed. Thompson agrees. "[Barth's approach is frequently] considered primarily as a negative approach denying that man by the light of reason, nature and history can attain to God, whereas what he is basically concerned to do is to affirm the truth of God in Jesus Christ."[91]

The Positive Epistemology of the Cross

To recap the opening statement to this chapter, positively for Barth "God is known through God and through God alone."[92] Barth says that he has made this "assumption and reckoned and worked with it all along."[93] God, being God, might have vested in the creature a capacity to independently attain the knowledge of God, a capacity standing over against divine revelation.[94] But evidently that is not what God has done. Rather the possibility of an anthropocentric starting point is undermined, relativised and set aside by the actual situation that exists: God makes himself known supremely in Jesus Christ.

Jesus Christ is "the light of life, the saving revelation of God, . . . the pronouncement, revelation and phenomenon of the truth, the truth

90. Busch, *Great Passion*, 27.
91. Thompson, *Christ in Perspective*, 120.
92. Barth, *Church Dogmatics* I/1, 296, and II/1, 179–80.
93. Ibid.
94. See Barth, *Church Dogmatics* II/1, 44. See also von Balthasar, *The Theology of Karl Barth*, 160.

itself".⁹⁵ He is the true starting point for authentic human knowledge of God. In his 1956 summary essay Barth draws this out. "Jesus Christ . . . comes forward to *man* on behalf of *God* . . . We do not need to engage in a free-ranging investigation to seek out and construct who and what God truly is, and who and what man truly is, but only to read the truth about both where it resides, namely, in the fullness of their togetherness, their covenant which proclaims itself in Jesus Christ."⁹⁶ Likewise Barth says, "[Our] starting point is not in any sense [reliant on] epistemological [science.] However man's capacity for knowledge may be described . . . the conclusion that God is known only through God does not have either its basis or its origin in any understanding of the human capacity for knowledge [but in] God revealed in his Word."⁹⁷

In that the knowledge of God is revealed in the man-God Jesus Christ, it shines in him most obviously, and so is revealed through him most clearly, at the point of the cross—in cruciform darkness and degradation. The remaining part of this chapter seeks to draw out the major aspects of this positive and integrally crucicentric epistemology. Mention is made first of Barth's approach to two systematic intersections: epistemology and Christology, and epistemology and pneumatology. Next his theology around two classically crucicentric motifs is explored: wisdom and foolishness, and hiddenness and revelation. Finally Barth's position concerning the creature's incorporation in the mind of Christ is outlined.

Crucicentric Epistemology and Christology

Several themes intermesh at the intersection of Barth's epistemology and Christology. These include: divine revelation to the creature, the personhood of Jesus Christ, the self-revealing God, Jesus Christ as the Word and truth of the cross, and the revelatory priority of the cross.

Divine revelation is always revelation *to* the creature. This notion does not rest for Barth on philosophic logic—the revealing subject necessarily requiring an object. Rather it rests properly theologically. Revelation has its basis and truth in the God who from eternity elects to reveal himself, whose "speaking is the basis of human hearing and

---

95. Barth, *Church Dogmatics* IV/3, 377–78.
96. Barth, "The Humanity of God," 47. Italics original.
97. Ibid.

confessing, and not *vice versa*."⁹⁸ This is a position Barth reiterates in many ways and places. For example he says, "[God] is and remains the One whom we know only because he gives himself to be known. He is and remains the light visible and seen only in His own light."⁹⁹ Similarly, "[In] the knowledge of God we have to do . . . with God Himself by God Himself."¹⁰⁰ Again, "Knowledge of God is knowledge completely effected and determined from the side of its object, from the side of God."¹⁰¹ And finally now, "God's revelation takes place among us and for us, in the sphere of our experience and of our thinking. But it has to be seriously accepted that it happens as a movement 'from God.' It is by the truth itself than in revelation we have to do with the truth itself. And it is only in the truth itself that, summoned and authorized and directed by it, we can effectively refer and appeal to the truth itself."¹⁰²

In his self-revelation God does what the creature "cannot do in any sense or way; he makes himself present, known and significant to [the creature] as God."¹⁰³ This also means that whenever God is really known by the creature, it is God who has disclosed himself to it and determined its knowledge. Thus Barth says conclusively, "The perfect work of truth will always be God's own work and not ours."¹⁰⁴

Bearing on this, Barth works out his theology of revelation in a series of interrelated models predicated on the threefold structure of the Trinity. Pertaining to all of them, he observes that, "*God* reveals Himself. He reveals Himself *through Himself. He* reveals *Himself.*"¹⁰⁵ These models may be summarized as follows:

- The self-revealing God reveals himself in unimpaired unity yet also in unimpaired distinction. As such he is Revealer, Revelation, and Revealedness.¹⁰⁶

---

98. Barth, *Church Dogmatics* IV/3, 411.
99. Ibid., II/1, 41.
100. Ibid., II/1, 181.
101. Barth, *Dogmatics in Outline*, 24.
102. Barth, *Church Dogmatics* II/1, 69.
103. Ibid., I/2, 362.
104. Ibid., II/1, 208.
105. Ibid., II/1, 296. Italics original.
106. See ibid., I/1, 295.

- The Word of God reveals himself firstly by speaking primarily and directly in the history of Israel culminating in Jesus Christ, secondly through the Witness of Holy Scripture, and thirdly through the proclamation of the church as it faithfully listens to Holy Scripture.[107]

- Divine revelation involves three realms of reality: the ultimate or primary realm in which God knows God, the secondary realm in which God makes God objectively known, and the tertiary realm in which the creature receives the knowledge of God mediated to it by God.

- The self-revelation of God can be understood in terms of subject, predicate and object. God the Father is the divine Subject who acts to reveal himself. God the Holy Spirit is the divine Predicate, the act of self-revealing. God the Son is the Object who is revealed.

- Related to the above, God may be understood as the Subject, the Act (or Power), and the Content and *Telos* of revelation. God is the Subject which discloses itself, the Act of self-disclosure; and the *Telos* and Content of that which is disclosed.

Behind these models lies a critical *crucicentric* idea: revealed knowledge is always "indirect and mediate, not immediate knowledge."[108] It is, as Barth lectures in 1922, knowledge channeled to the creature by way of Jesus Christ.[109] This also means methodologically that Barth's Christology and epistemology are profoundly intertwined. To turn to this dogmatic intersection three matters are now quickly reviewed,

---

107. See ibid., I/1, 111.

108. Ibid., II/1, 57.

109. Barth says here, "*Faith* and *revelation* expressly deny that there is any way from man to God and to God's grace, love, and life. Both words indicate that the only way between God and man is that which leads *from* God *to* man. Between these words—and this is the inner kernel of the theology of Paul and the Reformation—there are two other words: *Jesus Christ* . . . We can only say that by these words Paul and Luther and, finally and most positively, Calvin . . . meant to point toward that way of God to man which is the channel by which all reality reaches us" (Barth, "Ethics Today," 179–80. Italics original.). This is one place where Calvin can fairly be said to exercise an important influence on Barth's crucicentric approach. In a lecture around the same time Barth says, "We need to note above all else that for Calvin there is no real distinction between the elements of knowledge, but that Christ is from the first the key with which he unlocks the whole." Barth, *Calvin*, 164.

the significance of Christology for Barth, his understanding of Christ's Personhood, and of Christ as Revealer.

Barth says, "strictly speaking there are no Christian themes independent of Christology."[110] His work consistently reflects this methodological conclusion, Christology providing the inner content and structure of his thought overall. Thompson summarises the point when he says, "In [Barth's] theology there is no Christology as such; on the other hand, it is all Christology . . . This is due to the fact that [his] theology as a whole and in every part is determined by its relation to Jesus Christ, his being and action, so that one cannot detach any aspect of it from its christological basis."[111]

But for Barth Christology is more than a body of doctrine, even a guiding one. It is a way of thinking, a listening approach, an orientation to the living Christ himself. So he explains, "For me thinking is christological . . . when it consists in the perception, comprehension, understanding and estimation of the living person of Jesus Christ as attested by Holy Scripture, in attentiveness to the range and significance of his existence, in openness to his self-disclosure, in consistency in following him as is demanded."[112] And similarly in a personal letter dated to 1952, "I have no christological principle and no christological method. Rather, in each individual theological question I seek to orient myself afresh to some extent from the very beginning—not on a christological dogma but on Jesus Christ himself (*vivit! regnat! triumphat!*) [He lives! He reigns! He triumphs!]"[113]

Significantly Barth holds that in Jesus Christ the human is the setting for the divine, and the divine for the human. It follows that, "The one Jesus Christ is unlimitedly and unreservedly both God and man."[114]

Jesus Christ is *God*. For Barth it is the humiliation of Christ in the cross which supremely discloses not only the deity of Jesus Christ, but the meaning of his deity in terms of his whole history, as also the significance of the cross itself as a divine epistemological instrument. Indeed, as we have seen, Klappert calls this Barth's "basic thesis," *viz.* "[Barth's] basic thesis [is] the character of the whole history of Jesus Christ as the

110. Barth, *Church Dogmatics* II/1, 320.
111. Thompson, *Christ in Perspective*, 52.
112. Barth, *Church Dogmatics* IV/3, 174.
113. Letter to B. Gherandini, 24 May 1952. See Busch, *Great Passion*, 30.
114. Barth, *Church Dogmatics* IV/2, 73.

history of humiliation on the cross[. This is] the center from which he interprets the early Christian confession of the deity of Jesus."[115]

This basic thesis can be seen operating in Barth's typically crucicentric perception that in the deepest humiliation of the cross the reign of *God* is to be found. It was *because* Jesus Christ finally suffered and was crucified, died and was buried, that (in the light of the resurrection) the gospels attest him as Lord. "It was here they found the coronation of the King."[116] Barth makes a similar point in his consideration of the way of the Son. "Who the one true God is, and what He is, i.e., what is His being as God, and therefore his deity, . . . we have to discover from . . . His obedience of suffering, i.e., (1) the obedience of the Son to the Father, shown (2) in His self-humiliation, His way into the far country, fulfilled in His death on the cross. [The] mystery that he is very God [is] completely closed and necessarily closed to any consideration or reflection which does not look at Him."[117]

It follows decisively for Barth that Jesus Christ is "an element in our knowledge of God. We cannot speak correctly of God in his being in and for himself without considering him always in this attitude[. He is] the actual relationship in which God has placed himself; a relationship outside of which God no longer wills to be and no longer is God, and within which alone he can be truly honored and worshipped as God."[118]

But in Jesus Christ God is equally the *human* God. Again it is the sacrificial work of the cross that supremely discloses this. Here Barth says for example, "[The man Jesus] perceives that the superior will of God, to which he wholly subordinates himself, requires that he sacrifice himself for the human race, and seeks [to glorify God] in doing this. In the mirror of this [sacrificial] humanity . . . the humanity of God enclosed in his deity reveals itself."[119]

---

115. Klappert, *Auferweckung des Gekreuzigten*, 154, cited by Thompson, *Christ in Perspective*, 52. For further comment on Klappert's notion of Barth's "basic thesis" see here p. 175.

116. Barth, *Church Dogmatics* IV/2, 290.

117. Barth, *Church Dogmatics* IV/1, 177.

118. Ibid., II/2, 6–7.

119. Barth, "The Humanity of God," 51.

Barth holds that the human nature of Jesus Christ is at once like and unlike that of the creature. It is *like* in its sheer humanity. But it is *unlike* in being totally determined by grace in its: origin, sinlessness, holiness, authority, mediatory work, dignity, glory, but above all in its unity with the Holy Spirit. This is so in Christ's: election, incarnation, resurrection, ascension and final exaltation.

Almost every chapter of Barth's mature theology contains explicit or implicit reference to this. For quick instance, "[The] height of freedom and the depth of love actual in God the Father, Son, and Holy Ghost; each perfection of true Godhead, holiness or mercy or wisdom, omnipresence or omnipotence or eternity—all this is unlimitedly and unreservedly proper to the One who as Son of God became also Son of Man."[120] "[The Son] became and was and is man. But because he did so as the Son of God He is from the very first, from all eternity in the election and decree of God, elect man . . . [He] became man like us, but genuinely and totally."[121] And finally now, "The fact . . . that God Himself, in His deep mercy and its great power, has taken it upon Himself to exist also in human being and essence in His Son, and therefore to become and be a man, and therefore this incomparable Thou [means that we] have to do with God Himself as we have to do with this man."[122]

Subsisting within the divine nature, the humanity of Jesus Christ nevertheless always remains distinctly and authentically *human*. Barth makes abundantly clear that in the human history of Jesus Christ there is not a simple correspondence between humiliation and exaltation. "The first, His humiliation as the Son of God, means that he became a man. But the second, His exaltation as the Son of Man, does not mean that [the Son of Man] became God."[123] Similarly, "The Son of Man is not deified by the fact that he is also and primarily the Son of God. He does not become a fourth in the Holy Trinity."[124] Or again, "[In] Jesus Christ, as he is attested in Holy Scripture, we are not dealing with . . . the man who is able with his modicum of religion and religious morality to be sufficient unto himself without God and thus himself to be God."[125]

120. Ibid., IV/2, 73.
121. Ibid., IV/2, 358.
122. Ibid., IV/2, 50–51.
123. Ibid., IV/2, 71.
124. Ibid., IV/2, 93–94.
125. Barth, "The Humanity of God," 46.

Behind this, and in typical crucicentric fashion, Barth guards against the false logic that because deity and humanity exist hypostatically in Christ's representative Person, his human nature becomes itself divine. He puts the hanging question explicitly, "[If] the humanity of Jesus Christ is by definition the humanity of all men, [does this] not mean that the essence of all men, human essence as such, is capable of divinization?"[126] In response he makes it clear that *if even in the circumstances of Jesus Christ* human nature remains human, so does the humanity of the creature patterned on him.

That Jesus Christ is fully God and fully human raises the further and ancient question as to how the two natures of Christ are related. Barth supports the companion patristic doctrines of *anhypostasia* and *enhypostasia*. The human nature of the man Jesus is anhypostatic, it has no hypostasis or personal locus of its own, it does not exist independently of his divine nature. Rather it is enhypostatically assumed and subsumed into the divine nature of the Son, so that Jesus Christ is human only as he is divine.

As the human God, Jesus Christ is representative of all other humans. Thus Barth writes of him, "He became and was and is the one real and true and living and royal man; and as such he represents us."[127] He is then the prototypical, if infinitely superior, representative human being, the pattern for all other human beings. Again, and reflecting Paul, Barth observes that, "It belongs to the distinctive essence of Jesus Christ of the New Testament that as the One He alone is He is not alone, but the royal Representative, the Lord and Head of many."[128]

It is then for Barth precisely because Jesus Christ is the God that he is, and the man that he is, that in his freedom he is able to reveal God to the creature, and enable the creature to receive this knowledge.[129] Jesus Christ is Revelation, the one who discloses and the knowledge disclosed. This answer does not change across Barth's long project. In his 1922 Romans commentary he proclaims Jesus Christ the revelation of God

---

126. Ibid., IV/2, 81.

127. Ibid., IV/2, 358.

128. Ibid., IV/2, 275.

129. Barth's protection of the sheer freedom of God accounts for his insistence on the divine prerogative in all aspects of the divine / human relation. Indeed, Barth says, "[Even] in the form which he assumes by revealing himself, God is free to reveal himself or not to reveal himself." Barth, *Church Dogmatics* I/1, 369.

broken into the world, "the gospel and the meaning of history."[130] In his 1956 retrospective essay he declares Jesus Christ to be "in his Person the covenant in its fullness, the Kingdom of heaven which is at hand in which God speaks and man hears, [and] the *Revealer* of them both."[131] And in countless places in between Barth proclaims Jesus Christ the revelatory Truth and Word of God, and as such the Word of the cross.

Jesus Christ is the self-disclosing Truth of God. In many places Barth refers to John 14:6 in which Jesus claims not just to speak the truth but to *be* the truth that is spoken. It is as *this* ontic and noetic Truth[132] that he discloses both the truth of God in Godself, and of God and the creature in their relation. Thus Barth says, "Who and what God is in truth and who and what man, we have not to explore and construct by roving far and near, but to read it where the truth about both dwells, in the fullness of their union, their covenant, that fullness which manifests itself in Jesus Christ."[133]

Noetic, ontic, definitively relational, this truth is grounded entirely in itself. It is therefore "the first and final truth behind which there is concealed no other or different truth."[134] For this reason it precedes and is the exclusive basis for all other truths. It cannot be measured by some other and greater standard, for there is no such standard. This exclusive truth is the complete truth of God. There is no hidden depth in God that Jesus Christ does not truly reflect and cannot truly convey. It is not that he reveals only a "part" of the truth, or certain truths and not others.[135] Anything less than full revelation of the truth by Jesus Christ would mean that what he reveals is different from God who is Truth, undercutting the actuality of divine revelation. Anything less would mean, and as Parker interprets Barth, that "we should . . . have to turn elsewhere for

---

130. Barth, *Romans*, 29.

131. Barth, "The Humanity of God," 47. Italics original.

132. Torrance further explains this, "[Noetic] truth . . . is only truth as it derives from and rests in the ontic truth of God's self-objectification for us, and his self-giving to us in the revelation of himself—it is truth that has an ontological depth of objectivity in the very being and nature of God in his Word." Torrance, *Karl Barth*, 46.

133. Barth, "The Humanity of God," 38–39.

134. Barth, *Church Dogmatics* IV/1, 51.

135. See Busch, *Great Passion*, 88.

our knowledge [of God.]"¹³⁶ Given the actual state of affairs that exists however, Barth considers such a turn to be emphatically *not* required.

Barth's theology of truth is intermeshed with his theology of untruth—of the *lie* therefore, in which the creature attempts to render the truth innocuous, to "work it over, to translate and reinterpret and transform it . . . into a less troublesome [word.]"¹³⁷ That is, into a word which "is well able to appropriate and domesticate even and especially the cross of Jesus Christ, and the Word of the cross: perhaps in such a way that the Word of His cross is changed into a word of the dramatic mortification which takes place and is fulfilled in man, . . . the new thing of God a practice of man[.]"¹³⁸

To return briefly to Barth's negative epistemology, for him this "domestication of the cross" is closely associated with modernity's tendency to relativise the God who is Truth. It presumes the existence of an *objective* point alongside God from which God can be so relativised, a point in the preserve of the creature. Just here Barth makes two observations. First, since only that which is equal to God can occupy a vantage-point over against God, the creature claiming such objectivity for itself necessarily equates itself to God. Second, in point of fact the creature is *not* God and possesses no such vantage-point. Thus it has been deceived. It has listened to a lie having its origins in that ontological untruth which deceives both the world and the worldly church, a lie which promises eternal glory but delivers only eternal death.¹³⁹ In contrast to this deception the truth proclaimed by the cross overcomes the lie, it unveils the veiled.¹⁴⁰ It discloses Jesus Christ positively as "the truth—not simply a truth."¹⁴¹

Jesus Christ is then the truth who exclusively makes the truth of God available to the creature. Granting this parameter, Barth yet allows the creature *already* in the community of Christ a certain capacity to discern truth. He inserts this proviso on properly theological grounds, rather than the merely logical ones that the creature in Christ has unique access to truth. By his Spirit Jesus Christ reveals his truth *directly* to each

136. Parker, "Barth on Revelation," 372.
137. Barth, *Church Dogmatics* IV/3, 442.
138. Ibid., IV/3, 442–43.
139. See Barth, *Church Dogmatics* IV/3, 437–38.
140. See Ibid., I/1, 133.
141. Ibid., II/1, 68.

member of his community,[142] calling her or him to think out what is received in the illuminating light of the Spirit.[143] For, Barth says, the person in Christ is not merely an automaton, as it were "a cog set in motion."[144] Behind this he is concerned that uncritical acceptance of ecclesial dogma could hinder the life of God from flowing freely through the church. Clearly too he has in mind the Reformation summons to individual freedom of biblical interpretation in the light of the Holy Spirit.

Parallelling his theology of Jesus Christ as the ontic and noetic Truth, Barth holds Jesus Christ to be the ontic and noetic *Word of God*— the Word which speaks and the Word therefore conveyed and received, for in Jesus Christ God speaks so as to be heard. Barth expresses this in many places. Revelation in Jesus Christ, he says for example, "means the incarnation of the Word of God."[145] It follows that in this divine "revelation, God's Word is identical with God himself."[146] Elsewhere Barth writes similarly, "Jesus did not just come to tell us about God—but is himself the Word of God to us."[147] "Those who hear Him, hear God."[148]

Jesus Christ is then for Barth the exclusive Word of God to the creature, and as such the one Word permissible to the church. Barth writes, "[The] community cannot take account of any other word that God might have spoken before or after or side by side with or outside this word, and that He willed to have proclaimed by it. It accepts and proclaims this one Jesus Christ as the one Word, the first and final Word, of the true God."[149] It follows that Jesus Christ "is the one Word of God that we must hear, that we must trust and obey, both in life and in death. If . . . Jesus Christ is alive, if His community is the company of those among whom this is seen and taken seriously, as the axiom of all axioms, then the community . . . accepts and proclaims this one Jesus Christ as

---

142. Barth says here, "The living Lord Jesus Christ deals directly with his living community, not indirectly, not through some system of representation, not along the path of a humanly concocted chain of authority." Barth in *Die Schrift und die Kirche*, 37, cited by Busch, *Great Passion*, 259.

143. See ibid., IV/4, 35.

144. Barth, *Church Dogmatics* IV/3, 35, c.f. II/2, 178.

145. Ibid., I/2, 168.

146. Ibid., I/1, 349.

147. Ibid., III/1, 38.

148. Ibid., IV/3, 411.

149. Ibid., IV/1, 346.

the One Word, the first and final word, of the true God.¹⁵⁰ But it is the first article of the Barmen Declaration which constitutes perhaps Barth's best known statement to this effect, the declaration itself being almost entirely his own work. The declaration states, "Jesus Christ, as he is attested to us in Holy Scripture, is the one Word of God whom we have to hear, and whom we have to trust and obey in life and in death."¹⁵¹ Indeed, the community of faith cannot have to do with Jesus Christ apart from this divine Word, or with this Word apart from Jesus Christ.

This ontology is then pressed by Barth to align the Word of God and the Word of the Crucified Christ with the Word of the cross. In his exploration of the witness of Jesus Christ Barth asks, "Assuming that there is such a thing as the *theologia crucis*, the Word of the cross, and that it denotes the reality of the prophetic work of Jesus Christ, what is meant by this *theologia* or Word?"¹⁵² He then proceeds to answer his own question, echoing the classical crucicentric theologians in doing so. This Word of the cross is not a neutral word but alive, Barth says. It speaks "as the Crucified, Dead and Buried, . . . from the place from which God alone has the power to speak,"¹⁵³ from the far side of death. It "speaks of the work of God accomplished in His death, or, as we may also say, accomplished by Him as the One who suffered and died on the cross."¹⁵⁴ So it announces the meaning of the cross as the meaning of Jesus Christ, and identifies these meanings absolutely.

The proof that this is so, that the divine Word speaks in this cruciform way, rests for Barth not in speculative deduction, nor first in theological dogma. Rather it rests in prayer. For in prayer God speaks, and in prayer there "may be given without hesitation, vacillation or doubt, without the slightest uncertainty, the answer that the crucified Jesus Christ does speak; [and] as he speaks God speaks."¹⁵⁵ The Word from the cross and the Word of God are thus the same.

But Jesus Christ is equally the Content of that which is spoken from the cross. For as the cruciform Word he reveals and conveys "not only the work done, but in and with this Himself, His divine person,

150. Ibid.
151. See Green, Barth, 149.
152. Barth, *Church Dogmatics* IV/3, 409.
153. Ibid., 1V/3, 411.
154. Ibid.
155. Ibid., IV/3, 410.

His divine essence ... Hence the content of the pronouncement of this slain man is both the work and also the person and essence of God."[156] This living cruciform Content is then absolute, concrete. Repelling all attempts to subjugate it to some form of creaturely subjectivity Barth declares that it would "fill heaven and earth"[157] even if there were no one to perceive it, even if there were no ear to hear its speech.

If it is true that Barth awards revelatory priority to the Word of the Crucified and the Content that Word conveys, does he preference the epistemological significance of the cross over the epistemological significance of other christological moments? What is his starting point? Differing judgments are offered here.

T. F. Torrance, for instance, finds that, "[Barth's] starting point, as he so often said, was the resurrection of Jesus Christ. The downright reality of the resurrection, the bodily resurrection, of Jesus Christ from the dead overwhelmed him. It constituted the absolutely decisive event in space and time on which he took his stand and from which he took his bearings."[158] A few pages further on Torrance broadens this finding, "[It] was the incarnation of the Son of God, the Word made flesh in this world of space and time, that [Barth] made central in his theological and epistemological reconstruction."[159]

Bromiley, on the other hand, finds Barth's epistemological starting point to be the threefold Word of God—Jesus Christ, Scripture, and ecclesial proclamation. Such a starting point solves the ancient theological dilemma before Barth "of having to choose between an ontic beginning in God and a noetic beginning in Scripture,"[160] for by it Barth does both at once.

Thompson is of help at this point. He concludes, "[In] the context of revelation, the Easter story is central [for Barth.] In it takes place the hidden work of Jesus Christ which is subsequently revealed and believed in his resurrection ... but it is from the event itself that this is known and interpreted."[161] In this Thompson's appeal is both to his own and to Klappert's reading of Barth. To paraphrase Thompson, Klappert's

156. Barth, *Church Dogmatics* IV/3, 412.
157. Ibid., IV/3, 409.
158. Torrance, *Karl Barth*, 164.
159. Ibid., 168–69.
160. See Bromiley, *Introduction to the Theology of Karl Barth*, 13.
161. Thompson, *Christ in Perspective*, 141 n.61.

position is that in contrast to every conception of the resurrection as a completion of the being and work of Christ, it is the revelation of the royal man exalted on the cross to which the resurrection points, that for Barth completes the being and work of Christ.[162] Thompson then concludes, "One must . . . begin (as Barth does) with the fact that the true God . . . is revealed precisely in the humiliation and contradiction of the cross."[163]

It would seem that Thompson and Klappert, rather than Torrance and Bromiley, read Barth correctly here. Barth emphasizes the epistemological priority of the cross throughout his mature theology. In the prolegomena to the *Church Dogmatics* he states, "From the Easter story, the passion story is of course inseparable. In it takes place the hidden work of Jesus Christ which is subsequently revealed and believed in his resurrection."[164] In the last volume of his *Church Dogmatics* he can still say, "The living Jesus Christ, who is this one Word of God, is the Crucified [and as such] the Word of the cross understood in the light of the resurrection".[165]

See also Barth's intervening discussions on *The Verdict of the Father*,[166] *The Direction of the Son*,[167] and *The Mystery of Revelation*.[168] In each of these the revelatory significance of the whole Easter event is crucial, but within this the cross takes precedence theologically and methodologically. Indeed for Barth the cross becomes an explanation and a metaphor for the whole existence of Jesus Christ, as he says directly. "[The] word 'cross' [is] a description of the whole existence and divine likeness and activity of the man Jesus. . . . There is . . . no post-Easter Jesus who is not absolutely identical with the One to whose pre-Easter experience this limit belonged. In the whole of the New Testament He is the Crucified, enclosing in himself the whole of his being within this limit."[169]

---

162. See ibid., 93–94. See also Klappert, *Auferweckung des Gekreuzigten*, 316.
163. Ibid., 162 n.81.
164. Barth, *Church Dogmatics* I/2, 122.
165. Ibid., IV/1, 346.
166. Ibid., IV/1, 283f.
167. Ibid., IV/2, 364f.
168. Ibid., I/2, 122.
169. Barth, *Church Dogmatics* IV/2, 250.

There is also perhaps more prosaic evidence suggesting the overriding significance of the message of the cross for Barth. As is well known he set before him as he worked a reproduction of Matthias Grünewald's *The Crucifixion of Christ*—produced 1512–1515. This startling interpretation of the broken dead Christ, and of his chief witness directed to the paramount message he conveys, deeply moves Barth. Referring to the work in 1920 he lectures, "John the Baptist . . . with his hand pointing in an almost impossible way. It is this hand which is in evidence in the Bible."[170]

As already noted, for Barth the resurrection points to the supremacy of the message of the cross. Thence he accords high significance to the resurrection—about this Torrance is undoubtedly right. In doing so Barth takes up and further develops an older crucicentric understanding. Whereas the classical crucicentric theologians recognized one moment of resurrection, Barth divides the resurrection into two discrete but inseparable moments, their relation patterned on the hypostatic union.

The first of these is the *Auferweckung* or *awakening*—being the act of the Father raising the Son from the dead, in the tomb. As Klappert explains, the awakening is for Barth "the true, original, typical form of the revelation of God,"[171] an "exemplary form," an "exclusive act of God."[172] This is so precisely because the awakening throws "a backwards light" etching Christ's deity in relief,[173] uncovering the meaning hidden *sub contrario* in the cross. The matter can be put conversely also. In that the awakening reveals the supreme meaning of the Word from the cross, the Word from the cross reveals its own meaning first and principally by means of the awakening.

The second moment of the resurrection Barth terms the *Auferstehung*, normally translated "*resurrection*," but for Barth connoting

---

170. See Busch, *Karl Barth, His Life from Letters and Autobiographical Texts*, 116. The painting forms a panel in the Isenheim altarpiece, and is now in the possession of the Musée d'Unterlinden, Colmar, France.

171. Ibid., IV/1, 301. See also Thompson, *Christ in Perspective*, 89.

172. Klappert says that for Barth, "The awakening is the revelation of the Subject of the atonement on the cross, the exemplary form of revelation and in this way an exclusive act of God." Klappert, *Auferweckung des Gekreuzigten*, 228, cited by Thompson, *Christ in Perspective*, 89.

173. Thompson writes that for Barth the awakening conveys "the knowledge of the true and distinctive character of revelation and so of the deity of Jesus Christ." Ibid., 88.

particularly Christ's resurrection appearances to the disciples including the ascension, subsequent to the awakening in the tomb.[174] This second moment supports the hermeneutical significance of the first moment. That is, the backward light of the resurrection appearances shines first on the revelatory meaning of the awakening in the tomb, and then further back again to disclose the paramount epistemological significance of the cross. Or as Barth puts this, the resurrection appearances of Jesus Christ "were simply a lifting of the veil . . . the authentic communication and proclamation of the perfect act of redemption once for all accomplished in His previous existence and history."[175]

If the resurrection points up the paramount significance of the cross, so too for Barth does the incarnation. Here Thompson is again instructive. "Some believe [Barth's starting point] is the incarnation in its traditional form with the atonement following. For Barth, while the incarnation is certainly central, it is not the starting point. [Rather it is the] event of the cross [which is] the key to the whole of Barth's theology and has far reaching consequences."[176] Thompson then explains that for Barth "reconciliation (atonement) [is] the place where we start and from which we view the whole. For it is here that we learn who Jesus Christ is *and so the meaning of the incarnation.*"[177] Put otherwise, the incarnation takes place that there be the cross, something which the cross itself makes plain by the very fact that grounded in the incarnation, it crowns the history of Jesus Christ.

The priority of the cruciform starting point for Barth is demonstrated also by his high regard for the New Testament witness to this; it points to Christ's self-witness to the ultimate significance of his own death. In his exposition on "the direction of the Son," for instance, Barth says decisively, "Everything points towards this cross. And everything took place in the crucifixion . . . Thus the whole existence of the royal man Jesus as it is attested in the gospels [stands] under this sign . . . The

---

174. Klappert adds, "The awakening as a pure act of the divine grace of the Father to and upon the Son reveals the act of obedience of the Son on the cross." Klappert, *Auferweckung des Gekreuzigten*, 307, cited by Thompson, *Christ in Perspective*, 91–92.

175. Barth, *Church Dogmatics* IV/2, 133.

176. Thompson, *Christ in Perspective*, 10.

177. Ibid., 14. Italics mine.

whole New Testament witnesses to Jesus, and He Himself as echoed or reflected in the witness, points to this death."[178]

Crucicentric Epistemology and Pneumatology

At the intersection of Barth's epistemology and Christology Jesus Christ is the revelatory Word of the cross. At the intersection of his epistemology and pneumatology the Holy Spirit reveals that this is the case. Or as Torrance explains Barth, it is "through Christ and in his Spirit alone that we have access to authentic knowledge of God."[179] To consider this further the discussion turns first to the general significance of pneumatology in Barth's project.

An oft-repeated criticism of Barth is that he neglects the doctrine of the Holy Spirit. He is said to do so both in comparison to his much fuller treatment of Christology, and in respect to the depth of the pneumatology that he does present. Macchia, for instance, accuses Barth of focusing narrowly on one aspect of the work of the Spirit, the revelation of the message of the cross from the perspective of the resurrection, at the expense of a fuller and more liberative pneumatology. "Had Barth replaced his emphasis in pneumatology on revelation with a dominant focus on new creation," Macchia says, "he would have recognized that the work of the Spirit in Christ's resurrection did a great deal more than proclaim justification."[180]

But the criticism that Barth neglects pneumatology has itself been criticized. Busch, for instance, writes, "[Barth's concern] was the critical reclamation of the knowledge of the deity of the Spirit. [This being so] it can hardly be claimed that he sought to remedy Neo-Protestantism's forgetfulness of the deity of the Spirit by himself forgetting the Spirit."[181] Busch then finds that the doctrine of the Holy Spirit permeates Barth's mature theology, if succinctly. Barth had planned to pursue pneumatology more concertedly in what is the missing final volume of the *Church Dogmatics*, to have been called *"Redemption,"* but that does not mean that what he has achieved pneumatalogically is somehow inadequate.[182]

178. Barth, *Church Dogmatics* IV/2, 291.
179. Torrance, *Karl Barth*, 15.
180. Macchia, "Justification through New Creation," 214.
181. Busch, *Great Passion*, 222.
182. See ibid., 54.

Similarly Torrance, who finds that "in answer to his critics on all sides [Barth presents] a full-orbed rehabilitation of the doctrine of God the Holy Spirit,"[183] one influenced by the patristic fathers and Calvin. This replaces "the Augustinian-Thomist conception of infused and created grace as the medium bridging the gap between God and men."[184]

Like Busch and Torrance, Rosato—in a major work on the matter—concludes that Barth is thoroughly pneumatocentric, his pneumatology being particularly to the fore in engagement with modern theology. In introducing this finding Rosato writes, "In crucial passages of Barth's longer essays on Schleiermacher, and in shorter references to him in almost all his major works through the years, pneumatology is the recurring theme."[185] In further introduction Rosato finds that this pneumatology is plainly influenced by Barth's "tireless effort to redeem the valid insights and to excise the dangerous errors of Schleiermacher's Spirit theology. That this one aspect of Schleiermacher's thought so fascinates Barth lends credence to the daring assertion that Barth himself gradually became more properly a pneumatocentric than a christocentric theologian."[186] In the present view Rosato's "daring assertion" cannot be substantiated by what Barth has done, but is fair comment on where he might have gone had he had further opportunity. Certainly in what proved to be the final year of his life, 1968, Barth is envisaging "the possibility of a theology of the third article, in other words, a theology predominantly and decisively of the Holy Spirit."[187]

In light of Busch, Torrance and Rosato it therefore appears that Barth's comprehensive treatment of Christology does not *ipso facto* undermine his pneumatology, the latter indeed being full orbed, as Torrance suggests, both in its pervasiveness and theological depth.

What or who then is the Holy Spirit for Barth? As Rosato effectively indicates, Barth works out his pneumatology over against the modern theology of glory, especially that of the nineteenth century. Barth engages Schleiermacher and the Liberal Protestants, but also the broader Romantic reaction to modernity itself.

---

183. Torrance, *Karl Barth*, 186.
184. Ibid.
185. Rosato, *The Spirit as Lord*, 3.
186. Ibid.
187. Barth, "Concluding Unscientific Postscript," 78.

Nineteenth century theology effectively splits the Spirit from the Trinity, opening the way for the merger of the human spirit and the Holy Spirit. In distinction Barth insists negatively that the Holy Spirit is not an independent "persona" in the Trinity apart from the Son and the Father.[188] Neither is the Spirit some "new instruction, illumination and stimulation of man that goes beyond Christ."[189] Pneumatology is *not* anthropology;[190] God and the creature are *not* the same. Busch further explains. For Barth the true Spirit "overturns the pillar of the modern doctrine of the spirit, namely, the assertion that there is a capacity for God as a given in the human person[. Indeed the] whole idea that the Holy Spirit sanctions the view that we are equal partners with God is unmasked as a lie."[191]

Barth opposes the nineteenth century Romantics along similar lines. The Spirit is not some sort of pantheistic principle enabling the intermingling of creature and Creator.[192] Again that would be to divinize the creature. But if the Spirit cannot be co-opted by either modern Liberal theology or by Romanticism, neither is the Spirit precisely the same as the Father or the Son. The question therefore remains, "For Barth, what or who is the Holy Spirit?"

Positively Barth understands the Spirit as: transcendence, light, liberation, peace, the power of eternal life dawning over all human being. But above all, and far from splitting the Trinity, Barth defines the Spirit as the "third mode of being of the one divine Subject or Lord."[193] As such the Spirit is the Spirit of the Father, in full unity with him. Equally

188. Barth says, "[Even] if the Father and the Son might be called 'person' (in the modern sense of the term), the Holy Spirit could not possibly be regarded as the third 'person' . . . He is not a third spiritual Subject, a third I, a third Lord side by side with the two others." Barth, *Church Dogmatics* I/1, 469.

189. Ibid., I/1, 452–53.

190. Barth writes, "[That is] precisely what is so deeply problematic about Schleiermacher, that he—brilliantly, like no one before or after him—thought and spoke 'from an anthropological standpoint!' . . . As if pneumatology were anthropology!" Barth, "Concluding Unscientific Postscript," 279.

191. Busch, *Great Passion*, 225.

192. Expounding Barth's section in the *Church Dogmatics* on "The Spirit as Basis of Soul and Body," Busch says, "The Spirit is not the principle of pantheism that intermingles Creator and creature in an exchange of roles." Ibid., 228. See also Barth, *Church Dogmatics* III/2, 344–66.

193. Ibid., I/1, 469.

he is the Spirit of the Son, Jesus Christ's own presence and action,[194] his sovereignly operative power of revelation, his Servant proceeding from Him.[195] Being "the Spirit of the Father and the Son"[196] therefore, the Spirit comprises the transitional force,[197] the eternal bond, the communication,[198] the love binding Father and Son together—which is real love since God is antecedently love in himself.[199] Barth effectively sums these ideas when he says that the Spirit "is Lord in inseparable unity with the Father as Lord and the Son as Lord . . . With the Father and the Son He is the one sovereign divine Subject, the Subject who is not placed under the control or inspection of any other, who derives His being and existence from Himself."[200]

It follows that Barth holds the Son and the Father tightly together—there cannot be two revelations. But at the same time he carefully avoids merging Father and Son. As the crucicentric theologians before him[201] he sees that without a firm theology of the distinctiveness of the Spirit

---

194. "He is the Holy Spirit in this supreme sense—holy with a holiness for which there are no analogies—because He is no other than the presence and action of Jesus Christ Himself". Ibid., IV/2, 323.

195. Ibid., IV/2, 318.

196. Barth writes, "God is God . . . concretely as the Father and the Son, and this in the fellowship, the unity, the peace, the love of the Holy Spirit, who is Himself the Spirit of the Father and the Son." Ibid., IV/2, 341.

197. See Bromiley, *Introduction to the Theology of Karl Barth*, 204.

198. Barth says, "The specific element in the divine mode of being of the Holy Spirit . . . consists . . . in the fact that he is . . . the common element, or, better, the act of communion, of the Father and the Son. He is the act in which the Father is the Father of the Son or the Speaker of the Word[,] and the Son is the Son of the Father or the Word of the Speaker." Barth, *Church Dogmatics* I/1, 469–70.

199. Busch explains Barth here. "[Barth holds that in] the Holy Spirit the One who has come to humanity already [in Jesus Christ] comes to us again. We are to see two acts in the one and same revelation . . . [This] thesis is a repudiation of the idea that there is a revelation of the Spirit separate from the revelation of Christ whose content is something new and totally different from the revelation of Christ." (Busch, *Great Passion*, 223.) It is for this reason—the avoidance of a split between the Son and the Spirit and so of the Trinity itself—that Barth defends the eleventh century western addition of the filioque clause to the Nicene Creed. Regarding the filioque clause see here p. 182, n. 42.

200. Barth, *Church Dogmatics* I/1, 469.

201. Paul, Athanasius, and Luther all see that the cross would be emptied of its power and the triunity of God eroded, should the truth of the distinctive deity of the Holy Spirit and of Christ, and the graciousness of the divine self-giving in Christ through the Spirit, not be securely established. As Torrance says, for these earlier theologians the very foundation of Christian theology is at stake. See Torrance, *Karl Barth*, 215.

Karl Barth's Modern Epistemology of the Cross   237

there can be no coherent theology of either the personhood of Christ or the triunity of God. For the Spirit is, above all, the Spirit of the trinitarian God. Torrance further explains Barth's position. "If what God the Father is toward us in Jesus Christ and in the Holy Spirit he is antecedently, inherently and eternally in himself, and what he is antecedently, inherently and eternally in himself he is towards us in Jesus Christ and in the Holy Spirit, then we cannot but affirm the essential Deity of Jesus Christ and the Holy Spirit, and thus the Triunity of God."[202]

In summary then, the very fact that Barth's pneumatology is interlocked with his pervasive Christology, sustaining an embracing Trinitarianism, lends further support to the major importance of pneumatology within his project.

At the intersection of pneumatology and crucicentric epistemology Barth extends the pneumatological epistemology latent in the classical crucicentric tradition. The Spirit is not only the power of transition between the Father and the Son. As "God knowing God" the Spirit is the power that—in Bromiley's words—"mysteriously and miraculously makes the transition between Jesus and us,"[203] disclosing Father and Son, and he himself. Torrance adds here, "As [Barth] expounded it, the Holy Spirit is the freedom of God to . . . adapt the creature and open it up to receive him in his self-communication to it."[204] Barth himself sets out this pneumatological epistemology in numerous places across his project. For example he writes, "The Holy Spirit is the Spirit of God, because He is the Spirit of the Word. And that is the very reason and the only reason why we acquire eyes and ears for God in the Holy Spirit."[205] Again, "Wherever there is knowledge of Jesus Christ, it takes place in the power of his witness, in the mystery and miracle, the outpouring and receiving, of the gift of the Holy Spirit."[206] Similarly, "[The] Holy Spirit as the Spirit of Jesus [is] the Giver and source of truth, *Creator Spiritus*: the Creator also of all knowledge of the truth, of all walking and life in it: the

---

202. Ibid., 193. See also Barth *Church Dogmatics* I/1, 466, where Barth says that what God is antecedently in himself he is toward the world in revelation, the converse also applying.

203. Bromiley, *Introduction to the Theology of Karl Barth*, 204.

204. Torrance, *Karl Barth*, 180.

205. Barth, *Church Dogmatics* I/2, 248.

206. Ibid., IV/2, 156.

Paraclete who really guides the community into all truth."[207] Or, finally now, "[The Spirit is the] Spirit in this supreme sense . . . that he enables men to see and hear and accept and recognize [Jesus Christ] as the Son of Man who in obedience to God went to death for the reconciliation of the world and was exalted in his humiliation as the Son of God, and in Him their own exaltation to be the children of God."[208]

Barth then queries how this pneumatological knowledge transfer to the creature is actually accomplished, "How does the Holy Spirit act? How does He encounter us? How does he touch and move us? What does it mean to 'receive' the Spirit and to 'have' the Spirit; to 'be' and to 'walk' in the Spirit?"[209] To recall the earlier discussion here on the transmission of faith,[210] he answers that—sent by the Father and the Son—the Spirit anchors the knowledge of God securely both at its points of generation and reception. From above and beyond the creature the Spirit graciously conveys the knowledge of God to the creature. From below and within the creature the Spirit graciously opens it to receive that knowledge. Or as Torrance explains Barth, "Knowledge of God takes place through a movement of divine revelation from the Father through the Son in the Spirit, and an answering movement . . . in the Spirit through the Son to the Father."[211] And similarly, "By embracing man within the [Spirit described] circle of his own presence of himself to himself, and thus through meeting himself from man's end and within him, God makes man open to his revelation, capable and ready for it beyond any possibility that he may be considered to possess it on his own merely as a rational human being."[212] It is then Jesus Christ who directs this Spirit described epistemological circle. He does so, Barth says, for three complementary reasons:

First, to remind the creature that its self-glorifying attempt to know as God alone can know leads inevitably to final death. Barth says, "The grace of God, Jesus Christ himself, gives us what we require, . . . the Holy Spirit of power [and of] discipline which will ever and again keep us

---

207. Barth, *Church Dogmatics* IV/2, 359.
208. Ibid., IV/2, 323.
209. Barth, *Church Dogmatics* IV/2, 360.
210. For discussion on the transmission of faith see here pp. 197–99.
211. Torrance, *Karl Barth*, 214.
212. Ibid., 210–11.

from forgetting . . . that to our ruin we of ourselves should like to be like God knowing good and evil."²¹³

Second, to summon the creature from death to true knowledge of God in Jesus Christ, and him crucified. Here Barth declares, "[For] in His death . . . God has manifested Him for all men . . . by the irresistible awakening power of the Holy Spirit."²¹⁴ And similarly, "[The Spirit] will ever and again drive us to look to [Jesus Christ] and listen to him as our Saviour."²¹⁵

Third—and to foreshadow discussion here on Barth's soteriology, to reveal the message of the cross concerning salvation. To this last Barth says in 1934 addressing Brunner, "Of his free mercy God gives to man, who of himself can do nothing toward his own salvation, to man, whose will is not free but in bondage, his salvation in the Cross of Christ[, and does so] by the Holy Spirit who enables him to assimilate this word of the Cross."²¹⁶

Two Crucicentric Motifs

Echoing the classical crucicentric tradition Barth's epistemology is informed by two recurring sets of dialectical relations, effectively forming motifs marking the presence of the crucicentric idea. Critically their polarities are not determined over against each other logically but rather *theo*-logically, each being rooted concretely in the truth of God revealed in the cross. To explain them the discussion turns first to Barth's understanding of wisdom and foolishness, and then to his juxtaposition of divine revealedness and hiddenness.

Positively wisdom has two critical meanings for Barth. First, and to quote him, "wisdom is plainly enough identified with Jesus Christ Himself."²¹⁷ Similarly, in explicating the several Pauline passages concerning wisdom, he says, "It is clear that in all these New Testament passages [Ephesians, Colossians, Corinthians] wisdom is nothing more nor less than God Himself turning to man in grace and mercy, God in His love but also in His freedom, in the fullness of His love but also in the

213. Barth, "Gospel and Law," 27.
214. Barth, *Church Dogmatics* IV/1, 753.
215. Barth, "Gospel and Law," 27.
216. Barth and Brunner, *Natural Theology*, 78.
217. Barth, *Church Dogmatics* II/1, 439.

fullness of His freedom."[218] Second, wisdom is for Barth a strictly human capacity, a logic recognizing that the knowledge and therefore Wisdom of God can be received only where and how God has made it uniquely available, in Jesus Christ and at the point of a cross, and not otherwise.

In both these conceptions Barth's position may be distinguished from that of Schleiermacher, for whom wisdom is purely a human principle, or subjective quality, but which is not orientated to recognizing the place and manner in which God makes himself known, and which does not understand wisdom as either objective or personified.

After Paul, Barth holds the converse of true wisdom to be the foolishness of the world. He finds that in applying "its own supposed wisdom, the world failed to recognize God . . . where His wisdom actually was",[219] it failed to see the crucified Christ. Instead it relied and relies on its presumed capacity to fathom out true knowledge of God, a capacity guided by reason. But, and as already indicated, definitively for Barth a created capacity cannot obtain the measure of its Creator. The irony, he thinks, is that in its epistemological self-delusion the world, believing itself wise and the epistemology of the cross foolish, actually falls into the very condition it congratulates itself on avoiding: foolishness, irrationality.

Barth explains this in exegeting 1 Cor 1:18—2:10. "[The] Word of the cross is foolishness to them that are perishing but the power of God to them that are being saved (v.18). How is this? Because the foolish . . . can obviously see in the news of the death of Jesus Christ . . . only the news of a further demonstration of the meaninglessness of human life . . . [But this wisdom of the world] is assuredly not what it claims to be, the art of living, worldly wisdom, but the exact opposite."[220] Rather it is the case that, "[Those] who accept the Word of the cross in faith [hear] . . . God's own wisdom: His wisdom which in this mystery (that of the cross of Jesus Christ) . . . God has appointed and foreseen [in] . . . Christ by which he was made wisdom for us."[221] In added emphasis Barth then reiterates the point. "[The truly wise] are those who accept the Word of the cross in faith . . . [They] are wise enough to hear wisdom where fools

---

218. Ibid.
219. Ibid., II/1, 435.
220. Ibid.
221. Ibid., II/1, 437.

think to hear folly, and because they are fools, can in fact only hear folly. ... [What] they hear is God's own wisdom."[222]

To conclude this examination of wisdom and foolishness in relation to Barth's epistemology, it can be said that Barth defines the really wise as those who begin where the Wisdom of God is actually to be found. They receive the Word from the cross that the Crucified *is* the Wisdom of God, and thus (unlike the really foolish) the really wise begin with him. Indeed the gulf between the actually foolish and wise is at its greatest extent in their differing responses to this cruciform Word. Ignoring it the foolish seek out the knowledge of God aided by a "logic" predicated on themselves. Behind that Barth perceives the old desire to bypass the revelatory cruciform Word and usurp the glory of God. With Paul he therefore warns that God, denying that desire, will bring to naught both the fools' false reasoning and the fools themselves. God will cause the wise to disclose the falsity of their logic, humbling them. No creature may glorify itself in the presence of God; no false and boastful epistemology can prevail over him! But the really wise, proclaiming the logic of the cross, will be established forever on a foundation of truth.[223]

Like the classical crucicentric theologians before him Barth finds mutually contrasting states: divine lowliness and majesty, divine humiliation and exaltation, and overarching them divine concealedness and revealedness, to be intrinsic to the man-God Jesus Christ. The second major crucicentric motif found in Barth's epistemology is then that of divine hiddenness and revealedness. Barth sees that in "revealing Himself [God] also conceals Himself . . . [Where] there is unveiling there is also veiling."[224] Once again, here Barth is *not* basing his position on a form of closed logic—hiddenness and revealedness dialectically dictating the existence of each other. Rather his argument is properly theological.

Generally Barth finds four reasons for divine hiddenness, and the manner of it. These are each predicated on the very nature and decision of God. First, hiddenness is of the very essence of the God who dwells in unapproachable light and glory. Second, in his holiness God is unable to

222. Ibid.
223. See ibid., II/1, 435–36. Beside Paul, here Barth also appeals to Jer 9:23f., "Let not the wise man glory in his wisdom, neither let the mighty man glory in his might, let not the rich man glory in his riches: but let him that glorieth glory in this, that he understandeth and knoweth me, that I am the Lord which exercise loving-kindness, judgement and righteousness, in the earth : for in these things I delight, saith the Lord."
224. Ibid., II/1, 55.

be uncovered by a sinful creature. Third, God deliberately hides himself where the creature—who naturally seeks an all-powerful deity—must least suspect his presence. For Barth, as for Luther, this means in the opposite place to that naturally expected, that is, in "invisibility, in repellent shame, . . . in the despicable and forbidding form of the Slain and Crucified of Golgotha."[225] Here above all God is *deus absconditus*. Fourth, God conceals himself *in order to reveal himself*. As Jüngel explains, for Barth the "*deus absconditus* is not a God who is hostile to revelation. [But precisely] as the *deus absconditus*, that is, in his hidden mode of being, God is the subject of revelation."[226] Here divine hiddenness *presupposes* revelation.

For Barth God is the God of revelation, *deus revelatus*, above all precisely where he is most hidden, at the point of the cross. Fiddes explains. "Those who offer a theology 'from the cross' affirm that the cross is not just an indication of an eternal truth about God, but that it actually expresses what is most *divine* about God. . . . From this Lutheran background Barth formulated the dialectical statement that the divinity of God is displayed more clearly in the lowliness of the cross."[227] Klappert makes a similar point. Barth, he says, holds that in the cross "the Son of God reveals himself, necessarily and essentially and not accidentally or by way of confirmation or completion, as the One he is."[228]

Indeed, for Barth the revelation of glory through humility is integral to the divine nature. He writes, "[When] we remember that the goal and climax in the epiphany of the Son of God in the man Jesus consisted of His death on the cross and that as the risen Lord He is still the man who died on the cross, we [see that . . .] he reveals his glory in this way."[229] The Son's glory is one with his cruciform humility, and thus his cruciform humility can and does reveal and prove his glory. Elsewhere Barth adds, "The definitive form of the elevation and exaltation of this man, of His identity with God's eternal Son, was that in which He gave human proof of His humility and obedience to the Father, of His humiliation, in His

---

225. Ibid., IV/3, 377.

226. Jüngel, *God's Being is in Becoming*, 31.

227. Fiddes, *Creative Suffering of God*, 30. See also Barth, *Church Dogmatics* IV/1, 204, 555–58.

228. Klappert, *Auferweckung des Gekreuzigten*, 159, cited by Thompson, *Christ in Perspective*, 52.

229. Ibid., II/1, 55.

human suffering and dying as a rejected and outcast criminal on the wood of curse and shame."²³⁰

Why does God so reveal himself? Here Barth carefully guards against any explanation relying on an "inadequacy of human knowledge that revelation would only correct,"²³¹ to quote Busch. The purpose of divine revelation is not to fill some unfortunate gap in a putative God-capable natural intellectual capacity! God graciously reveals himself in the cross that, glorious as he is, he be apprehensible by the creature. Or as Barth explains, "In His revelation in Jesus Christ, the hidden God has indeed made Himself apprehensible. Not directly, but indirectly. Not to sight, but to faith. Not in His being, but in sign [that is, that the Word was made flesh.] Not, then, by the dissolution of His hiddenness—but apprehensibly."²³²

To sum up, it has been the force of this discussion on Barth's use of characteristically crucicentric dialectical motifs to show that for him the creature cannot naturally perceive what God alone can see, God hidden in the cross of Jesus Christ. It cannot naturally know what God alone can know, where and in whom divine wisdom and truth are ultimately vested. There is no way for it to naturally discover these things. But for proper perception the creature requires access to God's own cognitive capacity.

Incorporation in the Mind of Christ

Of the several areas in which Barth reflects the general epistemological ethos of the classical crucicentric tradition, the last considered here concerns his theology of the creature's union with the mind²³³ of Christ. In explaining this Barth's basic epistemological observation is recalled. As Torrance interprets this, Barth holds that by its natural powers and capacities the fallen creature is unable to achieve that "*cognitive union with God which true knowledge of him requires.*"²³⁴ Hence Barth's questions, "[How] can the unknown become for us the known reality, reality

---

230. Ibid., IV/2, 290.

231. Busch, *Great Passion*, 43.

232. Barth, *Church Dogmatics* II/1, 199.

233. To repeat an earlier note, by *mind* here is meant not only the intellect, but also the psychic disposition towards or away from God.

234. Torrance, *Karl Barth*, 143. Italics mine.

in truth? How can there be a perception of Jesus Christ . . . the Crucified: the Servant who was and is the Lord; the Humiliated who was and is Exalted; the King of Gethsemane and Golgotha?"[235]

In answer Barth considers that before the creature can receive true knowledge of God in Jesus Christ, it must be redeemed from its mental alienation from God, its mind renewed and reconciled with God.[236] Thence he appeals to the ancient Pauline notion of cognitive union with the mind of Christ. "To know God in [Jesus Christ according to Paul's bold] expression (1 Cor 2:16) is to receive and have the [mind] of Jesus Christ Himself, and thus to know in fellowship with the One who is known and in whom are hid all the treasures of wisdom and knowledge (Col 2:3)."[237] In this Barth emulates the sheer boldness of Paul's insight. While he doesn't teach that the creature loses its creatureliness in being united with the mind of Christ, nevertheless he does suggest that a *real* union between the creature's mind and that of Christ takes place. In coming to share in Christ cognitively the creature is made, as Busch expresses Barth, to participate in "the truth of Christ's knowledge of himself."[238] It comes to reason with *Christ's* reason.[239] It receives *his* knowledge.[240] Its ways of knowing and what it knows are uniquely and ontologically founded. So it is joined "in fellowship with the One . . . in whom are hid all the treasures of wisdom and knowledge (Col 2:3)."[241] This union with its cognitive reorientation and transformation culminates eschatologically; it comprises an eternal reality. Its advent is then entirely consequent on the grace of God;[242] it is not dependent on the creature's own prowess.

But how does such union come about? Barth holds with Paul that it is possible only as the creature's inauthentic mind is negated, its self-assumed capacity "to know God as God knows God" submitted to the

235. Barth, *Church Dogmatics* IV/2, 297.

236. See Torrance, *Karl Barth*, 143–44.

237. Ibid., IV/3, 185.

238. Busch, *Great Passion*, 63–64.

239. Barth says, "[In] virtue of His life in us we have His reason." Barth, *Church Dogmatics* , IV/3.2, 543.

240. Barth states, "Note should be taken of what is included in the knowledge of Jesus Christ according to Eph 1:18, 'That the eyes of your understanding should be enlightened'". Ibid., IV/3.1, 185.

241. Ibid.

242. See ibid.

same spiritual circumcision that Christ himself underwent.²⁴³ Only by *dying* with Christ is the human mind renewed and enlightened. Only in *this* way does it depart from its old orientation toward itself and put on Christ's orientation to God. Outside of death its old ways of knowing are unchanged, and ignorance and alienation continue unhindered.

Barth considers that in all its stages this process of cognitive death, union, and reorientation in Christ, is directed and empowered by the Holy Spirit. Thence he appeals to Paul where the evangelist writes, "[In] relation to all those who by the Spirit have been given to know what is given them by God there is made the immeasurable claim, 'We have the mind of Christ' (1 Cor 2:16)."²⁴⁴ Here possession of the mind of Christ and possession of the Holy Spirit are completely intertwined, the presence of the one indicates the presence of the other. It follows for Barth that, "The spiritual man is distinguished from the merely physical man by the fact that he has the [mind of Christ]."²⁴⁵

This cognitive possession marks the culmination of the Spirit directed revelatory work of the cross, and thence the climax of the cruciform message. It also culminates and completes the epistemological dimension of Karl Barth's modern crucicentric theology.

Conclusion

Two key principles inform *classical* crucicentric epistemology. These are the general principle that God alone is glorious, and the specific principle that "the knowledge of God as God is in Godself" is exclusively in the possession and gift of God. In identifying the nature of the various strands within Barth's negative and positive epistemology the foregoing discussion has illustrated Barth's adherence to these principles. It has also evidenced the similar orientation of his epistemology to that of the classical crucicentric tradition.

Negatively Barth rejects all anthropocentric starting points for the knowledge of God, including those provided by: philosophy,

---

243. Paul writes, "In him also you were circumcised with a spiritual circumcision, by putting off the body of the flesh in the circumcision of Christ (Col 2:11)." Interpreting this Barth explains, "By His circumcision—the context clearly shows that the reference is to [Christ's] death." Barth, *Church Dogmatics* IV/4, 14.

244. Ibid., IV/3, 543, c.f. IV/4, 14.

245. Ibid.

metaphysics, human reason, natural theology, and felt human experience. From his perspective the human attempt to reach up to the knowledge of God has two equally undesirable consequences. By attempting to know what God alone can know the creature necessarily mounts an attempt on the glory of God; God alone can know God. By looking to its own capacity to know, the creature necessarily circumvents the true Word of God proclaimed from the cross of Jesus Christ.

The multiple aspects of Barth's positive epistemology have also been indicated. Across his project his epistemology intersects extensively with Christology, but also with pneumatology. It makes use of dialectics, synthesizing epistemologically significant pairs of contraries—especially "wisdom and foolishness" and "revelation and hiddenness"—not logically but *theo*-logically in the actual cross of Jesus Christ. But Barth's positive epistemology also makes use of analogy, not now that drawn on the creature to God, but that drawn on Jesus Christ to God—an analogy sharpened acutely at the point of the cross. This epistemology culminates in the cognitive union of the human mind with the mind of Christ.

The discussion has also indicated the distinctively *modern* character of both the negative and positive dimensions of Barth's epistemology. Negatively he counters the modern centering of ultimate truth in the creature. At the same time, positively, he reflects the influence of modernity's focus on empiricism by beginning reasonably in the place where God makes Godself known. Barth summarises this procedure in his 1962 American lectures. "The dominant presupposition of [theology's] thought and speech," he says, "is *God's* own proof of his existence and sovereignty."[246] This proof is contained in "the one history of salvation and revelation"[247] announced in Jesus Christ, and him crucified.

An endeavor has now been made to sketch the intrinsically crucicentric and modern way in which Barth understands the one history of revelation, a perception shaping his epistemology. In the next chapter a parallel attempt will be made in respect to his understanding of the one history of salvation, as this shapes his soteriology.

---

246. Barth, "Evangelical Theology: An Introduction," 14. Italics original.
247. Ibid., 32.

8

Karl Barth's Modern Soteriology of the Cross

[The] Word of the cross is not the wisdom of the world . . . [but] God's own wisdom: His wisdom which in this mystery (that of the cross of Jesus Christ) is just as concealed (for the world) as it is revealed (for believers); the wisdom which before all worlds God has appointed and foreseen for our glorification.

—Karl Barth[1]

Right from the beginning of his project, in 1922, Barth declares his intention to recover and build on the dialectical soteriology of Paul and the Reformation, and here Luther rather than Calvin.[2] He adds, "We may and we must develop from them much deeper and more inclusive meanings, but the main principle of our thought will always be the vast reversion—from the end to the beginning, from sin to grace, from doom to righteousness, from death to life, from man to God, from time to eternity."[3] How well he succeeds can be judged by his similar approach to the Reformers, as also his development of their positions. This involves Barth in a lifelong[4] engagement with the essential contraries of the

---

1. Barth, *Church Dogmatics* II/1, 437. Round brackets original.
2. For the crucicentric influence on Barth of Luther as against Calvin, see here pp. 189–90 and associated notes.
3. Barth, "Ethics Today," 174.
4. Earlier reference was made to the "McCormack–Gunton debate," in which McCormack argues that the dialectical approach of Barth's earlier theology extends into Barth's mature work. See here pp. 186–87.

human condition as these are radically resolved in the crucified Christ, and with this a careful attention to the Word from the cross which announces exactly this resolution.

As Paul and Luther and the tradition they bracket, Barth develops his soteriological explanation of this cruciform Word around two deaths—that of Jesus Christ and that of the creature, and in relation to three forms of glory—that of God and the false and the true glory of the creature. Barth echoes the earlier crucicentric soteriology in other ways too. For him the justifying message of the cross is not merely a word about the God of the cross, but the divine Word of the cross himself speaking. Salvific grace is not merely imparted by God: Father, Son, and Holy Spirit, but identical to precisely this God. Justification does not mean that the creature circumvents the cross, but that it passes through it. Moreover in his explanation of these themes Barth adheres to the same order of salvation as that adopted by the classical crucicentric theologians, and does so for the same reasons.

To extend this last point and to recap a previous discussion, the classical crucicentric theologians hold God alone able to sanctify. The creature cannot sanctify itself so as to merit justification.[5] Could it do so three theologically untenable circumstances would prevail: God's electing decision would be conditionable, Christ and the grace of his cross would be relativised by the saving work of the creature, the creature would equate itself with God. But such circumstances do *not* prevail. Rather in the processes of salvation *justification comes before sanctification*—justification depending solely on the gracious Person and act of Jesus Christ. Accordingly in their theory of salvation the crucicentric theologians assert exactly this salvific order, reversing the western *ordo salutis* thereby.

In this regard in his Göttingen lectures the young Barth levels particular criticism at medieval scholasticism. The scholastics exhibit the trappings of orthodoxy, for example they hold the creature to be sinful and in need of healing, that it is grace which makes human action good, that salvation requires Christ. Indeed the scholastic church has all the appearance of "a real saving institution in which something is set up and achieved . . . [in] virtue of the infinite merit of Christ's sacrificial death . . . In it grace is present and is dispensed and outside it [there is] no

---

5. For discussion on the western and crucicentric orders of salvation see here pp. 71–73.

salvation."⁶ Yet, Barth says, exactly this church by its careful placement of sanctification before justification rushes headlong past the actual person and sacrificial work of Jesus Christ.

Barth goes on to explain that in declaring justification to be the precursor of and single basis for sanctification, the Reformation undercuts the salvific order of the scholastic church. It lets "God be God, the one object that no bold human grasping or inquiry or approach"⁷ might co-opt. It teaches that the creature is saved by dint of its *sinfulness* and not by its assumed sanctity, by sheer mercy"⁸ and not by purchased merit, by the gracious work of the cross and not by the work of the church. Thus proclaiming the glory of God and not the creature the Reformation puts an "end to the theology of glory,"⁹ or more exactly the theology of the cross does so via the Reformation's offices.

Now Barth recasts the tradition which culminated in the Reformation, freshly articulating the pneumatological and eschatological priorities within its crucicentric foundations. In this his aim is to correct error, especially now the nineteenth century's identification of the human spirit with the eternal Spirit of God, effectively making the creature its own Savior.¹⁰ So he offers a distinctively modern and faithful pneumatological and eschatological soteriology of his own.

Before introducing the negative and positive dimensions of this modern crucicentric soteriology two quick notes are useful. i) The discussion will be assisted by reference to two key lectures, the first delivered by Barth in 1922 at the commencement of his project, and the second delivered in 1935 near the beginning of his mature theology.¹¹ Taken

---

6. See Barth, *Calvin*, 34–35.

7. Ibid., 39. Barth further explains. "The Reformation did not really engender any new thoughts about God. It did the simple thing of underlining that *He*, God, is the point of the whole enterprise . . . The Reformation, too, knew of the glory of God and could speak about it. But it said: To God alone by the glory! That put an end to the theology of glory." Ibid., 39–40. Italics original.

8. Ibid., 40.

9. Ibid.

10. For the modern identification of the human spirit with the Spirit of God, see here p. 235.

11. Lecture One: "The Problem of Ethics Today." In *The Word of God and the Word of Man*, 136–82. By *ethics* Barth means principles of behavior rooted in obedience to the law of God. Barth delivered this lecture to a conference of ministers at Wiesbaden in September 1922. The work is interesting for his engagement with a nation desperately asking what it should do in the wake of military defeat, economic collapse, and political chaos.

together these comprehensively illustrate Barth's forensic theology, as also his debt to Paul and Luther in its regard. ii) Again the discussion is conducted in the hermeneutical light shed by the classical crucicentric tradition.

The Negative Soteriology of the Cross

As the crucicentric theologians before him, in his negative soteriology Barth opposes the self-glorifying attempt by the creature to condition God.[12] But the atmosphere in which he does so, and so the challenge before him, is quite different from that facing those earlier theologians. The salvation anxiety and concomitant attempt to merit divine approval Luther knew, for instance, no longer exists. Rather Barth must oppose those confidant that they already satisfy divine law so as to merit salvation, certain of their capacity to bend an already approving God to their will—even dangerously certain.[13] It is exactly this subtle self-congratulatory attitude to the command of God by those in the contemporary church that so distresses Barth. "Compared with that," he asks rhetorically, "what is the sin of the man who has not encountered God's law,"[14] who does not know of the divine claim on human obedience?

Barth thinks that the presenting problem (not excuse) for Christians behaving in this way is that although resident in the community of

---

Lecture Two: "Gospel and Law." In both *God, Grace and Gospel*, 3–27, and *Community, State, and Church*, 71–100. This address has an interesting history. Barth, a theological professor at Bonn when Hitler came to power in 1933, refused any legitimacy to the regime. He was to have presented the lecture at a conference of the Confessing Church in Barmen in 1935. Instead it was read by another while the Gestapo escorted Barth himself to the Swiss border. Later that year it was published and became something of a parting shot by Barth, aimed first at the apostate German-Christians. Initially the lecture attracted considerable debate. Subsequently it became all but lost, until 1956 when to mark Barth's seventieth birthday it was reprinted, first in its original German, and shortly thereafter in two complementary English translations (references above). It is now widely regarded as one of the most important of Barth's shorter writings.

12. In his early Göttingen lectures Barth explains that in questioning work righteousness Luther questions not merely "the subsidiary teaching of a Thomas . . . or an Eckhardt, but what was best and highest and most inward and vital in them." Barth, *Calvin*, 43.

13. See the earlier note here where Oberman suggests that lack of a proper fear of God facilitates the commission of atrocities. Barth would likely have agreed with Oberman here p. 105, n. 129.

14. Barth, "Gospel and Law," 15.

Christ, they are yet resident in a sinful world. Here there "is no security, not even religious security."[15] They cannot reach past their sinful situation to God anymore than they could before entering the community. Christ's forensic work has formally pronounced guiltless; significantly "it does not make guiltless."[16] Barth puts this bluntly, "Man's will is and remains unfree: he lives and will live to the end of his days under the annihilating effect of the fall; his goals from the least to the highest will be of a different kind from the final goal, his conduct will be evil, and his achievement not only incomplete but perverted."[17]

Thence Barth asks a series of rhetorical questions.[18] Why do those who know of their justification, who claim the benefits of Christ's cruciform work, yet refuse wholehearted submission to his lordship? Why (echoing Luther) do they call good "evil" and evil "good," sinfully preferring their own way, indeed making a virtue of doing so? Certainly arrogance, certainly pride, certainly a strange self-confidence, certainly too a denial of their own base imperfection, a deep-rooted refusal to humble themselves in response to Christ and to beg forgiveness. But really why is this? Why do those *already in the church* misuse the things of God in order to sanctify themselves according to their own idea of sanctity—even as they profess to know the power of God to conform them to Jesus Christ? Why do they "have a zeal for God but not according to knowledge[?]"[19]

Barth locates his answer in the wish of Christians to credit their salvation to themselves, and in the desire lying beneath that wish, the desire to be as God. He thinks that undergirding desire for glory would be a serious fault in those without awareness of Jesus Christ, or who like Israel explicitly reject him. But in those only "a small and immaterial step"[20] away from Israel it is even more reprehensible. *Christians* claim Christ, but "conceal [his] healing and hallowing grace in order to strengthen, to establish, to exalt, to exhibit [themselves] as worthy fellow-workers of God."[21] Secretly wanting their own lordship, they will not really have

15. Barth, "Ethics Today," 171.
16. Ibid., 170.
17. Ibid.
18. See Barth, "Gospel and Law," 17.
19. Ibid.
20. Barth, "Gospel and Law," 19.
21. Ibid., 17.

the first commandment to love and obey the Lord, therefore they will not have all the rest. Instead they (mis)use the law making a show of fine obedience, relegating Christ's cruciform work thereby.

Thence Barth unleashes his disgust. His attack bears quoting at length both for its content, and for the power of its rhetoric—even in translation.

> Now, indeed, with all the passion of that triumphant self-will, . . . with all the passion of his evil conscience, and certainly, most certainly, following the line of least resistance, man precipitates himself upon the law, one man upon this letter and fragment of it, another upon that. Each turns to that bit which seems to promise him most success, and each triumphs because with his letter and fragment in his hand he achieves sooner or later—at least in men's eyes—something in the nature of a special justification of his existence. Here we see one going furiously at his work. Here one cultivating an exemplary life as citizen and as family man. Here one on the hunt for "interesting" ideas, experiences, encounters and relationships. Here one in a showy simplicity and moderation. Here one gipsying it in the masterfulness claimed for genius. Here one in a contentious Church orthodoxy and theological preciseness. Here one going about with a radiant smile in evangelical freedom. Here one fussing at philanthropic work for "lame ducks" of all kinds among his fellows, or more agreeably still, directing their lives for them. Here one undertaking wild schemes of general world betterment. Here one stressing his individuality, decking out a private existence according to his very own pattern. Here one getting his ideas of justice from the multitude and from the trend of the times. Here one in a refined way directly opposed to it. And here one engaged on the fantastic plan of trying out absolute honesty, absolute purity, absolute unselfishness and absolute love.[22]

If this is true of its individual members, so too of the Christian community as a whole, even that community which, looking back to nineteenth century theology's accommodation with modernity, esteems very highly God's grace, patience and forgiveness. Regarding it Barth continues acerbically:

> [This community] would not like to abandon grace, but to keep it as a counterweight, and to temper its zeal for God which is without knowledge; it would even be glad to make use of grace

22. Ibid., 17–18.

and be served by it. But what does grace mean here? Jesus Christ, who bestows all things on his people in that he is the majesty of God Himself [stepped] into our place, has here become a mythical half-God who ostensibly imparts to them powers, a sort of magical endowment . . . Jesus Christ, the indispensable attendant, the useful lever, and, last but not least, the stop-gap in our efforts at justifying ourselves. Jesus Christ, the personification of the wonderful ideas which in keeping with the spirit and taste of our century, we are accustomed to fashion with a view to this justification. Jesus Christ the great creditor who is just sound enough to give us ever and again the necessary cover for our own undertakings and righteousness.[23]

It is then the particular sinfulness of the Christian community that it purports to keep divine law so satisfactorily that there can be no grounds for accusation against it, no judgment upon it, no need for rescue, and still less need for the sanctifying path of God. It holds itself legally entitled to full acceptance by, and partnership with God. It justifies its justification on its own grounds, and not that of the cross of Jesus Christ. It is in its own eyes glorious, lord to itself, without a genuine submission or worship before the actual God of glory. Its manufactured deity—all-powerful, transcendent and approving—becomes a useful polemical and would-be spiritual tool to aid its self-determination and self-sanctification. But such is not the triune God of Christianity. Of this community and its members Barth declares, "Here Christ has died in vain (Gal 2:21) . . . Here, bluntly, is enmity to the Cross (Phil 3:18)."[24] To this he adds icily, "Now it is more than ever, that Jesus Christ is nailed to the Cross with the help and to the honor of God."[25] "Vanity of vanities! Whatever else? To what a pitch can things be brought when once the faith which God in Jesus Christ demands for *Himself*, and for Himself *alone* is overlooked and omitted! Then there appear a thousand works of the law—of the law torn into a thousand pieces . . . A harmless desire? . . . No; for it is just out of this desire that issue [those things] which brought Christ to the Cross, and brings him within Christianity (Heb 6:6) again and again to the Cross."[26]

---

23. Ibid., 19.
24. Ibid., 19–20.
25. Ibid., 23.
26. Ibid., 17–18. Italics original.

When, individually and corporately, those claiming allegiance to Jesus Christ obey the law so as to assist God to glorify them, when, even more amazingly, they believe God just worthy enough to assist them in their justification of themselves, they are in grave error. When they fail to recognize the truth, that they could not and cannot keep the law perfectly and so break it entirely, and are therefore rightly condemned, and that the crucified Christ is not a second way to God beside their own laudable effort, but over against them[27] *the* lawful Way, then they reject their salvation and are again subject to death and hell![28] Indeed Barth says the "fallen man can no more raise himself than Satan can to the dignity of the being created and sustained by God, to a positive and independent existence of his own."[29]

It is just here that Barth finally advances a positive word. Even so at first glance his position still seems forbidding. As will be seen, he too insists that divine law, with its rules and its deadly penalty, never ceases to apply.

The Positive Soteriology of the Cross

Major soteriological themes associated with Barth's positive crucicentric soteriology include justification, sanctification, resurrection, and eschatological glorification. Each of these incorporates a number of contributing notions. In setting out this material the following discussion is patterned once again on the gracious *ordo salutis*.

Justification

In Luther's crucicentric understanding of justification Barth detects the high opening note of the Reformation. To paraphrase Barth slightly he explains that, "It was the theology of the cross as a theology of justification of sinners that Luther rediscovered. With this concept, which basically included all others, a reformation of Christendom, the church, and theology, had in fact begun. We are in fact forced to say that this

---

27. Jesus Christ, Barth lectures, "is the Crucified, the scandal, the strange work of God which threatens our works at their very root." Barth, *Calvin*, 47.

28. See ibid., 22.

29. Barth, *Church Dogmatics* II/2, 451.

one concern in all its one-sidedness is indeed the true essence of the Reformation."[30]

In terms of the present discussion what is helpful about these remarks is not first Barth's (certainly valid) insight into the significance of justification in Luther's *theologia crucis*. They are important here because they reveal Barth's accord with Luther's crucicentric soteriology. They also disclose his own view of the theology of the cross as a radical theological approach in which the soteriological placement of justification plays a critical role. To consider this crucicentric outlook on justification further, the discussion turns first to Barth's theology of the twin laws of death and of life, then to his understanding of the atoning work of Jesus Christ, and finally to his position on the number of the elect.

To again recap an earlier discussion, generally in the classical crucicentric tradition the law of God has two aspects, *alien* and *proper* to use Luther's nomenclature. In its alien aspect the law provides a standard of faultless conduct to which it holds the creature accountable, and against which it judges and condemns transgression. In its proper aspect the law provides for its judgment and inevitable condemnation to be worked out on behalf of the creature by One uniquely equipped to do so. Thence the creature is made *just* (guiltless) before it—*justified* therefore.

Barth understands the purpose of the law similarly. He does though have a particular dispute with Luther and his successors in one respect of it. Whereas for them the law in its graceless legalism is superseded by the gracious freedom of the gospel,[31] Barth insists that the law be held tightly to the gospel. (His 1933 lecture *Gospel and Law* is something of a critical footnote on Luther in this regard.)

The background here is that Luther separates the law from the gospel (and the state from the church) in order to restrain the medieval church from using the law of God in pursuit of civil power. Centuries later however Lutheran theology adapts Luther's position in the service of a very different objective, namely the formal *removal* of the constraint of the gospel on civil power. In the Germany of the 1930s Barth sees that this development permits the rise of a criminal state not only to go unchallenged, but to be actively supported by the vast majority of German Lutherans.[32] In refusing the relegation of divine law before the gospel

---

30. Barth, *Calvin*, 47. Slightly paraphrased.

31. For Luther's prioritizing of the gospel of grace over law see p. 90, n. 64.

32. See Busch, *Great Passion*, 154. Again see here p. 105, n. 129, where Luther's biographer Heiko Oberman makes an analogous observation.

therefore, he mounts a necessary challenge to the German Christians, (a move strangely missed by those who would accuse him of neglecting the theological importance of current questions). Where the gospel applies, the law applies. Indeed the good news of the command of God is the last word in every aspect not only of the Christian community, but of the *civil domain* and its operation.

But contemporary political impetus aside, there are for Barth important theological reasons for holding the gospel and the law together, even as the gospel and the law are not the same. The law is for him, "nothing else than the necessary form of the gospel, whose content is grace."[33] That is, it is the type of the Word of God which formally and graciously structures the gospel. Conversely this means that "the gospel . . . contains and encloses the Law as the ark of the covenant the tablets of Sinai,"[34] as the swaddling clothes the babe in the manger.[35] Thence, "The one Word of God is both Gospel *and* Law. It is not Law by itself and independent of the Gospel."[36] And neither can the gospel be the gospel without the law.

In structuring the gospel the law accomplishes two things. First, the law tethers the gospel securely to the righteousness of a holy God. Second, in line with the gospel the law brings the creature to the end of itself, so as to point it to the good news of God in Jesus Christ. In doing so the law operates in several ways including: exacerbating human sinfulness to underscore the incapacity of the creature to obey, revealing the righteous command and claim of God on creaturely obedience, warning the disobedient creature that it stands under due judgment and condemnation, and by extension advising the creature that it has need of One who will save it from the penalty pertaining to that judgment. Each of these mechanisms deserves further explanation.

By defining the boundaries outside which non-compliance with its commands exists, the law goads and exacerbates exactly that non-compliance. In explanation here Barth appeals to Paul, "Our sin makes use of the law as a spring-board (Rom 7:8,11), and it is only when in this way it gathers force (Rom 20), when it becomes 'exceeding sinful'

---

33. Barth, "Gospel and Law," 10. For further definition of the law see here p. 41, n. 28.

34. Barth, *Church Dogmatics* II/2, 511. Italics original.

35. See Barth, "Gospel and Law," 10.

36. Barth, *Church Dogmatics* II/2, 511. Italics original.

(Rom 7:13), when by its misuse of the law itself it serves up, so to speak, its masterpiece, turning the good, nay, the best, into its opposite (Rom 7:13), working a deception with it (Rom 7:11), that it celebrates its resurrection (Rom 7:8f), and as 'sin that dwelleth in us' (Rom 7:20), as sinful 'law in our members' (Rom 7:23), becomes active and recognizable (Rom 7:7)."[37]

The related point follows. Goading disobedience the law yet holds all creatures individually and corporately responsible for keeping its precepts. For the law is perfect, and the creature is responsible.

Being perfect the command of God necessarily includes the requirement that its precepts be perfectly obeyed. After Paul and Luther, Barth finds that any lesser demand by the law would mean that the law itself was compromised. It could not be a concrete standard of righteousness, it could not be the standard of a holy God. Equally any lesser compliance by the creature would mean no compliance at all.

Regardless of the temptation facing it, the creature is a responsible being. Barth explains, "[It is as God] makes Himself responsible for man that God makes man, too, responsible."[38] And, "[Man] as man is irresistibly compelled to acknowledge that his life is the business for which he is responsible, [and that divine truth must be] the ultimate governor of his conduct."[39] It follows for Barth that the perfect standard of the law is irreducible, and the penalty for its breach likewise! The fact of temptation provides no excuse. Legal compulsion to obey lays a heavy burden on the responsible creature.

In this situation the difficulty facing the creature is that although God holds it responsible before the law, it itself is without natural capacity to obey. It lives and moves and has its being in a fallen and antinomian world, a world acknowledging neither duty nor care in respect to the law, a world claiming its independence from the command of God, a world contaminating those resident within it with its impossible sinfulness. It is true that this contamination has its foundation in an even older reality, one reaching back beyond the beginning of human history to ancient rebellion in the universe. In Barth's words, "[Creaturely lawlessness] does not stand or fall . . . within the world of existing things, and certainly not with yesterday's, today's, or tomorrow's attempt at

---

37. Barth, "Gospel and Law," 15.
38. Barth, *Church Dogmatics* II/2, 511.
39. Barth, "Ethics Today," 138.

solving it. Its roots reach beyond its temporal beginnings and beyond all its actual and possible temporal solutions."[40] Nevertheless the fact of that ancient reality, indeed of both realities, corrupting environment and pernicious evil, does not excuse the creature from grappling with the ethical difficulty facing it: how temporally and eternally it might exist before the just command of a holy God.

In his early lecture on ethics Barth draws the problem out. "When men venture to ask themselves the simple question, What ought we to do? they take their place before this perfection and put themselves at its disposal, in its service; they enter into relationship with it—a relationship in comparison to which all other intercourse with the heavenly or demonic powers of the supersensual world fades to insignificance. For this question asks how man ought to live and move and have his being not only in this but in all possible worlds."[41]

The problem itself is then as unavoidable as it is unwanted. Barth continues, "We must still be clear upon one fact: we have no choice as to whether or not *we* will take up the ethical problem . . . [The] problem is *given us* and we must *accept* it . . . There is no moment in which we may hope to be free from the burden of it.[42] Neither can the creature solve its dilemma—how to get round law it cannot obey—by investing in its own arbitrary and changing standards of right conduct. By definition such standards never equate to divine standards. As Barth says, "[Every] random and temporal 'What shall we do?' contains a 'What' to which no random and temporal 'That' can give a satisfying answer."[43]

In its desperate predicament the creature brings two apparently opposing strategies to bear. First it attempts to comply perfectly with the just command of God. As already clear given the intrinsic nature of human sin logically this strategy cannot succeed; Barth says with Luther that even, perhaps especially, the creature's *best* works fail to comply. Then the creature attempts to avoid the command of God utterly, which proves equally impossible. In fact, both strategies—nomianism and antinomianism—entail the same sinful presumption to direct the electing decision of God. They are forms of work righteousness, they bespeak the

40. Ibid.
41. Ibid., 139.
42. Ibid., 140–41. Italics original.
43. Ibid., 141.

Karl Barth's Modern Soteriology of the Cross 259

old two-pronged desire: to be independent of God promulgating one's own law, and to be as God, glorious. And they inevitably fail.[44]

Thus the law simultaneously accomplishes several objectives. It points to the real poverty and self-glorifying perfidy of the creature's conduct, and so of the creature itself. It emphasizes the creature's incapacity to escape its founding predicament, and commensurate need of One who can effect its escape. Thereby, albeit obliquely, the law suggests the identity of that Person.[45] In this manner the law serves the gospel. Yet the creature, fallen and deceived, rejects the One to whom the law points and the astonishing offer that he makes.

So what happens to the law of God when in ignorance and sinfulness the creature fails to keep it perfectly and therefore at all? What happens when the creature then refuses to acknowledge that it stands in contravention of the divine precepts and tries to circumvent the law, taking to itself the capacity to be as God knowing good and evil? What happens when, nevertheless, the creature is presented with the gracious offer of One who can and is continually willing to assume its place so as to release it from the burden of the law, but it rejects this offer? Barth's point is chilling. *The law must take its course.* Inexorably the law, which is still God's holy, just, and prevailing law and an instrument of the gospel, will take its course. Or, as Barth himself explains, "[The law] continues to be God's claim on man even when man makes it subservient to his own claims."[46] "Its grave demands and obligations [are] unslackened."[47] Unless and until the burden of the law is removed from the creature, its full juridical weight continues to apply. Anything less would make a nonsense of the law.

First the law questions "all actual and possible forms of human conduct, all temporal happenings in the history both of the individual and of society."[48] Then the law judges.[49] Every act of the creature's life is weighed on the divine balance.[50] Then the law condemns. Indeed the creature which rejects the command of the law and in its pride looks to

44. See Barth, "Gospel and Law," 20.
45. See ibid., 15.
46. Ibid., 21.
47. Barth, "Ethics Today," 170.
48. Ibid., 139.
49. Ibid., 178.
50. See ibid., 140.

its own "measure of the good," by the very imperfection of that human measure effectively annihilates itself.[51] Or as Barth puts this, "[Man] condemns himself to death by his question about the good, because the only certain answer is that he, man, is *not* good, and from the viewpoint of the [real] good, is powerless [to be good.]"[52] Here there can be "no counsel, no consolation, no help."[53] The self-determining godlike creature is an impossibility. In the sight of God and of the law it can only perish.[54] Thus Barth, "It is simply that over against man's confidence and belief in himself, there has been written, in huge proportions and with utmost clearness, a *mene, mene, tekel*. [Aramaic: *It has been counted and counted, weighed and divided.*]"[55]

The creature, particularly the modern creature, is first deeply offended by the judgment against it, and then terrified and in crisis. It is first offended by the exposure of its actual powerlessness and incapacity for God, and by the revelation of its self-glorifying deception and duplicity. It is then terrified before the penalty it properly faces. It knows it cannot survive, but it does not wish to die. It is caught, Barth says, between the Scylla and Charybdis,[56] the rock and the hard place. Given this, the law comprises "a responsibility that cannot be borne: a deadly *aggression* against man. Either it puts to man a question to which for *him* there are only such answers as themselves become questions; or it gives him an answer for which he cannot ask . . . And he cannot live upon an answer which is so final that for him it is no answer at all."[57]

In this increasingly impossible situation the creature redoubles its attempt to avoid the demand of the law. First it feigns submission to the judgment of the law against it—the cruciform demand on its life, all the time converting that judgment and demand to a harmless word.[58] Then it openly attacks, repudiating the claim of the cross and the lordship

---

51. See ibid.
52. Ibid., 167–69.
53. Barth, "Gospel and Law," 23.
54. See Barth, "Ethics Today," 140.
55. Ibid., 149.
56. Ibid., 167–68.
57. Ibid., 152. Italics original.
58. In the nineteenth century this harmless word calls for brotherly love under the fatherly love of God. In the twentieth century it demands social justice under a just God. But in neither century does it proclaim the need for death to self, ontological transformation, and total submission individually and corporately to Jesus Christ.

of the Crucified. But these ploys too do not prevail. The creature is in fact already defeated, its future unknown to it.[59] Thus Barth, "From *this* lookoff we learn nothing as to whether we are cast away or *elected*—as to whether there is a *reality* awaiting our final words or not—as to whether, [if this is so], we may live adventurously or must live despairingly."[60] Finally brought to the end of itself, the creature dies.[61] The law, indeed God's *holy* law, has become for it the law of death!

But now for Barth something astonishing takes place. Just here, at the point of the creature's greatest ignorance and despair, in the face of God's righteous anger and implacable "No!" to human disobedience, an even greater "Yes!" comes in.

It is now that Barth's Christology must again be considered, this time at its intersection with soteriology. The heart of this intersection comprises the atoning work of the cross—atonement being the second element (after the law) in Barth's crucicentric understanding of justification. Hunsinger serves to introduce it: "The cross, as Barth understands it, occurred as the event of salvation by virtue of the true humanity and true deity of Jesus Christ. In his true humanity Jesus Christ was at once the embodiment of grace and the victim of human enmity toward grace. He . . . took the place of humankind before God in a positive sense, enacting obedience and service to God on humankind's behalf. Yet in the course of fulfilling this role, Jesus Christ was at the same time rejected and slain, becoming the victim of humankind's enmity toward the very grace which he embodied."[62]

Barth himself says, "[Jesus Christ] is God become man . . . [but] as such he is to be understood by the other fact that he is the one who was crucified, dead, and buried, who descended into hell, but rose again

---

59. See Barth, "Ethics Today," 169.

60. Ibid., 178. Italics original.

61. In his consideration of the judgment of God Barth spends some time arguing that if the death of the creature is only nominal then the creature has not really been changed. Rather it *really* dies in and with Jesus Christ so that it can *really* rise in and with him, new-made. Barth sums the point, "We speak of the proclamation of Jesus Christ, of the happening of His death on the cross . . . It is all true and actual in Him and therefore in us." Barth adds forcefully, "We have not invented all this. We have found it at the place where it is reality and truth, the reality and truth which applies to us and comprehends us, our own reality and truth. We have found it where we ourselves are and not merely appear to be." Barth, *Church Dogmatics* IV/1, 549.

62. Hunsinger, *How to Read Karl Barth*, 116.

from the dead. It is this . . . that Paul and the others meant when they spoke of Jesus Christ and him alone. *This* is the reason . . . they dared speak of a salvation."⁶³ He continues, "But note that forgiveness always takes the *way from God to man* and never otherwise. And note that there is no other way to this way but that the way is itself the way to this way. I am the way!"⁶⁴ For in Jesus Christ *God* has become like the creature so as to do for it what it cannot do for itself. Christ bears its sinful humanity before the law, and the condemnation duly pronounced on that sinfulness, and the penalty of the law therefore, satisfying the law on human behalf. Or as Barth himself says, "Grace, and so the content of the gospel, consists therefore simply in this: that in Jesus Christ with His humanity . . . He Himself and He absolutely alone—stands for us with our humanity."⁶⁵

This divine ontology and work proclaim and make the creature just *de jure* (by legal right) before God. In exchange for Christ's assumption of its nature it now stands in *his* relation to God, guiltless and unimpeded by the law, its condemnation lifted, its debt forgiven. The one for whom no defense existed has had a sound defense duly provided. The one for whom there was no freedom has been formally freed. No further charge against it stands. Barth calls this new state of affairs "a *justificatio forensis* [forensic justification], a *justificatio impii* [justification of sinners], a surpassing paradox; . . . the positive relation of God's will to man's conduct."⁶⁶ Now the law, indeed the same law by which the sinful creature had been judged and condemned, has become for it the law of life!

But the forensic importance of Christ's cruciform work is greater still. As Barth further explains, "He who accepted death as the wages of sin—and by that very act vindicated His sinlessness—was not able to be holden of death; His life had to swallow up death and did swallow it."⁶⁷ In consequence those represented in Christ likewise cannot be held by temporal death! He has forged for them a passage through death into his risen life, which is the very life of God. Barth stresses the point, "*Through* our doom we see therefore what is beyond our doom, God's

63. Barth, "Ethics Today," 181–82. Italics original.
64. Ibid., 181. Italics original.
65. Barth, "Gospel and Law," 6–7.
66. Barth, "Ethics Today," 170.
67. Barth, "Gospel and Law," 6.

love; *through* our awareness of sin, forgiveness, *through* our death and the end of all things, the beginning of a new and primary life."[68]

Barth continues to speak comprehensively of his astonishment at what Jesus Christ has done. Recalling Paul's own amazement he says emphatically, "[According] to the remarkable verses in Col 2:14f., God has blotted out the handwriting of ordinances that was against us, He has taken it out of the way, nailed it to His cross, spoiled principalities and powers, made a show of them openly (as prisoners), and triumphed over them—and all this in Him, in the circumcision of Christ, [which is therefore the circumcision] of His people."[69] Recalling Luther, he observes that it is exactly "when man is most remote from God that God in his mercy seeks out and finds him."[70] This happens in the crucified Christ; in him alone are human sinfulness and the rejection which it attracts fully weighed and fully dealt with. So a note of wonder sounds in Barth. "The fact that the will of God is also the will which rejects the world because of its sin cannot possibly be ignored or denied by Jesus Christ. On the contrary, it is only in Him that it is taken seriously, that it is genuinely real and revealed as God in His humanity makes Himself the object and sacrifice of this rejection."[71]

That God alone can and wonderfully does deal with human sin raises a related point. As is already clear Barth's concern right across his project is to forestall each and every suggestion that of itself the creature can somehow, even passively, condition the law; that would make it equal to God. Nevertheless he thinks that the creature is not a passive participant in the processes of salvation. In a measured sense human action *is* involved. Careful explanation is required here. Barth is not suddenly, surprisingly, bowing to the theology of self-glorification! His point is that justification is not simply an external process but affects the creature ontologically. The creature does not initiate its justification, but it *is* caught up in it. If this were not so it could not be transformed.

In 1922 Barth states this as follows. "If the primary and positive relation of man to God is brought out by a last wholly negative and

---

68. Barth, "Ethics Today," 169. Italics original.

69. Barth, *Church Dogmatics* IV/1, 255. The circumcision of Christ is regarded by Paul, and by Barth following him, as a proleptic sign foreshadowing Christ's death. See here p. 245, n. 243.

70. Barth, "Gospel and Law," 6.

71. Barth, *Church Dogmatics* II/2, 421.

annihilating crisis, then evidently the whole conduct of man, since it *is* determined and disrupted by this valley-of-death crisis, participates in justification."[72] In the same lecture Barth says that to encourage this participation God waits for "the submissiveness which gives to him the glory due his name, [and then for] the *desperatio fiducialis*, the confident despair in which man joyfully gives himself up for lost."[73] This creaturely salvific activity is, however, "of such a kind that the infinite separation of the righteousness of God from that of humankind is *not* reduced by [it,] but all the more clearly brought out."[74]

Much later in his project—at a time when he finds himself freer to emphasize not only the otherness but also the humanity of the God who is *pro nobis*—Barth insists "that the initiative and the decisive action in the happening described as atonement are both with God (as in John 3:16)."[75] But then he immediately adds, "This is not to say that man's part is only passive[, but through Jesus Christ] it is God himself who intervened to act and work and reveal."[76] The creature's necessary participation in its justification notwithstanding, human action connected with justification is always first that of the man-God Jesus Christ.

In interim conclusion then, the theology of the cross stands at the heart of the junction between Christology and soteriology in Barth's thought. But this is not only true methodologically. Theologically, actually, the Word of the cross both proclaims the meaning of the atoning work of Jesus Christ, and is itself that meaning. It announces that Jesus Christ does for the creature what the creature cannot do for itself, he meets the condition of its freedom. The Word of the cross is then a living Word which, in actively paying the price of creaturely freedom, involves the creature in its activity so that the creature is really ontologically freed.

The third substantive matter in relation to Barth's theology of justification concerns the number benefiting from the cruciform work of Jesus Christ.[77] Barth's answer to the question of the elect demonstrates two significant marks of his soteriology: his desire to protect the free-

---

72. Barth, "Ethics Today," 170. Italics original.

73. Ibid., 169. Italics original.

74. Ibid. Italics original.

75. Barth, *Church Dogmatics* IV/1, 74.

76. Ibid.

77. For discussion on the question of the salvation of all in the classical crucicentric tradition, see here pp. 99–105.

Karl Barth's Modern Soteriology of the Cross 265

dom of God to elect, and his powerful emphasis on the sheer liberality of grace. His answer also indicates his debt to the classical crucicentric tradition.

Barth has often been accused of betraying his reformed background by effectively opting for universal election [*apokatastasis*].[78] At first glance there appear some grounds for this accusation. On the basis of Paul and the general witness of the New Testament Barth opposes the idea of limited atonement. He insists that Jesus Christ dies on the cross for all sinners. Indeed, and as Torrance says, on the basis of Paul, Barth holds that the whole of creation has been formally redeemed and sanctified in Jesus Christ.[79] Certainly some "remain ignorant of their justification"[80] and therefore election. But given the sovereign freedom of God and the encompassing nature of divine grace, the ignorant may yet become aware of their election so as to witness to it. If they remain in ignorance and do not witness to their election, even so creaturely ignorance does not impinge on the electing decision of God, any more than creaturely knowledge might do so.

As the crucicentric theologians before him Barth finds salvific grace outpoured everywhere. There is for example a lovely passage in the *Church Dogmatics* suggesting at least the possibility of eternal existence for animals—given their "being originally and decisively with Jesus," and because what happens in the human sphere is "valid and effectual for all other spheres."[81] The argument then goes that the God who wants to protect *all* creatures on the basis of his incarnate being and act, is not likely to reject those with whom he most immediately and ontologically identifies.

In many other places too Barth speaks of the limitless reach of the work of the cross. For instance in discussing the continuing fact of human sinfulness he includes *all* human beings in the category of those benefiting from Christ's cruciform work, "[All] of us, Christians and non-Christians alike, sin in evil thoughts and words and deeds as though we were not those who were justified and sanctified in [Jesus Christ's] life

---

78. Bromiley, for instance, finds that Barth does "not deal well with the solid and consistent witness of Scripture to eternal perdition as well as eternal salvation." Bromiley, *Introduction to the Theology of Karl Barth*, 97.

79. See Torrance, *Karl Barth*, 236.

80. Barth, "Gospel and Law," 16.

81. See for instance Barth, *Church Dogmatics* III/2, 136f.

and death."[82] Elsewhere Barth points out that even in the case of Judas, the New Testament does not make an example of the "embodiment of the temporal and eternal rejection of certain men."[83]

Universal election is also implied when, following Paul, Barth gives "the many" the force of "all." For example, Barth writes, "It belongs to the distinctive essence of the Jesus Christ of the New Testament [that he is] the Lord and Head of *many* . . . [The] decision which has been taken in [Him applies to the world and] all those who live in it, . . . whether they have known Him or not[. The ignorant] are only provisionally and subjectively outside Him and without Him . . . for objectively they are His, they belong to Him, and they can be claimed as His *de iure*."[84] And similarly, "Jesus Christ . . . is not for Himself, or for His own sake, but [constitutes] the reality and the revelation of the will of God on behalf of *an unlimited number of other men* . . . He is elected, therefore, to be for them the promise and proclamation of their own election."[85]

Barth also appears to teach universal election when he insists that the divine decision to elect cannot be reversed or changed or rejected by the creature, the latter has neither the formal right nor the natural ability to do so. Indeed since the right of election is reserved exclusively to God, any attempt by the creature to reject its election is just as presumptuous and just as doomed as the attempt to merit it. Part of Barth's reasoning here runs as follows

> In defiance of God and to his own destruction [the individual man] may indeed behave and conduct himself as isolated man, and therefore as the man who is rejected by God. But he has no right to be this man, for in Jesus Christ God has ascribed this to Himself with all that it involves and therefore taken it away from man. What man can do with his negative act can only be the admittedly real and evil and fatal recollection and reproduction of that which has been removed from him; but for all its wickedness and disastrous result this negative act as such can never be other than impotent."[86]

---

82. Ibid., IV/3, 362.
83. Ibid., 11/2, 476.
84. Ibid., IV/2, 275. Italics mine. For Paul's use of "many" see here p. 100.
85. Ibid., II/2, 421. Italics mine.
86. Ibid., II/2, 316–17.

Thus for Barth it is not God's will to reject any human creature; of his wisdom and patience he elects rather than annihilates the creature intent on rejecting him.[87]

On these grounds too Barth deeply opposes positions associating election and predestination, his opposition further suggesting a sympathy towards a theory of broad election. He cites Calvin's doctrine of predestination for rejection as well as election—the notable "doctrine of double predestination," for "the serious distortion of the biblical message which this involves, [and for] its inhumanity."[88] Predestination in either direction impinges on God's continuing freedom to elect whomsoever and however many God chooses, including *all*. Barth proceeds to rework Calvin's doctrine christologically, recognizing in Jesus Christ the one predestinate man, the one man predestined for rejection and election.

It would seem then that the charge that Barth is universalist is fairly founded. Or is it? In his discussion on the election of the individual Barth directly denies universalism, doing so for the same reason that he refuses predestination for rejection—that is, the protection of divine freedom. "If we are to respect the freedom of divine grace, we cannot venture the statement that it must and will finally be coincident with the world of man as such (as in the doctrine of the so-called *apokatastasis*).[89] No such right or necessity can legitimately be deduced. Just as the gracious God does not need to elect or call any single man, so He does not need to elect or call all mankind."[90]

Barth's rejection of universalism may be demonstrated in other ways also. It is present in his denial of the abstract argument that since Christ dies on behalf of the whole world, the whole world must be elected. The first statement—which is true, does not necessarily imply the

---

87. See ibid., II/2, 450.

88. Ibid., IV/2, 520. By means of an excursus here Barth sharply rejects Calvin's doctrine of predestination.

89. Further to an earlier discussion, Barth's constant image is of the world as a large circle and the community of the elect—Israel and the church—as smaller open circles within this. These circles' common centre comprises the crucified and risen Lord of the church. Given the unlimited number of the elect the size of the inner circle of the church is not fixed; the election of each individual enlarges it. Given the graciousness of the God of the cross the possibility that the inner circle might expand to fill the outer circle cannot be excluded.

90. Ibid., II/2, 417f.

second—the truth of which cannot be deduced. If it did, the free grace of God would dissolve into a metaphysical system. For the same reason Barth denounces modern theology's "optimistic estimate of man"[91] which holds that no one can be divinely rejected. That position reshapes "the freedom of divine grace into a compulsion, and the divine judgment over sin into a light-hearted appeasing."[92] In short *obliging* God to elect all undermines divine freedom, as it underplays the utter gravity of sin. Indeed obliging God in *any* way resurrects the theology of glory—only God can oblige God.

In the final analysis therefore, Barth neither posits nor denies universal election. As just seen, to dictate either position is to dictate the action of God. But neither (contra critics such as Bromiley) is Barth ambivalent or nuanced concerning the possibility of universal election. That possibility exists for him concretely. Like the crucicentric theologians before him he leaves the question open *deliberately*. He does so with the clear expectation that given the boundless grace of God in the cross of Jesus Christ, the number of the elect is neither determinable by the creature nor likely limited by God. Barth himself comments that:

> [There] is no good reason why we should forbid ourselves, or be forbidden, openness to the possibility that in the reality of God and man in Jesus Christ there is contained . . . the supremely unexpected withdrawal of that final threat, i.e., that in the truth of this reality there might be contained the super-abundant promise of the final deliverance of all men . . . If we are certainly forbidden to count on this as though we had a claim to it, . . . we are surely commanded the more definitely to hope and pray [for it.]"[93]

Barth thus instructs the church to hear and proclaim the Word of the cross, balancing its teaching on election toward the overwhelming grace of the God who in the cross of Jesus Christ has overcome the deadly consequences of human sin.

The Word of the cross is both judgment and promise of life. The community which hears this one Word, Barth says, will not be afraid when it proclaims the cruciform message of judgment. But equally the community will herald the cruciform "Yes!" spoken to the world in the

---

91. Ibid., II/2, 295.
92. Ibid.
93. Ibid., IV/3, 478.

death of Jesus Christ.[94] In consequence, "The Church will not preach *an apokatastasis*, nor will it preach a powerless grace of Jesus Christ or a wickedness of men which is too powerful for it. But without any weakening of the contrast and also without any arbitrary dualism, it will preach the overwhelming power of grace and the weakness of human wickedness in face of it."[95]

Sanctification

Two crucicentric principles bear on Barth's theology of sanctification. These are that God alone is glorious, and that the God who alone conditions salvation alone sanctifies the saved. These principles are typically crucicentric not merely because they also inform the classical crucicentric tradition, but because together they expose the attempt by the creature to sanctify itself as an attempt on the glory of God. With these principles in view major strands in Barth's theology of sanctification are now reviewed. These include: Spirit-directed acknowledgement of Christ's justifying work, the trustful moment, the environs of Golgotha, creaturely death and suffering, and the receipt of new and sanctified life.

For Barth it is by the Holy Spirit that the salvific Word from the cross is appropriated to and actualized within the creature. By calling, gathering and enlightening *certain* individuals, the Spirit makes that which has taken place objectively in Christ for *all* people, subjectively valid for certain people.[96] Subsequent to Christ's justifying work, and it must be *subsequent to*, the Spirit creates an entry for himself where there was none.[97] He penetrates and indwells the creature, disclosing to it that which Christ has done for it and why. The Spirit then causes the creature to receive this disclosure and to respond to it. This receipt and response mark a continuing process of sanctification, wherein the creature is conformed to Jesus Christ—to his death and to his resurrection.

---

94. See ibid., IV/1, 347.

95. Ibid., II/2, 477.

96. Torrance says, "[For Barth this] is what takes place as we are baptized by the Holy Spirit, [we] are born again, called, gathered and enlightened." Torrance, *Karl Barth*, 180.

97. See Barth, *Göttingen Dogmatics*, 197.

Barth describes this Spirit directed sanctification in several places. For example, "Subjective revelation can consist only in the fact that objective revelation . . . comes to man and is recognized and acknowledged by man. And that is the work of the Holy Spirit."[98] Again, "[The] fact that God gives His *pneuma* to man or that man receives this *pneuma* implies that God . . . discloses Himself to man and man to Himself."[99] And similarly, "The work of the Holy Spirit is that our blind eyes are opened and that thankfully and in thankful self-surrender we recognize and acknowledge that it is so."[100]

An integral element of this recognition and acknowledgement is the retrospective acknowledgement of human sinfulness, the seriousness of which can be measured, Barth thinks, "by the fact that nothing less than God's eternal Word had to befriend us in this depth, and so befriend us as to step into our place."[101] The creature sees that its sinfulness rightly merits death, but that in his cruciform work Jesus Christ has lifted the eternal effect of this consequence from it. It sees too that this does not mean that it has escaped death, but that rather *it has already died*! It has already—and here Barth echoes Paul and Luther—*been crucified with Christ*.[102] It has already—and here a marked similarity to the *Theologia Germanica* exists—passed through "the door of death and hell."[103]

Like the classical theologians this is something Barth can put personally, "The sentence which was executed as the divine judgment in the death of Jesus Christ is that we are those proud creatures, that I am the man of sin, and that this man of sin and therefore I myself am nailed to the cross and crucified (in the power of the sacrifice and obedience of Jesus Christ in my place), that I am therefore destroyed, . . . that as the

---

98. Barth, *Church Dogmatics* I/1, 239.

99. Ibid., I/1, 450. Italics original.

100. Ibid., I/2, 239.

101. Barth, "Gospel and Law," 14.

102. Barth says here, "And Jesus Christ . . . enters in in such a way that man's own humanity, as Paul is fond of saying, is dead . . . 'I have been crucified with Christ' (Gal 2:19f.)" "Gospel and Law," 7.

103. Barth, "Ethics Today," 168. This quotation reads in context, "And can man conceivably enter into him except through *the door of death and hell* which is the perception of his remoteness from him, his condemnation by him, and his powerlessness before him?" Italics mine. For the *Theologia Germanica*'s use of similar terms, see here p. 60.

Karl Barth's Modern Soteriology of the Cross

one who has turned to nothingness I am done away in the death of Jesus Christ."[104]

In this new situation the creature finds itself standing guiltless before God, a prisoner released. Thus it is freed from anxiety in the face of the law. As Barth puts this, "If God is for us, if he has 'locked us up' in unbelief in order to have mercy upon us . . . who can be against us? Certainly not the right and power of his own law."[105]

The creature sees too, and *retrospectively*, that it could never have justified itself, not even by a prayer of surrender, not even by faith of its own devising. (Authentic prayer for Barth is always the work of the Holy Spirit, as faith is always the gift of God.) It sees that its justification and liberation are "altogether the work of God and not man."[106]

In response to all this, in answer to the promise contained in the Bible,[107] what Barth terms "the trustful moment" takes place. At long last the "godless man makes that transition as and to the extent that he hears and believes the promise. He turns his back on his life as a rejected man and turns to his proper life as an elected man."[108] At long last "the desire and love for the will of God are fitting and natural."[109] At long last the one who was turned to self-adulation turns to God, to be patterned by the Spirit on Jesus Christ. Thence the elected man "now lives that which he is in Jesus Christ independently of his own will and conduct and apart from all his own or other desire. He now lives by the fact that in Jesus Christ his rejection, too, is rejected, and his election consummated. He now lives—the futile beneath him; the significant and true above him; his arrogant isolation of himself from God and all its consequences

---

104. Barth, *Church Dogmatics* IV/1, 515.

105. Barth, "Gospel and Law," 26.

106. Barth, *Church Dogmatics* IV/1, 74.

107. As indicated, Barth teaches that both testaments of the Bible work together to proclaim the covenantal promise of God to lift his people out of slavery and reconcile them to himself. The First Testament announces the promise to come, and the New Testament proclaims the promise fulfilled in Jesus Christ. Equally both testaments command obedience to the law—obedience not in order to condition receipt of the promise, but in gratitude for having already freely received it. Supporting his position Barth refers to such texts as: Exod 20:2; Deut 5:6, 6:4–5; and Mark 12:29–31.

108. *Church Dogmatics*, II/2, 322.

109. Ibid., II/2, 772.

behind him as an eternal past; his justification before God as an eternal future before him."[110]

It is precisely now, *after* justification, *after* the moment of turning to Christ in trust, that—by dint of the Spirit—the deadly claim and command of the cross is pressed upon the creature all the more. For though the creature has died *de jure* to its desire for glory, it must now die to that desire *de facto*. This does not mean that the creature must die a *second* time, as it were. As seen, in the death of the representative man Jesus Christ the creaturely intent on self-glorification has already been formally judged, condemned, and negated. It does mean however that the transformation wrought formally in the cross must be made actual in the creature's own being. There must be ongoing ontological change if the creature is to be really patterned on Jesus Christ, actually sanctified.

In the process that now commences the deepest interior battle of the creature's existence begins, deeper still than that which took place prior to its initial acknowledgement and trust. What God requires is nothing less than its total submission, the utter negation of its old ways of being. Only then can what has been done for it formally begin to be worked out in it actually. Only then can the sanctifying life of Christ be securely grounded within it. Only then can Christ's lordship be securely established over it. But the elect creature—who would certainly obey Christ within reason—is nevertheless yet resident in a fallen world and as such unwilling to give away its very self, its independence, its life.

It is precisely here that the Holy Spirit leads the creature to do what it cannot do in its own power, work out its salvation practically. The Spirit directs the creature to take up its own cross,[111] to die more and more to its old pursuit of glory, and commensurably to live more and

---

110. Ibid., II/2, 322.

111. In distinguishing "the cross of Christ" from "our cross" Barth puts and answers a question, "Is it not inevitable that the effectiveness of God's intervention should involve our seeing and feeling and experiencing and suffering . . . as [Jesus Christ] Himself has suffered [the judgment of God] for us? Not in the same way as He has suffered it, for He alone has suffered the eternal death which we have deserved. Our cross is not the cross of Calvary [but] alongside the cross of Christ there is our own cross, alongside His suffering our suffering, alongside His death our death." (Ibid., II/1, 405–6.) Elsewhere Barth says similarly, "Jesus . . . prevents us from going back or looking back, demanding that we should take up our little cross—our cross not His—and follow Him, but follow Him where He Himself has long since carried His own, by way of Golgotha to the throne of God." Ibid., IV/1, 345.

more in penitence[112] and new obedience. It is in this cruciform way that the creature is really conformed by the Spirit to Jesus Christ, actually sanctified.[113]

This cruciform existence, which is authentically *Christian* existence, takes place in the locale of the cross of Jesus Christ. This Barth variously terms the *environs* and the *neighborhood* of Golgotha.[114] He says that outside this location there can be no true growth in trust, no real exercise of faith, no actual experience of salvation. Thus, he concludes, "We do not believe if we do not live in the neighborhood of Golgotha."[115]

This also means that for Barth, as for Luther, the command from the cross to ongoing death in the environs of Golgotha exists at the centre of soteriology; this is so right across Barth's project. In his 1922 lecture on ethics Barth finds the fact of cruciform claim *on those who already acknowledge their justification* reiterated down the history of the church, being proclaimed with particular clarity in the Reformation. He restates that deadly claim, adding with thick irony, "My critics certainly have in their libraries copies of the New Testament and editions of Luther; yet to most of them this type of thought seems incredibly new."[116] Some three decades later, in 1955, Barth still firmly declares that "the first thing that is true of those who [belong to Jesus Christ is that they] stand under the sign and direction of His cross. The 'must' of his passion extends to them too."[117] And four years later in 1959 he writes, "The narrow way of the Christian who belongs to [Jesus Christ], which leads through the strait gate of discipleship, means neither more nor less for man than that in order to win his life he should give it up for lost and really lose it . . . This is what we cannot ignore in this encounter, yet also cannot of ourselves

---

112. Recalling the difference between the western and gracious orders of salvation, Busch reports that for Barth, "penitence is not the condition but the consequence of the gracious pardon of the sinner and makes it possible to begin with" (Busch, *Great Passion*, 213). For the classical placement of penitence in the processes of salvation, see here pp. 71, 104.

113. The *pneuma* of God is called "holy," Barth teaches, "because its purpose is the sanctification, i.e., the setting apart, the seizing, appropriating and distinguishing of men who receive it." Ibid., I/1, 450.

114. Barth explains that, "[The] environs of Golgotha . . . are Israel, the Church, the world, and our own lives." Barth, *Church Dogmatics* IV/2, 360.

115. Ibid., II/1, 406.

116. Barth, "Ethics Today," 174. Clearly here Barth has Luther's *theologia crucis* in mind.

117. Barth, *Church Dogmatics* IV/2, 263. Italics original.

accept."[118] Death is the heritage of those in Christ. It is at this point that Barth's understanding of sanctification intersects with his understanding of Christian suffering.

As the cultured intellectual and religious worlds of the first century, generally modern theologians find the suggestion that human suffering might in any way be *positive*, at once inhumane and theologically suspect. Barth however rejects that assessment. As the crucicentric theologians before him he holds that, properly understood, suffering plays a significant role in sanctification.[119] Although no longer under divine condemnation, the Christian community exists within a fallen world, within the cruciform shadow of divine judgment. Suffering—again defined as pain and the endurance of pain—is the hallmark of this locale of the cross. Barth puts this with utmost seriousness. "The afflictions of Israel, the Church, the world and ourselves are all announcements and echoes of the reality of divine judgment [which] is only what happens at Golgotha. But it did really happen there. We therefore find its traces and tokens, its announcements and echoes in the environs of Golgotha. These environs are Israel, the Church, the world, and our own lives."[120] And in the same place he writes, "We . . . cannot live in the neighbourhood of Golgotha without being affected by the shadow of divine judgment, without allowing this shadow to fall on us. In this shadow Israel suffered. In this shadow the Church suffers. That it suffers in this way is the Church's answer to the world on the question of a 'theodicy'—the question of the justice of God in the sufferings inflicted on us in the world." Barth goes on to say that it is by suffering that the creature is begotten again.[121] For Barth too, therefore, the process of sanctification proceeds via suffering.

The end of old self-glorifying ways of being is always painful, but it leads to certain benefits for the believer. These include increasing identification with the crucified Christ, and realized victory over the ontological root of all suffering, sin and death. In illustrating this Barth appeals to Luther's understanding that suffering, being first always that of Christ himself, "stands at the heart of life and speaks of sin and folly, death and

118. Ibid., IV/3, 442. See also ibid., IV/3, 39.

119. For a discussion on the classical crucicentric understanding of the suffering of believers, see here pp. 111–17.

120. Barth, *Church Dogmatics* II/1, 405–6.

121. Ibid., 406.

hell."[122] He then agrees with Luther that, "These fearful things of God, his strange work, the crucified Christ, . . . are the theme of true theology."[123] In his mature reflection Barth is to continue his explanation of suffering and consequential benefit, setting this theme within the wider frame of the sanctifying work of God, "Our suffering and death [comprise] the path through sin to resurrection which we travel in Christ and with Christ and in imitation of Christ, penitently and obediently,"[124] he writes in 1940 as war tears at the world again. Later as the cold war rages his opinion does not change. "[To be in Jesus Christ] is to be like Him, to be His brothers, to have a share in that in which He is quite unlike us, [which means] in His obedience to God."[125]

But for Barth human suffering is emphatically *not* a virtue, a way to God, an end in and of itself. Rather in certain people the Holy Spirit can take the life-suffering to which all are heir, and make of it a cruciform passage to new life. Barth stresses this life-giving pneumatological function. The Spirit is variously, "The Spirit of God, . . . the sole source of life";[126] "God in His freedom to be present to the creature, and therefore to . . . be the life of the creature";[127] "Christ's presence with his people as the earnest of their inheritance of eternal life, as their sure companion on the way as well as himself being the way."[128]

Temporally the receipt of this new Spirit directed life of Christ takes place over the remainder of believers' earthly lives. They are clothed in Christ's sanctified humanity more and more, to be increasingly conformed to him. As such they live because the life of Christ conveyed by the Spirit flows within them.[129] Barth can put this negatively also, *viz.* "lack of the Spirit means [believers] must die."[130]

---

122. This comment falls within an early lecture on the Heidelberg Disputation. Barth, *Calvin*, 46.

123. Ibid.

124. See ibid., II/1, 406.

125. Ibid., IV/2, 270.

126. Ibid., III/2, 353–54.

127. Ibid., I/1, 450.

128. See ibid., IV/3, 351–52.

129. Barth makes it clear that the spirit of the creature is not a third thing alongside its soul and body, but something given. "It belongs to [the creature's] constitution as . . . its superior, determining and limiting basis." Ibid., III/2, 354.

130. Ibid., III/2, 360.

The Spirit is the creature's sole means of spiritual life. Given this, there can be no possibility that the life formally granted believers in Christ may be received via any other means, or from any other source. Believers do not retain some portion of themselves beyond the reach of divine grace so as to enliven and restore themselves.[131] If that were so there would be no need for the life conveyed by the Spirit, no need either for Christ's cross as the crucible of that new life, or for the creature to die to itself in receiving it. Rather it would keep the keys to its own life and death. But for Barth this is not the case.

A comment by Barth serves to conclude this discussion on his approach to sanctification. He touches on both sanctification's methodology and its goal when he says that those who are conformed by the Spirit to Jesus Christ become "that which in and of themselves they neither are nor can be, men who belong to God, who are in real fellowship with Him, who live before God and with God."[132] They become those who look to their resurrection in and with the resurrection of Christ.

Resurrection and eschatological glorification

Having considered justification and sanctification, the last part of this discussion on Barth's crucicentric soteriology considers his theology of resurrection and true glorification eschatologically. A number of familiar crucicentric themes are again present and now reviewed. These include: the promise and hope of resurrection from the dead, the return of Jesus Christ, the true *theologia gloriae*, and with this last the eternal service of the creature. Brief mention is also made of the significance of triumph in Barth's crucicentric thought. In explicating these themes Barth continues to adhere to the same principles that informed classical crucicentric soteriology. He insists that the sovereign glory of God may never be usurped by the creature, not even eschatologically, and that the creature which could not condition its salvation cannot condition its transformation in the future God has prepared for it.

To preface discussion of these themes a matter touching on the intersection of Barth's soteriology and *eschatology* is first addressed. Recalling

---

131. Contra Brunner, Barth insists that it is not possible for the creature to restore itself as a "motor-car that has come to grief and been successfully 'repaired'" (Green, Barth, 166–67). See previous note on the Barth-Brunner debate, p. 203, n. 38.

132. Ibid., I/1, 450.

a similar estimation of his pneumatology, it concerns the frequent criticism that Barth's eschatology lacks depth. In Jenson's words the "*eschatological* character of God's reality and work, so clear in Scripture, does not determine the structure of Barth's vision as it should."[133] But is this really so? Certainly Barth's stated intention is not to downplay eschatology. In 1922 he writes, "[If] Christianity be not altogether thoroughgoing eschatology, there remains in it no relationship whatever with Christ."[134] Neither is this a position from which he is to depart. Across his project the whole reason for creation and reconciliation and redemption is the eternal decision in God that there should be Jesus Christ, that by his death, his circumcision as Paul calls it and Barth agrees,[135] a new and everlasting covenant between God and the creature be cut.

Further evidence for Barth's deep eschatological concern exists in the fact that he intended a concerted treatment of eschatology (as also pneumatology) in *Redemption*—the culminating volume planned for the *Church Dogmatics*, but unfortunately never produced. According to Busch, Barth did "not leave any indications on how he would have handled"[136] the missing eschatology. Busch himself reliably suggests that Barth would have developed it in trinitarian fashion, and have included explanation of the final revelation of humankind as the eternal validation of the divine covenant established in Jesus Christ. In the present view, as part of such a discussion Barth would likely also have worked out humankind's eschatological service of witness and proclamation, and have incorporated its participation in the rule of Christ over his eternal kingdom—Barth's extant view of these matters to be discussed further here. But however that may be, the loss of the proposed volume does not mean that what Barth does do with his eschatology is therefore inadequate, either in terms of itself or in regards to its influence on later theologians.

It would seem then that the criticism by Jenson and others that Barth lacks an adequate eschatology cannot be sustained. Indeed the reverse appears to be the case. Barth can be fairly credited with encouraging eschatology's move from the relatively peripheral position it holds in the classical crucicentric tradition and in the older dogmatics gener-

---

133. Jenson, "Karl Barth," 34. Italics original.
134. Barth, *Romans*, 314.
135. Regarding circumcision see here p. 245, n. 243; p. 263, n. 69.
136. See Busch, *Great Passion*, 54.

ally, to the central place it now enjoys in late-modern crucicentric theology, as also the liberation theologies. Witness for example the works of Hall, Kärkkäinen, and Moltmann, all of which look back to Barth in this regard.

To turn directly to this still influential eschatology, at its interaction with soteriology Barth locates a three-part divine promise: of creaturely resurrection, of Christ's final return, and of true creaturely glory.

The first part of the eschatological promise is that at the close of earthly life all temporal barriers will be overcome, and the sanctified creature lifted into the fullness of Christ's resurrection life. Such fulfillment is entirely the work of the One who by "his promise alone creates something absolutely new."[137] This is so since the capacity to fulfill the re-creative promises of God belongs exclusively to the God who alone can transcend death. He alone can create new and resurrected life out of nothing, "the idea of the resurrection of the dead [being contiguous] with that of the *creatio ex nihilo*."[138]

It follows for Barth that fulfillment of the promise of resurrection is not conditional on creaturely merit, anymore than fulfillment of the great promises of justification and sanctification were earlier. He writes, "the final question of the possibility of man before God . . . certainly cannot be ascribed to [the creature] as a possibility from within."[139] If it could, then once again the creature would be as the One who summons it into the promise. Rather, Barth says, in connection to his resurrection the truly "biblical man recognizes and confesses his own creatureliness,"[140] and waits on God to fulfill his promise. By implication the non-biblical man, the one who sinfully and foolishly attempts to condition his resurrection and who therefore embraces a false theology of glory, misses the meaning of the promise entirely.

Fulfillment of the resurrection promise to believers is certain. This is so because, from another perspective, it is *already* taking place. In the realm of the cross with its ongoing exchange of death for the risen life of Christ, Christ's future has *already* broken into the present lives of believers, therefore they are *already* present in his future. It is on this actuality that believers' future hope is founded. This for Barth is not hope based

---

137. Barth, *Church Dogmatics* III/2, 156.
138. Ibid.
139. Ibid.
140. Ibid.

on wishful thinking, as it were, but tethered concretely in what actually is the case. Before the followers of Christ there is certainly "nothing but resurrection and eternal life."[141]

This also means that the creature resident in the environs of the cross does not exist between "the now and not yet" but between "the now and already."[142] That is, "the already" not only of personal resurrection but of the *Parousia*, being the return of the One who is the first and the last Word of God. Or as Barth himself says, "The eschatological perspective in which Christians see the Crucified and Resurrected ... is not the Minus-sign of an anxious 'Not-Yet,' which has to be removed, but the Plus-sign of an 'Already' ... in virtue of which they here and now recognize in him who is the first Word[,] the final Word."[143] The return of Christ comprises the second part of the eschatological promise.

To explain this further, Barth views the *Parousia* in three moments.[144] It has already commenced with Easter and Pentecost. It will culminate with the *Eschaton*, with Christ's final appearing at the end of history when he will judge the living and the dead, defeat all enemies finally and forever, and establish an eternal reign of equity and peace. No less than creaturely resurrection the advent of the Eschaton is certain, and for a similar reason. Barth argues here that the Son's enacted coming as Jesus of Nazareth in the past, and his being in the present, do not simply foreshadow his coming again. Rather the God who in these ways has *already* begun to fulfill his pledge to return, who moreover does not partially honor his promises, *will* complete what he has started.[145]

According to Barth, in this certain *Parousia* "we too are manifested as those who live, as those who are united with [Jesus Christ], as those

---

141. The context of this quotation from Barth is, "[Our] humanity, in so far as it is ours [is] condemned and lost ... but, in so far as it is the humanity of Jesus Christ, what we see ... is nothing but resurrection and eternal life." Barth, "Gospel and Law," 6.

142. Barth's eschatological insight into the "now and already" temper of existence in the cross represents an advance on classical crucicentric understanding. Broadly speaking the latter does not develop the eschatological implications of Christ's being in the present to the same extent.

143. Barth, *Church Dogmatics* IV/1, 327. See also Thompson, *Christ in Perspective*, 31.

144. Barth understands three moments in the *Parousia*: first *Easter*, second *Pentecost*—as the present, active presence of Jesus, third *the Eschaton*—as the final "coming again" in which the future hope generated by the first two moments is fulfilled.

145. See Barth, Karl, *The Christian Life*, 247. See also Barth, *Church Dogmatics* III/3, 154f., and IV/3, 914–15.

who cannot be separated from Him either in His lowliness *or in His glory*."[146] After its concerns with the themes of creaturely resurrection and Christ's final return, the third and major section of the gracious eschatological promise concerns true creaturely glorification.

As seen, the crucicentric tradition is characterized by concern with three sorts of glory, that of God, and the false and true glory of the creature. To be properly aligned with this tradition it is not enough to oppose the possibility of human self-glorification as *false* theology, there must be a developed position concerning the other polarity of the dialectic. The *true* theology of human glory must be proclaimed.

Godsey assists in introducing such a positive *theologia gloriae* in Barth. He chooses the following quotation from the *Church Dogmatics* as putting Barth's "whole endeavor into perspective."[147] "The election of grace is the eternal beginning of all the ways and works of God in Jesus Christ. In Jesus Christ God in His free grace determines Himself for sinful man and sinful man for Himself. He therefore takes upon Himself the rejection of man with all its consequences, *and elects man to participation in His own glory*."[148]

The observation that Barth's focus on human glory as the outworking of grace puts his "whole endeavor into perspective" is interesting because it does not appear to have been made elsewhere. But this time,[149] and in the present view, Godsey is quite right. A true and gracious *theologia gloriae*, one reminiscent of that advanced by the classical crucicentric tradition, not only is present in Barth but culminates his theology. In so doing it further verifies his own crucicentric credentials. For this reason it will be considered here at some length.

Again as seen, Barth rejects any suggestion that the creature is, or in its future might of itself become, divine. To recall an earlier discussion he does not support kenotic theories which, in emptying Jesus Christ of deity, risk divine nature changing into human nature.[150] Neither does he

146. Ibid., IV/2, 301. Italics original.

147. Godsey, "Barth and Bonhoeffer," 19.

148. Barth, *Church Dogmatics* II/2, 94. Cited by Godsey, "Barth and Bonhoeffer," 19. Italics mine.

149. As noted in the second literature review, Godsey appears to miss the mark in another way however. He fails to understand the true *theologia gloriae* as a strand *within* the crucicentric tradition, citing its presence in Barth as evidence of Barth's departure from that tradition. See here pp. 179–80.

150. For Barth's theology of the personhood of Christ, see here pp. 221–24.

raise Christ's human nature to become divine nature. In either of these circumstances the hypostatic union is split, losing its power to save, and, as seriously, destroying the infinite distinction between God and the creature. Instead and like the classical crucicentric theologians before him, Barth thinks that if *even in the circumstances of Jesus Christ*[151] human nature is not divinized, then the human nature of the creature resident in Christ certainly cannot be so.

At the close of his great section on glory in the *Church Dogmatics*[152] Barth calls the distinction between the glory of Jesus Christ and the creatureliness of the creature "the fundamental law of human existence,"[153] the *raison d'être* of the community which proclaims it. He adds immediately, "[We] must just as certainly miss the glory of God in ourselves as we may find it in Jesus Christ, and . . . we may find it just as certainly in Jesus Christ as we must miss it in ourselves. For the confirmation of this fundamental law, for the sake of this limit and promise, the Church [exists, its proclamation here being] the most urgent task in human existence and history."[154] He could hardly put it more strongly!

Nor is this a position from which Barth is to depart, even in his eschatology. In speaking of the future claim of God he says directly:

> [There] can be no question of a conformity which means equality, or anything in the nature of a deification of man, of making him a second Christ. The correspondence [between God and man] . . . cannot *and will not* mean abolition of 'the infinite qualitative difference' between God and man. It is a question . . . of a correspondence in which God and man are in clear and inflexible antithesis . . . The covenant, the partnership remains, but there is no development of an identity between God and man . . . Jesus Christ will reign and man will be subject to Him, and they will be different in and in spite of the closest fellowship between Him and his imitators . . . Even [in the eschatological] kingdom of perfection this relationship will be maintained. [Then there will be no more suffering and no more hell, and God and his people

---

151. Barth thinks Christ's deity is most visible in the cross, this being an advance on the classical crucicentric tradition which sees only Christ's humanity at work there, Luther's doctrine of *communicatio idiomatum* notwithstanding. See here p. 96.

152. Ibid., II/1, 608f. This "paragraph" is entitled "The Eternity and Glory of God."

153. Ibid., II/1, 677.

154. Ibid.

will meet face to face.] But even then we shall not be gods, let alone God Himself.[155]

Given all of this, given that it is Barth's dedication to distinguishing God and the creature from each other that marks the chasm between the theologian of glory and his own approach, how is it that Barth can then go on to speak of a true *theologia gloriae*?

Barth is not suddenly arguing that the creature somehow finally leaves its creatureliness behind to become substantially divine. But (as Godsey says) he does maintain that in Jesus Christ God "elects man to participation in His own glory."[156] Note "*His* own" not "*its* own" glory, the creature is still not glorious in and of itself. Neither can the creature bring about its proper glory in any way. As with justification and sanctification the process of creaturely exaltation is entirely the work of God. In Thompson's explanation of Barth here it involves "a movement from man to God but one which is wholly determined by God's movement to and for man and is in fact identical with it."[157] This divine action is the culmination of all God's ways and works towards humankind. Moreover the exaltation of the human creature to share in Christ's glory is certain for the same reason that creaturely resurrection is certain. That is, it has *already* taken place in the man-God Jesus Christ, therefore it *already* applies to those in him.[158]

In these ways Barth's debt to the earlier crucicentric tradition—which takes a very similar view—is apparent. But he also extends that tradition at the point where it understands a cruciform exchange to take place between divine abasement and creaturely *justification*. Barth proposes that by "his own abasement God has [also] elected and achieved man's *exaltation*,"[159] so relating divine abasement and creaturely exaltation to glory dialectically. This is an exchange not based on a necessary relation so as to ground it anthropocentrically, but set properly theologically in the prior decision of God.

Creaturely glorification is referred to positively by Barth in many places. For instance he writes, "Man's position and course under grace

---

155. Barth, *Church Dogmatics* II/2, 577–78. Italics original.
156. Ibid., II/2, 94.
157. Thompson, *Christ in Perspective*, 17.
158. See Ibid., II/1, 673.
159. Ibid., IV/1, 6. Italics original.

are . . . to be defined as the position and course of one, in place of whose humanity steps Jesus Christ with His assumed, obedient and glorified humanity."[160] And again, "human essence in all its nature and corruption . . . has now become and is participant in [Christ's] elevation and exaltation."[161] Crucially here human "essence" is not transposed into divinity, but the creature is made fully and gloriously *human*—as Hunsinger in his own interpretation of Barth also notes. "We are made glorious, not divine but fully human. We are [included in Christ's] being, in his humanity, in his history, in his transition from shameful death to glorious resurrection, in his transformation of the old creation into the new."[162]

Barth himself summarises the matter when he says that as a result of Christ's cruciform work, "We not only have a *theologia crucis*, but [consequently] a *theologia resurrectionis* and therefore a *theologia gloriae*, i.e., a theology of glory of the new man actualized and introduced in the crucified Jesus Christ."[163] Put otherwise, the Word from the cross proclaims that Jesus Christ is the crucified, recreated, resurrected and glorious man, and that the creature's re-creation, resurrection and true glorification are consequent on being caught into his cruciform death, resurrection and glory. Barth stresses the point; deriving from the *theologia crucis* of Jesus Christ the true *theologia gloriae* announces "a theology of the promise of our eternal life which has its basis and origin in the death of this man."[164]

The fulfilment of the eternal plan of God to lift the creature, individually and corporately into Christ's risen glory, applies to the redeemed *world*. As T. F. Torrance explains, "Barth [speaks of] the will of God that at last the peoples and nations of the world shall . . . share together in the glory of the Lord."[165] In this extension to the nations of the promise of glory Barth's development of the implications of Christ's abasement in the cross is far reaching. (It also represents a significant advance on classical crucicentric thought.)

160. Barth, "Gospel and Law," 7.
161. Barth, *Church Dogmatics* IV/2, 270.
162. Hunsinger, *How to Read Karl Barth*, 124–25.
163. Ibid., IV/2, 355. For an earlier discussion on this passage in relation to Godsey see here p. 179.
164. Ibid.
165. Torrance, *Karl Barth*, 81–82.

Fulfilment of the divine plan for human glory applies first however to the community in Christ, the church militant and triumphant. For Barth the church militant is the earthly preparatory form of the glorified community to be. He thinks this has implications for the Christian community's present being and act. The earthly church participates in the divine "self-glorification: no less really in this form than in the future form which here and now we still await and to which the Church moves."[166] Or more roundly, "We are not here and now excluded from the glory of God. But the form in which we are surrounded by it, and in which we participate in it, is the form of the Church, proclamation, faith, confession, theology, prayer."[167]

That constitutive ecclesial work, proclamation, prayer and so on, focuses down to two divinely set tasks by which the earthly church practically anticipates its eschatological glorification and service. Firstly it is called to reflect the glory of God back to God; secondly it is called to reflect the glory of God to the world.

The earthly church, meaning also each of its individual members, is called both in being and act to reflect the glory of God back *to God*. This dynamic reflection is the *telos* of the eternal decision that there should be the community and the creature whose "destiny is to be the image of God."[168] Herein quite simply the "meaning and purpose of all creation."[169] Indeed the "whole point of creation is that God should have a reflection in which he reflects Himself and in which the image of God as the Creator is revealed, so that through it God is attested, confirmed and proclaimed. For this reflection is the centre and epitome of creation concretely represented in the existence of man."[170]

Barth then elaborates on this ecclesial reflecting. "Where there is light [that is, Jesus Christ who is light] and the light shines, there is an illuminating and an illumination. This means that another object [the creature] is illuminated, . . . echoes and reflects the glory of the Lord."[171] It does so in the same way that the moon reflects sunlight back to the

---

166. Barth, *Church Dogmatics* II/1, 75.
167. Ibid.
168. See Thompson, 17, for further discussion of Barth here.
169. Barth, *Church Dogmatics* II/1, 676.
170. Ibid.
171. Ibid., II/1, 648.

sun. Or "in the same way . . . an echoing wall [repeats and broadcasts] the voice which the echo 'answers.'"[172]

In this Barth carefully excludes the possibility of a self-glorifying *analogia entis*. The creature can reflect the glory of God *not* because it shares commonality with God, but sheerly because God of his freedom graciously lights it. The function of those glorifying the risen Son "is bound to his person."[173] It is exclusively "God's self glorification which is accomplished . . . in His glorification by the creature."[174]

It follows for Barth that presently the "revelation of [Christ's] majesty discloses also the relative and subordinate but genuine majesty to which we are elected and called in Him."[175] The creature "is permitted to serve the divine self-glorification, and [only] in this way and to this extent what it does can have a share in God's own glory."[176] This subordinate status does not however mean that the glory reflected by the creature is inferior to the glory that God shines forth directly. It is still the glory *of God*, originating in God and used by God to glorify God.

The second task laid on the earthly preparatory form of the church, and so its individual members, is that of reflecting the glory of God *to the world*. It is to do so by witnessing to Jesus Christ in its being and act, or more deeply conceived, by being present to Jesus Christ as he witnesses to and glorifies himself through its being and act. This requires the throwing down of creaturely self-glory and the pessimism and unbelief feeding it, and in their stead acceptance of the free gift of faith. The preparatory form of the church is then the community of those whom, having passed through the cross, by faith "expect and finally receive eternal life [now]."[177] Its members know that in the crucified and risen Christ their justification, sanctification, resurrection, and glorification have already taken place formally, *de jure*. In response they are to forgive as they have been forgiven,[178] dwell in mutual love, and look toward

---

172. Ibid., IV/2, 363.
173. Ibid., II/2, 425.
174. Ibid., II/1, 672.
175. Ibid., IV/2, 300.
176. Ibid., II/1, 670.
177. Ibid., II/2, 423.
178. Barth says, "Since there is such a thing as forgiveness (which is always forgiveness of *sin!*), there is such a thing as human conduct which is justified . . . There is an effective *brotherly love* [which] begins with our forgiving our debtors—with empty hands!—as we also are forgiven." Barth, "Ethics Today," 172–73. Italics original.

the *de facto* completion of their resurrection and glorification with sure hope—the very hope of Easter. So Barth declares, "The Christian community is the Easter community. Our preaching is Easter preaching, our hymns are Easter hymns, our faith is an Easter faith."[179]

Barth holds that in its earthly preparatory form the church community participates in the divine "self-glorification: no less really in this form than in the future form which here and now we still await and to which the Church moves."[180] But this also means that the fulfillment of the glorious eschatological destiny to which that earthly community is called, and for which it is to look, still lies ahead.

It is not until the Eschaton that creaturely glory will be fully revealed. Only then, Barth says, will those risen in Christ be fully clothed in the Son's "true and incorruptible and immortal being."[181] Only then will "the promise and faith of the future revelation of [man's] participation in God's glory"[182] be fully worked out. Only then will the present destiny of those in Jesus Christ be fulfilled. Barth bases his position on the "New Testament community [which hopes for] the glorification of the creature which is latent and implicit in [Christ's] glory, initially revealed in His resurrection, and [is] finally to be revealed in His return."[183] Or as Thompson neatly captures this, "Our future is in and with him who brings us to glory, the true end of salvation."[184]

In his discussion on "the determination of the elect" Barth takes this yet further. He finds the traditional account of the future of believers impoverished.[185] Certainly the elect finally "go to heaven,"[186] but he thinks much more is implied in the scriptural record. The notion of heaven misses "the biblical view [which]—in a deeper understanding of what is meant by the clothing of men with God's eternal glory—opens at

---

179. Ibid., IV/2, 355.

180. Barth, *Church Dogmatics* I/1, 675.

181. Ibid., IV/3, 928. This reference falls within a remarkable discussion concerning the end of creaturely life.

182. Ibid., II/1, 648–49. See also Busch, *Great Passion*, 288.

183. Ibid., III/2, 490.

184. Thompson, *Christ in Perspective*, 132.

185. Contra Jenson and others, Barth's conclusion that traditionally eschatology has been treated inadequately would seem to mitigate against the likelihood that he himself would neglect it. For an earlier discussion on this matter see here pp. 277–78.

186. Barth, *Church Dogmatics* II/2, 423.

this point another door."[187] Barth then proceeds to walk through it. The "concern of those who have reached their goal in the coming age does not seem to be a passive, functionless enjoyment of their eternal innocence, justification and blessedness,"[188] he suggests. On the contrary, just because they have been clothed in Christ's glorious humanity their function stands or falls with the fact that they render him service eternally.[189] This eternal service extends that already begun by the elect temporally. (On this point once again Barth is making an advance on traditional crucicentric understanding.)

The prior eschatological task of the glorified is to continue to magnify the risen Christ by reflecting his glory back to him. Here Barth ascribes to them the exultant cry of the exiled John, "Thou art worthy, Oh Lord, to receive glory and honor and power."[190] In great shout and adulation the glorified will cast down their own crowns before Christ, disclaiming all homage toward themselves, and acknowledging that that glory they do show forth derives from, and properly belongs, entirely to him.

The second eschatological task of the glorified is to continue to witness to the crucified Christ in his risen glory, *viz.* to "that mighty voice from heaven."[191] Or rather they are to continue to serve as conduits through which he witnesses to his own glory. He is then both the glorious content and the actual proclamation of their eternal witness. Or as Barth puts this, "He is Himself the kingdom of God [and the] good news of that kingdom."[192]

But the scope of this eschatological witness extends even further. In the matter of "the future life of those who . . . have become partakers of the grace of God,"[193] the elect of God, Barth appeals to Paul and to the writer of Revelation. Those whose earthly lives have been spent in the shadow of Christ's cross will also *reign* with him. They will possess

---

187. Ibid.
188. Ibid., II/2, 424.
189. See ibid., 425
190. Ibid., III/1, 13. (John 4:11)
191. Ibid.
192. Ibid., II/2, 423–24.
193. Ibid., II/2, 344.

"a definite share in his kingship."[194] They "will judge even the angels."[195] It follows that in this glorious future, which even now is beginning, "in them He recognises Himself."[196]

Vitally for Barth, the glorified perform their service not primarily as isolate beings, but corporately. It is again first the Christian community, now in its final and eternal form, that participates forever in the divine self-glorification. The church triumphant is then the primary locus of the glory of the risen Christ; *he glorifies it that it glorifies him*. Herein for Barth the summit of the word of human glory proclaimed from the cross—the true *theologia gloriae*.

Barth then notes with some surprise that that true *theologia gloriae* is often overlooked in the contemporary church. He identifies three specific reasons for this neglect.

First, Christ's cruciform humiliation necessarily hides his glory, and with it the true glory of the creature in Christ. Barth says, "The knowledge of the reality of . . . our participation in [Jesus Christ] and in [his] exaltation . . . is not self evident, either from our own standpoint, or especially from that of Jesus Himself, whose exaltation (and with it our own) has indeed taken place, but is also concealed in his crucifixion and therefore his humiliation."[197]

Second, the false *theologia gloriae* with its promises of Godhood and independence and its denial of the need to die to self, tempts believers away from the true *theologia gloriae*. Thence Barth warns that, "The *theologia crucis*, in which the true *theologia gloriae* has its roots, may easily be destroyed by a false *theologia gloriae*."[198] (Barth thinks the contemporary Christian community, indebted as it is to the self-glorifying theology of the nineteenth century, particularly vulnerable in this respect.)

Related to this, the third reason for the neglect of true human glorification stems from the fact that traditionally crucicentric theologians

---

194. Ibid. The context of this quotation is, "As created beings they are completely and utterly other than God, completely and utterly dependent upon Him, and therefore made by Him alone into what they are: but as the elect of God they are not strangers to Him, but possess a definite affinity with Him and *a definite share in His kingship.*" Italics mine.

195. Ibid.

196. See ibid., 345.

197. Ibid., IV/2, 360.

198. Ibid., IV/2, 9.

have very powerfully rejected the false *theologia gloriae*. But this has meant that their proclamation of the true *theologia gloriae* has been comparatively marginalized. It has been even less likely than the falseness of the false *theologia gloriae* to gain the broad attention of the church.

Later in his project, the false *theologia gloriae* being well dismissed, Barth sets about remedying this situation. He proclaims the true *theologia gloriae* clearly to the church—as seen. This proclamation is however not without opposition. Accordingly he defends his action. He begins with the questions against him:

> The exaltation of man to God? . . . Is this not the way of theological humanism, moralism, psychologism, synergism, and ultimately an anthropocentric monism—a way which in the last thirty years Evangelical theology has scarcely begun to learn again to see and avoid in all its aridity? . . . Is not the supposed summons to take it up a temptation which we do well simply to avoid in view of all that happened in the 18th and 19th centuries, and further back in the Middle Ages and even in the Early Church, not to forget the constant warning [presented by the errors] of Roman Catholicism?"[199]

Barth's answer entails yet further questions. How can the creature really know of its glorious destiny? How is it that "we are endowed and adapted to receive grace of His fullness, or even to realise [in ourselves] the presence of the fullness of divine, and therefore of human glory?"[200]

He then presents his solution. Simply put, the Bible witnesses to this truth. "In the Bible . . . there are men who are in different ways exalted by the grace of God. We cannot ignore this fact. Indeed, we are forced to take it very seriously. It is part of the revision and correction which the Church and its proclamation must always be ready to accept from Scripture."[201]

Now on the pattern of Paul and Luther, Barth does what the theologian of the cross must always do where there is error. He corrects. For the Church to declare the claim of the cross but forego the proclamation of the true *theologia gloriae* leaves the doctrine of reconciliation "hollow and empty and unreal on its objective side."[202] Whereas the church

---

199. Ibid., IV/2, 8.
200. Ibid., IV/2, 354.
201. Ibid., IV/2, 7.
202. Ibid., IV/2, 10.

rightly rejects the false *theologia gloriae*, it is *not* to neglect the proclamation of the true. A "committed mistake is not put right by committing the opposite mistake,"[203] Barth says. The church "does not know grace as a whole, which means that it does not know it at all, if it tries to escape this side of its biblical attestation."[204] For the exaltation of the creature has already taken place formally, and is now taking place actually. "We deny the whole of the third article of the creed, and blaspheme against the Holy Spirit, if we reject this answer."[205] Therefore the church must positively announce the Word from the cross concerning true creaturely glory. Taking this action is of critical importance. If eternal participation in the glory of Jesus Christ is the *telos* of God's redeeming love, the final "Yes!" of God to the creature, a proper proclamation of the gospel demands that it do so.

To draw this discussion on Barth's true *theologia gloriae* toward its close, an earlier observation is recalled. Luther emphasizes the divine proscription on the false *theologia gloriae* to correct, and Paul emphasizes the true *theologia gloriae* to encourage. In so doing each takes a legitimate crucicentric position. Barth though is called both to correct and to encourage. He deals with a weakened church captive to an intellectual age which rejects the logic of the cross altogether, a church intent on glorifying itself. Thence Barth's whole project becomes "a silver trumpet of enormous dimensions"[206] with which he cries a definite "No!" not only to Brunner but to the false glory of the church itself. That said, Barth must equally address a church which—in the face of the immense civil and ideological upheavals of the twentieth century and of frank persecution—is in great need of encouragement. Thence Barth's "No!" is the sharper just because he encloses it in the glorious "Yes!" of God to humankind. This is a "Yes!" echoing the Word of the cross itself, a "Yes!" worked out eternally in the creature via justification, sanctification, and triumphant participatory glorification. Moreover here the familiar methodological point applies. Barth's conception of the true *theologia gloriae* with its eschatological emphases once again picks up and considerably develops the like notion advanced by the classical crucicentric theologians.

203. Ibid.
204. Ibid., IV/2, 7.
205. Ibid., IV/2, 355.
206. See "No! Answer to Emil Brunner," in Green, *Barth*, 166.

There is one final matter for discussion, brief but important. As seen many commentators point to a "note of triumph" in Barth's soteriology, citing for example his theology of true creaturely glory. For some of them this triumphant approach necessarily disqualifies Barth as a crucicentric theologian.[207] In the present view however, the element of triumph in Barth's work does not negate but rather seals his crucicentric credentials. Theologically it stresses the high meaning of the Word from the cross: that by dint of the cross the creature is made triumphant over evil, sin and death, as also the false glory of the world. Methodologically it comprises an important device for underscoring positive crucicentric polarities, supporting the Word of the cross structurally. All this means that Barth cannot be dismissed as a theologian of the cross on triumphal grounds. The real problem here is that those who think he can fail to comprehend the triumphant theology from the cross themselves.

Conclusion

Viewed in the hermeneutical light of the classical *theologia crucis*, it appears that in the modern age Karl Barth vitally recovers the crucicentric system, including its several soteriological elements, so as to present an authentically modern and crucicentric soteriology of his own.

For Barth is a *modern* theologian. This is so not simply by dint of birth, but because he develops his position in dialogue with both the modern age and the theological response that age inspires, particularly the nineteenth century theological response. Barth then criticizes that earlier reply. Modern soteriology has made of the saving God a prisoner either of rationality or felt experience, while presuming to humankind the godlike power to dictate the terms of salvation. Thence he cites it for what it actually is, the reactionary resurgence of old, self-glorifying intent. In its place Barth asserts a peculiarly modern, fresh, and responsive soteriology of his own, one that accounts for human nature individually and communally, one that preferences reason in proclaiming the exclusivity of the glory of the electing God.

But Barth is also a *crucicentric* theologian. In his soteriological formation he adheres to the same key principles as those guiding classical crucicentric soteriology. These are the general principle maintaining a

---

207. For example Berkouwer—see here pp. 174–75, and Godsey—see here pp. 179–80.

categorical distinction between God and the creature, and the specifically soteriological principle that God alone can determine the creature's eternal relation to God.

The elements Barth sets around these principles likewise reflect those found in the earlier crucicentric tradition. In the order discussed here these are as follows. Negatively—the creaturely attempt to use the law to condition salvation, and with this opposition to the false *theologia gloriae*. Positively—under justification: the laws of death and of life, the atoning work of Jesus Christ, and the methodological question of the number of the elect. Under sanctification: Spirit directed acknowledgement of Christ's justifying work, the trustful moment, the environs of Golgotha, creaturely death and suffering, and the receipt of new and sanctified life. Under resurrection and eschatological glorification: the promise and hope of resurrection from the dead, the return of Jesus Christ, the true *theologia gloriae* and with this the eternal twofold service of the creature. The significance of triumph in Barth's soteriology is also noted.

In discussing these elements the study has recalled Barth's strong pneumatological and eschatological emphases, these resulting from his development of strands nascent in the earliest period of the crucicentric tradition. Incidentally the suggestion has been that these advances critically influence the direction of important late-modern theologians of the cross, not least Hall, Kärkkäinen and Moltmann.[208]

An early comment by Barth reveals the distinctly crucicentric tenor of the soteriology he then pursues for nearly fifty years. As such it serves as an apt conclusion to this account of that soteriology and its modern and crucicentric orientation. In 1922 Barth lectures, "There is an *obedience unto salvation* which begins when we come down from our high places, from our High Place . . . and declare a thorough-going religious and moral disarmament."[209] It would seem that not since Martin Luther has anyone given material form to the *obedience unto salvation* more faithfully, or in the modern age set the logic governing *the need to disarm* before the church more powerfully, than Barth himself.

---

208. A note by Thompson instances this, "Moltmann's views show a new awareness of the place of the cross as basic to Christian faith and theology and is a strong confirmation of Barth's emphasis, *theologia crucis*." Thompson, *Christ in Perspective*, 162 n.81.

209. Barth, "Ethics Today," 172–73. Italics original.

9

In Final Conclusion

Theologia crucis is not a single chapter in theology, but the key signature for all Christian theology. It is a completely distinctive kind of theology. It is the point from which all theological statements which seek to be Christian are viewed.

—Jürgen Moltmann[1]

From the Apostle Paul and the earliest period of the Christian tradition, through Athanasius and then a defined group of medieval mystics, up to and including the Reformer Martin Luther, a thin line of theologians collate, relate, and convey the crucicentric idea—or in strict theological terms they relay it from the cross. For this idea is that the cross itself proclaims a self-disclosing and a saving Word, each dimension paralleling the other, each of equal theological significance. Luther, uncovering and codifying the ancient system predicated on this idea, retrospectively calls it what it is: *theologia crucis*. In turn this *Word from the cross* and the system conveying it provide a guiding foundation within the modern evangelical theology of Karl Barth.

The forgoing investigation has sought to investigate the nature of the theology of the cross and to overview the tradition carrying it. In so doing it has responded to two substantive proposals. The first of these considers:

---

1. Moltmann, *The Crucified God*, 72.

> That the theology of the cross (*theologia crucis*) is an ancient system of Christian thought conveying the message of the cross of Jesus Christ, that in it alone all—necessarily self-glorifying—creaturely attempts to know and be as God are overcome, that the proper glorification of human knowledge and being may proceed.

On the basis of its investigation of the relevant primary and secondary literatures, the conclusion to Part One of this discussion proposes the systematic shape and content of the classical theology of the cross diagrammatically, and lists the marks of its theologians. There is no need to summarize all this material now, but the classical tradition's guiding principles do bear reiteration.

The overarching crucicentric principle holds that God alone is glorious. Contingent on this two further principles parallel each other. An epistemological principle holds that any attempt by the creature to know God as God alone can know God is necessarily the attempt to usurp the glory of God; rather God alone can know God in Godself so as to reveal God. A soteriological principle holds that any attempt by the creature to condition the divine electing decision as God alone can condition it is necessarily the attempt to be as God; rather God alone can determine the election of the creature.

The foregoing investigation has found that in accord with its guiding principles, classical crucicentric theology advances the crucicentric idea both negatively and positively. Negatively, it rejects all self-glorifying methodologies—epistemological and soteriological, and therefore the theological system supporting them, *viz.* the *theologia gloriae*. Positively, it proclaims the theology from the cross of Jesus Christ: that on the basis of the cross the creature's noetic and ontic presumptions to glory are *already* defeated. In their place a way has been made for the creature to be really drawn into the glorious self-knowledge and humanity of the risen Christ. The positive aspect of classical crucicentric theology encompasses its negative aspect, not doing away with the latter's seriousness, but placing it in the proper context of God's overwhelming grace and love toward the creature.

Part One of the presentation concluded that enough had been done to validate the first substantive proposal. That suggestion stands.

The second substantive proposal in the current investigation holds:

That the crucicentric system provides a pervasive, pivotal, and generative influence in the twentieth century orthodox theology of Karl Barth, who crucially recovers, reshapes, and reasserts it as a peculiarly modern instrument—in so doing further advancing the system itself.

"Dogmatics is possible only as a theologia crucis."[2] Barth opens his mature theology with this proposition and it has been the burden of the second part of this discussion to discover what this implies for his project. To date the possibility of a significant crucicentric proclamation (however understood) within Barth's project has been largely ignored by the relevant secondary literatures. Given this, in the current investigation it has been necessary to search out pertinent secondary comment "in the crevices." But there it is present, if peripherally so in terms of its immediate context. These materials, along with selected sections of the primary literature, have been viewed in the hermeneutical light of the classical crucicentric tradition. This has allowed Barth's crucicentric status in terms of that tradition to be ascertained.

As many scholars observe, Barth dialectically engages the whole stretch of Christian theological tradition preceding him, as also the succession of intellectual paradigms with which Christian tradition intersects. But he pays particular attention to modernity and the various theological responses to it preceding his own.

Within this broad ambit Barth encounters the classical crucicentric tradition by way of its theologians, Paul and Luther especially but also others whom they bracket. What is less often noticed, including by Barth himself, is that indirectly, via Luther, this line of influence touches on a contrary strand within medieval mysticism.[3] In Barth's thought its print

---

2. Barth, *Church Dogmatics* I/1, 14. Also see here p. 1.

3. Barth is suspicious of mysticism, regarding it as a creaturely instrument in the false quest for glory, and the antithesis of the theology of the cross. In 1922 he writes, "Jesus Christ is *least of all* an object of religious and mystical experience. So far as he is this to us he is not Jesus Christ" (Barth, "Ethics Today," 181; italics original). The same year he lectures, "Neither Bernard, Tauler[, nor others,] could really get beyond the picture of Jesus as the model of our seeking of God and as the invincible head of all [who do so. But the] ideal of medieval piety that mysticism equated with Christ . . . could not coexist with the theology of the cross, which summoned precisely this ideal of piety to judgment and sought to bring freedom from preoccupation from the self" (Barth, *Calvin*, 60). Barth correctly estimates medieval mysticism's false quest for glory, but he fails to recognize fully that a radical strand within medieval mysticism—represented by Bernard, Tauler and others—also perceives the falsity of that quest, and

is detectable, for example in his juxtaposition of cruciform hiddenness and revealedness, or in his *analogia fidei*, or in his heralding of true human glory.

The current study finds that under all these stimuli, positive and negative, it is supremely Barth who recovers the crucicentric tradition for the twentieth century and beyond. In doing so he balances properly the vertical and horizontal axes of the cross, the way of the God of the cross toward the creature, and the way of the creature before this God. Epistemologically Barth denies the ancient *analogia entis*, while also bringing out crucicentric theology's inherent logic. Soteriologically he re-emphasizes the crucicentric tradition's chief insights, not least the deadly claim of the cross consequent on the creaturely presumption to glory, and therefore the value of *death* as the one passage to true and glorious life.

Barth locates the truth of God and true creaturely glory where these may reasonably be found. That is, not in ancient analogy drawn from the creature to God, not in the self-sanctification forwarded by the western *ordo salutis*, and certainly not in the anthropocentric spirit of the age. Rather divine truth and true human glory are available in the man-God Jesus Christ, and him crucified. He is the noetic and ontic Word from the cross, and the Content of the Word so proclaimed. Thence the opening to Barth's mature theology already noted: dogmatics, the formal explication of Christian faith, *is* only possible as a *theologia crucis*.

But Barth also reforms and extends the classical crucicentric tradition by building on its ancient christological, pneumatological and eschatological foundations. Christologically, he holds Christ's divine as well as human nature to be fully involved in the work of the cross. Soteriologically, he presents the Holy Spirit empowering the in-breaking Word of the cross: its transmission, receipt, and transformative effect. Eschatologically, building on Paul, he develops the eternal goal of life in the cross as eternal participation in the glory of the risen Christ.

Barth is then an eminently *crucicentric* theologian. In his high regard for reason, for the human, for the individual, he is also a *modern* one. Barth critically engages both modernity itself and the modern, particularly nineteenth century, theological reaction to modernity. He

stands implacably against it. Its own starting point is not the creature but the crucified; its piety rests not in determining but in being determined, and its positive crucicentric influence reaches immediately to Luther.

argues that the modern age must be accommodated to the Gospel and not vice versa. The anthropocentric starting point for the knowledge of God and the way of salvation is unreasonable, foolish. It does not start in the cruciform place where that knowledge and way are made available. The human is not the precursor of the divine. Neither is the modern individual the center of reality. Indeed modern individualism is but a cipher for independence from God and isolation from others. Barth is therefore a modern theologian in a quite different way to those who precede him, or to their twentieth century descendants.

Additionally the second substantive proposal suggests that the classical crucicentric system provides a generative influence in the twentieth century orthodox theology of Karl Barth. The implication is that the crucicentric idea influences not only Barth's own project, but later projects taking their lead from his. It must be admitted that this aspect of the second proposal has not been concertedly examined here. Within the recent secondary literature there are certainly hints that Barth's crucicentric orientation forms a critical foundation enabling the late twentieth century crucicentric renaissance to proceed as it has, but the precise nature of that renaissance's link back to Barth has yet to be explored. Likewise, the mooted connection between Barth's modern theology of the cross and late-modern liberation theologies is yet to be fully investigated. These provisos aside however, it does appear that the second substantive proposal here has been proved.

A subsidiary proposal affirms:

> That where the crucicentric nature of Karl Barth's project has been missed or misassigned, and therefore he himself not considered crucicentric, there has likely been failure properly to comprehend the shape and content of the system structuring the crucicentric tradition, and to perceive the marks of its theologians.

Given that Barth's broad debt to major figures in the classical crucicentric tradition is well established, and his own general importance for those widely held to be late-modern theologians of the cross equally so, it seems curious that his own status as a theologian of the cross should remain relatively unremarked. The above proposal forwards a reason for this. But does ignorance of the shape and content of the theology of the cross really correlate with failure to perceive it in Barth?

Relating the analyses of the two databases used in this investigation is helpful in reaching an answer. One commentator takes an extended view of the theology of the cross and does not accept Barth's crucicentric status: Bayer (1995). Two commentators take a confined view of the theology of the cross and do not accept Barth's crucicentric status: Godsey (1987) and Barker (1995). Considering this very small sample, on balance it would seem that a confined conception of the theology of the cross *does* mean that its presence is likely to be overlooked in Barth. To this extent the subsidiary proposal can be affirmed.

Only three commentators take an extended view of the theology of the cross and accept Barth's crucicentric status: Thompson (1978), Bauckham (1988), and Tomlin (1999). The more significant finding is that eight others: Klappert (1971 and 1994), Fiddes (1988), Wells (1992 and 2001), Schweitzer (1995), Hinlicky (1998), Hunsinger (1999), Richardson (2004), and Vorster (2007), lean toward a confined view of crucicentric theology and accept Barth's crucicentric status. That is, they each define the theology of the cross differently, and they each assign a theology of the cross to Barth that accords with their particular definition of it. When however the various crucicentric conceptions they attribute to Barth are *put together*, the fully orbed nature of his actual theology of the cross, along with its similarity to the classical *theologia crucis*, comes into view. It follows that the commentators concerned have each ascribed a theology of the cross to Barth on partial evidence. Their ignorance of the true shape and content of the theology of the cross indeed does correlate with failure to perceive it properly in Barth—and further affirms the subsidiary proposal here.

The fact that Barth presents a comprehensive theology of the cross does not of itself make him a theologian of the cross; his status as a crucicentric theologian does not depend on closed logic. Rather it relies on the material reason that he subscribes to particular positions marking the theologian of the cross down the history of the church. As delineated in the conclusion to Part One of this investigation, these traditional crucicentric marks include:

- Primary attendance to the Word from the cross.
- A particular way of seeing, that is, *through* the cross and not around it.
- Adherence to three central principles: the prior principle that God alone is glorious; contingent on this the epistemological principle that God alone can truly know God in Godself so as to reveal God

truly; and the soteriological principle that God alone can condition the salvific will of God.

- A wise regard for reason, beginning where God is and not where God is not.
- A profound realism methodologically and theologically.
- Two stances toward human glory, negative and positive.
- A particular watchfulness at the threshold of the church and the world.
- Insistence that the Gospel take priority over the age.
- Existence in the realm of the cross.[4]

There can be no doubt that the principal theologians mentioned in this investigation, including Barth, satisfy these criteria. But there is one other mark they fulfill, that is, submission to the summons of the cross personally. Indeed the greatest Christian theologian of the modern age is not above preaching to the inmates of Basel Prison. At Easter 1961 Barth speaks movingly of the intimate relation between cruciform claim and consequent freedom in his own life.

> In my lifetime I have been a parish minister of twelve years and a professor of theology for nearly forty years now, but I have again and again had hours and days and weeks—and have them continually—during which I feel myself abandoned by God, . . . but the truth of Easter Day, like the truth of Good Friday—is this, that God holds us fast whoever we are and whatever our situation . . . The truth is that he is completely and utterly ours and that we may be completely and utterly his. That is the Easter message. And celebrating Easter means that we should submit to this Easter truth."[5]

The current investigation into this Truth, the marks both general and personal of its theologians, and the shape and content of the system associated with those marks, has needed to move in numerous directions. In doing so several matters have arisen which suggest productive possibilities for future investigation.

---

4. For greater detail concerning the classical crucicentric marks see here pp. 131–34.
5. Barth, Karl, *New Sermons from Basel Prison*, 54–55.

First, it appears that one of the reasons the theology of the cross has not commonly been seen in its multivalent dimensions is that a wide angled lens is required to see these altogether. The current investigation has used such a lens. The intention has been to overview the whole crucicentric system, rather than deeply consider a few of its elements but miss the wider view. This also means, though, that scope remains for more concerted investigation into particular crucicentric elements and their inter-relations, and into particular crucicentric periods and their theologians.

Second, and stemming from the last point, medieval mysticism attracts a broad secondary literature, yet so far comparatively little attention has been accorded the fine crucicentric strand running within it. Further investigation might better draw the lines between broad and narrow mystical strands, as also between crucicentric mysticism and dogmatic theology.

Third, the crucicentric status of Reformer John Calvin warrants further investigation.

Fourth, the so-called "note of triumph" in Barth's theology is often commented on but seldom connected to his crucicentric orientation. It would be interesting to explore this connection more concertedly than has been possible here.

Fifth, there appears to be a lack of understanding as to the nature and place of the true *theologia gloriae*, whether in connection to the crucicentric tradition broadly, or to Barth specifically. Added explanation here could be helpful.

Sixth, as already indicated questions exist concerning Barth's influence on late-modern theologies of the cross, not least his significance for their eschatological and pneumatological concerns.

Seventh and finally now, allied to the above the links and distinctions between Barth's modern theology of the cross and late-modern liberationist perspectives, while hinted at in the literature, bear further elaboration.

What then is the contribution of the present investigation? To the extent that the hidden structure (shape and content) of the classical crucicentric system at the centre of orthodox Christian thought has not previously been diagrammatically described, and the marks of its theologians not delineated as such, in assisting in these developments this discussion breaks fresh ground. The classical crucicentric system has been found to shed a hermeneutical light by which the crucicentric status of *any* theological project, or theologian, might be evaluated. Examination of Karl Barth's modern orthodox project in this light has enabled a further and crucicentric way of reading him to be brought to the fore. It has also firmly established Barth's pivotal place in the modern crucicentric tradition.

In final conclusion, this discussion began with the observation that the term "the theology of the cross" (*theologia crucis*) is intriguing; it forms a definite feature within the contemporary theological landscape even as its heritage seems little understood. Untethered to the long tradition that at the outset of the Reformation finally produced it, the nomenclature lies open to whatever sense its users wish it to bear. Tethered to that classical crucicentric tradition however, on the basis of the present investigation the term appears to have two complementary meanings. First, the theology of the cross is a defined system of epistemological and soteriological Christian thought. This system carries the revelatory message from the cross of Jesus Christ concerning the unbreachable exclusivity of divine glory, and regarding false and true human glory and the deadly passage that lies between. Second, the theology of the cross is the cruciform message itself, the noetic and ontic Word of the cross upon which the crucicentric system is founded formally. This living cruciform theology is foreshadowed in the writings of ancient Israel, and in the power of the Holy Spirit reiterated by a thin line of theologians including: Paul, Athanasius, a discrete group of medieval mystics, Luther, and in the modern age Karl Barth. Via them, and in inimitable glory, it sounds through all the world and to the end of the earth.[6]

---

6. A remark of Barth's is drawn on here. Ontologically identifying the Word of Jesus Christ, the Word of the cross, and the dynamic Glory of God, he says approvingly, "Paul was thinking of His Gospel which for him was identical with the Word of the cross, when in Rom 10:18 he cited the passage in Ps 19:3f. which speaks of the glory of God going through all the world and to the end of the earth[.]" Barth, *Church Dogmatics* IV/3, 409.

Bibliography

A Religious of CSMV. *"On the Incarnation," by Saint Athanasius, With an Introduction by C. S. Lewis*. Mowray, 1963 [cited 2008]. Online: http://www.spurgeon.org/~phil/history/ath-inc.htm.

Althaus, Paul. *The Theology of Martin Luther*. Philadelphia: Fortress, 1966.

Anatolios, Khaled. *Athanasius: The Coherence of his Thought*. London: Routledge, 1998.

———. *Athanasius*. London: Routledge, 2004.

Audi, Robert, ed. *The Cambridge Dictionary of Philosophy*. Cambridge: Cambridge University Press, 1995.

Aulen, Gustaf. *Christus Victor*. New York: Macmillan, 1951.

Avis, Paul D. L. "Karl Barth: The Reluctant Virtuoso." *Theology* 86 (1983) 164–71.

Baillie, John, John T. McNeill, and Henry P. Van Dusen, eds. *Calvin: Theological Treatises*. Library of Christian Classics 2. Translated by J. K. S. Reid. London: SCM, 1954.

Balds, David L. "Apokatastasis." In *Encyclopedia of Early Christianity*, edited by Everett Ferguson, et al, 78–79. London: Taylor & Francis, 1998.

Balthasar, Hans Urs von. *Mysterium Paschale: The Mystery of Easter*. Edinburgh: T. & T. Clark, 1990.

———. *The Theology of Karl Barth: Exposition and Interpretation*. Translated by Edward T. Oakes. Communio Books. San Francisco: Ignatius, 1992.

Barker, Gaylon H. "Bonhoeffer, Luther, and Theologia Crucis." *Dialog* 34.1 (1995) 1–17.

Barth, Karl. *Against the Stream: Shorter Post-War Writings*. Translated by E. M. Delacour and Stanley Godman. London: SCM, 1954.

———. *Anselm—Fides Quaerens Intellectum: Anselm's Proof of the Existence of God in the Context of his Theological Scheme*. Translated by Ian W. Robertson. Richmond: John Knox, 1960.

———. *Call For God: New Sermons from Basel Prison*. Translated by A. T. McKay. London: SCM, 1967.

———. "Christian Community and Civil Community." In Karl Barth, *Community, State and Church: Three Essays by Karl Barth with an Introduction by Will Herberg*, 149–89. Garden City, NY: Doubleday, 1960.

———. *The Christian Life: Church Dogmatics IV/4—Lecture Fragments*. Translated by Geoffrey W. Bromiley. Grand Rapids: Eerdmans, 1981.

———. *Christmas*. Translated by Citron Bernhard. London: Oliver & Boyd, 1959.

———. "Church and Culture." In *Theology and Church: Shorter Writings 1920–1928*, 334–54. London: SCM, 1962.

———. *Church Dogmatics*. Edited by Geoffrey W. Bromiley and T. F. Torrance. 4 vols in 13 part vols. Edinburgh: T. & T. Clark, 1936–1969.

———. *Church Dogmatics: A Selection with Introduction by Helmut Gollwitzer*. Translated by Geoffrey W. Bromiley. Edinburgh: T. & T. Clark, 1961.

———. *Community, State and Church: Three Essays*. With an Introduction by Will Herberg. New York: Anchor, 1960.

———. "Concluding Unscientific Postscript on Schleiermacher." In *Karl Barth: The Theology of Schleiermacher: Lectures at Göttingen. Winter Semester of 1923/24*, edited by Dietrich Ritschl, 261–79. Grand Rapids: Eerdmans, 1982.

———. *Credo*. Translated by J. Strathearn McNab. London: Hodder & Stoughton, 1936.

———. *Deliverance to the Captives*. Translated by Marguerite Wieser. London: SCM, 1961.

———. *Die Schrift und Die Kirche*. Zürich: Evangelischer Verlag, 1947.

———. *Dogmatics in Outline*. Translated by G. T. Thomson. London: SCM, 1993.

———. *God Here and Now*. Translated by. Paul M. van Buren. London: Routledge & Kegan Paul, 1964.

———. *The Epistle to the Philippians*. London: SCM, 1962.

———. *The Epistle to the Romans*. Translated by Edwyn C. Hoskyns. 6th ed. London: Oxford University, 1968.

———. *Evangelical Theology: An Introduction*. Translated by Grover Foley. London: Collins, 1965.

———. "Evangelical Theology in the Nineteenth Century." In *The Humanity of God (Three Essays)*, 11–33. Richmond: John Knox, 1960.

———. "Evangelical Theology in the Nineteenth Century." In Karl Barth, *God, Grace and Gospel: Three Essays by Karl Barth* (Scottish Journal of Theology Occasional Papers no. 8), 55–74. Edinburgh: Oliver & Boyd, 1959.

———. "Fate and Idea in Theology." In *The Way of Theology in Karl Barth. Essays and Comments*, edited by H. M. Rumscheidt, 25–61. Princeton Theological Monograph Series 8. Allison Park, PA: Pickwick, 1986.

———. *God, Grace and Gospel: Three Essays by Karl Barth*. Translated by James McNab. Scottish Journal of Theology Occasional Papers, no. 8. Edinburgh: Oliver and Boyd, 1959.

———. *God in Action*. Translated by E. G. Hornrighausen and Karl J. Ernst. New York: Round Table, 1993.

———. "Gospel and Law." In *God, Grace and Gospel* (Scottish Journal of Theology Occasional Paper, no. 8), 3–27. London: Oliver & Boyd, 1959.

———. *Göttingen Dogmatics*. Vol. 2. Translated by G. W. Bromiley, edited by H. Reiffen. Grand Rapids: Eerdmans, 1990.

———. *The Holy Spirit and the Christian Life: The Theological Basis of Ethics*. Translated by R. Birch Hoyle. Louisville: Westminster John Knox, 1993.

———. *How I Changed My Mind*. Richmond: John Knox, 1966.

———. "The Humanity of God." In Karl Barth, *God, Grace and Gospel: Three Essays by Karl Barth* (Scottish Journal of Theology Occasional Papers, no. 8), 31–52. Edinburgh: Oliver and Boyd, 1959.

———. "The Humanity of God." In Karl Barth, *The Humanity of God (Three Essays)*, 37–65. Richmond: John Knox, 1960.

———. "The Interpretation of the Lord's Prayer according to the Reformers." In *Prayer and Preaching*, 24–63. London: SCM, 1964.

———. *A Late Friendship: The Letters of Karl Barth and Carl Zuckmayer*. Grand Rapids: Eerdmans, 1982.

———. *A Letter to Great Britain from Switzerland*. London: Sheldon, 1941.

———. *Letters, 1961–1968*. Grand Rapids: Eerdmans, 1981.

———. *Prayer and Preaching*. London: SCM, 1964.

———. "The Problem of Ethics Today." In *The Word of God and the Word of Man*, 136–82. New York: Harper, 1957.

———. *Protestant Theology in the Nineteenth Century: Its Background and History*. Introduction by Colin E. Gunton. Translated by John Bowden and Brian Cozens. Grand Rapids: Eerdmans, 2001.

———. *Protestant Thought: From Rousseau to Ritschl*. Translated by Brian Cozens. New York: Harper & Row, 1959.

———. *The Resurrection of the Dead*. Translated by H. J. Stenning. 1933. Reprint, Eugene, OR: Wipf and Stock, 2003.

———. "'Ten Articles on the Freedom and Service of the Church' (Barth's evaluation of this East German Church Statement)." *Scottish Journal of Theology* 19 (1966) 392–98.

———. *Theological Existence Today: A Plea for Theological Freedom*. Translated by R. Birch Hoyle. London: Hodder & Stoughton, 1933.

———. *Theology and Church*. With an Introduction by T. F. Torrance. Translated by Louise Smith. London: SCM, 1962.

———. *The Theology of John Calvin*. Translated by Geoffrey W. Bromiley. Grand Rapids: Eerdmans, 1995.

———. *The Theology of Schleiermacher: Lectures at Göttingen, Winter Semester of 1923–24*. Edited by Dietrich Ritschl. Translated by Geoffrey W. Bromiley. Grand Rapids: Eerdmans, 1982.

———. *The Word of God and the Word of Man*. Translated by Douglas Horton. New York: Harper, 1957.

Barth, Karl, and Emil Brunner. *Natural Theology: Comprising "Nature and Grace" by Professor Dr. Emil Brunner and the reply "No!" by Dr. Karl Barth*. Introduction by John Baillie. Translated by Peter Fraenkel. 1946. Reprint, Eugene, OR: Wipf and Stock, 2002.

Bauckham, Richard. "'Only the Suffering God Can Help': Divine Passibility in Modern Theology." *Themelios* 9.3 (1984) 6–12.

———. "Cross, Theology of the." In *New Dictionary of Theology*, edited by Sinclair B. Ferguson, et al., 181. Leicester, UK: InterVarsity, 1988.

Bayer, Oswald. "The Word of the Cross." *Lutheran Quarterly* 9 (1995) 47–55.

Berkouwer, G. C. *The Triumph of Grace in the Theology of Karl Barth: An Introduction and Critical Appraisal*. Translated by Harry R. Boer. Grand Rapids: Eerdmans, 1956.

Berquist, Jon L. "What Does the Lord Require? Old Testament Child Sacrifice and New Testament Christology." *Encounter* 55 (1994) 117–18.

Bettis, Joseph D. "Is Karl Barth a Universalist?" *Scottish Journal of Theology* 20 (1967) 423–36.

Bonhoeffer, Dietrich. *The Cost of Discipleship*. Translated by R. H. Fuller and Irmgard Booth. New York: Simon & Schuster, 1995.

———. *Letters and Papers from Prison*. Edited by Eberhard Bethge. New York: Touchstone, 1971.

Bornkamm, Heinrich. "Die theologischen Thesen Luthers bei der Heidelberger Disputation 1518 und seine theologia Crucis." In *Luther, Gestald und Wirkungen, Schriften des Vereins für Reformationsgeschichte* 5.188 (1975).

———. *Luther's World of Thought*. Translated by Martin Bertram. St Louis: Concordia, 1965.

Brecht, Martin. *Martin Luther: His Road to Reformation, 1483–1521*. Translated by James Shaaf. Philadelphia: Fortress, 1985.

Bromiley, Geoffrey W. *An Introduction to the Theology of Karl Barth*. Grand Rapids: Eerdmans, 1979.

Brown, Alexandra R. "Apocalyptic Transformation in Paul's Discourse on the Cross." *Word and World* 16 (1996) 427–36.

Brunner, Emil. *The Christian Doctrine of Creation and Redemption, Dogmatics*. Vol. 2. Translated by Olive Wyon. Philadelphia: Westminster, 1952.

———. *The Mediator: A Study of the Central Doctrine of the Christian Faith*. Translated by Olive Wyon. Philadelphia: Westminster, 1957.

Bultmann, Rudolf. *Theology of the New Testament*. Translated by Kendrick Grobel. 2 vols. New York: Scribner, 1955.

Burgess, Andrew R. *The Ascension in Karl Barth*. Aldershot, UK: Ashgate, 2004.

Busch, Eberhard. *The Great Passion: An Introduction to Karl Barth's Theology*. Translated by Geoffrey W. Bromiley. Grand Rapids: Eerdmans, 2004.

———. *Karl Barth, His Life from Letters and Autobiographical Texts*. Translated by John Bowden. Grand Rapids: Eerdmans, 1994.

Calvin, John. *Institutes of the Christian Religion*. Translated by Henry Beveridge. Vol. 1. Grand Rapids: Eerdmans, 1975.

Chavannes, Henry. *The Analogy between God and the World in Saint Thomas Aquinas and Karl Barth*. Translated by William Lumley. New York: Vantage, 1992.

Clough, David. *Ethics in Crisis: Interpreting Barth's Ethics*. Aldershot, UK: Ashgate, 2005.

Cornwall, Robert D. "The Scandal of the Cross: Self-Sacrifice, Obedience, and Modern Culture." *Encounter* 58.1 (1997) 1–17.

Cousins, Peter. *A Christian's Guide to the Death of Christ*. London: Hodder and Stoughton, 1967.

Crawford, R. G. "The Atonement in Karl Barth." *Theology* 74 (1971) 355–58.

Dalferth, Ingolf. "The Visible and the Invisible: Luther's Legacy of a Theological Theology." In *England and Germany: Studies in Theological Diplomacy*, edited by S. W. Sykes. Frankfurt: Lang, 1981.

Davidson, Ivor. J. "*Crux-probat-omnia*: Eberhard Jüngel and the Theology of the Crucified One." *Scottish Journal of Theology* 50 (1997) 157.

———. "Response to Bishop John Spong." *Stimulus* 11.2 (2003) 29–31.

Dawson, R. Dale. *The Resurrection in Karl Barth*. Aldershot, UK: Ashgate, 2007.

Denney, James. "The Death of Christ." Carlisle, UK: Paternoster, 1997.

Duke, James O, and Robert E. Streetman, eds. *Barth and Schleiermacher: Beyond the Impasse*. Philadelphia: Fortress, 1988.

Dunn, James D. G. "Paul's Understanding of the Death of Jesus." In *Reconciliation and Hope*, edited by Robert Burke. Grand Rapids: Eerdmans, 1975.

———. *The Theology of Paul the Apostle*. Grand Rapids: Eerdmans, 1998.

———. *The New Perspective on Paul*. Rev. ed. Grand Rapids: Eerdmans 2008.

Ebeling, Gerhard. *Luther: An Introduction to His Thought*. Translated by R. A. Wilson. London: Collins, 1970.

Eckhart, Meister. *Meister Eckhart: The Essential Sermons, Commentaries, Treatises, and Defence*. Translated by Edmund College and Bernard McGuinn. Classics of Western Spirituality. New York: Paulist, 1981.

Edwards, David L, and Stott, John. *Essentials: A Liberal-Evangelical dialogue*. London: Hodder & Stoughton, 1988.

Elwell, Walter A., ed. *Evangelical Dictionary of Biblical Theology*. Grand Rapids: Baker, 1996.

Ferguson, Everett, et al. *Encyclopedia of Early Christianity*. London: Taylor & Francis, 1998.

Ferguson, Sinclair B., David F. Wright, and J. I. Packer, eds. *New Dictionary of Theology*. Leicester, UK: InterVarsity, 1988.

Fiddes, Paul S. *The Creative Suffering of God*. Oxford: Clarendon, 2002.

Ford, David F. *Karl Barth: Studies of His Theological Method*. Edited by Stephen Sykes. Oxford: Clarendon, 1979.

———, ed. *The Modern Theologians: An Introduction to Christian Theology in the Twentieth Century*. 2nd ed. Oxford: Blackwell, 1997.

Forde, Gerhard O. *The Law-Gospel Debate: An Interpretation of its Historical Development*. Minneapolis: Augsburg, 1969.

———. "On Being a Theologian of the Cross." *Christian Century* 114 (Oct, 1997) 947–49.

———. *On Being a Theologian of the Cross: Reflections on Luther's Heidelberg Disputation*. Grand Rapids: Eerdmans, 1997.

Forsyth, Peter Taylor. *The Work of Christ*. Eugene, OR: Wipf and Stock, 1996.

———. *The Cruciality of the Cross*. Eugene, OR: Wipf and Stock, 1996.

Gaebelein, Frank E. G., and J. D. Douglas, eds. *Expositor's Bible Commentary Electronic Version*: Zondervan, 2002.

Galvin, John P. "The Death of Jesus in Contemporary Theology, Systematic Perspectives and Historical Issues." *Horizons* 13.2 (1986) 239–52.

Gerber, U. "Review of *Die Auferweckung des Gekreuzigten*." *Theologische Literaturzeitung* 102.3 (1977) 224–26.

Gill, John. *The Cause of God and Truth*. Part 4, Section 14—Athanasius. The Hall of Church History. Online: http://www.pbministries.org/books/gill/Cause_of_God_and_truth/Part%204/chapter2/chap02_section14.htm.

Godsey, John D. "Barth and Bonhoeffer: The Basic Difference." *Quarterly Review: A Scholarly Journal for Reflections of Ministry* 7.1 (1987) 9–27.

Gollwitzer, Helmut. "Kingdom of God and Socialism in the Theology of Karl Barth." In *Karl Barth and Radical Politics*, edited by George Hunsinger. Philadelphia: Westminster, 1976.

Green, Clifford, ed. *Karl Barth: Theologian of Freedom*. Minneapolis: Fortress, 1991.

Gregory of Nazianzus. *The Fourth Theological Oration, which is the Second Concerning the Son*. Christian Classics Ethereal Library. Online: http://www.ccel.org/ccel/schaff/npnf207.iii.xvi.html.

Gregory of Nyssa. *On the Christian Mode of Life*. Translated by Virginia Woods Callahan, *The Fathers of the Church*. Washington, DC: Catholic University of America, 1967.

Gunton, Colin E. *The Actuality of Atonement: A Study of Metaphor, Rationality and the Christian Tradition*. Edinburgh: T. & T. Clark, 1988.

———. "Bruce McCormack's Karl Barth's Critically Realistic Dialectical Theology: Its Genesis and Development 1909-1936." *Scottish Journal of Theology* 49 (1996) 483-91.
———. "Salvation." In *The Cambridge Companion to Karl Barth*, edited by john Webster, 143-58. Cambridge: Cambridge University Press, 2000.
———. *The Barth Lectures*. London: T. & T. Clark International, 2007.
Gutierréz, Gustavo. "Liberation Praxis and Christian Faith." In *The Power of the Poor in History*, edited by Gustavo Gutierréz. Maryknoll, NY: Orbis, 1983.
Hagan, Kenneth. "Luther on Atonement—Reconfigured." *Concordia Theological Quarterly* 61 (Oct 1997) 251-76.
Hall, Douglas John. "The Theology of Hope in an Officially Optimistic Society." *Religion in Life* 40 (1971) 376-90.
———. *Lighten Our Darkness: Towards an Indigenous Theology of the Cross*. Philadelphia: Westminster, 1976.
———. *Thinking the Faith: Christian Theology in a North American Context*. Minneapolis: Fortress, 1989.
———. "Luther's Theology of the Cross." *Consensus* 15.2 (1989) 7-19.
Hamilton, Kenneth. *To Turn From Idols*. Grand Rapids: Eerdmans, 1973.
Hartwell, Herbert. *The Theology of Karl Barth: An Introduction*. London: Duckworth, 1964.
Hasel, Frank M. "The Christological Analogy of Scripture in Karl Barth." *Theologische Zeitschrift* 50 (1994) 41-49.
Hasselmann, Karl-Behrnd. "Review: 'Analogia entis oder Analogia fidei: Die Frage der Analogia bei Karl Barth' by Horst Georg Pöhlmann: Göttingen: Vandenhoeck & Ruprecht, 1965." *Lutheran World* 13 (1966): 245.
Hendel, Kurt K. "Theology of the Cross." *Currents in Theology and Mission* 24 (1997) 223-31.
Heron, Alasdair I. C. *The Holy Spirit: The Holy Spirit in the Bible, the History of Christian Thought, and Recent Theology*. Philadelphia: Westminster, 1983.
———. *A Century of Protestant Theology*. Cambridge: Lutterworth, 1993.
Hinlicky, Paul R. "Luther's Theology of the Cross—Part One." *Lutheran Forum* 32.3 (1998) 46-49.
———. "Luther's Theology of the Cross—Part Two." *Lutheran Forum* 32.4 (1998): 58-61.
Hinson, David F. *Theology of the Old Testament—Theological Education Guide No 15*. London: SPCK, 1994.
Hoffman, Bengt, ed. *The Theologia Germanica of Martin Luther*. New York: Paulist, 1980.
Hunsinger, George. *Disruptive Grace: Studies in the Theology of Karl Barth*. Grand Rapids: Eerdmans, 2000.
———, ed. *For the Sake of the World: Karl Barth and the Future of Ecclesial Theology*. Grand Rapids: Eerdmans, 2004.
———. *How to Read Karl Barth: The Shape of His Theology*. New York: Oxford University Press, 1991.
———. "Karl Barth and Liberation Theology." In *Disruptive Grace: Studies in the Theology of Karl Barth*, edited by George Hunsinger. Grand Rapids: Eerdmans, 2000.
———. "Karl Barth's Christology: Its basic Chalcedonian character." In *The Cambridge Companion to Karl Barth*, edited by John Webster, 127-42, 2000.

———. "The Politics of the Nonviolent God: Reflections on René Girard and Karl Barth." *Scottish Journal of Theology* 51 (1998) 61–85.
———. "What Karl Barth Learned from Martin Luther." *Lutheran Quarterly* 13 (1999) 125–55.
Iserloh, Erwin. "Luther's Christ-Mysticism." In *Catholic Scholars Dialogue with Luther*, edited by Wicks, Jared. Chicago: Loyola University Press, 1970.
Jensen, Gordon A. "The Christology of Luther's Theology of the Cross." *Consensus* 23.2 (1997) 11–25.
Jenson, Robert W. "Karl Barth." In *The Modern Theologians: An Introduction to Christian Theology in the Twentieth Century*, edited by David F. Ford, 23–49. 1st ed. Oxford: Blackwell, 1989.
———. "Karl Barth." In *The Modern Theologians: An Introduction to Christian Theology in the Twentieth Century*, edited by David F. Ford, 21–35. 2nd ed. Oxford: Blackwell, 1997.
John of the Cross, Saint. *John of the Cross: Selected Writings*. New York: Paulist, 1987.
Jones, Cheslyn, Geoffrey Wainwright, and Edward Yarnold, eds. *The Study of Spirituality*. London: SPCK, 1986.
Jüngel, Eberhard. *God as the Mystery of the World: On the Foundation of the Theology of the Crucified One in the Dispute between Theism and Atheism*. Translated by Darrell L. Guder. Edinburgh: T&T Clark, 1983.
———. *God's Being is in Becoming: The Trinitarian Being of God in the Theology of Karl Barth. A Paraphrase*. Translated by John Webster. Grand Rapids: Eerdmans, 2001.
———. "Gospel and Law; The Relationship of Dogmatics to Ethics." In *Karl Barth: A Theological Legacy*, 105–26. Philadelphia: Westminster, 1986.
———. *Karl Barth: A Theological Legacy*. Translated by Garrett E. Paul. Philadelphia: Westminster, 1986.
Kärkkäinen, Veli-Matti. "'Evil, Love and the Left Hand of God': The Contribution of Luther's Theology of the Cross to an Evangelical Theology of Evil." *Evangelical Quarterly* 74 (2002) 215–34.
Kiecker, James G. "*Theologia Crucis et Theologia Gloriae*: The Development of Luther's Theology of the Cross." *Lutheran Quarterly* 92.3 (1995) 179–88.
Kitamori, Kazoh. *Theology of the Pain of God*. London: SCM, 1966.
Klappert, Bertold. *Die Auferweckung des Gekreuzigten: Der Ansatz der Christologie Karl Barths im Zusammenhang der Christologie der Gegenwart*. Neukirchen-Vluyn: Neukirchener, 1971.
———. *Versöhnung und Befreiung: Versuche, Karl Barth kontextuell zu verstehen*: Neukirchen-Vluyn : Neukirchener Verlag, 1994.
Koperski, Veronica *What Are They Saying about Paul and the Law?* Mahwah, NJ: Paulist, 2001.
Kortner, U. H. J. "Was Everything Just a Play? Legitimacy and the Limitations of Dramatic Doctrine in Theology." *Neue Zeitschrift für Systematische Theologie und Religionsphilosophie* 38 (1996) 198–218.
Lauber, David. *Barth on the Descent into Hell: God, Atonement and the Christian Life*. Aldershot, UK: Ashgate, 2004.
Lienhard, Marc. *Luther: Witness to Jesus Christ*. Translated by Edwin H. Robertson. Minneapolis: Augsburg, 1982.
Loewenich, Walther von. *Luther's Theology of the Cross*. Translated by J. A. Bouman. Minneapolis: Augsburg, 1976.

Lull, Timothy F., ed. *Martin Luther's Basic Theological Writings*. Foreword by Jaroslav Pelikan. Minneapolis: Fortress, 1989.

Luther, Martin. *Luther's Works*. Edited by Jaroslav Pelikan. Philadelphia: Fortress, 1958–1986.

———. *Martin Luther: Faith in Christ and the Gospel (Selected Spiritual Writings)*. Edited by Eric W. Gritsch. New York: New City, 1996.

———. *Martin Luther's Basic Theological Writings*. Foreword by Jaroslav Pelikan. Edited by Timothy F. Lull. Minneapolis: Fortress, 1989.

———. *Martin Luthers Werke: Kritische Gesamtausgabe, Briefwechsel*. Vol. 1–18. Weimer: Böhlau, 1912–1921.

———. *Martin Luthers Werke. Kritische Gesamtausgabe. Weimarer Ausgabe*. Weimar: Böhlau, 1883–.

McCormack, Bruce. "Barth in Context: A Response to Professor Gunton." *Scottish Journal of Theology* 49 (1996) 491–98.

———. "Historical Criticism and Dogmatic Interest in Karl Barth's Theological Exegesis." In *Biblical Hermeneutics in Historical Perspective*, edited by M. S. Burrows and P. Rorem. Grand Rapids: Eerdmans, 1991.

———. *Karl Barth's Critically Realistic Dialectical Theology: Its Genesis and Development 1909–1936*. Oxford: Clarendon, 1995.

McDowell, John C., and Mike Higton, eds. *Conversing with Barth*. Aldershot, UK: Ashgate, 2004.

McGrath, Alister. *Christian Theology: An Introduction*. Oxford: Blackwell, 1994.

———. *The Enigma of the Cross*. London: Hodder & Stroughton, 1996.

———. *Luther's Theology of the Cross: Martin Luther's Theological Breakthrough*. Oxford: Blackwell, 1985.

———. *Making Sense of the Cross*. Leicester, UK: Inter-Varsity Press, 1992.

McGuckin, John Anthony. *St. Cyril of Alexandria: The Christological Controversy : Its History, Theology, and Texts*. New York: St. Vladimir's Seminary, 2004.

———. *The Westminster Handbook to Christian Theology*. Louisville: Westminster John Knox, 2004.

McIntyre, John. *The Shape of Soteriology*. Edinburgh: T. & T. Clark, 1992.

McKim, Donald K., ed. *The Cambridge Companion to John Calvin*. Cambridge: Cambridge University Press, 2004.

———, ed. *How Karl Barth Changed My Mind*. Grand Rapids: Eerdmans, 1986.

Mackintosh, H. R. *Types of Modern Theology: Schleiermacher to Barth*. London: Nisbet, 1937.

McLeod Campbell, John. *The Nature of the Atonement*. London: Macmillan, 1873.

Macchia, Frank D. "Justification through New Creation: The Holy Spirit and the Doctrine by Which the Church Stands or Falls." *Theology Today* 58 (2001) 202–17.

Mangina, Joseph L. *Karl Barth on the Christian Life*. Issues in Systematic Theology 8. New York: Lang, 2001.

Mattes, Mark C. "Gerhard Forde on Re-envisioning Theology in the Light of the Gospel." *Lutheran Quarterly* 4 (1999) 373–93.

Mechels, E. "Die Auferweckung des Gekreuzigten. (Review)." *Evangelische Theologie* 38 (1978) 450–58.

Meredith, Anthony. *The Cappadocians*. London: Chapman, 1995.

Metzger, Bruce M., and Murphy, Roland E., eds. *The New Oxford Annotated Bible with the Apocrypha: An Ecumenical Study Bible Completely Revised and Enlarged (New Revised Standard Version)*. New York: Oxford University, 1994.

Meyendorff, John. *Byzantine Theology: Historical Trends and Doctrinal Themes*. 2nd rev. ed. New York: Fordham University Press, 1983.

Meyer, Ben F. "A Soteriology Valid for All." In *The Early Christians: Their World Mission and Self-Discovery*, 114–58. Wilmington, DE: Michael Glazier, 1986.

Meyer, John R. "Athanasius' Use of Paul in his Doctrine of Salvation." *Vigiliae christianae* (1998) 146–71.

Miell, David K. "Barth On Persons In Relationship: A Case For Further Reflection." *Scottish Journal of Theology* 42 (1989) 541–55.

Migliore, Daniel L. *Faith Seeking Understanding: An Introduction to Christian Theology*. Grand Rapids: Eerdmans, 1991.

Molnar, Paul D. "The Function of the Immanent Trinity in the Theology of Karl Barth." *Scottish Journal of Theology* 42 (1989) 367–99.

Moltmann, Jürgen. "The Crucified God." *Interpretation* 26 (1972) 278–99.

———. *The Crucified God: The Cross of Christ as the Foundation and Criticism of Christian Theology*. Translated by John Bowden and R A Wilson. London: SCM, 1995.

———. *Theology of Hope: On the Ground and the Implications of a Christian Eschatology*. Minneapolis: Fortress, 1993.

Morse, Christopher. "Raising God's Eyebrows: Some Further Thoughts on the Concept of the *Analogia Fidei*." *Union Seminary Quarterly Review* 37 (1981–82) 39–49.

Neufeld, Franceen (Vann). "The Cross of the Living Lord: The Theology of the Cross and Mysticism." *Scottish Journal of Theology* 49 (1996) 131–46.

Newman, John Henry, and Robertson, Archibald, ed.s. *"Four Discourses Against the Arians," by Saint Athanasius*. New Advent, 1892 [cited 2008]. Online: http://www.newadvent.org/fathers/2816.htm.

Norris, Christopher. "Modernism." In *The Oxford Companion to Philosophy*, edited by Ted Honderich, 583. Oxford: Oxford University Press, 1995.

———. "Post-modernism." In *The Oxford Companion to Philosophy*, edited by Ted Honderich, 708. Oxford: Oxford University Press, 1995.

Norris, Frederick W. "Cappadocian Fathers." In *The Dictionary of Historical Theology*, edited by Hart, Trevor A., 111–15. Grand Rapids: Eerdmans, 2000.

Nugent, Donald Christopher. "What Has Wittenberg to Do with Avila?" *Journal of Ecumenical Studies* 23 (1986).

Nwatu, Felix. "The Cross: Symbol of Hope for Suffering Humanity." *African Ecclesial Review* 39 (February 1997) 2–17.

Oberman, Heiko A. *Luther: Man Between God and the Devil*. Translated by Walliser-Schwarzbart, Eileen. New York: Image Doubleday, 1992.

Pailin, David A. "Deism." In *A New Dictionary of Christian Theology*, 148. London: SCM, 1993.

Pangritz, Andreas. *Karl Barth in the Theology of Dietrich Bonhoeffer*. Translated by Barbara and Martin Rumscheidt. Grand Rapids: Eerdmans, 2000.

Parker, T. H. L. "Barth on Revelation." *Scottish Journal of Theology* 13 (1960) 372–73.

———. *Calvin: An Introduction to His Thought*. London: Continuum, 1995.

———. *Karl Barth: A Biography*. Grand Rapids: Eerdmans, 1970.

Pettersen, Alvyn. "Athanasius." In *The Dictionary of Historical Theology*, edited by Trevor A. Hart, 41–42. Grand Rapids: Paternoster, 2000.

Placher, William C. *Readings in the History of Christian Theology: From Its Beginnings to the Eve of the Reformation*. Vol. 1. Philadelphia: Westminster, 1988.

Plass, P. "The Concept of Eternity in Patristic Theology." *Studia Theologica* 36 (1982) 11–25.

Prenter, Regin. *Luther's Theology of the Cross*. Philadelphia: Fortress, 1971.

Rae, Murray. *The Cross of Jesus Christ in Christian Theology*. Unpublished notes. Undated.

Richardson, Alan. "Theologia Crucis: Theologia Gloriae." In *A New Dictionary of Christian Theology*, edited by Alan Richardson and John Bowden, 566. London: SCM, 1993.

Richardson, Kurt Anders. *Reading Karl Barth: New Directions for North American Theology*. Grand Rapids: Baker Academic, 2004.

Rosato, Philip J. *The Spirit as Lord: The Pneumatology of Karl Barth*. Edinburgh: T. & T. Clark, 1981.

Salter, Emma Gurney, ed. *The Vision of God, by Nicholas of Cusa*. New York: Ungar, 1960.

Sarot, M. "Patripassianism, Theopaschitism and the Suffering of God—Some Historical and Systematic Considerations." *Religious Studies* 26 (1990) 363–75.

Sauter, G. "Why is Karl Barth's Church Dogmatics not a 'Theology of Hope'? Some Observations on Barth's Understanding of Eschatology." *Scottish Journal of Theology* 52 (1999) 407–29.

Schaff, Philip. *Contra Gentes. Nicene and Post-Nicene Fathers, by Saint Athanasius*, 1892 [cited 2008]. Online: http://www.newadvent.org/fathers/2801.htm.

———. "Festal Letter 4," by Saint Athanasius, 1892 [cited 2008]. Online: http://en.wikisource.org/wiki/Nicene_and_Post-Nicene_Fathers:_Series_II/Volume_IV/Letters/Letters/Festal_Letters/Chapter_4.

———. "Festal Letter 5," by Saint Athanasius, 1892 [cited 2008]. Online: http://www.ccel.org/ccel/schaff/npnf204.xxv.iii.iii.v.html.

———. "Festal Letter 7," by Saint Atthanasius, 1892 [cited 2008]. Online: http://en.wikisource.org/wiki/Nicene_and_Post-Nicene_Fathers:_Series_II/Volume_IV/Letters/Letters/Festal_Letters/Chapter_7.

———. "The Life of Antony," by Saint Athanasius. *Select Works and Letters*. Vol IV. Christian Classics Ethereal Library, 1892 [cited 2008]. Online: http://www.ccel.org/ccel/schaff/npnf204.xvi.ii.i.html.

Schleiermacher, Friedrich. *The Christian Faith*. Edited by H. R. Mackintosh and J. S. Stewart. Edinburgh: T. & T. Clark, 1968.

Schreiner, Thomas R. *Paul: Apostle of God's Glory in Christ—A Pauline Theology*. Downers Grove, IL: InterVarsity Press, 2001.

Schwarzwäller, Klaus. "Review of 'On Being a Theologian of the Cross: Reflections on Luther's Heidelberg Disputation, 1518', by Gerhard O. Forde." *Lutheran Quarterly* 13 (1999) 109–14.

Schweitzer, Don. "Douglas Hall's Critique of Jürgen Moltmann's Eschatology of the Cross." *Studies in Religion* 27 (1998) 7–25.

———. "Jürgen Moltmann's Theology as a Theology of the Cross." *Studies in Religion* 24 (1995) 95–107.

Schwöbel, Christoph. "Theology." In *The Cambridge Companion to Karl Barth*, edited by John Webster, 17–36. Cambridge: Cambridge University Press, 2000.

Shrady, Mary, ed. *Johannes Tauler: Sermons*. New York: Paulist, 1985.
Snyder, Howard A. "On Second Thought—is God's Love Unconditional?" *Christianity Today* 38 (July 17, 1995) 30.
Sobrino, Jon. *Christology at the Crossroads: A Latin American Approach*. Translated by J. Jurry. Maryknoll, NY: Orbis, 1978.
———. "The Importance of the Historical Jesus." In *Jesus in Latin America*. Maryknoll, NY: Orbis, 1987.
Solberg, Mary M. "Notes Towards an Epistemology of the Cross." *Currents in Theology and Mission* 24 (1997) 14–27.
Spence, Alan. "John Owen." In *The Dictionary of Historical Theology*, edited by Trevor A. Hart. Grand Rapids: Eerdmans, 2000.
Stott, John R. W. *The Cross of Christ*. Leicester, UK: Inter-Varsity Press, 1989.
Sykes, Stephen. "Barth and the Power of the Word." In *The Identity of Christianity: Theologians and the Essence of Christianity from Schleiermacher to Barth*, 174–208. London: SPCK, 1984.
———. *The Identity of Christianity: Theologians and the Essence of Christianity from Schleiermacher to Barth*. London: SPCK, 1984.
———, ed. *Karl Barth: Centenary Essays*. Cambridge: Cambridge University Press, 1989.
———. "Karl Barth on the Heart of the Matter." *Gregorianum* 67 (1986) 679–91.
———, ed. *Karl Barth: Studies of his Theological Method*. Oxford: Clarendon, 1979.
———. "Theology through History." In *The Modern Theologians*, edited by David F. Ford, 229–51. Oxford: Blackwell, 1997.
Tamez, Elsa. *Amnesty of Grace: Justification by Faith from a Latin American Perspective*. Translated by Sharon H. Ringe. Nashville: Abingdon, 1993.
———. *Bible of the Oppressed*. Translated by Matthew J. O'Connell. Maryknoll, NY: Orbis, 1982.
Taylor, Charles. *The Malaise of Modernity*. Concord, ON: Anansi, 1991.
Thompson, John. *Christ in Perspective: Christological Perspectives in the Theology of Karl Barth*. Grand Rapids: Eerdmans, 1978.
———. *Modern Trinitarian Perspectives*. Oxford: Oxford University Press, 1994.
———. "Modern Trinitarian Perspectives." *Scottish Journal of Theology* 44 (1991) 349–65.
Thomson, Robert W. *"Contra Gentes and De Incarnatione" by Saint Athanasius*. Oxford: Clarendon, 1971.
Tinsley, E. J. "Mysticism." In *A New Dictionary of Christian Theology*, 387. London: SCM, 1993.
Tomlin, Graham. "The Theology of the Cross: Subversive Theology for a Postmodern World?" *Themelios* 23 (October 1997) 59–73.
———. *The Power of the Cross: Theology and the Death of Christ in Paul, Luther and Pascal*. Carlisle, UK: Paternoster, 1999.
Torrance, Alan. *Christian Experience and Divine Revelation in the Theologies of Friedrich Schleiermacher and Karl Barth*. Unpublished notes. Aberdeen: University of Aberdeen, undated.
Torrance, Thomas F. "Athanasius: A Study in the Foundations of Classical Theology." In *Theology in Reconciliation*, 215–66. Grand Rapids: Eerdmans, 1976.
———. "The Atonement and the Holy Trinity." In *The Mediation of Christ*. Edinburgh T. & T. Clark, 1992.

———. "The Atonement and the Oneness of the Church." *Scottish Journal of Theology* 7 (1954) 245–69.

———. "The Foundation of the Church: Union with Christ Through the Spirit." In *Theology of Reconstruction*, 192–208. London: SCM, 1965.

———. *The Incarnation*. Edinburgh: Handsel, 1981.

———. *The Mediation of Christ*. Edinburgh: T. & T. Clark, 1992.

———. *Karl Barth - Biblical and Evangelical Theologian*. Edinburgh: T. & T. Clark, 1990.

———. *The Mediation of Christ*. Edinburgh: T. & T. Clark, 1992.

———. *Theology in Reconciliation: Essays Towards Evangelical and Catholic Unity in East and West*. Grand Rapids: Eerdmans, 1976.

———. *Theology in Reconstruction*. Grand Rapids: Eerdmans, 1965.

Tripp, David. "Theologia Germanica." In *A Dictionary of Christian Spirituality*, edited by Gordon S. Wakefield, 376–77. London: SCM, 1983.

Vorster, Nico. "The Problem of Theodicy and the Theology of the Cross." *Die Skriflig* 41 (2007) 191–207.

Wace, Henry. *Gregory of Nazianzus (Entry in the Dictionary of Christian Biography and Literature to the End of the Sixth Century)* 1911. Online: http://en.wikisource.org/wiki/Dictionary_of_Christian_Biography_and_Literature_to_the_End_of_the_Sixth_Century/Dictionary/G/Gregorius_Nazianzenus,_bp._of_Sasima_and_Constantinople.

Wainwright, G. "Recent Foreign Theology - Historical and Systematic." *Expository Times* 92 (1981) 166–71.

Ward, Bendicta. "The Study of Spirituality." In *The Study of Spirituality*, edited by Jones, Cheslyn, Wainwright, Geoffrey and Yarnold, Edward, 283–91. London: SPCK, 1986.

Ware, Robert. C. "The Resurrection of Jesus: Theological Orientations (Part 1)." *Heythrop Journal* 16 (1975) 22–35.

———. "The Resurrection of Jesus: Theological Orientations (Part 2)." *Heythrop Journal* 16 (1975) 174–94.

Watson, Francis. "The Bible." In *The Cambridge Companion to Karl Barth*, edited by John Webster, 57–71. Cambridge: Cambridge University Press, 2000.

Webster, John. *Barth*. London: Continuum, 2000.

———. *Barth's Earlier Theology*. London: T. & T. Clark, 2005.

———. *Barth's Ethics of Reconciliation*. Cambridge: Cambridge University Press, 1995.

———. *Barth's Moral Theology: Human Action in Barth's Thought*. Grand Rapids: Eerdmans, 1998.

———, ed. *The Cambridge Companion to Karl Barth*. Cambridge: Cambridge University Press, 2000.

———. "Ethics and Politics." In *Barth*, 141–163. London: Continuum, 2000.

———. "What Is the Gospel?" In *Grace and Truth in the Secular Age*, edited by Timothy Bradshaw. Foreword by George Carey. 109–18. Grand Rapids: Eerdmans, 1998.

Webster, John, and George P. Schner, eds. *Theology after Liberalism: A Reader*. Oxford: Blackwell, 2000.

Weinandy, Thomas G. *Athanasius: A Theological Introduction*. Aldershot, UK: Ashgate, 2007.

———. "Origen and the Suffering of God." In *Papers Presented at the Thirteenth International Conference on Patristic Studies, Oxford, 1999*, edited by Wiles, M. and J., Yarnold E. Leuven: Peeters, 2001.

Wells, G. A. "Dietrich Bonhoeffer's Christianity Without Religion and 'Nach Zehn Jahren.'" *German Life and Letters* 39 (1985) 65–75.

Wells, Harold. "The Holy Spirit and Theology of the Cross: Significance for Dialogue." *Theological Studies* 53 (1992) 476–92.

———. "Theology of the Cross and the Theologies of Liberation." *Toronto Journal of Theology* 17 (2001) 147–66.

Westerholm, Stephen. *Israel's Law and the Church's Faith: Paul and His Recent Interpreters*. Grand Rapids: Eerdmans, 1988.

———. *Perspectives Old and New on Paul : The "Lutheran" Paul and His Critics*. Grand Rapids: Eerdmans, 2004.

———. *Understanding Paul: The Early Christian Worldview of the Letter to the Romans*. Grand Rapids: Eerdmans, 2004.

Wigley, Stephen D. "The von Balthasar Thesis: A Re-examination of von Balthasar's Study of Barth in the Light of Bruce McCormack." *Scottish Journal of Theology* 56 (2003) 345–59.

Willis, Robert E. "Bonhoeffer and Barth on Jewish Suffering: Reflections on the Relationship between Theology and Moral Sensibility." *Journal of Ecumenical Studies* 24 (1987) 598–615.

Winkworth, Susanna. *Theologia Germanica*, c. 1350 [cited 2007]. Online: http://www.passtheword.org/DIALOGS-FROM-THE-PAST/theogrm1.htm.

Wood, Donald. *Barth's Theology of Interpretation*. Aldershot, UK: Ashgate, 2007.

Young, Robert. *Young's Literal Translation* BibleGateway.com, 1898. Online: http://www.Biblegateway.com/versions/index.php?action=getVersionInfo&vid=15&lng=2.

Subject and Name Index

act, 1, 80, 95, 99, 199, 210–11, 220, 231–32, 236, 248, 259, 264–65, 284–85
age, 6–7, 48, 59, 67, 134, 150, 155–56, 160, 167, 211, 214–16, 287, 291, 296, 299
analogia entis, 49, 51, 73, 132, 139, 193, 200, 206–8
analogia fidei, 49, 73, 132, 139, 187, 192–93, 296
analogy, 47, 49, 63, 73, 132, 139, 187–88, 206, 236, 246
Anatolios, Khaled, 33, 38, 47, 58, 78–80, 87, 93, 98, 106, 114
Antony, Saint, 38, 54
apokatastasis, 102, 265, 267, 269 *see also* universalism
Arians, 76, 89, 93–94, 98, 102, 106, 110, 122–23, 127
Athanasius, Saint, 3, 6, 33, 37–38, 40, 47, 53–55, 58, 61, 64–65, 68, 76–81, 87–89, 92–95, 98, 100–103, 106, 109–10, 114, 121–24, 127, 236, 293, 301
atonement, 7, 16–17, 20, 23, 25, 140–41, 143, 145, 151, 231–32, 264
awakening, 175–76, 231–32

Barker, Gaylon H., 16, 22, 66, 131, 171, 173, 185, 194, 298
Barth, Karl
    assessment of nineteenth century theology, 157–58, 160, 207, 213, 235
    Christian suffering, 274
    crucicentric status, 2, 171, 178–79, 182, 186–88, 191–93, 295, 298
    developmental phases, 168, 173–74, 179, 181, 187
    divine suffering, 171
    eschatology well developed, 277
    extends classical *theologia crucis*, 190
    modern theologian, 149, 155–56, 160–61, 164, 180, 291, 297
    natural theology, 202, 208, 296
    pneumatology well developed, 233
    theologia crucis, 1, 19, 28, 168, 170–74, 176–83, 185–86, 188, 190–93, 228, 255, 283, 288, 291–92, 295–96, 298
    the value of philosophy for theology, 206
    view of Luther, 165, 254
Bauckham, Richard, 17, 95, 171, 173, 180–81, 195, 298
Bayer, Oswald, 16, 23, 80, 113, 119, 173, 184, 194, 298
believers (*see also* Christians), 20, 55, 58, 62, 111–16, 121–23, 126, 129, 151, 247, 274–76, 278
Berkouwer, G. C., 173–75, 177–79, 194, 291
Bernard, Saint, 61, 110, 116, 295
Bible, 51, 85, 121, 153, 155, 217, 231, 271, 289
blood, 61, 92–93, 100–101
Bonhoeffer, Dietrich, 19, 22, 66, 131, 139, 162, 168, 185
Bromiley, Geoffrey W., 229–30, 236–37, 265, 268

318 Subject and Name Index

Busch, Eberhard., 46, 155–56, 169, 192, 194, 200–201, 205, 207–9, 215–17, 221, 225, 227, 231, 233–36, 243–44, 255, 273, 277, 286

Calvary *see* cross
Calvin, John, 96, 99, 104, 150, 166, 189–90, 220, 234, 247
Cappadocian Fathers, 78, 124
    Basil of Caesarea, 16–17, 94, 124
    Gregory of Nazianzus, 78, 95
    Gregory of Nyssa, 94, 102–3, 124
Christendom, 6, 41, 90, 254
Christian Life, 116
Christian truth, 18, 101, 133
Christianity, 18, 154, 215–16, 253, 277
Christians (*see also* believers, the Righteous), 38, 66, 85, 98, 109–10, 203, 213, 250–51, 256, 265, 279
christocentric theologian *see* theologian of the cross
Christology, 13, 22, 92, 137, 176, 178, 185, 218, 220–21, 233–34, 246, 264
church (*see also* community), 15, 21, 79, 85, 93, 98, 103, 105, 108, 110, 112, 127, 133, 139, 142, 153, 161–62, 165, 199, 203, 213, 215, 220, 227, 244, 249–50, 254–55, 267–69, 273–74, 281, 284–86, 289–90, 292, 298–99
Church Dogmatics, 8, 49, 178–79, 184, 265, 277, 280–81
co-crucifixion, 20, 98
cognitive union, 34, 42, 66–67, 69, 243–44, 246
commandments, 86, 88, 141–42, 144, 199 *see also* law
community (*see also* church), 20, 165, 203, 227–28, 238, 250–53, 267–68, 281, 284–85
creation, the, 37, 42–43, 47–48, 50, 53–55, 61, 67, 95, 101–2, 127, 141–42, 186, 196, 200, 265, 277, 284

Creator, 46–47, 49–50, 53–55, 58, 61, 71–73, 81, 87, 104, 132, 139, 196, 206, 235, 237, 240, 284
creatureliness, 124, 126, 244, 278, 282
cross, 4–5, 17–18, 20, 23, 41, 43, 45, 50, 54, 62, 82, 111, 115, 121, 138, 174, 178, 242, 244, 269, 272–74, 292
crucicentric system, 2, 5, 8, 17, 23, 56, 129–32, 136, 195, 291, 295, 297, 300–301
crucicentric theologian *see* theologian of the cross
crucifixion, 59, 62, 65, 74, 77, 79, 86, 91, 96, 105, 122, 179, 181, 184, 231–32, 288
curse, 86, 243

Dalferth, Ingolf, 15, 18–19, 22, 40, 49, 51–53
Davidson, Ivor J., 44, 60
de-creation, 87–88, 106
death
    continuing, 129, 134
    creature's vicarious, 4–5
    physical, 120
    real, 132
    sanctifying process of, 4
deification, 57, 120–21, 123, 126, 158, 181, 281 *see also* glorification
Deity of Christ, 215
deus absconditus, 62, 165, 193, 242
dialectics, 7, 16, 18, 28, 34, 41, 49, 55–56, 59–60, 68–69, 79, 115, 119, 130–31, 137–39, 164, 169, 174, 181, 185, 187–88, 193, 211, 239, 241–43, 246–47, 280, 282, 295
divine judgment, 268, 270, 274
divine revelation, 3, 52, 55, 58, 63, 69, 217–18, 220, 225, 238, 243
divinity (*see also* Jesus Christ), 37–38, 75, 81, 94, 96, 106, 111, 122, 129, 142, 190, 215, 283
Dunn, James D. G., 67, 83, 97–98, 101

Subject and Name Index 319

Earth, the, 58, 65, 100–101, 118, 153–54, 241, 301
Eckhart, Meister, 42–44, 124
election, 97, 99–102, 104–5, 132, 223, 265–68, 271, 280, 294
Enlightenment, 9, 152, 163, 193, 211–12
epistemology, 3–4, 8–9, 13, 16, 20, 22–23, 25, 33–34, 40–42, 46, 49, 51, 54–55, 57–59, 64, 66, 68–70, 73, 129, 138–39, 161, 171, 184, 193, 195–99, 206, 209, 211, 216, 218, 220, 226, 233, 237, 239–41, 245–46
eschatological participation in Christ, 123, 126–27, 288
eschatology, 13, 29–30, 120, 276–78, 281, 286
exaltation, creaturely, 176, 238, 282, 288–90
experience, 39–41, 80, 113, 152, 180, 193, 210–13, 219, 252, 273, 291
Experience, Christian, 208–12, 216

faith, 1, 4, 18–19, 25, 35, 37–40, 44–45, 50–53, 65, 71–72, 82, 86–87, 99–100, 102–3, 109, 112, 116–17, 121, 123, 126, 129, 137–39, 141, 151, 153, 161, 165–66, 188, 192, 196–99, 206, 208–9, 214–15, 220, 228, 240, 243, 253, 271, 273, 284–86
    eyes of, 36, 60, 62
    knowledge of, 193, 198
    object of, 39, 206
    transmission of, 197–99, 238
    work of, 198
false *theologia gloriae*, 126, 132–33, 166, 288–90, 292
Father, 3, 9, 37–38, 54, 58, 65, 68, 77–78, 88–89, 91, 93–96, 98, 102, 110, 118, 123–24, 127, 140, 160, 182, 184, 220, 222–23, 230, 232, 235–38, 242, 248
Festal Letter, 78, 92, 94, 98, 110, 114, 122
Fiddes, Paul S., 15, 20, 171, 173, 180–81, 195, 242, 298

followers of Christ, 106, 108–9, 120 see also believers
foolishness, 20, 34, 36, 52, 55–58, 61, 69–71, 73, 75–76, 79, 99, 102, 129, 138, 218, 239–41
fools, 75, 240–41
Forde, Gerhard O., 13–14, 16, 24, 29–30, 35, 63, 111–12, 131, 136–37, 141, 194
freedom, 26, 78, 95, 97, 102–3, 114, 144, 183, 212, 224, 237, 239–40, 262, 264, 275, 285, 295
freedom of divine grace, 267–68

glory, of God, 42, 50, 55, 60, 63, 66, 71, 87, 105, 121, 127, 133, 138–39, 151, 241, 246, 249, 269, 281, 284–85, 294, 301
God, true knowledge of, 5, 20, 33, 40, 45–47, 49, 150, 164, 201, 239–40
Godsey, John D., 19, 153, 161–62, 173, 179–80, 194, 280
Golgotha *see* cross
Gospel, 15, 20, 24, 27, 34–35, 66–67, 85, 90, 92, 105, 113, 127, 134, 151, 154, 164, 207, 215, 225, 232, 255–56, 259, 262, 297, 299, 301
grace, 19, 21, 37, 46–47, 49, 72, 79, 86–88, 90–91, 100–104, 123, 130, 136, 139–41, 143, 145, 151–52, 164–65, 174–75, 178, 183–84, 190, 201–3, 207, 220, 223, 232, 234, 238–39, 244, 247–48, 250–53, 255–56, 261–62, 265, 267–69, 276, 280, 282, 287, 289–90, 294
Greeks, 38, 56–57, 74–76, 84, 95–96, 99, 108, 112

Hagan, Kenneth, 16, 25, 50
Hall, Douglas John, 6, 14, 16, 20, 27, 162, 168, 173, 177–79, 194, 278, 292
Heidelberg Disputation, 3–4, 7, 14, 18, 24, 30, 35, 54, 61–63, 89, 96, 119, 127, 130, 135–37, 139–41, 143, 145–46, 164, 193, 197–98, 275

Hendel, Kurt K., 16, 24, 112
hermeneutic, theology of the cross as, 10, 30, 131, 175, 179, 185, 194–95, 232, 250, 291, 295, 301
Hinlicky, Paul R., 16, 55, 103, 172, 188, 191, 195, 298
historico-critical methodologies, importance of, 153
Holy Spirit, 8, 37–38, 65, 131, 151, 181–82, 198–99, 220, 223, 227, 233–37, 239, 245, 248, 269–72, 275, 290, 296, 301
homoousion, 78
human nature, creaturely, 86, 92, 103–4, 121, 123, 281, 291
Hunsinger, George, 8, 15, 28, 49, 72–73, 96, 139, 149, 160, 172, 188–90, 192, 195, 206, 261, 283, 298

incarnation, 3, 39, 58, 64, 77–78, 91–92, 96, 98, 122, 128, 223, 227, 229, 232
individual, the, 79, 104, 112, 152, 157, 161, 164
individuality, 124–25, 252
Israel (*see also* Jews), 21, 85–86, 101, 105, 118, 220, 251, 267, 273–74, 301

Jenson, Robert W., 39, 161, 163, 277
Jesus Christ, 2, 5, 7, 14, 17–18, 20, 22–24, 29–30, 34, 36, 38–40, 42–43, 45, 47–48, 50–1, 54–67, 69–73, 76–82, 86, 89–91, 94, 96, 98–100, 103–8, 111, 115–16, 118, 120–21, 128–32, 134–35, 137–41, 143–45, 150, 152, 155, 158–59, 162, 171–72, 174–76, 178–83, 188–90, 193, 196–208, 215, 217–18, 220–33, 236–41, 243–44, 246–49, 251, 253–56, 260–73, 275–77, 279–86, 288, 290, 292, 294–96, 301
    the Center, 40
    circumcision of, 245, 263
    crucified, 1, 4–5, 18, 36, 52, 60–62, 64, 67, 75, 104, 106, 111–12, 115, 120, 130, 132–33, 137, 160, 165–66, 176–79, 181, 188, 228, 240, 248, 254, 263, 274–75, 283, 287
    cruciform work, 67, 71, 90, 99, 101, 105, 108, 262, 265, 283
    death, 38, 98, 108, 114, 120, 144, 146, 178
    divinity, 53, 58, 64, 81, 90, 120, 122, 171, 180, 189–90, 222–24, 227, 242, 262, 266, 280–82
    exaltation, 77, 223, 241–42, 283, 288
    faith of, 5, 40, 198
    glory, 66, 120, 122, 127, 133, 174, 282
    grace, 145
    human nature, 81, 93–96, 121–23, 223–24, 280–81, 296
    humanity, 98, 121, 190, 281
    life, 28, 107, 115, 118, 145, 275
    Parousia, 279
    resurrection, 77, 233
    revelation of, 52, 236 *see also* revelation
    risen glory, 29, 283
    sanctifying life, 107, 272
    Son, 18, 37–38, 58, 61, 64–65, 68, 77–78, 89, 91–96, 98, 101, 106, 119, 122–24, 127, 140, 150, 176, 180, 182, 184, 198–99, 220, 222–24, 229–32, 235–38, 242, 248, 279, 286
    two natures, 78, 81, 94, 96, 171, 180, 224
Jews, 56–57, 74–76, 84, 99, 105, 162 *see also* Israel
justification, 42, 71–72, 82, 84, 86, 90, 97, 99, 104–8, 111, 117, 127–29, 132, 140, 143, 145, 233, 248–49, 251, 253–55, 262–65, 271–73, 276, 278, 282, 285, 287, 290, 292
    precedes sanctification, 71–72, 90, 117, 129, 132, 143, 248–49
justification by faith, 72, 117

Kiecker, James G., 4, 16, 22–23, 142

Subject and Name Index   321

Klappert, Bertold, 131, 171, 175–78, 182–83, 194–95, 229–32, 242, 298
knowledge
    of God, 4, 16, 18, 30, 33–37, 40–42, 45–49, 51–55, 57, 59–60, 62, 64, 66, 68, 74, 131–33, 138–39, 152, 154, 156, 184, 196–202, 204, 206–9, 214, 217–20, 222, 238, 241, 245, 297
    theological, 65, 206
knowledge of God, true, 5, 20, 33, 40, 45–47, 49, 139, 150, 164, 201, 204, 239–40, 244

law (*see also* commandments), 40–41, 55–56, 61, 68, 71, 74–75, 82–91, 93, 97, 105–7, 109, 113, 127–28, 137, 140–41, 143–45, 199, 249, 252–63, 271, 292
    of death, 88–89, 128, 137, 144, 261
    of life, 89, 128, 137, 144, 262
    penalty for breaking, 84–86, 88–91, 128, 140, 143–45, 183, 256–57, 260, 262
Liberal Protestantism, 153–55, 157–58, 162, 172, 199
liberation theology, 29, 191–92, 278, 297
life, eternal, 109, 118, 128–29, 144, 262, 275, 278–79, 283, 285
light, 34, 38, 43, 45, 48, 55, 59, 64, 66, 79, 109, 115, 125, 159, 167, 170, 175, 180, 217, 219, 227, 230–32, 235, 241, 250, 284–85, 291, 295, 301
logos, 20, 47, 56–57, 59, 73–76, 95, 97, 135, 139, 145, 163, 240–41, 290, 292, 296
Luther, academic versus mystical theology, 44–45
Luther, Martin, 3–7, 13–30, 32–36, 38–42, 44–46, 48–52, 54–55, 58–66, 72–73, 75, 77, 79–80, 82–84, 89–90, 94–97, 99–100, 103–5, 107–8, 111–12, 115–17, 119–20, 125–27, 130–31, 135–46, 149–55, 157, 159–61, 163–67, 169, 171–82, 185–86, 188–93, 195, 197–98, 208, 220, 236, 242, 247–48, 250–51, 254–55, 257–58, 263, 270, 273–75, 281, 289–90, 292–93, 295–96, 301
    philosophical position, 50
    theologia crucis, 14, 17, 19, 21–25, 28–30, 32, 35, 41, 44–45, 61, 126, 135–36, 143, 149, 166, 171–73, 179, 181, 185–86, 188, 190, 193, 198, 255, 273
    theology, 21, 25, 28, 44, 66, 89, 105, 149, 175
Luther scholarship, 3
Lutheran theology, 28, 149, 255

man-God Jesus Christ, 120, 155, 188, 196, 218, 241, 264, 282
Mattes, Mark C., 16, 29–30, 63, 80
McCormack, Bruce, 187, 247
McCormack-Gunton debate, 187–88, 247
McGrath, Alister, 14, 41, 64, 77, 79, 89, 107, 109, 111–12, 121
McIntyre, John, 7
Meyer, Ben F., 76, 92, 98, 122
mind
    of Christ, 56, 66–67, 69, 218, 244–46
    creaturely, 4, 34, 42, 244
    of God, 34, 66, 68
Modern Soteriology, 247, 249, 251, 253, 255, 257, 259, 261, 263, 265, 267, 269, 271, 273, 275, 277, 279, 281, 283, 285, 287, 289, 291
modern theology, 19, 27, 160, 164, 192, 216, 234, 268, 297, 300
modernity, 9, 149, 153–54, 156, 158, 160–61, 164, 234, 252, 295–96
Moltmann, Jürgen, 15–16, 18–19, 21–23, 26, 186, 196–97, 199, 201, 203, 205, 207, 209, 211, 213, 215, 217, 219, 221, 223, 225, 227, 229, 231, 233, 235, 237, 239, 241, 243, 245, 278, 292
mysticism, 13, 41, 44, 68, 118, 295

narrow tradition *see* thin tradition

natural creation, 45, 53–55, 69, 202
natural theology, 40, 46, 53, 55, 68, 132, 161, 196, 199–201, 203–4, 206, 246
negative epistemology, 4, 40, 199, 216, 226
Neufeld, Franceen (Vann), 15, 42–44, 48
Nicholas of Cusa, Saint, 6, 42, 48–49, 118
nineteenth century theology, 156–57, 199–200, 209, 211, 214, 216, 234, 260, 288, 291, 296

Oberman, Heiko A., 105, 117
Object, divine, 8–9, 35, 38–39, 157, 159–60, 176, 185, 198, 200–201, 204–6, 208–10, 212–13, 216, 218–20, 249, 263, 284, 295
ontological, 5, 14, 23, 26, 39, 55–56, 68–69, 75, 88, 98, 106, 114, 119–20, 123, 126, 128–29, 132, 137, 143–44, 149, 197, 205, 225–27, 229, 244, 260, 263–65, 272, 294, 296, 301
ordo salutis
 gracious, 71, 73
 western, 71–72, 132, 136, 141, 143, 248, 296
Origen, Patristic Father, 94–95, 101–3

participation in Christ *see* eschatological participation in Christ
Paul, Apostle, 6, 44, 56, 66, 70, 130, 188, 293
persecution, 112–14
philosophy, 9, 45–46, 49–52, 55, 68, 184, 199, 204–6, 245
 idealism, 187, 205
 realism, 87, 133, 205, 207, 299
pneumatology, 13, 218, 233–35, 237, 246, 277
prayer, 228, 271, 284

Rae, 72
resurrection, 3–4, 21, 45, 61–62, 64–65, 71, 77–79, 82, 109, 111, 117–21, 126–29, 144, 146, 173, 176–79, 181–82, 184, 186, 192–93, 222–23, 229–31, 233, 254, 269, 275–76, 278–80, 282–83, 285–88, 292, 294, 296
revelation (*see also* Jesus Christ), 49, 55, 60–61, 63–66, 69, 178–79, 196–97, 199–203, 214, 217–20, 224–25, 227, 229–31, 233, 236–38, 242–43, 246, 260, 266, 285–86
 general, 46, 61
Richardson, Alan, 15, 30, 49, 172, 192–93, 195, 298
Righteous, the, 140–41
righteousness, 72–74, 85–87, 90, 104, 122, 141, 241, 247, 253, 256–57
Romanticism, 159, 211–12, 234–35
Rosato, Philip J., 234

salvation, 4–5, 7, 17, 24, 43, 45, 71–81, 84, 92, 97–104, 106–7, 109, 112–14, 121–22, 124, 131, 136, 141–45, 150, 154, 184, 239, 248–49, 254, 261–64, 272–73, 276, 286, 291–92, 297
sanctification, 16, 72, 82, 107, 111, 117, 120, 128–29, 132, 165, 249, 254, 269, 273–74, 276, 278, 285, 290, 292
Schleiermacher, Friedrich, 153, 157, 200, 209, 211–16, 234–35, 240
 the Christian religion, 211–13
 theology, 209, 214, 216
Schreiner, Thomas R., 83, 92, 100–101
Schweitzer, Don, 16, 21–22, 26–27, 171
secondary literature, 2, 10, 13, 121, 131, 167–69, 189, 194, 295, 300
sin, 24, 27, 43, 45, 47, 54, 72, 77–81, 83–88, 92, 95, 97, 113, 130, 136, 140–44, 164–65, 168, 188, 208–9, 247, 250, 256, 262–63, 265, 268, 270, 274–75, 285, 291
Solberg, Mary M., 16, 25–26
Son of God *see* Jesus Christ, Son
soteriology, 3, 5, 7–8, 13, 16, 41, 43, 56, 70, 79, 99, 120, 129, 140, 173,

176, 178, 183–84, 195, 246, 261, 264, 273, 292
soul, 37, 39, 43, 45, 48, 53, 59–60, 74, 78, 81, 103–4, 115–16, 124–26, 235, 275
Spirit *see* Holy Spirit
suffering, 1, 7, 13, 15–16, 19–24, 27–29, 35–36, 45, 54–55, 59–60, 62–63, 68–69, 78, 82, 85, 90–96, 107, 111–17, 124–25, 128–29, 138–39, 151, 162, 168, 171–75, 179–81, 185, 189–90, 193–95, 210, 222, 242–43, 269, 272, 274–75, 281, 292
   Christian, 15, 274
   of God, 15, 28–29, 59, 91, 93–95, 171, 174–75, 180, 189, 242
   human, 13, 111–15, 194, 243, 275

Tauler, Johannes, 44–45, 48, 59, 115, 125, 295
theologia crucis (*see also* theology of the cross), 1–4, 10–11, 14, 16–17, 19, 21–25, 28–30, 32, 35, 41, 44–45, 61, 126, 130–31, 133–36, 143, 149, 166, 168–74, 176–83, 185–86, 188, 190–93, 195, 198, 228, 255, 273, 283, 288, 291–96, 298, 301
Theologia Germanica, 6, 42, 44–45, 48, 60, 81, 98, 118, 124, 151, 270
theologia gloriae (*see also* theology of glory), 7, 18, 29–30, 82, 117, 120–21, 126–27, 129, 132–33, 138, 166, 168, 177, 179–80, 193, 276, 280, 282–83, 288–90, 292, 294, 300
theologia resurrectionis, 179–80, 283
theologian of glory, 35–36, 43, 116, 130, 139, 282
theologian of the cross, 1–2, 7–8, 10, 13–14, 19, 24, 28, 30, 33, 35–37, 41, 55, 62–63, 65–66, 77, 79–80, 82, 90, 99, 107, 111–12, 116, 120, 127, 129–31, 133–34, 136–39, 141, 150, 170, 172–74, 178–81, 183, 186, 191–92, 194, 196, 198, 228, 231, 241, 248, 290–92, 297–98
theology of glory (*see also theologia gloriae*), 4, 19–20, 43–44, 50, 65, 70, 72, 77, 99, 133, 165–66, 172, 174, 177, 180, 195, 197, 207, 213, 234, 249, 268, 278, 283
theology of the cross (*see also theologia crucis*), 1–6, 10, 13–31, 34, 38, 40–41, 44–45, 55, 66, 74–75, 89–90, 92, 111–12, 121, 126–27, 134, 149, 160, 167–81, 183–86, 188–91, 193–95, 249, 254–55, 264, 293–95, 297–98, 300–301
thin tradition, 6–7, 25–26, 46, 105, 150, 152, 191
Thompson, John, 131, 161, 170, 178–79, 185, 194–95, 204, 217, 229–32, 286, 298
Tomlin, Graham, 6, 14, 16, 25–26, 28, 44–45, 61, 108, 172, 190, 195, 298
Torrance, Thomas F., 40, 65, 78, 92, 156, 164, 169–70, 181, 192, 194, 196, 200, 202, 204, 206–8, 210, 225, 229–31, 233–34, 236–8, 243, 265, 269, 283
Trinity, doctrine of, 18, 123, 182, 219, 235–36
true theologian *see* theologian of the cross
truth, 19, 26, 34, 37–39, 41, 46, 48–51, 53–54, 57, 59, 63, 76, 78, 84, 113, 141, 143, 146, 160–61, 177, 197, 201–2, 209, 217–19, 225–28, 236–38, 241, 243–44, 254, 261, 268, 272–73, 289, 299

universalism, 82, 99–100, 103, 105, 129, 267

via antiqua, 49–50
via moderna, 49–50, 103
von Balthasar, Hans Urs, 169, 187, 217

von Loewenich, Walther, 3, 14, 16–18, 21, 30, 34, 38–39, 44, 50, 52, 58, 61–63, 65–66, 75, 97, 116–17, 121, 125–27

weakness, 22, 47, 60–61, 76, 91–92, 94, 107–8, 269
Webster, John, 156, 160, 162, 164, 192
Weinandy, Thomas G., 65, 87, 94, 106, 110, 123
Wells, Harold., 6, 15, 20, 22, 29, 34–35, 101, 111, 171–72, 182, 191–92, 195, 298
Westerholm, Stephen, 83–84
wisdom, 34–35, 38, 52, 54–59, 69, 71, 73, 75–76, 79, 99, 121, 127, 129, 143, 165, 187, 218, 223, 239–41, 247, 267
   human, 20, 34, 57, 75, 163
   worldly, 75, 240
Wisdom of God, 58, 75, 240–41
Word from the cross (*see also* Word of the cross), 10, 46, 58, 128, 131, 136, 150, 231, 241, 248, 269, 283, 290–91, 293, 296, 298
Word of God, 37, 58, 71, 79, 88–89, 123, 126, 160, 179, 193, 199, 206, 208–11, 220, 225, 227–30, 248–49, 256
Word of the cross (*see also* Word from the cross), 23, 26, 47, 55–58, 70, 75, 97, 127, 139, 149, 184–85, 198, 225–26, 228, 230, 233, 239–40, 247–48, 264, 268, 290–91, 296, 301
work
   alien, 45, 99, 119, 138, 144, 167, 255
   proper, 119, 144
work of the cross, 18, 25, 53, 78, 95–96, 108–9, 116, 119, 121, 125, 137, 176–77, 182, 184, 222, 245, 249, 261, 265, 296
works righteousness, 83